Essentials of Sociology

Third edition

Essentials of Sociology

Third edition

Leonard Broom

Australian National University
and University of California,
Santa Barbara

Philip Selznick
University of California, Berkeley

Dorothy H. Broom
Australian National University

F. E. PEACOCK PUBLISHERS, INC.
ITASCA, ILLINOIS 60143

Contents

Acknowledgments

First and foremost, we wish to record our debt to the late Gertrude Jaeger, whose collaboration endures and whose standards of teaching and scholarship continue to guide and challenge us.

For generous collaboration on *Essentials of Sociology* or the several editions of the parent book, *Sociology: A Text with Adapted Readings,* we express our obligation to a number of colleagues: Robert Blauner, Charles M. Bonjean, Burton R. Clark, Donald R. Cressey, Saul Geiser, Norval D. Glenn, Helen Beem Gouldner, Paul Jacobs, F. Lancaster Jones, Yuriko Kitaoji, John I. Kitsuse, William Kornhauser, Sheldon Messinger, Richard T. Morris, Philippe Nonet, Jerome H. Skolnick, and Ralph H. Turner. We also acknowledge the guidance and assistance of many other colleagues, and specifically for this edition, Leonard Beeghley, Larry H. Long, Larry Lyon, and Terrence Tutchings. Other intellectual obligations are recorded in citations and credit lines, but we especially express indebtedness to the authors of the original works upon which our Adaptations are based.

Gretchan N. Broom in her customary fashion insisted that what was said must be worth the saying and must be said clearly. When in doubt she filled her own prescription.

The first four editions of *Sociology* owed much to the high editorial standards and indefatigable efforts of Phyllis M. Barnett. We are conscious of her continuing imprint and we remain grateful for her patient guidance and personal commitment.

Ted Peacock proved that bureaucracy is not necessarily a dirty word by mobilizing a capable editorial team that worked with good spirit and dispatch: Elizabeth Hovinen, copy editor; Linda Pierce, art editor; Randi Brill and Sandy Mead, designers; W.L. Parker, indexer; and Joyce Usher, managing editor.

Last but not least, we express our thanks to the students and instructors who were moved to write to us about their experiences in using earlier editions of *Sociology* and *Essentials of Sociology.* Their suggestions have been carefully taken into account even when it may seem they have not been followed.

L.B.
P.S.
D.H.B.

To the Student

Please take a few minutes to read these suggestions on how to get the most out of this book. First, look carefully at the table of contents and you will see that the structure of the book is clearly signposted. The eleven chapters are logically grouped into four main Parts, and the chapters are divided into numbered sections.

You will find that there are fourteen adapted readings, a special feature of this book called Adaptations, which are numbered to the chapters in which they are located. The Adaptations are self-contained units that illustrate sociological ideas or research findings. Most of them are based on studies previously published in scholarly books or journals. If the material was originally written in technical language, we have simplified and condensed it to make it more comprehensible for students beginning sociology.

Some information is easier to grasp if it is presented in graphs or tables. Such visual aids are concise forms of communication, but in spite of their simple appearance, they require the same attention as pages of words. Adaptation 2.1, Reading a Table, and Adaptation 2.2, Understanding a Figure, are guides to help you make the best use of charts and tables.

Throughout the text when the most important terms are introduced for the first time, they are printed in heavy **boldface** type. All of these key terms are listed with short definitions beginning on page 235. The chapter in which the term appears first is given in parentheses.

Each chapter ends with a summary, which should help when you prepare your study outline. Your personal chapter outline would include the titles and numbers of sections, the main headings under each section, plus your own notes from the text, from lectures, and outside readings. To get ready for exams, carefully reread the summaries as well as reviewing the chapters.

At the end of each chapter we have included a few books as suggested readings. Citation references in text are identified in parentheses by author, publication date, and often the page of the source. This reference style is commonly used in sociological publications and reduces the number of footnotes without losing bibliographic information. References fulfill the scholar's duty to record where ideas and information come from and also provide leads to further reading on a specific topic. The complete reference listings are to be found in the back of the book. In a few cases two publication dates are given: (1904/1976). This means that the original printing, the first date, is less likely to be available in the library, so reference is made to a later printing.

You will find fewer photographs here than in other introductory sociology texts. We feel that at the college level, each picture must carry its own weight, not just lend visual relief. It must also be a good example of the photographer's art. Most important, it must help to develop a sociological point.

Factual information in this text emphasizes North America, but other examples range from preliterate cultures to the postindustrial societies of Western Europe and Japan. We introduce these materials because it is important for the student to gain a feeling for the variety of human social life. Furthermore, we can often better understand our own way of life if we see how it contrasts with different cultures. One of the founders of sociology, Emile Durkheim (1858 – 1917), stressed that comparisons are essential to understanding the nature of human society.

If you ever have an impulse to write to the authors of your texts, we would be glad to hear from you. Good luck in your study of this challenging subject.

Leonard Broom
Philip Selznick
Dorothy H. Broom

Part One

Sociological Perspectives

Chapter 1

Introducing Sociology

Section One
The Discipline of Sociology

Academic subjects are known by the questions they ask and by the ways they search for answers. Confronted by the common concerns of high levels of unemployment, social scientists approach the problem in very different ways: an economist might measure the ability of a city to provide relief to the unemployed, a political scientist the pressure groups seeking to protect industries threatened with bankruptcy and the loss of more jobs, a sociologist might study the impact of prolonged unemployment on family relations, and a psychologist how losing a job affects the person's self-image.

It will help to grasp the special emphasis of sociology if we begin with an overview of the other social sciences and note the links between them and sociology.

SOCIOLOGY AND THE SOCIAL SCIENCES

Sociology is one of the family of social sciences—anthropology, economics, geography, history, political science, and social psychology. All the social sciences engage in systematic study of social behavior and its products, and there are no clear boundaries between them. Indeed, some of the most worthwhile studies are done when people from different fields work together. However, even when they study the same problems, the various social sciences emphasize different aspects.

Anthropology is partly a biological and partly a social science. Physical anthropology deals with the biological origins of humanity and with variations in the human species, including race. Some anthropologists specialize in studies of the great apes; an example of this approach is research on dominance and submission among primates (Pfeiffer, 1978:241–244).

Social and cultural anthropologists study the ways of life of preliterate communities. We have drawn on such studies in this book when we compare present-day industrial cultures with Third World and preliterate cultures. (For example, see Adaptation 4.1.) In recent years increasing numbers of anthropologists have turned their attention to such topics as interpersonal relations in urban areas, and this trend represents a convergence between anthropology and sociology.

Economics deals with cost and price, savings and investment, supply and demand, and the production, distribution, and consumption of goods and services. When economists construct models of how the economy works, they often assume that people make economic decisions on the basis of certain goals, for example, to earn the maximum income with the least effort or least investment. Such assumptions are essentially psychological and sociological because they refer to personal preferences and social values. However, the assumptions may or may not correspond with reality. Sometimes people choose leisure over money or a future goal over an immediate goal, and these noneconomic facts limit the applicability of economic generalizations.

The economy is also related to and dependent on noneconomic institutions and forces, including government, the family, population change, and public opinion. Both sociologists and economists are interested in the problems of poverty and income distribution, which are discussed in Chapter 9.

Geography, like anthropology, spans the natural and social sciences. The early human geographers were chiefly concerned with how the physical environment influenced the location of human activities and the use of resources. Modern geographers give more attention to social and economic factors, and one geographer describes the discipline as "a social science emergent" (Cox, 1976:182). Geography coincides with the concerns of sociology on such topics as population distribution, urban ecology, and the use of natural resources.

History is both one of the social sciences and one of the humanities. Historical documents are valuable in sociological research, and sociological analyses are of interest to historians. In recent years, the development of social history has led to fresh insights on such subjects as slavery and family life. Historians have also tried to apply social science research techniques to earlier periods, for example, in studying such topics as occupational change and inheritance.

Political science is primarily concerned with the

study of government, and traditionally it has had a strong legal and administrative emphasis. But because politics and government are rooted in culture and social organization, political scientists have become interested in exploring social influences on administrative decisions and political behavior. The growing role of political decisions in many areas of social life has also stimulated interest in political sociology.

Social psychology is largely concerned with the links between group life and the psychology of the individual. Both sociologists and psychologists contribute to this area of knowledge. In their attempts to understand individual behavior and personality, social psychologists investigate interpersonal relations and group behavior. They study social roles, the development of personality, the meaning of social attitudes, and the dynamics of small groups. In this book, aspects of social psychology are treated in connection with behavior in small groups and the processes by which the human animal becomes a human person.

THE SOCIOLOGICAL VIEWPOINT

Sociology examines aspects of social life that might otherwise be overlooked or taken for granted. Its large and challenging agenda includes efforts to discover the basic structure of human society. Sociologists seek to understand the conditions that promote social conflict and stability, the forces that strengthen or weaken groups, and the sources of social change.

Some aspects of social life are familiar to most people from personal experience. Everyone has firsthand knowledge of a variety of social situations: a family, a work setting, a group of friends, a community. Sociologists often use this common-sense knowledge in research, for instance, when they interview people to learn about their social experiences and attitudes.

Although experience is supposed to be a good teacher, few people have enough experience to make accurate generalizations about a broad problem. For example, while everyone is aware of prejudice and discrimination based on age and sex, in the course of everyday life an individual would not learn much

about the historical sources and social bases of prejudice. No one person can have enough direct experience to form an accurate idea of how widespread and deeply felt age and sex discrimination are, how these attitudes are expressed, how they differ from one group to another, and whether they are increasing or decreasing.

In facing such questions, sociological research goes beyond common sense and sometimes contradicts popular beliefs. Sociology draws together many observations made by different people in different situations. Using this information, it builds theories and tests them. In doing so, it often develops concepts that are special applications of everyday ideas. For example, *friendship* is a common-sense term, but as we point out in Chapter 5, the sociological concept of *primary group* includes much more than the idea of friendship. Likewise, such sociological concepts as *deviance, stratification,* and *role* permit more precise analysis than is possible with everyday terms.

Section Two
Sociology and Social Policy

As a scientific field, sociology is both academic and applied. Like all scholars, sociologists try to be exact. As a result, they have developed ways of studying social life that may seem remote from urgent human concerns. This does not mean that sociologists do not care. Most want to help solve social problems, but if research is to be socially useful, it must be sound and objective. Thus, the sociologist is pulled in two directions: toward careful, well-designed studies and toward efforts to solve pressing social problems. The tension between these two priorities is expressed in a debate that has been going on for more than a generation. Two early influential statements that argued for a vigorous sociology committed to social improvement are *Knowledge for What?* (Lynd, 1939) and *The Sociological Imagination* (Mills, 1959).

There is no longer any argument that sociology has a legitimate role in helping to solve social problems. Although some sociologists continue to be primarily concerned with basic research and theory building, others contribute directly to social change by acting as consultants or employees of business, government, and other organizations. The application of sociology, ranging from large-scale policy research to critical evaluations of specific social programs, has developed rapidly in the last two decades. Courses in applied sociology, policy research, and evaluation research are now offered by many colleges and universities.

Nothing is more central to the scientific spirit than the idea of self-correction. Social scientists do not claim to be purely objective. They inevitably bring some element of choice to what they work on and how they carry out their work. To some extent they are all limited in their ability to look at the world objectively. But science does not insist on absolute objectivity. It does require that as a whole a discipline be receptive to new ideas and alternative approaches and that there be opportunities for criticism of findings and interpretations.

POLICY RESEARCH

Some people who have been trained in sociology get jobs in government or industry, where their skills are applied to practical problems. For example, consider these questions: Would the construction of a new freeway break up a long-established neighborhood and destroy community facilities? If so, could the neighborhood be protected by changing the route of the freeway, by building pedestrian bridges, or by rebuilding community facilities? Highway planners may not consider such questions until after the damage has been done. Sociologists think of these problems as the first order of business, to be evaluated fully before the route is laid out.

Sociological training leads policy analysts to look beyond official goals (such as highway construction) and anticipate their effects (such as neighborhood destruction). Urban planners may recommend that a new factory be built in a region of chronic unemployment. The sociologist's task would be to discover whether the unemployed population could qualify for the kinds of jobs that would be created or whether other workers would move in from the outside, making matters worse.

The skills of the social researcher are also used when an agency wants to measure its own performance. For example, do prisoners who take part in a work release program commit fewer crimes afterwards because the program was effective or because they were chosen from the "better-risk" group?

Relevance

As part of the social world, sociology is caught up in major events and crises. Much research has been done on racial conflict, sex discrimination, crime and delinquency, and population pressures. These and other urgent social issues give focus and direction to sociological research. In responding to changing conditions and pressing social problems, sociology attempts to be relevant to the modern world and most sociologists stay out of ivory towers.

Sociologists are aware of the contradictions between ideals and action. During the 1920s and 1930s, before the society of the United States was ready to let down the barriers of segregation, most sociologists opposed racial prejudice and discrimination. In their classrooms, they helped pave the way for massive changes that have taken place. One of the most influential documents in this area —*An American Dilemma* (Myrdal, 1944)—brought an understanding of racism and the heritage of oppression to a large audience. The book represents the work of many social scientists over many years. Again in the 1960s, sociologists helped lay the foundations for social programs like Head Start, which reflects sociological research on the importance of the early learning environment. Sociological research has also brought home to the public the reality of child abuse (Pfohl, 1977), battered wives, and attacks on old people.

RESEARCH AS A SOCIAL ISSUE

Most scientists face ethical problems in the course of their work. Physicists are concerned about balancing the destructive aspects of nuclear power against the peaceful uses of nuclear energy. Physiologists must weigh the value of new knowledge against the suffering of experimental animals. Chemists may worry about the environmental damage caused by useful synthetic substances. But because sociologists, psychologists, and anthropologists study human beings, they are confronted by a different set of problems.

Who should do research?

Anyone with the impulse, the time, and the money can conduct social research: You don't need a license to do research. When we are subjects in a study, however, most of us want to know whether the investigator is qualified. We want the researcher to be trained to conduct research competently and to follow ethical and professional standards.

Someone with a strong personal interest in the results of a study may not be a good investigator. Too much involvement in the outcome of research can lead to unintentional distortion of the information or conscious faking of evidence. A cigarette factory employee who wants to keep a job might not be an impartial interviewer for a survey on smoking and health.

However, it is hard for social researchers to be completely neutral about their subject matter. They do research because they think a problem is interesting and important. Sociologists who study race relations have personal feelings about racism and discrimination: Most believe that racism is destructive, that discrimination violates human rights, and that these attitudes and behaviors should be changed. Such feelings do not necessarily disqualify people as researchers. Sociologists are free to let their values influence their choice of research projects, but they must guard against letting their values influence the results. Scientific integrity and objectivity come first.

Some radical critics claim that in order to study a group, the researcher must be a member of it: thus one must be black to study blacks, only a Navajo can understand Navajos, and men cannot study women. This argument arises out of two issues: ethics and competence.

The ethical issue is whether outsiders have the right to observe a group or ask questions of its members. It requires the researcher to ask, ''What right do I have to invade the privacy of this group (or this person) with my questions? Why should these people cooperate with me?'' The competence issue is whether outsiders can do such research. Since they

Researcher and subject or invader of privacy? Margaret Mead as a young field worker among the Manus of the Admiralty Islands.

are foreign to the group, they might not ask the right questions or fully understand the answers.

On the other hand, if social research is to guard against accepting commonsense explanations as if they were scientifically proved, the investigator must always be an outsider to some extent. A committed member of a group may find it hard to be objective about the group's way of looking at the world. Sympathetic understanding of the group's point of view, which is essential to the research process, is not the same as accepting it uncritically.

Who should be studied?

As in the case of who should do research, there are few limits on who may be studied. In general, the people who are studied most are those who are least able to protect themselves. The poor have a hard time fending off social researchers. People who have unlisted phone numbers, receptionists, and servants are better able to protect their own privacy.

There is some justification for research on the poor and powerless. Programs to reduce poverty and disadvantage require information that can be obtained only from research on those who are intended to benefit from such programs. On the other hand, ''studying down'' neglects equally important topics such as how wealth is accumulated and passed on, or how the powerful gain and protect their positions. A sociology that studied only people at the bottom of the hierarchy could be criticized for serving the status quo. It would also give a lopsided and incomplete view of society.

Confidentiality and the use of findings

At every step in the project, from the start of study design to the final writeup, the researcher must face the issue of how to protect the people who have taken part in the study. In large-scale survey research, where results are reported in summary statistics and proper safeguards are used, respondents can be fairly sure of their privacy and anonymity. In studies of smaller groups or communities, it is harder to preserve anonymity. Subjects' names are sometimes disguised, but this tactic does not always work.

In addition, researchers must consider the potential uses of the results of their studies. They also need to be sure that the form in which results are published will not discredit or embarrass people or violate their privacy. A group that permits a researcher to study it obviously does not grant permission for the results to be used against its members.

Videotaping poses additional risks. There is a serious possibility that the subjects will be seen by people who know them and might expose them to criticism or ridicule. Because videotaping is so simple and convenient, it requires special safeguards to protect the privacy of subjects.

Section Three
Levels of Analysis

Sociology analyzes social life at three levels: interpersonal, group, and societal. Each level is more complex and involves a larger number of people than the one before it. Figure 1.1 presents the three levels, the social forms, or elements, found at each level, and examples of each.

THE INTERPERSONAL LEVEL

An **interpersonal relation** is the social connection between two or more persons, such as friend-friend, leader-follower, or neighbor-neighbor. *Interpersonal* means ''between persons'' but does not imply that the relations involved must be close or cordial. They may be friendly or hostile, close or distant, deep or superficial. Most daily life consists of interpersonal relations. Every interaction between persons is built on past experience and understanding. We know what to expect because we have an identifiable, named relationship to the other: we are friends, business competitors, fellow students, parent and child, or buyer and seller. In Chapter 5 this topic will be explored in more detail.

Adaptation 1.1 analyzes the quality of friendship in the black ghetto of Washington, D.C., and suggests how economic deprivation leads to impoverished human relations. It is an in-depth account of the pattern of interaction in a social setting called Tally's Corner. Although the men on Tally's Corner give their lives meaning by making friends, the instability and insecurity of ghetto life does not allow their social ties to mature into deep and lasting relationships. Their friendships are quickly made and quickly broken.

Life in the black ghetto does not encourage the self-confidence and self-esteem on which stable relationships grow. If the men could improve their job skills and find continuing employment, if they could live in one place long enough to feel that they would be there the next month or next year, if their friends would not disappear without explanation, perhaps then some of the basic conditions would exist that might lead to more stable interpersonal relations.

Level	Elements	Examples
Interpersonal	Patterned interaction Role behavior	Leader-follower Student-professor
Group	Primary groups Organizations Group relations	A group of friends A college Labor-management
Societal	Large-scale social patterns Communities and societies	Slavery Australia

Figure 1.1 Levels of Sociological Analysis

THE GROUP LEVEL

The next level of analysis deals with groups and group relations. Two major examples are person-centered groups, which are discussed in Chapter 5, and impersonal organizations, which are examined in Chapter 6.

The word **group** has a very general meaning. It can include everything from a family to a nation. Two persons form a group if they are friends or partners, that is, if they are held together by mutual interests or dependency and set apart from others by their relationship. A college is a group, since it has boundaries, a way to identify its members, and symbols that distinguish it from other colleges. Groups can be highly organized and stable, such as the Supreme Court, or they can be fluid and temporary like the gathering at a cocktail party or a political demonstration.

People who have similar incomes or are alike in other ways, such as age, occupation, or reading habits, do not necessarily form a social group. Instead, they are called statistical aggregates or **social categories.** Sometimes such categories are transformed into social groups, and the process by which this transformation occurs is of great interest to sociologists.

The aged are an example of a social category that is in the process of forming social groups. There is growing self-awareness among the old and growing concern about the kinds of groups that older people are likely to form or accept (Pratt, 1976). Is there an old-age life-style that can serve as a basis for separate housing? Or do older people have little in common despite their similar age and state of dependence? Political groups that lobby for the interests of older people, such as the Townsend movement of the 1930s and the Gray Panthers in the 1970s and 1980s, have sprung up from time to time. Should more—and more active—groups of this sort be expected as older people make up a larger percent of the population? What effect will they have on politics? Such questions indicate the kinds of problems that arise when we consider how social categories can form social groups.

THE SOCIETAL LEVEL

The third level of sociological analysis dealing with whole communities or societies is called the **societal** level. A society that is characterized by persistent and distinct patterns of social organization is a **social order.** The slave-based society of the South before the Civil War was a distinctive social order. More recently, religious leaders in the Middle East have attempted to organize a national political community around religious principles.

A kin-based society is another kind of social order. In many societies, kinship is the most important social bond and the family is the basis of social organization. The family firm and the family farm are examples of economic activities based on kinship. Only a few decades ago, before the rise of the corporation, many businesses and most farms were run by families.

Societies are **familistic** when the family is the main type of social group and is responsible for keeping order, producing goods, and performing religious duties. In a familistic society, relatives depend on each other. They give each other practical financial aid and guidance, and they also hold the keys to social esteem because the family itself has high or low prestige. Thus, interests of the family—wealth, honor, continuity—cannot be separated from those of the family's members. Modern societies, by contrast, are individualistic rather than familistic.

Societies and large organizations are not studied separately from small-scale situations. A comprehensive analysis would involve research at all three levels: the interpersonal and the group as well as the societal. Activities at each level express influences originating at other levels and in turn shape activities at those levels.

For example, the social organization of modern medicine reaches into the research laboratory, the drug industry, the hospital ward, and the doctor's office. It affects relations among doctors, nurses, technicians, and patients. It also influences interactions among druggists, doctors, and patients; among executives of pharmaceutical firms, their researchers, and government regulatory agencies; among health insurers, hospital administrators, and the supervisors who handle Medicare and Medicaid claims. Interpersonal relations are influenced both by the organization of hospitals and by drug companies and in turn influence them. Relations among doctors, nurses, and staff pattern the activity in hospitals, and communications among doctors influence their willingness to accept a new drug, thus in turn affecting the drug industry.

(Text continued on p. 13)

Adaptation 1.1

Liebow/The View from Tally's Corner

The New Deal Carry-out Shop—a neighborhood food store and eating place in a blighted section of downtown Washington, D.C.—was a point of entry for a participant observer study of the day-to-day lives of 24 adult black men. The subjects of the study were neither derelicts nor stable participants in the labor force, but casual and unskilled workers who were often unemployed. The fieldwork was done during 1962 and 1963.

At the Carry-out Shop, food is taken out or eaten standing up because there is no place to sit down. But customers gather in the 10-by-12-foot standing area for business and pleasure. On top of the cigarette machine, for example, the Carry-out's numbers-man-in-residence conducts his dealings with the white numbers backer, who comes daily to settle accounts with him and with other numbers men in the neighborhood.

Despite his rootlessness and instability, each man has a network of interpersonal relations, and these often resemble kinship relations even though no kin ties may be involved. The networks do not add up to a single unified group; rather, they consist of loose, shifting interrelations. Friendships are quickly made, and they take on a significance that would develop much more slowly in a more stable environment. To give their relationships meaning and depth, the men sometimes create fictional kinship bonds or imaginary personal ties of long duration. However, these friendships may dissolve as quickly as they develop.

FRIENDS AND NETWORKS

Perhaps more than most other worlds, the street corner world takes its shape and color from face-to-face relations of the people who live in it. On the street corner, each man has his own network of interpersonal ties: a weblike arrangement of man-to-man and man-to-woman relationships in which he is selectively attached in a particular way to a definite number of persons.

At the edges of this network are those persons with whom his relationship is emotionally neutral, such as area residents whom he has seen around but does not know except to nod or say "Hi" to as they pass on the street. Responses to these persons are limited to simple recognition.

In toward the center are those persons he knows and likes best, with whom he is "up tight":* his "walking buddies," good or best friends, girl friends, and sometimes real or supposed kinsmen. These are the people with whom he is in more or less daily, face-to-face contact and to whom he turns for emergency aid, comfort, or support in time of need or crisis. He gives to them and receives from them goods and services in the name of friendship. Routinely he seeks them out and is sought out by them. They serve his need to be with others of his kind and to be recognized as a unique human being, and he in turn serves them the same way. They are his audience and his fellow actors.

It is with these men and women that he spends his waking, nonworking hours, drinking, dancing, engaging in sex, playing the fool or the wise man, passing the time at the Carry-out or on the street

Casual encounter in the ghetto.

corner, talking about nothing and everything, about philosophy or Cassius Clay (Muhammad Ali), about the nature of numbers or how he would have it made if he could have a steady job that paid him $60 a week with no layoffs.

Friendship is sometimes anchored in kinship, sometimes in long-term associations, which may reach back into childhood. Other close friendships are born locally, in the street-corner world itself, rather than brought in by men from the outside. Such friendships are built on neighbor or co-worker relationships, or on a shared experience or other event or situation which brings two people together in a special way.

---

*This usage differs from the nonghetto "hip" meaning.
Source: From *Tally's Corner: A Study of Negro Streetcorner Men* by Elliot Liebow. Copyright © 1967 by Little, Brown and Company. By permission of Little, Brown and Company.

In general, close friendships tend to develop out of associations with those who are already in one's network of personal relationships: relatives, men and women who live in the area and spend much of their time on the street or in public places, and co-workers. The result is that the street-corner man tends to use the same individuals over and over again: He may make a friend, neighbor, and co-worker of his kinsman, or a friend, co-worker, and kinsman of his neighbor.

THE KINSHIP MODEL

One of the most striking aspects of these overlapping relationships is the blurring of kinship and friendship. Most of the men and women on the street corner are unrelated to one another, and only a few have kinsmen in the immediate area. Nevertheless, kinship ties are frequently manufactured to explain, account for, or even validate friend relationships. One can begin with kinship and build on this or, conversely, begin with friendship and build a kin relationship.

The most common form of pseudo-kin relation is known as "going for brothers." This means, simply, that two men agree to present themselves as brothers to the outside world and to deal with one another as brothers. Going for brothers appears as a special case of friendship in which the claims, obligations, expectations, and loyalties of the friend relationship are publicly declared to be at their maximum.

Only the most important members of one's personal network can distinguish between real and pseudo-kin relationships, partly because the question of whether two men are really brothers or are simply going for brothers is not considered relevant. The important thing for people to know in their interaction with the two men is that they say they are brothers, whether they are or not.

Pseudo-kinship ties are also invoked in certain man-woman relationships. "Going for cousins" avoids the implication of romantic or sexual connection. Indeed, this seems to be the primary purpose behind going for cousins. It is a way of saying, "This woman (or man) and I are good friends, but we are not lovers." Given the taboo against cousin marriage, going for cousins permits an unrelated man and woman to enter into a close-friend relationship without threatening their actual romantic or sexual attachments. It is a public disclaimer of romantic or sexual content in a cross-sex, close-friend relationship.

Sometimes pseudo-kinship is relied on to sharpen and lend structure to a relationship which is otherwise vague. Occasionally, one hears "He just calls her his sister" or "They just call it brother and sister" or even "They just go for brother and sister." Such was the case of a man whose young daughter was living with a married woman. In caring for his child, the woman was, of course, doing what sisters sometimes do. The assignment of the label *sister* to one who is performing a function, which is often associated with that label, was an easy step to take. A vague relationship was rendered specific; it was simplified, and the need for explanations was reduced. This may also have served to discourage public suspicion about the nature of the relationship. In these respects, perhaps, going for cousins would have served them equally well. And, as in the case of going for brothers, whether they were in fact brother and sister was less important than the fact that they called themselves so. The woman's husband, we must assume, knew that they were not related. But because they called themselves brother and sister, the husband's interests and status were not jeopardized.

MUTUAL AID

Most friendships are thus born in relationships or situations in which individuals confront one another day by day and face to face. These friendships are nurtured and supported by an exchange of money, goods, services, and emotional support. Small loans, ranging from a few pennies up to two or three dollars, are constantly being asked for and extended. Although records of debts and credits are not made, in fact debts are remembered and claimed in time of need or when friendships break down.

Each person plays an important part in helping and being helped by those in his network. Since much of the cooperation between friends centers on basic daily activities, friends are of special importance to a sense of physical and emotional security. The more friends one has or believes himself to have, and the deeper he holds those friendships to be, the greater his self-esteem and the greater the esteem for himself he thinks he sees in the eyes of others.

The pursuit of security and self-esteem pushes him to romanticize his perception of his friends and friendships. He wants to see acquaintances as friends, and not only as friends but as friends with whom he is up tight, walking buddies, best friends, or even brothers. He prefers to see the movement of money, goods, services, and emotional support between friends as flowing freely out of loyalty and generosity and according to need, rather than as mutual exchange resting on a quid pro quo basis. He wants to believe that his friendships reach back into the distant past and have an unlimited future, that he knows and is known by his friends, that they can trust one another, and that their loyalties to one another are almost unbounded.

Friendship is at its romantic best when things are going well for the persons involved. But friendship does not often stand up well to the stress of crisis or conflict of interest, when demands tend to be heaviest and most insistent. Everyone knows this. Pledges of aid and comfort between friends are, at one level, made and received in good faith. But at another level, fully aware of his friends' limited resources and the demands of their self-interest, each person is prepared to look to himself alone.

The recognition that, at bottom, friendship is not a bigger-than-life relationship is sometimes expressed as a repudiation of all would-be friends. There may be a denial that friendship as a system of mutual aid and support exists at all.

INSTABILITY

A similar attitude leads to the assessment of friendship as a fair-weather phenomenon. Attitudes toward friends and friendships are thus always shifting, often ambivalent, and sometimes contradictory. One moment, friendship is almost sacred; the next, it is

the locus of exploitation: "Friends are good only for money."

These shifts and apparent contradictions arise from the fact that, at any given moment, the relationships that comprise an individual's network may be at widely different stages of development or degeneration. They arise, too, from the ease with which a casual encounter can ripen into an intense man–man or man–woman relationship and the equal ease with which these relationships break down under stress.

The overall picture is one of a broad web of interlocking, overlapping networks in which the incumbents are constantly shifting and changing positions relative to one another. This fluidity is reflected in neighbor, kin, family, and household relationships —indeed, in the whole social structure of the streetcorner world, which rests so largely on the primary, face-to-face relationships of the personal network of the individual.

FICTIONAL HISTORIES

In support of the economic, social, and psychological forces arrayed against the stability of personal networks is the intrinsic weakness of friendship itself. Whether as cause, effect, or both, the fact is that friendships are not often rooted in long-term associations, nor do the persons involved necessarily know anything of one another's personal history prior to their association. The man would like to think—and sometimes says—that his friendship with so-and-so goes back several years or even into childhood, but this is not often so. Their relationship rests almost entirely in the present. A man may have detailed knowledge of his friend's present circumstances and connections, but little else.

He knows, from looking into himself, the characteristic features of the friend's personal history. He knows that his friend was raised principally by women and that he holds these women dear, that he was brought up to love and fear God, that he had little formal education, that he had few if any job skills and has worked in different towns and cities, that in one or more of these towns he fathered a child whom he has probably never seen, that he first came here because he has an uncle or aunt here, because he met this girl, because he heard about this job, or because he was wanted by the police or someone else. But he does not know the details. He does not know whether it was his friend's mother, grandmother, or father's sister who raised him, how far he went in school, which towns and cities he lived and worked in, and what experiences he had there. Much of this comes out in the course of casual talk and hanging around, but much does not. Especially lacking is an exchange of secret thoughts or private hopes and fears.

Friendship thus appears as a relationship between two people who, in an important sense, stand unrevealed to one another. Lacking depth in both past and present, friendship is easily uprooted by self-interest or by external forces.

The recognition of this weakness, coupled with the importance of friendship as a source of security and self-esteem, is surely a principal source of the impulse to romanticize relationships, to upgrade them, to elevate to friendship what others see as a casual acquaintanceship, and to upgrade friendship to close friendship. It is this, perhaps, that lies behind the attempt to ascribe a past to a relationship that never had one and to borrow from the bony structure of kinship (going for brothers) to lend support to a relationship that is sorely in need of it. It is as if friendship were an artifact of desire, a wish relationship, a private agreement between two people to act "as if," rather than a real relationship between persons.

Section Four
Contrasting Models of Society

Although most sociologists share a general perspective, there are important differences of emphasis and outlook. Many scholars place bets, so to speak, on one or another approach in the hope that it will offer a key to sounder knowledge or greater insight. As a result, the newcomer to sociology soon hears competing voices that express different views of human society (Coser, 1976).

CONSENSUS VERSUS CONFLICT

One may begin the study of society by asking: What holds it all together? What keeps it steady? Or one may ask: What pulls society apart? What makes for change? These alternative starting points seem neutral enough, but they contain the seeds of controversy (Dahrendorf, 1959).

No sociologist seriously doubts the importance of conflict in society. But some take conflict for granted and give their main attention to what they consider the fundamental sources of social cohesion: shared ideas, shared traditions, shared ways of perceiving and understanding the world. These ingredients of social order are summed up in the assumption that every group is held together by a consensus, by agreement on basic rules and values—agreements that extend to the details of everyday life, the assumptions people share even when they sit down together at the dinner table.

The **consensus model** emphasizes social stability and the persistence of shared ideas. Major social change is thought to come rather slowly and to depend on large-scale shifts in attitude and belief. Hence consensus has a conservative overtone. It suggests that many proposals for change are unrealistic because they do not sufficiently take account of community beliefs. For example, it might be argued that any effort to promote socialism among American workers would run up against strongly held beliefs about individualism and free enterprise.

The **conflict approach,** on the other hand, holds that the most important aspect of social order is the domination of some groups by others. In this perspective society is understood as an arena of actual and potential conflict, and that when things look peaceful, it is only because someone is sitting on the lid. Conflict theorists do not ignore consensus and belief, but they emphasize that popular attitudes are often sustained and manipulated by groups in power. They focus attention on who controls the communications media or the educational system.

A conflict model appeals to proponents of change for two reasons. First, it identifies the potential for change, especially the rise of new groups capable of challenging existing institutions. Second, the conflict model suggests that a strategic shift in power can decisively affect social history. These themes are prominent in the writings of Karl Marx, whose work is the clearest example of the application of a conflict model to the study of society. (See pp. 176–177.) Broadly speaking, conflict theorists in modern sociology tend to be influenced by Marxism, although they do not necessarily accept all of it. Consensus theorists are more likely to follow in the tradition of the French sociologist Émile Durkheim.

Most sociologists would say that they are sensitive to both consensus and conflict. Only a minority identify themselves exclusively with one approach or the other. However, there is a tendency for sociologists to lean toward the consensus model because an awareness of the ''social''—the influence of shared values and shared experiences on the human mind and self—has been such a large part of the sociological tradition. The conflict model serves to correct an overemphasis on consensus.

STRUCTURE VERSUS PROCESS

To analyze society is to break it up into elements for study: social roles, social strata and classes, institutions, culture, organizations, communities. These concepts identify *structural* units of society. Yet in the last analysis, society is made up of individual human beings. To discuss abstract social units, necessary though it may be, carries the risk that the human individual may be neglected.

One school of thought that concentrates on *process* and tries to keep the individual at the center of attention is known as **symbolic interactionism** (Blumer, 1969). Symbolic interactionists argue that the core of social reality is the active human being

trying to make sense of a social situation and give it meaning. Individuals respond to the social world on the basis of how their own acts and the acts of others are interpreted. Experience gains meaning (that is, its symbolic character) through interaction: The same gift can be interpreted as a friendly gesture or as a bribe. Symbolic interactionism calls attention to the person-centered processes that take place within the larger units of society.

Strictly speaking, structure and process are not in opposition. They are different ways of looking at the same social reality. A structural perspective projects an image of society in which individuals are controlled by the forces that play upon them, by their social backgrounds, and by the groups to which they belong. An interactionist perspective studies social life from the standpoint of how the actor makes sense of experience and copes with the environment.

Conclusion

The conflict model and symbolic interaction speak to the same basic issues. They are voices of resistance to an image of society as stable and self-renewing, capable of imposing a common mold on its members. Insofar as people derive from sociology such a restricted and faulty image of the social world, the criticism is justified. On the other hand, social knowledge cannot proceed without analysis of structure; and an understanding of what holds society together is necessary even for those who dislike the bonds and would gladly break them. Consensus *and* conflict, structure *and* process remain major themes of sociological inquiry.

Chapter 1   **Summary**

Section 1/**The discipline of sociology**

Academic subjects are known by the questions they ask and by the ways they search for answers. Sociology and the other social sciences (anthropology, economics, geography, history, political science, and social psychology) have much in common. They are all involved in the systematic study of social behavior and its products, but they emphasize different aspects of society even when they study the same topic or problem.

Although sociology deals with subjects that people experience in their everyday lives, the sociologist studies social life more systematically and precisely than is possible on the basis of direct personal experience.

Section 2/**Sociology and social policy**

As a scientific field, sociology is both academic and applied, and these two purposes sometimes conflict. The value of sociology's contribution to understanding social issues is based upon the objectivity and exactness of sociological analysis. When applied to policy research, sociology directs attention beyond official goals toward the long-run consequences of political or social action.

Because social scientists study human beings in real life social settings, they are challenged by ethical issues that are even more pressing than those that concern physical and biological scientists. It is difficult or impossible for social researchers to be completely neutral about some issues and they must guard against letting their values influence their results. Who should do research is not a question that sociology can automatically answer.

Who should be studied is also a lively question. The protection of subjects' privacy must always be balanced against what can be learned in a research project.

Section 3/**Levels of analysis**

Sociology analyzes social life at three levels—interpersonal, group, and societal. The interpersonal level is concerned with the social connections between two or more persons. Adaptation 1.1 analyzes friendship in a black ghetto and suggests how economic poverty can impair human relations. The group level deals with both person-centered groups and impersonal organizations. It also studies the processes by which a social category—a set of people who are similar in some way—may be changed into a social

group. The societal level deals with whole communities or societies.

Section 4/**Contrasting models of society**

Two sets of competing theoretical perspectives are the consensus model versus the conflict model and structure versus process. The consensus approach emphasizes social stability, suggests slow change, and tends to be conservative. The conflict approach emphasizes the potential for change and shifting power.

A structural perspective concentrates on relatively abstract social units such as strata, classes, and institutions. Symbolic interactionism reacts against the structural approach and emphasizes the processes by which persons respond to and interpret the social world in which they live. A comprehensive science of society includes both pairs of competing perspectives: consensus/conflict; structure/process.

Suggested Readings

Becker, Howard S.
1981 *Exploring Society Photographically*. Evanston, Ill.: Northwestern University Press.

Berger, Peter L., and Brigitte Berger
1976 *Sociology: A Biographical Approach*. Revised edition. Harmondsworth: Penguin.

Blumer, Herbert
1969 *Symbolic Interactionism: Perspective and Method*. Englewood Cliffs, N.J.: Prentice-Hall.

Coser, Lewis A.
1977 *Masters of Sociological Thought*. Second edition. New York: Harcourt Brace Jovanovich.

Hollander, Paul
1973 *Soviet and American Society*. New York: Oxford University Press.

Homans, George C.
1974 *Social Behavior: Its Elementary Forms*. Revised edition. New York: Harcourt Brace Jovanovich.

Merton, Robert K.
1967 *On Theoretical Sociology*. New York: Free Press.

Mills, C. Wright
1961 *The Sociological Imagination*. New York: Oxford University Press.

Nisbet, Robert A.
1966 *The Sociological Tradition*. New York: Basic Books.

Schneider, Louis
1975 *The Sociological Way of Looking at the World*. New York: McGraw-Hill.

General References

Gould, Julius, and William L. Kolb (eds.)
1964 *Dictionary of the Social Sciences*. New York: Free Press.

1968 *International Encyclopedia of the Social Sciences*. New York: Macmillan.

Theodorson, George A., and Achilles G. Theodorson
1969 *A Modern Dictionary of Sociology*. New York: Thomas Y. Crowell.

Chapter 2

Doing Sociology

Section One
The Research Process

Depending on the kind of information they seek, sociologists use a variety of research techniques. These include questionnaires and interviews; the analysis of official statistics and government records; the study of diaries and letters; and observation of individual behavior and face-to-face interactions.

Much sociological research is not very different from the way people ask and answer questions in everyday life. For example, a couple may think their second child adjusted to school better than their first child. This impression might lead them to ask other parents if they had found the same to be true of their children, and they might also talk with the children's teachers. Although such questioning is not the same as systematic study, in some ways it resembles scientific research.

SYSTEMATIC STUDY

Suppose a sociologist turns the parent's observation into a generalization: "Other things being equal, children with older brothers and sisters adjust to school better than firstborn children." Now the problem is stated in a form that can lead to research. It is now a testable **hypothesis,** which may be supported or rejected by the examination of evidence.

Having framed a testable hypothesis, sociologists would review scientific books and journals to see what other researchers have written on the topic. They might go to a school and observe the children. They would also talk with parents and teachers to find out what new pupils do when they are upset or insecure. From this exploration they would develop a classification of behaviors to identify children who adapt to school easily and those who have trouble. Crying, clinging to the parents, or refusing to join in school activities might be examples of problem behaviors.

Since some children adapt better or more quickly than others, we say that their adjustment varies: Adjustment to school is one major **variable** in this imaginary study. Birth order is the other major variable. The object of the research is to determine the

connection between the two variables, adjustment to school and birth order. In this study, birth order would be called the **independent** variable because it is presumed to influence behavior in school, which is the **dependent** variable.

The next step would be to select a small number of young children from several schools. The sample children would be identified as either firstborn or later born. The researchers would then observe the children in a systematic way and keep records of their behavior. **Controls** would be designed to rule out the possible influence of other factors that might affect the results. To control for time, observations would be made during the same hours of the school day, on the same days of the week, and at the same times of the school year. These procedures should insure that variations in the children's behaviors were not related to the timing of the observations.

It would also be advisable to control for sex. To take an extreme case, if all the firstborn children were boys and all the later-born children were girls, differences in adjustment to school might be related to differences in the ways boys and girls are brought up at home rather than to birth order. By including both boys and girls in both birth-order groups and recording the sex of each child along with the child's behaviors, the researchers could identify sex differences in adjustment. The resulting sample might look like the one in Table 2.1, which was made up for this example.

Table 2.1 Birth Order and Sex Composition of an Imaginary Sample

Birth order	Boys	Girls	Total
Firstborn	20	20	40
Later-born	20	20	40
Total	40	40	80

At this point, the sociologists would be ready to deal with the question of whether firstborn or later-born children have more trouble adjusting to school. Table 2.2 (which was also made up for this example) shows that firstborn children cry at school more often

Table 2.2   Adjustment to School, by Birth Order

Frequency of crying per day	Birth order		Total
	Firstborn	Later born	
More than twice	34	10	44
Twice or less	6	30	36
Total	40	40	80

than later-born children. Boys and girls are combined in this table because for the purpose of this simplified example we assume that there are no sex differences in adjustment. If frequency of crying is an accurate measure of adjustment problems, the data support the hypothesis. On the basis of this evidence, we could say that children with older brothers and sisters tend to adjust to school more easily than do firstborn children. To test the hypothesis more fully, the researchers would repeat the study in different schools, and similar studies would be done using different measures of adjustment and larger samples.

Scientific research should always be tentative and open to revision. A satisfactory scientific report clearly states its hypotheses and research procedures, and presents its conclusions in retestable form. A clearer statement of the problem, a better sample, or better controls may ultimately throw doubt on findings that once looked solid. Or earlier conclusions can be strengthened by later research and improved evidence. The objective of science is to present testable conclusions, not absolutely final answers.

MAKING SENSE OF DATA

Real data are rarely as cooperative as those in our imaginary example. Usually a research plan covers more than two variables, and those variables can usually be analyzed in several ways. The results of the research may not be obvious—facts rarely speak for themselves. In the adjustment to school study, what is to be counted as crying? Must it include tears? Or is a crying noise a sufficient indicator? Will the crying be measured by length of time? By

loudness? These are examples of practical research decisions.

Turning to a more typical sociological topic, such as social inequality, a researcher must decide how to measure income: as exact dollar amounts, or grouped in categories such as hundreds or thousands of dollars, or grouped in rough categories such as low, medium, and high? Once the data have been sorted into categories and tabulated, we can begin to interpret the results and test the hypothesis. It is often helpful to summarize the findings in the form of a table or graph. Adaptation 2.1 explains the layout of a table in detail. Adaptation 2.2 shows how to interpret statistical data that are presented in graphic form.

When a difference makes a difference

Since social research often involves comparing two or more groups, sociologists have to decide whether an observed difference is big or small. One way to solve this problem is to compare the size of the difference with the size of the numbers on which it is based.

In early 1980, for example, 55 percent of black women were working or looking for work, compared to 51 percent of white women, a difference of 4 percentage points. This difference is not very large in itself, but it is a long-standing difference: For many years, black women have been more active in the labor force than white women. Also in early 1980 the unemployment rates were roughly 10 percent for black women and 5 percent for white women (U.S. Bureau of Labor Statistics, 1980: Tables A33, A59). Again, 5 percentage points may not look like a big difference. But this difference says that the unemployment rate for black women was double the rate for white women. Thus, when the labor-force participation rates are subtracted (55 − 51 = 4), the result is almost the same as when the unemployment rates are subtracted (10 − 5 = 5). While the absolute differences (4 or 5 percent) are similar, the 4 percent difference between 55 and 51 percent is relatively small but the 5 percent difference between 5 and 10 percent is relatively big. By 1982 the labor-force participation rates of black and white women had converged (56 and 53 percent). The unemployment rates for black and white women had sharply increased, but the rate for black women (17 percent) was still nearly double that for white women (9 percent) (U.S. Bureau of Labor Statistics, 1982: Table A3).

Another way to decide whether a difference is big or small is to consider its social impact. Does the difference make a difference? One candidate may get only a few votes more than another, but the winner wins as definitely as if the election were a landslide. The high rate of unemployment among black women is socially significant because it is a source of stress for a great many households.

Some sociological research does not produce any numbers. Studies like those by Liebow (see Adaptation 1.1) and Goffman (see Adaptation 5.1) depend on the insight of a patient, sensitive observer. (Liebow, for example, spent a year associating with a group of black men in a Washington, D.C., neighborhood.) In such studies, the researchers must decide what information is relevant to their study and what is just "noise" in the social environment. They organize extensive notes to uncover underlying patterns in dozens or hundreds of separate events and interactions. If every observation were given equal attention, the basic patterns would simply drown in the data.

Description and explanation

A *description* of something tells what it is like: how big, how long, how many, where, which one, who did what. A sociological description is usually an account of the facts, a summary of the characteristics of a person or group. For example, there are several ways to describe life expectancy in the United States. We can say that on the average persons born in the United States can expect to live more than 70 years. We can also say that longevity has increased during the past 100 years, so that today people live longer than they did a century ago. We can also compare the longevity of men and women and report that on the average women outlive men.

But knowing what happens does not tell why it happens. Why is life expectancy over 70 years, not under 60 or over 80? Why has longevity increased

in the past century? Why do women live longer than men? The answers to these "why" questions are *explanations*. Women may live longer than men because men are exposed to more occupational disease and injury, because of biological differences between the sexes, because women take better care of themselves, or for some other reason or combination of reasons. To improve longevity, we need to know why the differences exist, not just what the differences are.

Sometimes we can use the information contained in a description without having an explanation. For example, in the 1800s Ignaz Semmelweiss, a Hungarian physician, found that he could prevent childbed fever by washing his hands in disinfectant before touching his patients. He did not know that bacteria caused the fever, nor did he need to know the reason in order to solve the immediate practical problem. In this case, *what* happened was more important than *why*.

SAMPLING

Except for research on small groups, it is impossible to study every person in a given category. Therefore, researchers choose a smaller number—a **sample**—of individuals for study. The sample represents the whole category.

The kind of sample selected depends on the goal of the research. Sometimes the purpose is to generalize the findings to a very large group. It may be possible to investigate only a few hundred people, but we may want the study to represent many thousands of people. In this case, the researcher chooses a **random sample.** Randomness avoids the risk of selecting subjects who are not representative of the whole group. In a simple random sample, every member of the whole group (**universe** or **population**) has an equal chance of being included in the sample. National public-opinion polls contact only a few hundred or a few thousand people, but they are chosen so as to represent the entire adult population.

Because they are not a random sample of the population, the use of college students as subjects for experiments is often criticized. A sample made up of students in an introductory course is biased by age, education, and family income, and the results of research using such a sample cannot be generalized to the population as a whole. However, if the researcher wants to find out how college freshmen form friendships, such a sample would be satisfactory. It would be even better to take a random sample of the whole freshman class in order to represent the students' varying backgrounds and fields of study.

A random sample is not well suited to all purposes. When little is known about the question to be researched, it may be better to use a **theoretical** or **purposive sample.** In this case, subjects for study are selected because they have some special characteristic, knowledge, or experience. If researchers wanted to study the causes of divorce, they would not start with a random sample of the entire population or even with a random sample of the population who had ever been married. Instead, they might take a random sample of the population of divorced people.

Researchers who already had some hunches about the causes of divorce could take two purposive samples: one of divorced pairs and one of still-married couples. To the extent possible, the two groups would be matched by age, length of marriage, education, and other characteristics. The matching would help bring out differences in the ways the spouses interacted and in the ways they adjusted to marriage. To keep things simple, it might be best to exclude divorced persons who had subsequently remarried, because they represent a different type of adjustment.

(Text continued on p. 25)

Adaptation 2.1

Reading a Table*

A statistical table is a labor-saving device. Quantitative data presented in a well-planned table are easier to understand than they would be if they were buried in several paragraphs of words. A table is not just a list of numbers; it is a statement of the way various factors are related to one another. In Table 2.3, the factors are age, race or ethnicity, and poverty.

Tables may present data in percents or numbers, and numbers may be given in units or thousands or millions. This table presents its data in percents, that is, rates per 100 persons.

ANATOMY OF A TABLE

A good table has clear signposts, and if you read these signs carefully, you can avoid needless work and confusion. Outside Table 2.3 are labels that identify the main features of a table. This adaptation deals with each of these features in turn. If you learn to follow the signs, you will know how to interpret the tables you will see in this textbook, in other books, and in magazines.

Title
The title of Table 2.3 says that it summarizes information on poverty among whites, blacks, and people of Spanish origin in the United States. It says that the data have been sorted into age categories and that they are presented as rates, that is, percents.

Headnote
The bracketed headnote explains that the rates apply to the money income of people who live alone as well as those who live in families.

Footnotes
Footnote *a* gives the poverty line for 1982 and tells the reader where to find more information about how

---

*Suggested by Wallis and Roberts, 1956:270–274.

Title	**Table 2.3** Poverty Rates, by Age, of Whites, Blacks, and Persons of Spanish Origin, United States, 1982

Headnote [Unrelated individuals and persons in families with money income below the poverty line in 1982][a]

	Percent in poverty			
Age	**White (Col. 1)**	**Black (Col. 2)**	**Spanish origin[b] (Col. 3)**	**Total[c] (Col. 4)**
Under 16	18	48	40	**22**
16 – 21	13	39	31	17
22 – 44	10	27	24	12
45 – 54	8	22	19	9
55 – 59	8	30	20	10
60 – 64	10	27	21	11
65 and over	12	38	27	15
All ages	**12**	**36**	**30**	**15**

Headings label the column group. *Stub* at the left. *Marginals* at the right edge and bottom row.

[a]In 1982 the poverty line for a family of four was $9,862. Payment in kind, such as free rent or farm produce, is not counted as money income. Nonmoney transfers, such as food stamps and health benefits, are also excluded. For explanations of money income and the poverty line, see original source, pp. 1 – 5 and 29 – 30.
[b]Includes persons of both Spanish and Spanish-American origin, who may be of any race. The word "Hispanic" is sometimes used instead of "Spanish origin."
[c]Persons of American Indian and Asian origin are not reported separately because of the small number in the sample.

Source: United States Bureau of the Census, *Current Population Reports*, Series P-60, no. 140 (Advance Report), July 1983: computed and compiled from Table 17. Basic data are from a Current Population Survey in which over 59,000 interviews were obtained from about 61,500 eligible households. The survey was conducted in March 1983 in order to secure data on income for 1982.

income and poverty are defined. Footnote *a* refers to the whole table, but footnotes *b* and *c* each refer only to a single column.

Source note

The source note points out that the data are taken from a large sample survey conducted by the Current Population Survey of the United States Bureau of the Census. The data on which Table 2.3 is based appear in the *Current Population Report* cited in the note. The table in the original source includes other age breakdowns and presents the data by sex, type of residence, region, and work experience. It also reports "raw" numbers and gives the percents to one decimal place. To construct Table 2.3, we chose a few of the most important facts presented in the original source and rounded the percents to whole numbers (for instance, 15 percent rather than 14.8 percent). The source note therefore says that the data were "computed and compiled" (that is, the original table has not been reproduced in the form in which it appears in the source). There is no set rule about where such explanations should be given, but they should be given somewhere. If they are not given in the table, they should be included in the text.

Headings and stub

The headings identify the information in the columns; the stub, which is the column at the left of the table, identifies the age brackets that label the rows.

Marginals

When you look at the numbers in a table, it is a good idea to work from the outside in. Begin by looking at the summary numbers in the margins called "marginals,'' which are usually found in the right-hand column and in the bottom row. The marginals in Table 2.3 are set in heavy type. In this example, column 4 shows the variation in poverty rates by age group for the whole population being studied. The overall rate for all ages, whites, blacks, and people of Spanish origin combined is given in the lower right-hand corner as 15 percent. Reading down column 4, you can see that the youngest age groups have the highest poverty rates and the oldest group the next highest rate. Reading across the bottom row, you can see that blacks have the highest poverty rate.

Cells

To make more detailed comparisons, look at various *cells* that is, the places where the numbers appear in the body of the table. For example, you might want to know whether blacks (column 2) of a certain age have a lower poverty rate than whites (column 1) of the same age. The table shows that in every age group blacks have higher poverty rates than whites. In fact, the highest rate for whites (18 percent for the youngest age group) is lower than the lowest rate for blacks in any age group (22 percent for blacks aged

45–54). Poverty rates for persons of Spanish origin (column 3) fall between those for blacks and whites but are closer to those for blacks. This comparison shows the extent of poverty among the largest minority groups in the United States.

FACTS FROM THE TABLE

Here are some of the important facts that can be found in this table:

1. The overall poverty rate for the United States population in 1982 was 15 percent.
2. There were wide variations by age and race/ethnicity, ranging from a high of 48 percent for blacks under age 16 to a low of 8 percent for whites aged 45–54 and 55–59.
3. Poverty rates were highest for the youngest and oldest age groups.
4. Poverty rates were highest for blacks and lowest for whites.
5. The poverty rates for persons of Spanish origin were between those of whites and blacks in each age group.

Adaptation 2.2

Understanding a Figure

Statistical figures are visual aids. They help the reader understand quantitative data more quickly than if they were presented in the form of tables or equations. Figures are especially useful for showing changes over time or differences between two or more groups on such characteristics as income or education. If exact data are needed, it is best to refer to the actual numbers.

Figure 2.1 presents in graphic form information that would otherwise require many words or a table with four columns of numbers. Like Table 2.3, Figure 2.1 compares poverty rates. However, the figure shows trends over time rather than a cross

section of the data at a single point in time.

Title

The title states that the figure traces the poverty rates for different groups over two decades.

Footnotes

Footnote *a* points out that there is a seven-year gap between the 1959 census figures for blacks and the figures for 1966, when the Current Population Survey began to report figures on blacks.

Footnote *b* indicates the starting date for poverty

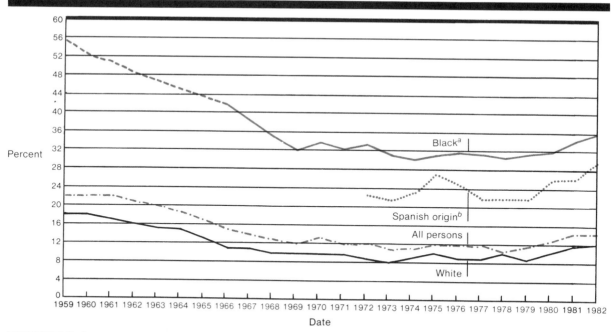

FIGURE 2.1 **Percentages of Whites, Blacks, Persons of Spanish Origin (Hispanic), and the Total Population in Poverty, United States, 1959-1982**

[a] Data for blacks in 1959 are from a 1:1000 sample drawn from the 1960 census. Separate sample survey data on black poverty were reported for the year 1966.

[b] Separate sample survey data on poverty among those of Spanish origin were first reported for 1972. Persons of Spanish origin may be of any race.

Source: U.S. Bureau of the Census, *CPR*, Series P-60, No. 140 (Advance Report), July 1983; collated from Table 17. Basic data are drawn from the Current Population Survey except as noted in footnote *a*.

data on persons of Spanish origin. It also mentions that they may be members of any racial group. Note that poverty data on whites, blacks, and persons of Spanish origin have different starting dates.

Source note

The source is another table in the *Current Population Report* that supplied the basic data for Table 2.3.

INTERPRETATION

In looking at trends, it is sensible to ask whether changes in the numbers are caused partly by changes in the methods used to collect or process data in different years. As is mentioned in footnote *a*, 1959 figures for blacks are from the 1960 census. The Bureau of the Census drew a 1:1000 sample (that is, one person in a thousand) from the 1960 census

results. All other data are from the Current Population sample survey.

The methodology of the Current Population Survey was revised in 1966, 1974, and 1979. As a result, the *Current Population Report* presents data gathered under both the old and the revised methodologies. The changes in method do not make much difference in this figure, but it is good practice for the source (and textbooks) to note anything that might influence the results. Sometimes changes in methods make differences that are big enough to show up as jogs in a graph.

Definitions of poverty

Poverty is discussed later in this book. Here we need only mention that inflation has been taken into account in setting the poverty line. For the 1982 definition, see footnote *a* to Table 2.3, page 22.

Facts from the figure

1. *Total population*. The poverty rate for the population as a whole fell quickly during the 1960s. There was little change until the recession of the 1980s led to a sharp increase in poverty.

2. *Whites*. The poverty rate for whites started from a lower level than did the rates for the other groups. It then decreased by half, and remained around 9 to 10 percent from 1968 through 1980 but showed an increase in the recession to 12 percent in 1982.

3. *Blacks*. In 1959, over half the black population was poor. From that time until the early 1970s the poverty rate of blacks declined, but there was little or no progress after that. Over one-third of all blacks lived in poverty in 1982.

4. *Persons of Spanish origin*. The short curve for persons of Spanish origin looks erratic, perhaps because it is influenced by continuing immigration. Statistics gathered over a longer period might give a better picture of the poverty status of this population.

5. *Hidden trends*. Stable percentages do not mean that there is no change in the number of people in poverty. Because the population is growing, the actual number of poor people increases when the percent remains the same. For example, the percent of the total population in poverty in 1976 was almost exactly the same as in 1972, but there were about half a million more poor people in 1976 than there were in 1972.

Section Two
Getting Information

Because sociologists are interested in all social behavior, sociological facts can be found in almost any human situation and researchers use a wide variety of methods.

OBSERVING

Often unaided eyes and ears are all the researcher needs. The most direct way to collect data is to look with a purpose—to look at people in social situations or to study the records of human activity. Polsky's research on pool-hall "hustlers" did not use questionnaires or other special techniques. Instead, Polsky used the pool hall itself and observed hustlers as they hustled. He watched them from the sidelines, played against them, and talked with them. His analysis of poolroom hustling was based on the information he obtained in this way (Polsky, 1967/1969: 31–108).

In Polsky's study, the observer was part of the social situation he was studying. This kind of research is therefore called **participant observation.** Often researchers are just observers and do not participate in the interactions under study. But the observer, whether a participant or not, must be careful to avoid influencing the situation. When the re-

Player? Hustler? Sucker?
Participant observer?

searcher's presence or behavior affects what is going on, the data obtained may be inaccurate. For example, people may be on their best behavior when they know they are being watched. This change is called the **guinea pig effect** (Webb et al., 1966:13). In most situations, people quickly get used to being observed. But careful researchers guard against the guinea pig effect by avoiding any unnecessary contact with the people they are studying.

Unobtrusive research

Some projects do not require the researcher to interact with the subjects. For example, if you wanted to find out which exhibits in a museum were the most popular, you would not have to talk with visitors to the museum. Instead, you could count the people who stop in front of each exhibit and clock the length of time they look at it.

An even less obtrusive approach (which would also save time) would be to measure the wear or dirt on the carpets around the exhibits. A study conducted in the Chicago Museum of Science and Industry used the museum's records of floor tile replacements. The study found that the tiles around the exhibit of hatching chicks had to be replaced every six weeks or so, but the tiles near some other exhibits did not have to be replaced for years (Webb et al., 1966:36–38).

STUDYING EXISTING RECORDS

There are many ways to get data without going ''where the action is.'' Some sociologists study documents in libraries, in private collections, or in the archives of newspapers or organizations such as unions or corporations. These materials are valuable for doing case studies of organizations or social histories of changing institutions.

For some purposes, a special technique, called **content analysis,** is used to code written material and identify patterns in the language and subject matter of books, articles, and other documents. For example, researchers studied prize-winning children's picture books to find out who the characters were and what they did (Weitzman et al., 1972). The study found that few of the stories were about girls

Observing the observers.

or women and that the females who did appear were inactive, weak, and dependent. Their roles were those of mother, wife, and in a few cases nurse or teacher. Content analysis can also be applied to paintings, films, television and radio programs, and other recorded material.

EXPERIMENTING

The most carefully controlled research design is the experiment. In an experiment, the subjects to be compared are identical in all ways but one. This one factor is the **experimental variable.** The purpose is to control all other factors that might affect the outcome. Then, at the end of the experiment, the researcher can claim that the differences found are probably due to the experimental variable.

Only a small number of sociological problems can be studied in experiments, which are often carried out in social-psychology laboratories where the researcher can control the environment. For example, social psychologists used a laboratory experiment to study the reactions of bystanders to an emergency—an accomplice pretended to fall off a chair (Latané and Darley, 1968). The people who heard the "accident" were arranged in groups of varying size. Factors other than group size, such as the sex and age of both "victim" and bystanders, were held constant (that is, controlled). The experimenters concluded that people in groups are less likely than lone bystanders to offer help to an accident victim.

In addition to conducting laboratory experiments, researchers sometimes conduct "natural" or **field experiments.** In such experiments, researchers do not control the variables directly. Instead, they take advantage of a real-life situation in which the variables are controlled by other agents or events. For example, a team of researchers who were interested in the effects of industrialization learned that a steel mill was going to be built in a small town. They studied that town and another one similar to it in size, economy, and social characteristics (Summers et al., 1969). By comparing the two towns before, during, and after the construction of the steel mill, they were able to compare a town that became industrialized with one that remained rural. Since the towns were similar and were exposed to similar influences— except for the steel mill—the researchers could assume that the differences they observed were largely caused by industrialization.

Section Three
Surveys and Polls

COMMUNITY SURVEYS

Large-scale social surveys are not new. Booth's seventeen-volume *Labour and Life of the People of London* (1889–1902/1970), a landmark of applied sociology, revealed the condition of the poor and near-poor in London during the nineteenth century. Although his methods would not meet modern technical standards, Booth broke new ground by using interviews to gather a large body of data.

In the United States, the best-known early community surveys are the Middletown and Yankee

City studies. The Middletown (Muncie, Indiana) surveys were conducted by Robert S. Lynd and Helen M. Lynd (1929 and 1937). They attempted to reveal the social life of a whole city. The findings were classified under six main headings: economic, family, education, leisure, religion, and community activities. The Lynds used several research methods including participant observation; study of public historical documents; analysis of statistics on employment, place of residence, membership in organizations, and recreation; and many formal and informal interviews. The Middletown studies applied research methods developed by anthropologists to a medium size American community (population under 5,000). Muncie was recently restudied with many of the same techniques used by the Lynds in the original Middletown studies (Caplow and Bahr, 1979; Caplow, 1980:50; Caplow et al., 1982. But for a critique of the 1982 reference, see Cherlin, 1982).

Research for the Yankee City series was carried out in Newburyport, Massachusetts, by W. L. Warner and his associates (Warner and Lunt, 1941, 1942; Warner and Srole, 1945; Warner and Low, 1947; Warner, 1959). It was part of a large research program comparing several kinds of American communities. The Yankee City monographs emphasized the influence of class distinctions on social behavior and beliefs.

The average citizen is well aware of established public-opinion polls, such as Roper and Gallup. There is much interest in the attempts of the polls to predict elections or to estimate the popularity of politicians. These polls, which are now conducted in many countries, are sample surveys. Other sample surveys gather data on consumer attitudes toward various products and are a standard marketing-research tool. In addition, governments use sample surveys to estimate population trends in the years between censuses. The United States Census uses sampling methods on some census questions.

Several times a year the Census Bureau also conducts a major sample survey called the Current Population Survey, which gathers data on such topics as school enrollment and poverty. These data are published in a series called *Current Population Reports*

(CPR)* and are widely used both in social science and public policy. For example, the data on poverty presented in Adaptations 2.1 and 2.2 supply objective information that a complex democratic society must have if it is to manage its problems in a humane way. Competent interpretation of that information is the responsibility of persons trained in the social sciences. They must identify underlying trends toward equality or inequality and the significance of the concentration of poverty in particular age-sex and ethnic groupings.

INTERVIEWS AND QUESTIONNAIRES

Asking questions is the best and cheapest way to get many kinds of information, and a lot of social research is based on interviews and questionnaires. The chief difference between interviews and questionnaires is whether respondents (persons answering the questions) answer directly on the questionnaire forms, like objective tests, or respond to questions asked by an interviewer. If an interviewer asks the questions, in person or on the telephone, the "questionnaire" is technically called an **interview schedule.**

Questionnaires are especially useful for collecting unambiguous information that people are well aware of, such as their education and work histories, how often they have moved, or their views on political issues. Questionnaire studies are cheaper than interviews, but replies may be less consistent, and many questionnaires, especially mailed questionnaires, are never returned to the researcher.

Interviews have a high response rate and more consistent replies. Schedules administered by trained interviewers may be highly organized, or structured, so that the responses will be easy to compare. On the other hand, to secure personal reactions from respon-

*When we refer to the *CPR* in this book, we do not use the *CPR's* "suggested citation" form: U.S. Bureau of the Census, *Current Population Reports,* Series P-60, No. 118, "Money Income in 1977 of Families and Persons in the United States." U.S. Government Printing Office, Washington, D.C., 1979. Instead, we shorten it to: *"Current Population Reports,* (or further abbreviate to *CPR), Series P-60, No. 118, March 1979."* With this information the reader should have no trouble finding the report in a library.

On the street, by telephone, and at home, survey interviewers and polling reports are standard features of modern life.

dents, questions may be open-ended, and the respondent is invited to express thoughts and feelings.

Many modern surveys include open-ended questions in addition to highly specific ones. Respondents may be asked how they feel about something, to describe an event in detail, or to talk about the future. Open-ended questions round out the picture drawn by more structured questions. Figure 2.2 shows two pages of a survey designed to investigate the quality of American life (Campbell et al., 1976). Questions C1 and C2 are completely open-ended. Subjects were asked to respond in their own words; there were no suggested answers. Two other open-ended questions (C5a and C7a) were asked only of certain respondents, depending on their answers to earlier questions. Respondents who said they did "not feel free" in the structured part of question C5 were asked in question C5a to indicate ways in which they did not feel free.

In question C3, respondents were asked to summarize their feelings about life in the United States. Table 2.4 presents some of the data gathered from this question. About half of the respondents answered that life was "about the same." Of the other half, more respondents thought that things were getting worse rather than better.

The limits of questionnaires

Interviews and questionnaires have some drawbacks. Sometimes people are unwilling or unable to answer questions. Sometimes there is a difference between what subjects say and what they do. To detect such differences, researchers may use more than one method. For example, LaPiere (1934) spent part of two years traveling with a Chinese couple. They were served in 184 restaurants and cafes and stayed at 66 hotels and auto camps, the forerunners of motels. They were refused service at only one place in nearly 10,000 miles of travel.

Six months later, LaPiere sent questionnaires to all the restaurants and hotels where they had been served and to a sample of similar places. Of the 256 that replied, all but one said that they would not accept Chinese guests or (in 18 cases) that it would "depend on the circumstances." Yet 128 of them had served such clients. The study concluded that interpretation of attitudes must "be derived from a study of humans behaving in actual social situations. They must not be imputed on the basis of questionnaire data" (LaPiere, 1934:237).

In the years since LaPiere's study, much progress has been made in attitude measurement and new laws have opened up the use of public facilities. However,

Table 2.4   Responses to the Question on the Quality of Life in the United States[a]

	Getting better (%)	Staying same (%)	Getting worse (%)	Number (100%)
All	17	47	36	2126
Sex				
Males	20	44	36	897
Females	14	51	35	1229
Education attainment				
Eighth grade or less	12	55	33	463
Some high school, no diploma	11	52	37	392
High school diploma	17	47	36	698
Some college, no degree	22	42	36	328
College degree(s)	27	38	35	234
Race				
White	17	47	36	1845
Black	17	50	33	221
Income				
Less than $3,000	12	52	36	290
$3,000 – 4,999	13	49	38	280
$5,000 – 6,999	15	50	35	265
$7,000 – 9,999	17	47	36	362
$10,000 – 11,999	16	47	37	264
$12,000 – 16,999	20	48	32	319
$17,000 or more	24	41	35	261

[a]See Question C3 in Figure 2.2

Source: From *The Quality of American Life: Perceptions, Evaluations, and Satisfactions,* by Angus Campbell, Philip E. Converse, and Willard L. Rodgers © 1976 by Russell Sage Foundation. Reprinted by permission of Basic Books, Inc., Publishers.

SECTION C: COUNTRY

C1. Now I have some questions on how you feel about life in this country as a whole.

Do you think that there are some ways in which life in the United States is getting worse? (How is that?) _____

_____

_____

_____

_____

_____

_____

_____

C2. Are there some ways in which you think life in the U. S. is getting better? (How is that?) _____

_____

_____

_____

_____

_____

_____

_____

C3. All things considered, do you think things are getting better, or worse, that they are staying about the same, or what?

| 1. BETTER | 5. WORSE | 3. SOME BETTER, SOME WORSE | 4. ABOUT THE SAME |

OTHER: _____

C4. People sometimes tell us that public officials in this country don't always treat them as fairly as they ought to. How about you—would you say that in general public officials treat you <u>very</u> fairly, fairly enough, not very fairly, or not fairly at all?

| 1. VERY FAIRLY | 2. FAIRLY ENOUGH | 3. NOT VERY FAIRLY | 4. NOT FAIRLY AT ALL |

Figure 2.2   Part of the Interview Schedule on the Quality of Life
Source: From *The Quality of American Life: Perceptions, Evaluations, and Satisfactions*, by Angus Campbell, Philip E. Converse, and Willard L. Rodgers © 1976 by Russell Sage Foundation. Reprinted by permission of Basic Books, Inc., Publishers.

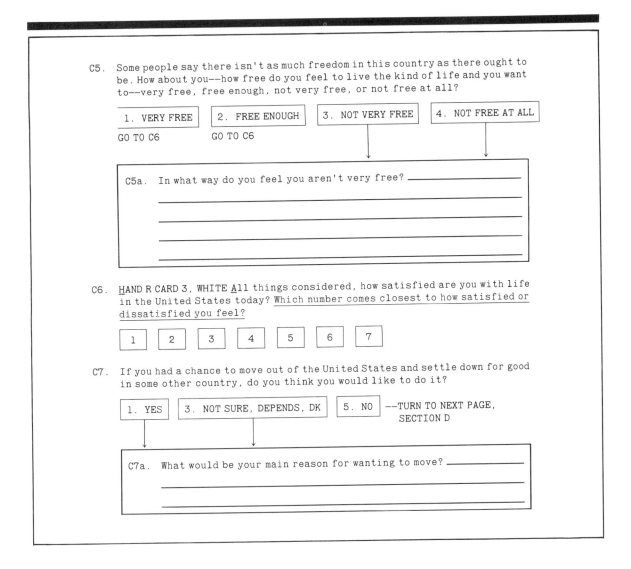

C5. Some people say there isn't as much freedom in this country as there ought to be. How about you—how free do you feel to live the kind of life and you want to—very free, free enough, not very free, or not free at all?

| 1. VERY FREE | 2. FREE ENOUGH | 3. NOT VERY FREE | 4. NOT FREE AT ALL |

GO TO C6   GO TO C6

C5a. In what way do you feel you aren't very free? _____

C6. HAND R CARD 3, WHITE All things considered, how satisfied are you with life in the United States today? Which number comes closest to how satisfied or dissatisfied you feel?

| 1 | 2 | 3 | 4 | 5 | 6 | 7 |

C7. If you had a chance to move out of the United States and settle down for good in some other country, do you think you would like to do it?

| 1. YES | 3. NOT SURE, DEPENDS, DK | 5. NO | —TURN TO NEXT PAGE, SECTION D

C7a. What would be your main reason for wanting to move? _____

the warning about the limitations on the interpretation of questionnaires still has merit, and the divergence between the attitudes individuals express and their behavior continues to be an important topic of sociological research.

Chapter 2   **Summary**

Section 1/**The research process**
All research begins with systematic questioning leading to a hypothesis, a statement that can be tested with evidence. It is often stimulated by the results of previous studies. To test a hypothesis a researcher gathers information on the variables under study: the independent variable or variables that are thought to be the cause and the dependent variable that is being influenced. Outside influences that might distort results are controlled.

Meaningful differences are not necessarily numerically large. A small percentage may be important if it represents a large number of people or reveals a significant impact on many lives.

Samples are used to study large groups in a systematic way. In a random sample every member of the population under investigation has an equal chance of being selected. In a theoretical or purposive sample subjects are chosen because they have characteristics relevant to the research.

Adaptation 2.1 reviews the characteristics of a table and how to interpret what is reported in the table. Adaptation 2.2 presents a similar set of instructions for statistical diagrams.

Section 2/Getting information

A wide range of methods are used to collect information. They include direct observation either as an active participant or an arm's-length observer and examining and codifying (systematically summarizing) existing records. Formal laboratory experiments are relatively rare in sociological research, but field or natural experiments are undertaken when opportunities arise.

Section 3/Surveys and polls

Community surveys, using almost the full range of research techniques from the examination of written records and printed documents to the statistical analyses of demographic data and sample surveys, try to gain a systematic overview of an entire community. The Middletown and Yankee City studies are the best-known American community surveys.

Public opinion polls are usually restricted to well-defined topics and require precise sampling so the small number of people interviewed can stand for the whole population. They usually call on the skills of trained interviewers and may be conducted either in person or by telephone.

Questionnaires filled out by the respondents are useful for collecting relatively simple information about which people are well aware but are of less value for subjective and more subtle topics.

Suggested Readings

Barnes, J. A.
1979 *Who Should Know What? Social Science, Privacy and Ethics.* New York: Penguin Books.

Converse, Jean M., and Howard Schuman
1974 *Conversations at Random: Survey Research as Interviewers See It.* New York: Wiley.

Freeman, Howard E., Russell R. Dynes, Peter H. Rossi, and William Foote Whyte (eds.)
1983 *Applied Sociology.* San Francisco: Jossey-Bass Inc., Publishers.

Hammond, Phillip E. (ed.)
1967 *Sociologists at Work: Essays on the Craft of Social Research.* Garden City, N.Y.: Doubleday Anchor Books.

Kaplan, Abraham
1964 *The Conduct of Inquiry: Methodology for Behavioral Science.* New York: Harper & Row.

McCall, George J., and J. L. Simmons (eds.)
1969 *Issues in Participant Observation.* Reading, Mass.: Addison-Wesley.

Moser, C. A., and G. Kalton
1971 *Survey Methods in Social Investigation.* London: Heinemann.

Sudman, Seymour, and Norman M. Bradburn
1982 *Asking Questions: A Practical Guide to Questionnaire Design.* San Francisco: Jossey-Bass Inc., Publishers.

Webb, Eugene J., Donald T. Campbell, Richard D. Schwartz, and Lee Sechrest
1966 *Unobtrusive Measures.* Chicago: Rand McNally.

Official Statistical Sources for the United States

Statistical Abstract of the United States (annual).

Historical Statistics of the United States: Bicentennial edition (1975).

Social Indicators.

Part Two

Elements of Analysis

Chapter 3

Culture

Section One
The Concept of Culture

In social science, the term **culture** refers to the shared ways of thinking and believing that grow out of group experience and are passed from one generation to the next (Kroeber and Kluckhohn, 1963; Williams, 1960). It is the way of life of a society, the knowledge, beliefs, customs, and skills available to its members. An Eskimo hunter, a Mexican midwife, and an American burglar all share in the general culture of their societies and possess the specialized knowledge of their occupations. Each gains and transmits his or her culture through the socialization process (see Chapter 4).

SYMBOLS

A **symbol** may be defined as anything that stands for or represents something else. The word *pencil* is a symbol: It stands for the idea of a pencil, or for a specific object. Meaning is given to a symbol by those who use it; that is, the meaning of a symbol is social in origin. While words are the most common symbols, acts or objects can also be symbols. For

Table 3.1 Two Types of Symbols

Idea or object	Referential	Expressive
A place to live	The word *house*	The word *home*
Flag	Storm warning	National emblem
Cross	Road sign for *intersection*	Emblem of Christianity
Law	Definition of a crime	Ideal of justice

example, a threatening gesture or a river that marks a boundary have social meanings just as words do.

Symbols may be referential or expressive (Sapir, 1934). Those that refer to specific things are called **referential symbols.** The word pencil denotes (refers to) a specific class of objects. **Expressive symbols** are less specific and limited. National flags carry overtones of feeling and social meaning. They connote abstract ideas such as patriotism rather than denoting specific objects.

The same word or object can be both referential and expressive. (See Table 3.1.) The word *professor* denotes a person who holds a position on a facul-

The Brooklyn Bridge as an expressive symbol.

ty, but the same word may connote authority and learning, or perhaps absentmindedness. The word *cross* denotes an arrangement of lines, but it connotes religious martyrdom and Christianity. The Brooklyn Bridge is a referential symbol when it refers to the fact that it is a bridge in a particular location. It has become an expressive symbol because it is recognized as an enduring thing of beauty and a remarkable engineering accomplishment.

Expressive (connotative) symbols play a special role in culture. *Home* is more expressive than *house*. Expressive symbols define and reinforce the shared ideals of a society. Referential symbols that are narrowly denotative—for example, a code for filing books in a library—have nothing to do with personal or group identity.

CULTURAL VALUES

A **cultural value** is a widely held belief or feeling about what is important to the community's identity or well-being. Privacy, individualism, equality, and freedom are examples of values that strongly influence the way people live, how they are governed, and what they feel is worthwhile. For example, in trying to balance the well-being of the community and the right to hold property, some cultures lean toward equality of income. Others reward people unequally for unequal effort or skill.

In the Anglo-American tradition, privacy is highly valued. How one lives at home, out of sight of the rest of the community, is no one else's business as long as it is not dangerous or does not bother others. The right to privacy is expressed in the ancient law that says "a man's house is his castle." Neither friend nor stranger may enter without permission, and even the police are supposed to have a good reason for doing so. In most cases they can enter only with a court order.

But no value is absolute. Privacy is under attack not only by its old enemies, gossips and snoops, but also by some new ones—electronic eavesdroppers, the mass media, and computer data banks. The values of efficient information management and free enterprise come into conflict with the value of privacy. How to manage electronic data files and at the same time preserve personal privacy is far from resolved.

NORMS

Cultural values are expressed in **norms,** or specific guides to conduct. Some norms apply to everyday activities, while others apply to situations that do not occur often. At funerals women, but not men, may wear a veil to hide their grief. Other aspects of the funeral ceremony require the guidance of a specialist, the funeral "director," since most mourners do not know exactly what is expected of them.

The most important cultural norms, for example those forbidding murder and incest, are called **mores*** (Sumner, 1906/1960:48). Weaker norms, such as those governing dress, are called **folkways.** Feelings about folkways are less intense than feelings about mores, and conformity with folkways is largely up to the individual. A person who does not conform with generally accepted norms of dress arouses little reaction in others except on formal occasions or in special situations, such as visiting a religious place.

CULTURE AND SOCIAL ORGANIZATION

Culture and social organization are linked together. **Social organization** is made up of relations between people and groups, and those relations are guided by cultural rules. For example, the family is a unit of social organization, but much family behavior is guided by culture. One culture may place a high value on a kind of family in which the father is dominant. Another may give the father a less dominant role. Thus, culture and social organization are interdependent. When sociologists discuss these subjects under separate headings, they do so to emphasize different aspects of social life.

---

*The Latin singular of *mores, mos,* is not used by sociologists, who usually say "one of the mores."

Architecture for privacy in an Algerian village.

The Tanala case

The connection between culture and social organization is illustrated by a famous study of the Tanala, a hill tribe on the island of Madagascar off the east coast of Africa (Linton, 1936:348–355; 1933). Originally, the Tanala engaged in dry rice cultivation. They cut down jungle growth and burned it to clear the land for planting. After one or two crops the land lost its fertility and had to be left alone until the jungle overran it again. This went on until there was no more fertile land around the village. Then the village was moved.

Under this system individuals did not own the land; the village as a whole controlled it. Within the village joint families (groups of households with a common head) were the chief units of organization. Joint-family members worked as a group and owned the crops from the land they cleared. The head of the joint family divided the crops among the households, and all households were more or less equal in terms of wealth. Forest products, such as game, belonged to anyone who took them.

However, the culture and social organization of the Tanala were changed when they learned wet rice cultivation, a different technique of rice growing, from another tribe. Adopting new traits or patterns as a result of culture contact is called **acculturation.** Wet rice was planted on small plots cultivated by single households. Unlike the dry rice system, the wet rice system allowed land to be cultivated over and over. The idea of individual ownership of land developed, but only a limited amount of land was suitable for wet rice cultivation.

As a result two classes were formed, the landowners and the landless. Those who held wet rice land no longer took part in jungle clearing, and they did not want the village to be moved. The landless, who continued to use the dry rice system, had to go so far into the jungle that they could not get back to the village at night. Therefore, they too began to develop separate households. Many other changes took place in the kinship and marriage system, in the practice of warfare, in the design of villages and village defense, in slavery, and in the distribution of authority.

The Tanala case shows how social relations are affected by changes in a group's activities. When the food-gathering technology changed, the social system also changed. The shift from dry to wet rice cultivation brought about major changes in social organization—less emphasis on the joint family, greater emphasis on the household, and the location of the village in a single place. Along with these changes came shifts in cultural values. The household replaced the joint family as the chief unit of organization, and land became something to be owned rather than just used temporarily.

Section Two
The Impact of Culture

The experience of the Tanala shows how culture and social organization interact. First, the technology, the material culture, changed as some of the Tanala adopted wet rice growing. Then, the wet rice culture influenced social organization: New social classes and different family forms emerged. In this case, the innovation in material culture was the source of the change; hence, culture is the independent variable. That which was changed (social organization) is the dependent variable. Subsequently the altered social patterns such as landownership influenced the cultural values attached to land. In this last example, social organization is the independent variable and the cultural values are the dependent variable.

CULTURE IS PERVASIVE

Cultural assumptions underlie thought and action, and culture touches every aspect of life. But for the most part, culture is taken for granted. Rational actions are subject to cultural definitions of what goals should be preferred and what means may be used to reach these goals. Emotional responses are governed by cultural norms as to where and how grief, pride, or love may be expressed. Culture even influences

A study of immigrant communities in New York described cultural variations in nonverbal communications.
Left, a traditional southern Italian gesture that can signify "Please, I pray you to shut up, I want to talk."
Right, a Jewish immigrant way of making a conversational point with a companion's hand. The study found that such gestural patterns were rapidly lost in succeeding generations.
Source: In *Gesture, Race and Culture* by David Efron, © 1972 by Mouton & Co. N.V., Publishers, The Hague. Sketches by Stuyvesant Van Veen. Reprinted by permission.

physiological responses. For example, people may be conditioned by their culture to feel nauseated by certain sights, smells, or tastes or to be sexually aroused by certain objects (Hall, 1959; 1966). Culture is a part of every social activity and institution.

LANGUAGE AND CULTURE

Language is usually thought of as a way to express ideas and feelings and to communicate messages: Any language can convey any idea. In this common-sense view, all of the world's languages are merely different ways to express the same underlying messages. Although different names and sounds are used, the things named and the thoughts expressed are assumed to be basically the same.

This view of language has been challenged by a number of linguists and anthropologists. Social scientists now believe that language is more than a vehicle for thought. In fact, it is a vital part of thought itself (Whorf, 1940/1956). Language is not simply a set of labels for objects that already exist —it *constructs* those objects out of experience. Different languages are not merely different codes for the same messages—they *shape* the kinds of messages that can be communicated and even the kinds of messages that can be conceived.

> Language is a guide to "social reality." . . . Human beings do not live in the objective world alone, nor alone in the world of social activity as ordinarily understood, but are very much at the mercy of the particular language which has become the medium of expression for their society. [Sapir, 1929/1958:162]

This statement may exaggerate the role of language, but it points to one of the most important ways in which culture influences thought.

Consider the word *accident*. It implies bad luck, a chance event that is beyond human control. Thus, a death in an auto crash is called an accident whether it was caused by poor road design, a pothole in the road, a defect in the car, drunken driving, a driver playing "chicken," or any of a number of other causes. Combining such varied causes under one heading makes it harder to think clearly about why road deaths happen, how they can be prevented, or how we can protect ourselves when we are on the road.

Selective attention

Language makes a person more sensitive to some features of the external world than to others. This may be seen in the use of verbs. In English a verb must have tense—past, present, or future. Therefore, the English speaker is aware of time whenever he or she uses a verb.

In Hopi, by contrast, the form of the verb depends on the source of information rather than the time of the action (Whorf, 1940/1956:217). The Hopi speaker who names an action must indicate whether he or she is describing a direct experience, a belief or expectation, or a generalization about experience. A Hopi who has just watched a boy running uses a word that expresses direct observation and that may be translated either "He is running" or "He ran." A Hopi who believes the boy is running but has no direct evidence for this uses the word that expresses expectation and that may refer to a past, present, or future action. Finally, a speaker who knows the boy has a habit of running —say, during a racing game—uses the word that

expresses a generalization or law. The Hopi speaker must always be aware of the sources of information.

Language and status

In Japanese, verbal forms indicate different attitudes. One form indicates a humble attitude toward the listener; the second shows politeness; and the third reveals a "plain" or abrupt attitude (Shodara, 1962:31–32). These forms require the speaker to know the status of the listener: The plain form is used with inferiors, the polite form with peers, and the humble form with superiors. Some European languages also have formal and intimate styles of address, for example the pronoun pairs in French *(vous-tu)* and German *(Sie-du)*.

Language can also express patterns of social dominance. Traditionally the English language has taken male dominance for granted, for example in the use of *man* as a synonym for *humanity* or *he* meaning a person of either sex. Like many others, the authors of this book recognize the problem and avoid words that imply female subordination. The trend to give the two sexes equal billing is now so widely accepted that the masculine tone of quotations written a relatively short time ago seems old-fashioned. Problems of equality between the sexes are discussed in detail in Chapter 7.

Section Three
The Diversity of Cultures

One of the lessons of history and anthropology is that humanity is both *one* and *many*. Human beings everywhere have the same biological and mental makeup. But their motivations, customs, and beliefs differ enormously. The uniformity and diversity of culture is the subject of this section. Cultural variation is present in every aspect of social life, from language to posture, from concepts of property to ways of making love, from great ideas to good manners. Readers of this book find many foreign customs reasonable or even attractive, for example, wearing a sari or perhaps having more than one spouse at a time. Others, such as circumcision rites for adolescents or eating live witchetty grubs, are hard to accept.

CULTURAL UNIVERSALS

Despite their great diversity, there is a striking uniformity among the world's cultures. Murdock has listed seventy-three elements, **cultural universals,** that are known to all cultures:

> age-grading, athletic sports, bodily adornment, calendar, cleanliness training, community organization, cooking, cooperative labor, cosmology, courtship, dancing, decorative art, divination, division of labor, dream interpretation, education, eschatology, ethics, ethnobotany, etiquette, faith healing, family, feasting, fire making, folklore, food taboos, funeral rites, games, gestures, gift giving, government, greetings, hair styles, hospitality, housing, hygiene, incest taboos, inheritance rules, joking, kin-groups, kinship nomenclature, language, law, luck superstitions, magic, marriage, mealtimes, medicine, modesty concerning natural functions, mourning, music, mythology, numerals, obstetrics, penal sanctions, personal names, population policy, postnatal care, pregnancy usages, property rights, propitiation of supernatural beings, puberty customs, religious ritual, residence rules, sexual restrictions, soul concepts, status differentiation, surgery, tool making, trade, visiting, weaning, and weather control. [Murdock, 1945:124]

When cultural universals and cultural variations are considered together, a more balanced view of strange customs is possible. The custom of wife lending is frequently cited. Among the Eskimo of northwest Greenland, a man may lend his wife to a friend for the night, and temporary exchanges of wives are common (Murdock, 1934:213). The idea of sexual property is maintained (the wife is not supposed to lie with another man without permission), but sexual exclusiveness is not highly valued.

The general idea of hospitality appears to be common to all cultures, but the specific form it takes is highly varied. Thus, hospitality may be offered in many different ways, of which wife lending is one. What makes Eskimo culture distinctive is its particular way of offering hospitality. In short, any culture is made up of unique variations. Cultural universals can be accounted for by the psychic unity of humanity and the limited number of possible solutions to common problems.

Psychic unity

Despite individual differences and cultural variations, human beings are alike in that we are all social creatures who have similar emotions, need security and response, and are able to use symbols. The psychic unity of humanity may be seen in the story of Ishi, the last "wild" American Indian, who spent the final years of his life in San Francisco. (See Adaptation 3.1.) Psychic unity does not make cultures the same, but it tends to create similarities.

Common problems, limited solutions

Action and choice always take place within a framework of limits. Some limits are set by the physical environment. The polar Eskimo could make shelters of snow or skins, but other materials were not available.

The fact that solutions are limited applies most clearly to the technical aspects of culture. There are many ways of making a boat or an oar, but certain conditions must be met if the boat is to float or the oar to pull. If, in addition, the need is for a speedy boat or an efficient oar, the limitations are more restricting. "The fewer the possibilities . . . the more likely are similar solutions" (Goldenweiser, 1937: 125). The principle of limited solutions also applies to language, which must have some sort of grammar, and to social organization, which must adapt to environmental and demographic conditions.

From a broad range of possibilities, each culture selects the ends and means that meet its needs. "All cultures constitute . . . somewhat distinct answers to essentially the same questions posed by human biology and by the generalities of the human situation" (Kluckhohn, 1962b:317). This means that every culture faces similar problems, but each culture solves those problems in its own way.

ETHNOCENTRISM

Each group tends to think of its way as the natural and best way. Strange people, beliefs, or practices are treated with suspicion and hostility simply because they are strange. This tendency is called **ethnocentrism.** It is the feeling that other cultures are inferior or even outlandish. Extreme ethnocentrism leads to the belief that some people are less than human.

In its milder forms, ethnocentrism is a sort of cultural nearsightedness. Even a book like this one might be accused of mild ethnocentrism because it uses the word *American* to mean a citizen of the United States of America. Latin Americans sometimes resent this use of a word that applies equally to them. Many Latin Americans call United States nationals *Norte-americanos,* which is itself an example of ethnocentrism in that it lumps together citizens of Canada and the United States. But there is no convenient name like *Canadian* or *Mexican* for a citizen of the United States of America.

Cultural relativism

Criticism of ethnocentrism is often based on the idea of **cultural relativism.** Sumner expressed this point of view when he said, "Everything in the mores of a time and place must be regarded as justified with regard to that time and place. 'Good' mores are those which are well adapted to the situation. 'Bad' mores are those which are not so adapted" (1906/1960:65). According to this reasoning there is no universal standard that can be used to evaluate cultures or norms as good or bad. Each culture must be seen in its own terms, and a custom can be evaluated only by its contribution to the culture of which it is a part. In that sense, cultural judgments are relative.

To make sense of a particular practice, whether it is cannibalism or television commercials, social scientists consider how it fits into its culture. Cultural relativism encourages both a tolerant attitude toward foreign ways and a greater effort to understand them. However, while cultural relativism is important for social science, two cautions should be noted:

1. It is sometimes said that cultural relativism makes it impossible to recognize values that are good for all humanity. On the contrary, cultural relativism itself is based on such a value: respect for cultural differences. This implies that all people need and deserve respect because of their common humanity.

2. Although it is proper to insist that cultural facts be judged in context, it is possible to identify aspects of morality that are cross-cultural:

> No culture tolerates indiscriminate lying, stealing, or violence within the ingroup. . . . No culture places a value upon suffering as an end in itself. . . . All cultures define as abnormal individuals who are permanently inaccessible to communication or who consistently fail to maintain some degree of control over their impulse life. [Kluckhohn, 1962a:294–295]

CULTURE SHOCK

To the extent that people are insensitive to and unaware of other values, they are said to be culture bound. To some extent, all of us wear the blinders of our own culture.

When they find their unquestioned cultural values being violated, people are likely to experience culture shock. **Culture shock** is the disorientation and frustration of those who find themselves among people who do not share their basic values and beliefs. Usually, differences in styles of dress, eating habits, and other everyday matters can be adjusted to fairly easily. Acute culture shock is most likely to occur when expectations about personal feelings and interactions are violated.

We can only guess at the culture shock felt by Ishi, the last of the Yahi Indians (Adaptation 3.1), who first encountered Western culture as a mature man. When he was captured, he was aware of white people only as a threat to his life. In time he learned that not all whites were dangerous, and that must have been a shocking, if welcome, discovery. For the last five years of his life he lived with whites who became his friends, teachers, and pupils. He slowly adapted to the strange new environment in which he lived, but there was much in the white culture that he could not understand. Even after several years in a protected situation, there must have been much that surprised him and for which he did not even have words.

(Text continued on p. 47)

Adaptation 3.1

Kroeber/Ishi in Two Worlds

On August 29, 1911, in the California gold country, an emaciated, middle-aged Indian was found crouched against a corral fence. The sheriff was called, saw that the "wild" man was near starvation and suffering from exhaustion and fear. When he was unable to communicate with Ishi, he took him to jail to protect him from curiosity seekers. Undoubtedly Ishi expected to be killed as a result of his capture by his enemy, the white man.

Anthropologist T. T. Waterman went to the jail and established a rudimentary communication with him with the aid of a phonetically transcribed list of Yana words, which were from a dialect of the language Ishi spoke. The University of California received permission from the Indian Bureau in Washington, D.C., to take Ishi to the University Museum of Anthropology in San Francisco, which became his home until he died four and a half years later.

Ishi was the last wild Indian in North America and the last surviving member of the lost tribe of the Yahi, a subgroup of the Yana nation, whose ancestral lands were in northern California. The coming of the white man brought death to the California Indians. In the single year of 1864, most of the two or three thousand Yana, other than the Yahi, had been murdered and massacred by white settlers. In 1865, when Ishi was a small child, the extermination of the Yahi began. By the 1870s, only a handful were still alive. In order to survive and to maintain their identity as a people, these few Yahi entered upon the Long Concealment. With rare exceptions they were never again seen by strangers. They hid in the brush of the canyons, avoiding all encounters, but their struggle for survival was doomed. By the turn of the century, apparently only five Yahi remained, among them Ishi, his mother, and his sister (or cousin). Finally, the only survivors were Ishi and his mother. After she died, he was without human companionship from November 1908 until August 1911.

THE UNSPOKEN NAME

The morning after Ishi's arrival at the museum he and Professor A. L. Kroeber, who would become his Big *Chiep* (Ishi pronounced *f* as *p*), met, and a friendship was born of their meeting. Reporters demanded to know his [the Indian's] name, refusing to accept Kroeber's word that the question was in the circumstances unmannerly and futile. Batwi [a "civilized" Yana who acted as interpreter and informant for the

anthropologists] intervened, engaging to persuade the wild man to tell his name—a shocking gaucherie on Batwi's part. The wild man, saving his brother

Source: Abridged from *Ishi in Two Worlds: A Biography of the Last Wild Indian in North America* by Theodora Kroeber (Berkeley and Los Angeles: University of California Press, 1961), pp. 124–128, 133, 138–139, 144–146, 162, 230, 236. Originally published by the University of California Press. Reprinted by permission of Theodora Kroeber and the Regents of the University of California.

Ishi, August 29, 1911.

A.L. Kroeber and Ishi, 1911.

Yana's face, said that he had been alone so long that he had had no one to give him a name—a polite fiction, of course. A California Indian almost never speaks his own name, using it but rarely with those who already know it, and he would never tell it in reply to a direct question.

The reporters felt, not unnaturally, that they were being given "the runaround." Kroeber felt more pushed than did his nameless friend, who remained relatively detached, not understanding most of what was said and standing quietly by Indian custom so far as he did understand. Said Kroeber, "Very

well. He shall be known as *Ishi*." He regretted that he was unable to think of a more distinctive name, but it was not inappropriate, meaning "man" in Yana, and hence not of the private or nickname category. Thus it was that the last of the Yahi was christened Ishi and, in historic fact, *became* Ishi.

He *never* revealed his own, private, Yahi name. It was as though it had been consumed in the funeral pyre of the last of his loved ones. He accepted the new name, answering to it reluctantly. But once it was bestowed, it took on enough of his true name's mystic identification with himself, his soul, whatever inner essence of a man it is which a name shares, that he was never again heard to pronounce it.

Kroeber says that the first impression of Ishi was of his gentleness and of a timidity and fear kept under severe control. Ishi started at the slightest sound. A stranger, the hearty type, burst into the room where Ishi was talking with Kroeber, grabbed Ishi's hand, and pumped hand and arm up and down in vigorous greeting. When released, Ishi stood, his arm frozen in the air for several seconds.

His shyness at first was acute. A blush, coming with a painful intensity, caused his face to mantle and cloud. He continued to blush easily even after he was no longer fearful and tense, covering his blushes with a deprecatory smile or a laugh and the placing of the fingers of one hand over his mouth, in that universal gesture of embarrassment.

A MAN APART

Deeper than shyness and fear was Ishi's awareness that he was alone—not as the unfriendly or too introverted or misanthropic are alone, for he was none of these. To be sure, he would sit, unbored, dreamy, and withdrawn into his own mystic center, but only if there was nothing to do, no one to talk to or to work with. He much preferred companionship, and he smiled readily, his smile beginning in the eyes and traveling from eyes to mouth. He was interested, concerned, amused, or delighted, as the case might be, with everything and everyone he knew and understood.

His aloneness was not that of temperament but of cultural chance, and one early evidence of his sophisticated intelligence was his awareness of this. He felt himself so different, so distinct, that to regard himself or to have others regard him as "one of them" was not to be thought of. "I am one; you are others; this is in the inevitable nature of things," is an English approximation of his judgment on himself. It was a harsh judgment, arousing in his friends compassion, then respect. He was fearful and timid at first, but never unobservant, nor did his fear paralyze his thinking as it paralyzed his gesturing. He faced the disparity of content between Yahi culture and white, and the knowledge that he could not begin from so far behind and come abreast. He would not try to. He would and did adapt as one of goodwill and breeding must adapt to one's host in dress, in the forms of greeting and leave-taking, in the use of knife and fork at table; these and other conventions of simple etiquette.

Meanwhile, he remained himself—a well-born Yahi, never unmindful of the code his mother and uncle had taught him. It might be conjectured that this position of aloofness and aloneness would have driven him into a depression, but such was not the case. Ishi had kept his morale through grief and an absolute solitariness; the impact of civilization could not budge it. Beneath the shyness and reserve he remained possessed of natural, temperamental, and unimpaired outgoingness and interest in people and phenomena, which he was able, day by day, to express ever more spontaneously, as the museum home became more and more *his* home.

His self-respect and pride no doubt prevented Ishi from acquiring a more rapid and facile command of English—he was reluctant to use a word or phrase until he was fairly sure of it—just as they hampered an easy fellowship with people he knew only slightly. But these character traits seemed not to have seriously cut him off from the people and activities he really valued, and they did serve to discourage even the least perceptive white person from the benevolent superiority of the civilized to the primitive, of the first-class citizen to the second-class. Many people, after awhile, laughed with Ishi. He was no king's jester; no one ever laughed *at* him.

CROWDS AND MOUNTAINS

A white man had been, until a few days [before Ishi came to the museum], a signal of mortal danger. He was becoming fairly at ease with his friends in the museum and concealed his sudden fears from them as best he could. But the crowding around of half a dozen people made his limbs become rigid; his first close-up of a group of perhaps 80 or 100 people left his faculties paralyzed. With time, he came to realize that crowds were not intrinsically menacing; his early terrible fear abated, but not his dislike of people in numbers such that the individual becomes lost in the faceless throng. He never liked strangers to come too close or to touch him. He learned to suffer the handshake as a custom universal to the white man and of friendly intent, and to acknowledge a proffered hand promptly and with courtesy. He never himself initiated a handshake.

No dream, no wildest nightmare, prefigured for Ishi a city crowd, its clamor, its endless hurrying past to be endlessly replaced by others of its kind, face indistinguishable from face. It was like a spring salmon run, one fish leaping sightlessly beyond or over another, and he disliked the sweaty smell of people in numbers. It suggested to him the odor of old deer hide.

One Sunday afternoon, Ishi was taken for an automobile ride through Golden Gate Park and to the ocean beach. The ocean is something every inland Indian has heard of, and has some sort of picture of in his mind. They speak of the ocean even when, like Ishi, they have never seen it, and it is likely to figure in myths and tales. Ishi was looking forward to seeing it, but when the car stopped on the bluff above, giving onto a wide view of ocean, surf, and beach, Ishi's breath drew in, not because of the great rolling Pacific, but because of the thousands of people who covered the beach below and spilled over into the surf—a Sunday afternoon crowd on a rare warm September day. He said over and over softly, half-whisperingly, *"Hansi saltu, hansi saltu!* Many white people, many white people!"* He had not known so many people could inhabit the earth at one time; the shock of sheer numbers obliterated every other impression. Kroeber thought to distract him by pointing out some of the taller office buildings as a less disturbing wonder to him. Ishi looked at them appraisingly, but without being greatly impressed, since, unlike his inexperience in estimating population figures, he had an adequate measuring rod for the height of a building. He had lived until now in the shadow of Waganupa and in sight of Mount Shasta and between the sheer walls of Deer Creek Canyon.

The vertical walls of a city are indeed puny, scarce worthy of comment, by comparison.

RITUALS OF RESPECT

Ishi did not venture off Parnassus Heights [site of the museum] alone until he had been in the city some time, but he went to various places with one person or another. His first such expedition was on the day after his arrival. Waterman took him across the bay to Berkeley where he saw the campus of the university and had dinner with the Watermans and their two children—his first dinner at a white man's table in a white man's home. He was there many times later, and of his first time Waterman reported only that Ishi so closely watched his hostess, imitating her in her choice of fork or spoon, in her use of a napkin, and in the amount of food she put on her plate, that his exactly similar motions appeared to be simultaneous with hers.

Anyone who has had California Indians as house guests will recognize this as very "Indian." Customs differed from tribe to tribe, but a strict etiquette of eating was observed by all of them. The shift to new food and a different way of serving it seems to be adroitly managed when the principle and habit of conventional behavior "at table" is already ingrained.

Getting into and out of a suit coat or topcoat he found unhandy at first, whereas a single demonstration was all he needed to learn to tie a four-in-hand cravat, since he was used to knotting and tying cords of hemp and hide. Pockets he appreciated; within three days of having them he had them filled, and with the usual male miscellany. With the clothes went the code: Ishi, to whom nakedness had been the normal and unmarked state, refused to have his picture taken except when he was fully dressed. Pictures of him in native undress had to await his return visit to the Lassen foothills.

ISHI'S TREASURE

[Because of work Ishi did at the museum, he was put on the university payroll.] He was good with his hands, and there was about this job as about every-thing he did what Kroeber called a ''willing gentle-ness.'' He was most grateful for the work, having observed that everyone in the white man's world had a regular job for which he received a regular wage. And he was pleased to have the *mahnee,* which permitted him to pay for his own food and whatever else he wanted instead of having it given to him. He was a proud person, to whom economic indepen-dence meant a great deal. Ishi now had a name, an address, and economic status.

[He learned to write his name so he could en-dorse and cash his paycheck.] Kroeber offered to keep Ishi's money, except for small amounts, in the safe. He showed him how the safe was operated and explained that only he and E. N. Gifford, the new curator, knew the combination and could open it.

Ishi had many times made a cache of valuables of one sort or another—food, arrows, tools, and the like—burying them under a pile of rocks or hanging them high in a tree. He was pleased to learn about the white man's cache and to put his silver there. He saw his money wrapped and stored, his own name plainly written on the outside of the package. The safe was closed. He twirled the combination and, trying to open it, saw that the box would not open. He was immensely satisfied; his treasure was now both well hidden and accessible whenever he wanted to get to it.

ISHI'S DEATH

To survive our civilization, an early and continuing immunization to it is necessary. [Ishi did not have the necessary immunization and died of tuberculosis in 1916.] Now the law reads that when a person dies intestate and without living blood relatives, such monies and property as may have been his at the time of death go to the state. The public administrator who is charged with responsibility to see that this transfer is actually made has, or had in 1916, certain discre-tionary powers also. Ishi's few personal possessions the administrator left with the museum. There was also Ishi's treasure in the safe in the museum office, his ''counting room''—520 half dollars in 13 film cases, each neatly filled to the top. The administrator took half this sum for the state. The other half went where Waterman knew Ishi wished his treasure to go. So it was that Doctor Moffitt, dean of the medical school, received 260 half dollars with a covering note from Waterman: ''This gift from Ishi is in actual cash, and I hope you will accept it, though of course it is no return for the medical and hospital attention that Ishi received. It will serve perhaps as a recogni-tion of his sense of obligation.'' Doctor Moffitt ac-knowledged the gift, thanking Waterman and ex-plaining that he was putting Ishi's money in a special fund rather than taking it as payment for hospital expenses, since there had never been any idea of charging him. In this way, Ishi's treasure continues to contribute its bit to the science of healing, a science for which Ishi himself had so great a curiosity and concern.

A COMMON HUMANITY

A century has passed since Ishi was born, yet he continues to engage the imagination. He was unique, a last man, the last man of his world, and his experi-ence of sudden, lonely, and unmitigated changeover from the Stone Age to the twentieth century was also unique. He was, further, a living affirmation of the credo of the anthropologists that modern man—*Homo sapiens*—whether contemporary American Indian or Athenian Greek of Pericles' time, is wholly human in his biology, in his capacity to learn new skills and new ways as a changed environment ex-poses him to them, in his power of abstract thought, and in his moral and ethical discriminations. It is upon this broad base of man's panhumanity that scientists and humanists alike predicate further progress away from the instinctual and primitive and subhuman strata of our natures.

Section Four
Diversity within Cultures

Complex societies like the United States contain not one culture but many ethnic, regional, and occupational subcultures with different values and norms, social relationships, and life chances. Some sociologists suggest that there is no American culture but only a large number of subcultures. American culture can be thought of in several ways: as including all the subcultures, as made up of the elements that all the subcultures share, or as limited to the values and attitudes of a dominant group or the majority of the population.

SUBCULTURES

A **subculture** is a pattern that is distinctive in important ways but has much in common with the dominant culture. In other words, a subculture contains some of the dominant cultural values but also has values or customs of its own. Every group has some distinctive patterns, but unless they affect the total life of the members, the patterns do not make up a subculture. A subculture has a general influence on attitudes and life-styles and tends to give a person a specific identity.

A subculture may be based on an occupation if that occupation is the context of the everyday life of its members. Such occupations as mining, police work, railroading, long-haul trucking, and logging are likely to develop subcultures.

More typical, however, is a subculture based on ethnic group or social class. These subcultures tend to be found in separate localities such as immigrant neighborhoods with their special shops, churches, and schools. Thus, they provide a setting for many of the activities of their members.

DIVERSITY AND CULTURE CONFLICT

It is easy to exaggerate the extent to which a society adheres to a single value system. Not everyone accepts the middle-class goals of wealth and success. Many groups and subcultures emphasize values and standards of behavior that are quite different from those of middle-class America. Therefore, many people are deviant not because of weakened social ties but because they belong to groups with different values and standards. Even conformity may lead to deviance when it results from participation in a **deviant subculture,** the norms of which run counter to those of the larger society. This aspect of deviance shows that deviant behavior is (1) learned; and (2) organized and maintained by groups.

The idea that deviant behavior is learned is the basis of the theory of **differential association** put forward by Edwin H. Sutherland (1883–1950). According to this theory, criminal techniques, criminal behavior, and the motives and justifications for criminal activities are learned mainly in small groups (Sutherland, 1939/Sutherland and Cressey, 1978: 81).

More is involved in differential association than the idea that bad company makes bad people. While some police officers and prison guards are affected by their daily association with criminals, most of them do not become criminals. The key factors in differential association are acceptance of criminal attitudes and learning specific types of criminal behavior.

One implication of Sutherland's theory is that deviance is more likely to occur and persist in societies that contain a variety of groups and subcultures. In the eyes of the larger society, subcultures are deviant to the extent that their norms and values differ from those of the dominant culture. Thus, because modern society is made up of groups with widely diverse backgrounds, some people become deviant merely by learning to conform to the norms of their group.

Lower-class deviance

Some boys from the slums grow up in a world that does not support self-discipline or deferred gratification. "There is little interest in long-run goals, in planning activities and budgeting time, or in activities to be acquired only through practice, deliberation, and study" (Cohen, 1955:30). Because they are not exposed to such values, these boys are ill prepared to compete in the middle-class school environment, where rationality, deferred gratification, and control of aggression are stressed. Unable to meet these standards, the boys experience disapproval, rejection, and damaged self-respect.

When large numbers of youth face the same problems over a long period of time, the stage is set for the formation of delinquent gangs. Such gangs are a response to rejection and failure. They hit out against middle-class culture and also set standards that the boys can meet, thus restoring their self-respect:

> The delinquent subculture functions simultaneously to combat the enemy within and the enemy without, both the hated agents of the middle class and the gnawing internal sense of inadequacy and low self-esteem. It does so by erecting a counterculture, an alternative set of status criteria. [Bordua, 1961:125]

For these reasons, membership and prestige in a juvenile gang often depend on standards that conflict with those of conventional society. The abilities to fight, hustle, and gamble are deviant by middle-class standards but carry high prestige in the delinquent subculture.

Some lower-class norms may encourage delinquency without being directly opposed to conventional values. The following are characteristics of some urban lower-class cultures: *toughness,* or concern with physical strength and masculinity; *smartness* (being street wise), or the ability to outsmart others and not be "taken"; *excitement,* or the search for thrills and kicks to relieve the routine of everyday life; *autonomy,* or the wish to be free from authority; and *fate,* or the belief that what happens to a person is due less to his or her own actions than to luck or fortune (Miller, 1958).

Thus, delinquent subcultures are not simply personal responses to blocked opportunities. They are organized, collective reactions that develop over time. Stable group norms and values exist before any particular boy enters the gang, and they continue long after he leaves it.

White-collar deviance

"Crimes committed by persons of respectability and high social status in the course of their occupations" are called **white-collar crimes** (Sutherland and Cressey, 1978:44). They include computer crime, insurance fraud, consumer fraud, bribery, and

the like. Though they are condemned by the criminal law, such crimes are widely tolerated and not often prosecuted. Indeed, bribery and fraud are a way of life in many businesses, professions, and governments. They become matters of public scandal from time to time, as in the case of the bribes paid by multinational corporations or the misuse of Medicare funds by physicians. More routine forms of dishonesty are seldom reported, though they may be dealt with privately by warning or dismissing employees.

White-collar offenders do not fit the image of the common criminal, and law enforcement officials are reluctant to treat them as such. Many offenses, such as tax evasion and business fraud, are not considered really serious, even though the white-collar criminal may be "by far the most dangerous to society of any type of criminal from the point of view of effects on human rights and democratic institutions" (Sutherland and Cressey, 1978:46). These are real dangers, but to the average citizen they seem remote compared with direct threats to persons or property.

Section Five
Culture Conflict and Change

This section discusses what happens when cultures come into conflict and are weakened or renewed.

CULTURE CONTACT

As we have seen, acculturation is the adoption of new culture patterns as a result of contact with another culture. Ideally, acculturation is the way one people learns from another. Although many primitive peoples lived in isolation, others traveled and traded extensively. Communicating with different peoples, they gained a wide range of knowledge and practices—from the techniques of navigation to ideas for tracing descent and inheriting property. Culture contact among peoples with roughly similar lifestyles is likely to be seen as an opportunity rather than a threat:

> Minor variations in cultures, when they appear and function in the historical contact of peoples, seem to be among the most powerful incentives of develop-

ment and progress. But there is a limit to the cultural disparity between two groups in contact which can be resolved with relative safety. [Goldenweiser, 1937:428]

Contacts between folk communities and more advanced societies put pressure on simpler societies, as illustrated by the problems of the Old Order Amish (Wittmer, 1971).

The Amish are a religious farming community that broke away from the Mennonites in the late seventeenth century before either group came to America. They believe that a simple, rural way of life is the road to salvation. However, their efforts to maintain a simple life-style have been frustrated at many points.

The Amish want to limit the education of their children so as not to spoil them for farm life. Compulsory-education laws that were a focus of culture conflict have been adjusted to the group's needs. The Amish have their own schools, and in Pennsylvania work on the farm and in the home to age 16 is accepted as equivalent to high school. They prefer the horse and buggy, but horses do not last long on hard-surfaced roads. They want to farm, but even here they run into problems:

> Until recently, Amish farmers have been able to buy farms from retiring non-Amish neighbors, often lending one another money at 2 or 3% in order to help the young Amish farmer obtain land. Non-Amish farmers in the community resent this. Perhaps for this reason, many public auctions of farm lands are now being held on Sunday, eliminating the Sabbath-abiding Amishman from the bidding. Because of the scarcity of land, many Amishmen have recently taken jobs in factories sanctioned by the church. Since the Amish religion does not permit a member to join the union, these jobs are usually short-lived. [Wittmer, 1971:106]

When the Amish try to isolate their children, they are protecting the authority of traditional norms. When they try to maintain a unified life-style, with everyone engaged in farming, they are following their religious convictions. When some of the members of the community go into factory work or commerce, their loyalty to the community and its way of life is undermined.

The Amish are a special case in that they are an ''intentional'' community. (See p. 92). For religious reasons they try to maintain a distinctive culture identity. Most preindustrial communities are not ''intentional'' and therefore are more receptive to outside influences.

Costs and benefits

The effects of acculturation can be evaluated only from the historical viewpoint. It cannot be assumed, for example, that the impact of European culture on preindustrial communities has always been destructive. A summary of the cultural changes that have occurred in the Mexican village of Tepoztlán since the Spanish conquest concluded that ''on the whole, but particularly in the field of material culture, the new culture elements in all periods did not supplant but were added to the old, making for a richer and more heterogeneous culture'' (Lewis, 1951:440). On the other hand, the same author notes:

> We have seen that in the increased contact with the outside world in recent years, Tepoztecans have taken many new traits of modern life. They now have Coca-Cola, aspirin, radios, sewing machines, phonographs, poolrooms, flashlights, clocks, steel plows, and some labor saving devices. They also have a greater desire to attend school, to eat better, to dress better, and to spend more. But in many ways their world view is still much closer to sixteenth-century Spain and to pre-Hispanic Mexico than to the modern scientific world. They are still guided by superstition and primitive beliefs; sorcery, magic, evil winds, and spirits still dominate their thinking. It is clear that, for the most part, they have taken on only the more superficial aspects and values of modern life. Can western civilization offer them no more? [Lewis, 1951:448]

In sum, cultural borrowing is always selective, but the crucial point is what is selected.

THE WEAKENING OF CULTURE

To refer to the weakening of culture, anthropologists use such terms as **cultural disorganization** (Redfield, 1941) and **spurious culture** (Sapir, 1924), which appear to pass judgment on the quality or worth of a culture. But the words can be used objectively if (1) it is understood that any culture is at risk during periods of social change, and (2) the supposed weaknesses and the forces that produce them are identified in detail so that they can be tested.

A study of cultural change in Yucatán (Redfield, 1941), compared four communities: an isolated Indian tribal village (Tusik), a peasant village (Chan Kom), a town (Dzitas), and a city (Mérida). These communities varied along a "folk-urban continuum." From Tusik at the "folk" end to Mérida at the "urban" end, there was a progressive weakening of traditional culture: People were more open to outside influences; their way of life was less steady and unified. The result was a breakdown of traditional culture, increased secularization, and a more individualized society.

Cultural disorganization, or loss of cultural unity, is illustrated by the effects of the conversion of some Chan Kom families to Protestantism. For these families, religious identity became separated from community membership. "The community no longer acted as a unit in its religious life, and the principal leaders, who remained Catholic, felt the weakness and often expressed their sorrow and chagrin" (Redfield, 1941:145). After a while, however, the Protestant families began to take part in some traditional Catholic rituals:

> While maintaining their separate prayer-meeting, the Protestants began to attend novenas of their neighbors. . . . When All Soul's Day came around, the Protestants held a prayer-meeting with a table decorated much as they had decorated tables on such occasions before conversion; and, while they did not set out food for the dead or call upon them by name, their prayer-meeting was felt to have the same ghost-averting function as its more traditional predecessor. . . . So the community remained a single community, although with alternate cults for certain classes of occasions, and with an unresolved conflict as to the sanctity and value of the santos. [Redfield, 1941:145]

Whenever institutions become specialized—for example, when religion is separated from government or family life from occupation—cultural unity tends to be weakened. Such weakening may be welcomed, however, if it strengthens other values such as individual freedom.

Secularization is loss of symbolic meaning—in church festivals, in growing and handling maize, and in other traditional occupations. Everyday life becomes less expressive and more instrumental. *Holy days* become *holidays,* occasions for feasting, visiting, and making money.

Individualization is seen in the breakdown of traditional forms of collective labor, the rise of individual rights in land, and the narrowing of kinship to closer relatives. "In the villages it is relatively easy to say 'the family did this' or 'the community did that'; in Mérida it is not so easy" (Redfield, 1941:354).

The preceding discussion is not meant to imply that all isolated villages are similar to Tusik in having a deeply rooted folk culture nor that exposure to outside influences always has damaging effects. The weakening of culture is a matter of degree and should be viewed in terms of its consequences. Industrial society has weakened folk cultures, but it has also opened up new opportunities for many people. Membership in a close-knit community can be a positive value, but it may also be limiting. Note, too, that a people may survive and even flourish despite cultural disorganization, secularization, and individualization.

THE DESTRUCTION OF CULTURE

A more tragic result of outside influences is the outright destruction of culture. A whole way of life can collapse when advanced societies overwhelm primitive communities, as they did in the period of European colonialism. Economic exploitation was only part of the story. Often the entire culture of a colony was shattered. Traditional crafts could not compete with Western technology, and old institutions were undermined.

The culture of Tahiti was destroyed in this way.

> The chief trouble was that there was now nothing for the Tahitians to do. Before the Europeans arrived they had their own occupations and had enlivened their days with their own rituals and entertainments, but now all these had been taken away from them, and the singing of Christian hymns was really not enough to compensate. In that soft soporific climate it was impossible to make the people work for

Cultural impoverishment in Las Vegas and in urban India.

long. . . . The missionaries imported a weaving machine, and for a month or two the girls worked it with great enthusiasm. Then the novelty wore off and the machine was left to rust away in its palm-leaf hut. It was the same with the attempts to start cotton and sugar-cane growing; after the first season or two the workers drifted away. Their own arts and crafts had long since been forgotten; no one could make cloth from the bark of a tree and there no longer seemed any point in building the great double-canoes with their high carved prows: a crude boat hacked out of a tree-trunk was good enough. [Moorehead, 1966:87–88]

When Captain Cook arrived in 1769, there were about 40,000 Tahitians. Less than a century later there were only 6,000. The destruction of the culture had a direct effect on health and longevity. "It almost seemed that the heart had gone out of the people, and that they had lost the will to survive. Pulled one way by the missionaries, another by the whalers, and now another by the French officials they subsided with a sigh" (Moorehead, 1966:93).

When everyday activities are robbed of their symbolic meaning, there is a loss of motivation. This, in turn, results in personal disorganization: inability to take care of oneself, relate to others, keep up a garden, hold a job, and resist self-destructive pleasures such as heavy use of alcohol. Especially when new diseases are introduced, the population may decline dramatically.

Early in this century the population of Melanesia fell rapidly. Some observers believed the decline was caused by the erosion of culture and "loss of interest in life" (Rivers, 1922: Chapter 8). It is hard to separate such influences from the disastrous effects of diseases introduced from outside. In any case, populations that appeared to be dying out have rebounded, and overpopulation has become a serious problem throughout the Pacific islands.

CULTURAL RENEWAL

Cultures do not always decline. To be sure, any change in social organization carries some risk that the traditional culture will be weakened. In many cases, however, new values and life-styles will emerge in the long run. Americans today are groping for ways in which to renew their culture. Among the

current trends in American culture the following have been identified (Bennis, 1970):

From	Toward
Achievement	Self-actualization
Self-control	Self-expression
Independence	Interdependence
Endurance of stress	Capacity for joy
Full employment	Full lives
Competitive relations	Collaborative relations

If the new values become part of the nation's social organization, they may lead to profound changes. But even if these ideals are widely accepted, the result will not be a return to an "old-time" culture, small in scale and slow in pace, based on stability, unity, and sacredness. They will be values of a "postindustrial" mass society continually striving to adjust to shifting technology and to unify many different peoples.

Chapter 3 **Summary**

Section 1/**The concept of culture**

The term *culture* refers to the shared ways of thinking and believing that grow out of group experience and are passed from one generation to the next. The essential features of any culture are contained in its symbols. There are two major categories of symbols: *referential,* those that denote specific things, and *expressive,* those that connote abstract ideas or feelings.

A cultural value is a widely held belief about what is important to the community's identity or well-being, such as freedom, equality, and individualism. Values are expressed in norms, or specific guides to conduct. The most important norms are the mores, e.g., the prohibition of murder. Weaker norms are called folkways, e.g., eating with a knife and fork.

Culture and social organization are linked together because the relations between people and groups are guided by cultural rules. The connections are illustrated by an example of culture change in which a new method of farming had far-reaching effects on social organization.

Section 2/**The impact of culture**

In the example of culture change leading to altered social organization, the causative factor (new farming techniques) is the independent variable and the changed social form (land ownership) is a dependent variable.

Culture touches every aspect of life, but for the most part it is taken for granted. It colors emotional responses, perceptions, and style of living as well as values. Language is more than a way to express ideas and feelings. It actually shapes ideas and the way the world is perceived. Language sensitizes people to certain features of the external world, the social environment, and relations with others.

Section 3/**The diversity of cultures**

The world's cultures are widely diverse, but there are universal elements. Such cultural universals can be explained by three facts: the psychological similarity of all human beings, the requirements of group life, and the limited number of possible solutions for common human problems.

Each social group tends to think of its own culture as natural and superior and that of others as somehow inferior—an attitude called *ethnocentrism*. Cultural relativism, on the other hand, suggests that a culture trait should be valued on its own terms within the culture of which it is a part, not by some outside standard. Sometimes when a person is confronted by a sharply different way of life, culture shock is experienced. Ishi, the subject of Adaptation 3.1, experienced culture shock in confronting American urban society.

Section 4/**Diversity within cultures**

Complex societies like the United States contain many ethnic, regional, and occupational subcultures with differing values and norms. A subculture is a pattern that is distinct in important ways but has much in common with the dominant culture. When the norms of a subculture run counter to those of the larger society, the subculture is called deviant. Deviant norms are learned and maintained by a subgroup in the same way as conventional norms are learned and maintained by the dominant population.

Section 5/**Culture conflict and change**

Acculturation takes place when one culture adopts traits or patterns from another. The results can be either beneficial, e.g., when more efficient production techniques are adopted, or negative, e.g., when a group's values and way of life are undermined. Culture disorganization refers to loss of culture unity, hopes, and ideals. Folk cultures are often weakened when they come into contact with advanced societies. On the other hand, culture change can bring about a restructuring and revitalization of traditional values.

Suggested Readings

Benedict, Ruth
1946/1964 *Patterns of Culture*. Baltimore, Md.: Houghton Mifflin.

Hall, Edward T.
1966/1969 *Hidden Dimension*. New York: Doubleday Anchor Books.

Hymes, Dell
1964 *Language in Culture and Society*. New York: Harper & Row.

Kluckhohn, Clyde
1944/1964 *Mirror for Man*. Greenwich, Conn.: Fawcett.

Murgía, Edward
1975 *Assimilation, Colonialism and the Mexican American People*. Austin: University of Texas Press.

Ryan, Bryce F.
1969 *Social and Cultural Change*. New York: Ronald Press.

Schneider, Louis, and Charles M. Bonjean (eds.)
1973 *The Idea of Culture in the Social Sciences*. Cambridge, England: Cambridge University Press.

Sumner, William Graham
1906/1960 *Folkways*. New York: New American Library.

Williams, Robin M., Jr.
1970 *American Society: A Sociological Interpretation*. Third edition. New York: Knopf.

Chapter 4

Socialization

Section One
The Basis of Socialization

Socialization can be looked at from two viewpoints: that of society and that of the individual. To society, socialization is the process of fitting new individuals into an organized way of life and teaching them the society's cultural traditions. Socialization transforms the human animal into a human being, a member of a society. Because of that transformation most babies grow up into fully functioning social beings, able to use the language of their parents and competent in their society's culture.

From the individual's viewpoint, socialization is the process of developing a **self.** Through interaction with others, a person gains an identity, develops values and aspirations, and, under favorable conditions, becomes able to make full use of his or her potential. Socialization is necessary for the growth of self-awareness and the formation of identity. Thus, it performs two functions: It transmits a social heritage and it creates a personality.

This section reviews the inborn qualities on which socialization depends. Sections Two and Three summarize socialization through the life course. In Section Four we look at the social self as a product of socialization and in Section Five at deviance and the failures of socialization.

THE FOUNDATIONS OF SOCIALIZATION

The human species is social by nature. Both the capacity and need for group life have been built into the human animal through its long evolution (Pfeiffer, 1978). Thus, socialization is both possible and necessary. That is, humans have the capacities that make social life possible and also a need for social life. But each generation and each individual must learn how to be social in a specific time and place.

Socialization is based on several inborn qualities. Among them are (1) the absence of instincts, (2) a long period of childhood dependency, (3) the ability to learn, (4) the capacity for language, and (5) the need for social contact.

The absence of instincts

The concept of instinct was formerly used to account for human behavior. Society was explained by a herding instinct, the role of women by a maternal instinct, property by an acquisitive instinct, war by an aggressive instinct, and so on. Instinct is no longer regarded as the cause of complex human behavior.

In a strict sense, **instinct** refers to behavior patterns for which some species are biologically programmed. Nest building by birds is instinctive. It contains both the impulse to build a nest (with suitable stimulation) and readiness to respond to the environment in patterned ways that result in building a particular kind of nest. The nests of different species of birds differ, but members of the same species build the same kind of nest.

Humans have **biological drives** rather than instincts. A *drive*, such as thirst, is a physical tension that is felt as discomfort or an impulse to action. Thirst needs to be relieved, but the drive does not determine what fluid is to be drunk, how, where, or with whom. Drives do not direct behavior toward specific goals or touch off a programmed sequence of activities leading to the satisfaction of a need. Unless drives are guided by learning, they tend to produce only restless and searching behavior. If humans had biologically fixed behavior patterns like the nest building of birds, our ability to learn would be limited and we would be less open to socialization.

Childhood dependency

By the standards of apes and monkeys, human infants are slow to become independent from their parents. Unlike apes, they cannot cling to a moving adult and cannot get to their mother's breast by themselves. Human babies need the protection and care of adults much longer than other primates. The need to learn the skills of social living further prolongs human dependency. This means that there is more time for socialization. Helplessness, therefore, makes extensive socialization of humans possible.

The ability to learn

Dependency contributes to socialization because humans can learn more and for a longer time than other animals. Although people have different abilities, all humans have the potential to be intelligent. At young ages, chimpanzees learn as well as or better than

Prolonged dependency of humans makes extensive socialization possible.

humans; but after infancy, the learning rate of apes declines compared with that of young children.

The capacity for language

The ability to learn and to solve problems is directly related to the capacity for language. Language enables people to think about what they have done, elaborate it, and communicate it as a general idea to others. Language can also be used to express feelings, values, and attitudes. It is the key to the creation of human society because it makes possible the symbolic interaction on which society depends.

The need for social contact

Becoming fully human requires social contact. Children who spend years in extreme isolation do not develop the qualities that are basic to social life. One such isolated child, Anna, was the second illegitimate child of a mentally retarded mother. Until the age of 6, she spent most of her time alone in a second-floor room. She was fed entirely on milk, and her physical needs were attended to in only a superficial way. Anna was thin and apathetic when she was

found, and there was doubt if she could even see or hear (Davis, 1940:555). ''She had no glimmering of speech, absolutely no ability to walk, no sense of gesture, not the least capacity to feed herself even when the food was put in front of her, and no comprehension of cleanliness'' (Davis, 1947:434).

Anna was placed in a county home where she began to recover and grow physically. However, she was cared for by a nurse who single-handed looked after more than 300 patients, so she still spent many hours alone. She was given little remedial care such as speech therapy, and as a result did not improve socially during the nine months she spent in the county home.

When Anna was placed in a foster home, she finally received from the foster mother the attention and care she needed, and in this setting she developed rapidly. After only three months she began to walk alone, responded to verbal instructions from her foster mother, and recognized people, although she did not speak. Less than a year later she was moved again, this time to a special school, where she gradually began to talk and develop coordination. She continued to make progress until she died from a blood disease at the age of 10.

The dehumanizing impact of isolation is also evident in less drastic cases. A study of social isolation compared the progress of 61 infants in a foundling home, where there was very little physical contact and social stimulation, with that of three groups of infants in more normal environments. A measure called the development quotient (DQ) was used to assess six aspects of personality: perception, body mastery, social relations, memory, relations to inanimate objects, and intelligence (Spitz, 1945 and 1947/1964).

The foundling-home infants had an average DQ of 124 for the first four months of their lives, the second-highest score among the four groups. During the first year, their average DQ fell to 72, but the DQs of the other groups did not change. By the end of the second year, the average DQs of the foundlings had fallen to 45, which ''would qualify these children as imbeciles'' (Spitz, 1964:418).

Two years after the end of the study, the foundling-home infants were observed again. Of the 21 children between the ages of 2 and 4 who were observed, only five could walk without help, only one dressed alone, and only one spoke in sentences. Most could not talk at all or knew only a few words. Lack of stimulation and contact in infancy appeared to retard the development of their learning ability.

Physical versus emotional isolation

Anna and the foundling-home babies were isolated and deprived of all emotional contact. Babies in a remote Guatemalan village are raised in a different kind of isolation. To protect them from the "evil eye," their mothers do not talk to them, play with them, or take them out of the bare, windowless hut in which the family lives. However, the babies are cuddled and fed. At first these children are retarded in their intellectual and motor development. But when they are brought into the social life of the village, they start to catch up. By the age of 11 they show no ill effects from their early isolation (Kagan, 1973:41–43). Even though they are given little stimulation, these Guatemalan babies receive body contact and emotional comfort from their mothers. They are isolated physically but not deprived emotionally. This research suggests that later social contact can make up for the damage done by isolation in the early years of life.

DYNAMICS OF SOCIALIZATION

Socialization is carried out in many different ways, by many people, and in a variety of social settings. Parents, playmates, teachers, fellow students, co-workers, lovers, spouses, and children contribute to socialization. Socialization may be intended or unintended, formal or informal. Usually it involves face-to-face encounters, but it also happens at a distance, through letters, books, and the mass media. The persons being socialized may be passive or active, depending on the extent to which they can influence the socializer.

Socialization may be carried out for the benefit of the person being socialized or for the benefit of the socializer. For example, children are given some chores to teach them useful skills but they are given other chores simply to relieve adults of drudgery. Often socialization goes along smoothly with little awareness that one person is influencing the other. But it can also be oppressive, even brutal, with both parties aware of pressure and conflict.

Section Two
Childhood Socialization

In modern society, the conventional child-rearing environment is the nuclear family, which is composed only of parents and their children living in a separate home. Parents tend to be the only adults with direct and constant access to infants and young children. Therefore, they are the only people to whom their children can turn for help, affection, and instruction.

ADULT-CHILD INTERACTION

In sharp contrast to many preliterate and folk societies, modern society often places responsibility for the day-to-day care of a young child in the hands of only one person—usually the mother. Mother and child form a socially isolated **dyad** (two interacting persons) for long periods. Both mother and child have limited opportunities to interact socially with their own age peers.

What goes on in the home is largely unseen by the rest of society. This fact means that parents must be self-controlled and resourceful. It also leaves young children vulnerable to their parents' psychological and social weaknesses. Few other societies place responsibility for the child so completely in the hands of the biological parents. Small wonder, then, that in Western society the parent-child relationship is highly emotional and is the most important factor in forming the child's personality.

There have always been many exceptions to this conventional pattern. Throughout most of human history, the energies of mothers were needed for productive work outside the home. Few mothers could devote much time or attention to children, and child care was much less intensive than it is today. Only in the twentieth century did motherhood become a full-time occupation for adult women (Rossi, 1964/1967:106).

When mothers must work, as is the case in most working- and lower-class families, care givers other than parents must become involved in child rearing. In recent years, growing numbers of children are being cared for at least in part outside the household as a result of the increase in one-parent families and working mothers. A diversity of individuals ·and agencies have taken on child care and consequently participate in early socialization.

The socialization of young children is a process of give and take between adult and child. Parents try to influence, guide, or control their children, but the children are not passive. Even newborn babies affect their parents through their appearance and behavior. Therefore, the study of parent-child interaction considers both the responses of the child to the parents and those of the parents to the child.

Many mothers who want babies are not so keen on children.

Parental responses to the child

The way an infant's needs are met is largely socially determined. Feeding patterns, for example, vary from one culture to another, from one social group to another, and from one mother to another. The infant may be fed whenever it wants, fed on a rigid schedule, or fed when it is convenient for the mother. It may be bottle or breast fed well into childhood, or it may be weaned after a few months. Some babies are picked up and carried whenever they "fuss," while others are handled less often and left to "cry it out."

No matter how a baby's needs are met, the adult's response to the infant is colored by emotion. As the infant grows, adults put less effort into satisfying the child's bodily needs and more into expressing approval and disapproval so as to encourage the development of self-control. There are also emotional responses to the child's appearance, intelligence, and temperament. Parents respond to the child in terms of their own psychological needs, their social class, and their ambitions for the child. In doing so, they communicate to the child their own attitudes toward social life.

The child's responses to parents

Infants and young children are almost completely dependent on their social environment, but they are active participants in their own socialization. A study of month-old infants showed that they initiated about four out of five mother-infant interactions. Surprisingly, during the stage of life when the child is most helpless it has the greatest influence over the adults in its environment: It demands attention by crying and usually gets a response. Never again will that person gain attention so easily. However, it appears that babies differ considerably in the frequency with which they cry, and, therefore, in the amount of attention they receive (Korner, 1974).

The earliest reactions of human infants are biological responses to their inner states of comfort and discomfort. Gradually, they associate crying with attention and satisfaction. They learn to cry with a purpose. By crying to get attention, the infant initiates interpersonal communication. Later the child learns to recognize the sensations of hunger and to say "I'm hungry" instead of crying.

The human ability to express feelings and emotions is central to socialization. Besides being able to participate in social interaction, even young infants can respond emotionally. This is the core around which human personality and social bonds develop. However, uncontrolled expression of emotion can be self-destructive and disruptive to society. Therefore, teaching the child how to cope with feelings and to express them in socially acceptable ways is one of the primary goals of socialization. Another goal is to enlarge the range and subtlety of human emotions.

Humans do not suffer deprivation and frustration passively. They might react with rage and aggression. As children grow older, they learn to manage their frustration and their aggressive impulses. This learning is a major task in the process of socialization.

Attachment

At the age of about six months, babies begin to show attachment behavior. They recognize certain individuals and respond differently to different people. The attachment pattern is limited to special adults called "attachment figures," who are usually, but not always, the parents. The infant shows delight when its mother or father appears and distress when the attachment figure leaves (Pilling and Pringle, 1978: 63–102). If the child is separated from an attachment figure for a long time or in distressing circumstances, a grief reaction sets in. In the end the child may become emotionally withdrawn (Rutter, 1972: Chapter 2).

Attachment is a two-way process between the infant, who comes to love its parents, and the mother and father, who love their baby. The human infant takes an active part in loving and being loved. The infant's ability to smile and make sounds plays a part in the formation of an affectionate and pleasant relationship between parent and child. In fact, children need to evoke positive feelings from their parents or care-givers.

When attachment patterns are seriously disrupted by rejection or long separation, the child may become psychologically disturbed. Clinical studies of delinquent and maladjusted children show that failure to evoke love in the parents may result in loss of the ability to love (Redl and Wineman, 1951). The child's obvious need for love, respect, and self-esteem suggests that these requirements are basic to human development (Maslow, 1965:33).

PATTERNS OF CHILD-REARING

Two broad patterns of socialization are presented in Table 4.1 as a set of contrasts (Bronfenbrenner, 1958; Kohn, 1977). The pattern that stresses obedience is called **repressive socialization;** the pattern that stresses involvement of the child is called **participatory socialization.**

Both reward and punishment play a part in all learning, but one may be stressed more than the other. Repressive socialization punishes wrong behavior; participatory socialization rewards good be-

Table 4.1   Two Patterns of Socialization

Repressive	Participatory
Punishing wrong behavior	Rewarding good behavior
Material rewards and punishments	Symbolic rewards and punishments
Obedience of child	Autonomy of child
Nonverbal communication	Verbal communication
Communication as command	Communication as interaction
Parent-centered socialization	Child-centered socialization
Child's perception of parent's wishes	Parent's perception of child's wishes

havior. In toilet training, for example, parents may scold when a child has an accident, or they may praise the child for self-control.

Participatory socialization gives children freedom to try things for themselves and explore the world on their own terms. This principle does not mean that the child is ignored. Supervision is needed, but the supervision is general. To be effective, repressive socialization requires even more (and more detailed) supervision. However, since no child can be watched all the time, punishment depends on whether the child is caught misbehaving and on whether the parent is in a mood to punish. From the child's viewpoint, such punishment may seem arbitrary.

Repressive socialization emphasizes obedience, respect for authority, and external controls. Communication tends to be downward from parent to child, often taking the form of commands or statements that discourage the child from responding (Silverstein and Krate, 1975:25). Gesture and nonverbal communication are frequent (Bernstein, 1958). The child must learn—by interpreting the parent's tone of voice, facial expression, and posture—to tell how serious a command is to ''shut up'' or ''get down.''

In participatory socialization, communication is a dialog in which children express their wants and needs as well as adjusting to those of adults. Participatory socialization is child centered rather than parent centered: The adult tries to identify the child's needs rather than expecting the child to comply with the parents' wishes. When cooperation is emphasized and goals are shared, socialization is less dependent on imitating adults and conforming to adult rules.

When attention is concentrated on controlling children's behavior, conflict between adults and children is inevitable. In some less developed societies where personal autonomy is a dominant value, there is less conflict between parents and their children. Children control themselves. They are not controlled by their parents, and children who misbehave are responsible for their own actions. Adaptation 4.1 describes practices in several societies that strongly value independence and self-respect, where a battle of wills between parent and child is a rare occurrence.

(Text continued on p. 63)

Adaptation 4.1

Lee/Beyond Permissiveness: Socialization for Autonomy

Western parents feel a conflict between the need to teach their children the rules of society and the desire to encourage independence. Punishment is thought to instill discipline at the expense of individuality. Permissiveness, on the other hand, is thought to encourage independence at the expense of self-control.

In some cultures, personal autonomy is so highly valued that there is little or no conflict between independence and social control. This study describes several societies in which child-rearing practices, cultural norms, and even language show respect for personal autonomy. In these societies there is no place for coercion in the rearing of children.

PERMISSIVENESS AND RESPECT

Many of us feel that to allow a child to decide for himself and to act according to his own wish, that is, to be permissive, is to show respect for the unique being of the child. Yet for many of the societies we know, it would be a presumption for any person to "allow" another to take what is essentially his prerogative—the right to decide for himself. These people do not "permit" others. When the children of the Wintu Indians of California ask "Can I?" they are asking for information on the rules of the structure; for instance, they may be seeking clarification about a religious taboo or social custom. They are saying in effect, "Is it permissible for me to . . . ?" and not, "Do you allow me to . . . ?" These people do not "give" freedom to their children, because it is not theirs to give. If they do not impose an external time schedule on their infants, but feed them when they are hungry, and put them to bed when they are sleepy, they are not being permissive; they are showing their deep-seated respect for individual worth and their awareness of the unique tempo of the individual.

Ethnographers have presented us with many incidents, apparently commonplace and trivial, which point out for us an amazingly thoroughgoing implementation of respect for personal quality. For instance, one anthropologist visiting a Sikh household noticed that a small child, asked to entertain his baby brother, merely went up to the playpen and put in a toy truck. He did not show the baby how the truck worked; he gave the truck silently. This amazed the visitor, since she knew that the Sikhs were a people of great empathy and warmth, and with a great love for babies. She knew, also, that the child in question had approached the baby with friendliness and affection. Then she remembered the personal autonomy of the Sikh and realized that the boy was acting consistently with the cultural

Source: Abridged and adapted from Dorothy Lee, "Individual Autonomy and Social Structure," *Personnel and Guidance Journal*, 35 (September 1956), 16–21. Copyright 1959 American Association for Counseling and Development. Published in this form by permission of Dorothy Lee and the AACD.

values; he was furnishing the baby with the raw material for experience and leaving him to explore without any attempt to influence him. He was expressing respect, not noninvolvement.

LANGUAGE AND PERSONAL INTEGRITY

Among the Wintu Indians, the principle of the integrity of the individual is built into the language. Many verbs which express coercion in our language—such as to take a baby to (the shade) or to change the baby—are formed in such a way in the Wintu language that they express a cooperative effort instead. For example, the Wintu would say, "I *went with* the baby" instead of "I *took* the baby." And they say "The chief *stood with* the people, which they have to translate into English as "The chief ruled the people." To *live with* is the usual way they express what we call possession, and they use this term for everything that they respect, so that a man will be said to live with his bow and arrows. In Wintu, every interpersonal reference is couched in grammar which rests on the principle of individual integrity. Yet, for this people, the emphasis on personal inviolability did not mean that the individual is an isolate. There was such pervasive empathy among them that this, too, was expressed in the grammatical forms; if a boy was sick, the father used a special form of *to be sick* and said "I-am-sick-in-respect-of-my-son."

GIVING ORDERS, FOLLOWING PRECEPTS

A corollary of the principle of individual integrity is that no personal orders can be given or taken without a violation of personal autonomy. The individual takes his cues from the impersonal system of norms, not from the commands of another. In this sense, personal autonomy is compatible with, and supported by, an intricately developed social structure. In Burmese monasteries, for example, where novices performed menial tasks, the monks did not give orders. Instead, the work was structured throughout the day; and all the monk said to get the work done was "Do what is lawful," reminding the novice to act according to the cultural tenet, not ordering him.

When the specific aspects of the structure are not

clear, the people in such societies can turn to authority for clarification. And here we often find, as with the Burmese or the Navaho Indians, that the authority of the headman, or the chief, or the leader, is in many ways like the authority of the dictionary, or of Einstein. There is no hint of coercion or command here; the people go to the leader with faith, as we go to a reference book, and the leader answers according to his greater knowledge, or clarifies an obscure point, or amplifies according to his greater experience and wisdom. He does not say ''You must do this because I order you to.'' Yet he does use the word *must* or its equivalent; he says, so to speak, ''As I see it, this is what must be done.''

In Navaho autobiographies we often find the phrase ''I followed the advice of my parents'' but rarely ''I obeyed my parents.'' The good Navaho does not command his child; and a mother who is aggressive toward her children, who ''talks rough'' to them, is strongly criticized. In teaching her children the tremendous number of taboos they have to learn for their well-being, the good Navaho mother does not say ''I will punish you if you do thus-and-thus'' but ''Such-and-such an unpleasant thing will happen to you.'' If a child breaks a taboo, he is not ''guilty.'' He has not committed a sin against the mother and is not in need of forgiveness. He has made a mistake which he must set right.

GUILT AND SELF-RESPECT

This attitude is basic to all Navaho relatedness. Man is not burdened with guilt, and does not feel apologetic toward human or divine beings. He is neither grateful nor abject to his gods. As a matter of fact, he must never humble himself before them, since the process of healing, of the recovery of harmony with the universe, involves identification with the appropriate god, who would be slighted if the patient humiliated himself. The Navaho has, and indeed must have, as much respect and value for himself as for others. This is the Navaho version of the principle, discovered so recently in our society, that we cannot accept and respect others until we learn to accept and respect ourselves.

THE COMPETENT CHILD

The Navaho do not differentiate between adults and children in the respect they show for personal autonomy. There is no minority status for children. For example, a good Navaho will not take it upon himself to speak for another, whether adult or child. A father, asked to sell his child's bow and arrow, will refer the request to a five-year-old boy, and abide by the child's decision not to sell, even though he knows the child is badly in need of the clothing that can be bought with the price of the toy. A woman, asked whether a certain baby could talk, said yes; and when the ethnographer was puzzled by the ''meaningless'' sounds the baby was making, she explained that the baby could talk, but she could not understand what the baby said. Traditionally, parents do not force their children to do what they unequivocally do not want to do, such as going to school or to the hospital; children are not coerced even ''for their own good.''

For the Navaho mother, personal autonomy means that the child has the freedom to make his own mistakes. And the child has his freedom because the mother has faith in him. This does not mean that she has high expectations of him, but that she trusts him. When the baby starts walking, the mother does not see to it that he is out of reach of the fire, and that all the sharp knives have been put away. The child gets burned a little and the mother helps him learn from this experience. By taking a chance on her child, the mother teaches him to be ready to meet and deal with danger, instead of warning him away from danger. This trust means that the child has freedom to move, to act, to undertake responsibility.

COERCION AND LEADERSHIP

So the individual remains inviolate. No one coerces another among the Navaho. There is no political coercion, and all leadership is traditionally incidental. Men do not seek leadership, and white employers have found that the Navaho are reluctant to become foremen, however able they may be. It is ''fundamentally indecent,'' according to Clyde Kluckhohn, a close student of the Navaho, ''for a single individual to presume to make decisions for the group.''

CONCLUSION

The societies referred to here are highly consistent in their respect for personal integrity. However, they were studied as homogeneous, traditional societies, and their cultures changed little over long periods. The children could gradually learn adult roles at home by sharing the life of their father and mother. They could take it for granted that they would live the same kind of life as their parents and hold the same values. These principles were supported by various aspects of the culture, even by the grammar of the language, as among the Wintu.

The practices of these societies are described not for others to copy but as evidence that: (1) personal autonomy and social control can exist together; (2) spontaneity is not necessarily killed by group responsibility; (3) respect for individual integrity is not something that can be achieved by following a simple formula; rather, it must be supported by deeply held values and by a way of life.

Section Three
Adult Socialization

Socialization continues throughout life. Adult roles require new learning, and changing social situations make new demands. The socialization of adults differs from that of children in what is learned, where the learning occurs, and how the person responds:

> In terms of *content*, socialization in childhood is . . . concerned with the regulation of biological drives; in adolescence, with the development of overarching values and the self-image; while in adulthood [it involves] more overt and specific norms and behaviors (such as those related to the work role), as well as more superficial personality features. [Mortimer and Simmons, 1978:423]

SOCIALIZATION THROUGH THE LIFE COURSE

Childhood socialization usually takes place in a situation that is specifically geared to teaching and learning. Adult learning, on the other hand, usually occurs on the job or in the family. Children tend to be emotionally involved with their socializers—parents, teachers, and peers—and this involvement makes the process more effective. Relations between adults and their socializers are less likely to be emotional. Adult socialization tends to be voluntary, and the adult can more readily than the child resist the socializing influence or withdraw from the situation (Mortimer and Simmons, 1978:424). Adult socialization takes place mainly in connection with employment or during changes and crises in the life cycle, which are discussed in Chapter 7.

The socialization associated with employment involves more than on-the-job training, professional education, or technical qualification. A less visible aspect of adult socialization can be called socialization *by* the job. Throughout the working career, a worker's personality is influenced by the kind of work he or she does. For example, independent, self-directed work encourages people to initiate actions and to be self-confident in their lives off the job (Kohn and Schooler, 1982).

In homogeneous societies, where the various groups that socialize the individual tend to have the same values, socialization can give a person a sense of living out an unbroken life cycle. Each stage leads naturally to the next, and every experience fits into a meaningful, predictable pattern. Different ways of learning and different agencies of socialization follow one another in a more or less orderly sequence as the person passes from one stage of life to the next.

In heterogeneous societies like the Western industrial nations, groups with different values compete with each other. The peer group may encourage disruptive behavior while the family and school urge conformity. As one group's influence increases and another group's influence fades, desocialization may occur: People are encouraged to reject their past socialization and the groups they used to belong to. In such societies, life can be a series of difficult choices and painful self-assessments rather than a smooth passage from birth to death.

RESOCIALIZATION

Throughout life, people change their attitudes, values, and self-images as they take on new roles and undergo new experiences. When this process is gradual and partial, it is called continuing socialization. **Resocialization,** by contrast, is more drastic. It involves giving up one way of life for another that is not only different from it but also incompatible with it. Examples of resocialization are brainwashing, rehabilitation of criminals, deprogramming, and religious conversion of "sinners." In these cases, the person breaks with the past and is "made over."

Certain occupations and callings require exten-

sive resocialization. Religious and military careers in traditional societies are good examples of occupations that require major retraining and reshaping of the person's life.

Total institutions

Resocialization of adults often takes place in what is called a **total institution,** an all-encompassing environment that is usually isolated from the community. A person who enters a monastery or nunnery makes a decisive break with the past and with secular society. Other examples of total institutions are mental hospitals, prisons, and some military units and political groups. Adaptation 4.2 discusses the fate of the self in such organizations that try to establish full control over the person.

While the Adaptation points to the similarities in such institutions, there are significant differences among them. The assault on identity that takes place in a prison or mental hospital may be similar in some respects to the mortification of a military recruit or a religious novitiate. However, when individuals voluntarily submit themselves to a changed life for religious or patriotic reasons, there may be little or no psychological damage.

(Text continued on p. 67)

Adaptation 4.2

Goffman/Stripping the Self

The recruit comes into the establishment with a conception of himself made possible by certain stable social arrangements in his home world. Upon entrance, he is immediately stripped of the support provided by these arrangements. In the accurate language of some of our oldest total institutions, he begins a series of abasements, degradations, humiliations, and profanations of self. His self is systematically, if often unintentionally, mortified. He begins some radical shifts in his moral career, a career composed of the progressive changes that occur in his beliefs concerning himself and significant others.

The processes by which a person's self is mortified are fairly standard in total institutions; analysis of these processes can help us to see the arrangements that ordinary establishments must guarantee if members are to preserve their civilian selves.

BREAKING WITH THE PAST

The barrier that total institutions place between the inmate and the wider world marks the first curtailment of self. In many total institutions, the privilege of having visitors or of visiting away from the establishment is completely withheld at first, ensuring a deep initial break with past roles. A report on cadet life in a military academy provides an illustration:

> For two months the swab (new recruit) is not allowed to leave the base or to engage in social intercourse with noncadets. This complete isolation helps to produce a unified group of swabs, rather than a heterogeneous collection of persons of high and low status. Uniforms are issued on the first day, and discussions of wealth and family background are taboo. The role of the cadet must supersede other roles the individual has been accustomed to play. There are few clues left which will reveal social status in the outside world.

PEOPLE PROCESSING

The inmate, then, finds certain roles are lost to him by virtue of the barrier that separates him from the outside world. The process of entrance typically brings other kinds of loss and mortification as well. We very generally find staff employing what are called admission procedures: taking a life history; photographing, weighing, fingerprinting, assigning numbers, searching, and listing personal possessions for storage; ordering the recruit to undress, bathe, and be disinfected; haircutting; issuing institutional clothing; instructing as to rules; and assigning to quarters. Admission procedures might better be called trimming or programming, because in thus being squared away the new arrival allows himself to be shaped and coded into an object that can be fed into the administrative machinery of the establishment, to be worked on smoothly by routine operations. Many of these procedures depend upon attributes such as weight or fingerprints that the individual possesses merely because he is a member of the

largest and most abstract of social categories, that of human being. Action taken on the basis of such attributes necessarily ignores most of his previous bases of self-identification.

THE OBEDIENCE TEST

Because a total institution deals with so many aspects of its inmates' lives, with the consequent complex admission procedure, there is a special need to obtain initial cooperativeness from the recruit. Staff often feel that a recruit's readiness to be appropriately deferential in his initial face-to-face encounters with them is a sign that he will take the role of the routinely pliant inmate. The occasion on which staff members first tell the inmate of his deference obligations may be structured to challenge the inmate to balk or to hold his peace forever. Thus these initial moments of socialization may involve an obedience test and even a will-breaking contest: An inmate who shows defiance receives immediate visible punishment, which increases until he humbles himself.

Admission procedures and obedience tests may be elaborated into "the welcome," a form of initiation where staff or inmates, or both, go out of their way to give the recruit a clear notion of his plight. As part of this rite of passage he may be called by a term such as *fish* or *swab,* which tells him that he is merely an inmate and, what is more, that he has a special low status even in this low group.

The admission procedure can be characterized as a leaving off and a taking on, with the midpoint marked by physical nakedness. Leaving off, of course, entails a dispossession of property, important because persons invest self-feelings in their possessions. What is perhaps the most significant of these possessions is not physical at all: one's full name. Whatever one is called thereafter, loss of one's name can be a great curtailment of self.

STANDARD ISSUE

Once the inmate is stripped of his possessions, at least some replacements must be made by the establishment, but these take the form of standard issue, uniform in character and uniformly distributed. These substitute possessions are clearly marked as really belonging to the institution and in some cases are recalled at regular intervals to be, as it were, disinfected of identifications. With objects that can be used up—for example, pencils—the inmate may be required to return the remnants before obtaining a reissue. Failure to provide inmates with individual lockers and the periodic search and confiscation of accumulated personal property reinforce property dispossession. Religious orders have appreciated the implications for self of such separation from belong-

ings. Inmates are sometimes required to change their cells once a year so as not to become attached to them.

IDENTITY KIT

One set of an individual's possessions has a special relation to self. The individual ordinarily expects to exert some control over the guise in which he appears before others. For this he needs cosmetic and clothing supplies, tools for applying, arranging, and repairing them, and an accessible, secure place to store these supplies and tools—in short, the individual needs an identity kit for the management of his personal front. He also needs access to decoration specialists such as barbers and clothiers.

On admission to a total institution, however, the individual is likely to be stripped of his usual appearance and of the equipment and services by which he maintains it, thus suffering a personal defacement. Clothing, combs, needles and thread, cosmetics, towels, soap, shaving sets, bathing facilities—all may be taken away or denied him, although some may be kept in inaccessible storage, to be returned if and when he leaves. In the words of the Rule of St. Benedict, which governs the Benedictine monks:

> Then forthwith he shall, there in the oratory, be divested of his own garments with which he is clothed and be clad in those of the monastery. Those garments of which he is divested, shall be placed in the wardrobe, there to be kept, so that if, perchance, he should ever be persuaded by the devil to leave the monastery (which God forbid), he may be stripped of the monastic habit and cast forth.

As suggested, the institutional issue provided as a substitute for what has been taken away is typically of a coarse variety, ill-fitting, often old, and the same for large categories of inmates. The impact is described in a report on imprisoned prostitutes:

> First, there is the shower officer who forces them to undress, takes their own clothes away, sees to it that they take showers and get their prison clothes. . . .
> There is not a sadder sight than some of the obese prisoners who, if nothing else, have been managing to keep themselves looking decent on the outside,

confronted by the first sight of themselves in prison issue.

In addition to being stripped of one's identity kit, loss of a sense of personal safety is common. Beatings, shock therapy, or, in mental hospitals, surgery —whatever the intent of staff in providing these services for some inmates—may lead many inmates to feel that they are in an environment that does not guarantee their physical integrity.

MORTIFICATION

Corresponding to the indignities of speech and action required of the inmate are the indignities of treatment others accord him. The standard examples here are verbal or gestural profanations: Staff or fellow inmates call the individual obscene names, curse him, point out his negative attributes, tease him, or talk about him or his fellow inmates as if he were not present.

Whatever the form or the source of these various indignities, the individual has to engage in activity whose symbolic implications are incompatible with his conception of self. In prisons, denial of heterosexual opportunities can induce fear of losing one's masculinity. In military establishments, the patently useless make-work forced on fatigue details can make men feel their time and effort are worthless. In religious institutions, there are special arrangements to ensure that all inmates take a turn performing the more menial aspects of the servant role. An extreme is the concentration camp practice of requiring prisoners to administer whippings to other prisoners.

Section Four
The Social Self

Self is an Anglo-Saxon word that originally meant "same" or "identical." It refers to a unique, lasting identity. To be human is to have a self, an inner identity. Thus, the self is the source of a person's thoughts, actions, and emotions. Every culture gives its members a self. The content of the self may vary, but the process by which it is created is universal.

IDENTITIES

Socialization provides individuals with identities, largely through the aspirations it encourages or discourages. An **identity** is a self-concept built up over a lifetime. It combines the definitions supplied by others with the individual's private self-definition. Young upper-class Englishmen, for example, were once taught upper-class etiquette by their valets. But knowledge of upper-class manners could not make the valet a member of the upper class, either in his own eyes or in the eyes of others. Although the valet knew how to act like a gentleman—sometimes better than the gentleman himself—he did not have the identity of a gentleman.

Special Olympics.
Bringing the handicapped in.

In modern industrial societies, aspirations are less firmly fixed than in traditional societies. One result is that people have less definite identities. Today a sense of identity seems to be achieved later in life than in the past. Individuals have more options, and socialization is less closely linked to such factors as sex, ethnic origin, and family status.

Who am I?

A technique used to investigate people's self-concepts is to have them answer the question "Who am I?" several times (Bugental and Zelen, 1950:483–498). The first few answers often include obvious characteristics such as name, age, height, weight, and ethnicity. Repeating the question fifteen or twenty times brings out more revealing responses. These may indicate the speaker's character, mood, salient status, and interpersonal style (Gordon, 1968:120–123). For example, although he was not responding to the question "Who am I?" Lyndon Johnson once described himself as follows:

> I am a free man, an American, a United States Senator and a Democrat, in that order. I am also a liberal, a conservative, a Texan, a taxpayer, a rancher, a businessman, a consumer, a parent, a voter, and not as young as I used to be nor as old as I expect to be—and I am all those things in no fixed order. [Gordon, 1968:123]

THE "LOOKING-GLASS" SELF

We are the way we are at least partly because of other people's reactions to us and to what we do. We are constantly picking up this feedback and incorporating it into our sense of self. Thus, the self is built up through social interaction. It is a social construction as well as a personal reality.

Charles Horton Cooley (1864–1929) called this aspect of the self "the reflected or looking-glass self." The **looking-glass self** has three elements:

> the image of our appearance to the other person; the imagination of his judgment of that appearance; and some sort of self-feeling, such as pride or mortification. [Cooley, 1902/1964:184]

People imagine not only how others see them and

their actions but also how they judge what they see— with approval, or with doubt or hostility. As a result, the looking-glass self is made up of feelings about other people's judgments of behavior. The self consists of a composite of more or less accurate assessments of others. To Cooley, this social self was the central element of sociology: "The imaginations which people have of one another are the solid facts of society" (1902/1964:121).

MEAD ON SELF AND SOCIETY

Nineteenth-century scholars developed the idea that the nature of the individual arises from social experience. According to this view, the content of human consciousness cannot be separated from the society in which it is formed. In the twentieth-century, the American philosopher G. H. Mead (1863–1931) carried this approach a step further. In contrast to those who stressed the impact of culture or social structure, Mead stressed the processes of day-to-day socialization. In tracing the way language, social interaction, and role taking create the human mind, he laid the foundations of social psychology.

While being socialized, the child learns facts and their social meanings at the same time. One might suppose that a fact could be taught simply as a fact, without any social meaning attached to it. However, as adults present children with facts, they cannot avoid also presenting attitudes toward those facts. In the process of responding to these attitudes, the child acquires a social self.

Mead stressed the part that *social others* play in creating the self.

> The individual experiences himself as such, not directly, but only indirectly, from the particular standpoints of other individual members of the same social group or from the generalized standpoint of the social group as a whole [Mead, 1934:138].

This view of the self is similar to the idea of a looking-glass self in which one imagines oneself reflected in the eyes of others.

The significant other

Mead thought that the self develops in two states. At first, the child is not mature enough to cooperate with others or understand shared goals. Young children relate only to specific individuals who are not merely others but **significant others.** At this stage, play consists largely of simple role taking. The child plays at being a parent, doctor, or letter carrier, reenacting the behavior and attitudes of the important individuals of his or her life.

The generalized other

Older children and adults respond not only to the significant other; they also respond to the collective attitudes of the larger group or community: the **generalized other.** Play is no longer limited to simple role taking but involves organized games that require the player to adjust to a number of others and to the rules of the game. In performing this role, the child responds to the generalized other. The young individual perceives the attitudes of others toward the roles and activities that make up social life. To Mead, society is more than a group of individuals. It is a complex organization of social attitudes which shape the developing self.

The self as "I" and "me"

Mead described the self as an organization of conventional social attitudes, but also as active, spontaneous, and creative (1934:178). He called the more conventional or socially controlled part of the self the "me" and the more active part the "I." If group life is restrictive, the "me" dominates the "I" and creativity is limited. But under the right conditions the "I" influences and may even restructure group life. Indeed, there are times when the "me" encourages free expression of the "I." These, Mead said, provide "the most exciting and gratifying experiences" (1934:213).

FREUD ON SELF AND SOCIETY

Sigmund Freud (1856–1939), the founder of psychoanalysis, had a stronger influence on present-day concepts of the self than did Mead. While Mead was teaching philosophy at the University of Chicago, Freud was practicing a new kind of psychotherapy in Vienna. As a philosopher, Mead explored the role of society in the development of rationality and selfhood. As a psychoanalyst, Freud stressed the role of

society in the development of mental and emotional disorders. Mead emphasized the cooperative aspects of group life as well as the potential unity of the self. Freud emphasized the conflicts that arise in group life and the struggles that go on within the self.

The self as id, ego, and superego

Freud divided the self into three parts. The **id** stands for gratification of impulses, the **ego** for rational self-preservation, and the **superego** for conformity. People become self-conscious when these demands are in conflict. In the course of coping with conflict, they develop a variety of selves, character types, and personalities.

According to Freud, the id is the biological core of the self; it stands for the animal nature of human beings. These drives, which Freud called instincts, are sexual and aggressive impulses that continually demand satisfaction. Therefore, the id is the part of the self that society tries to control.

The ego is the ability to take account of the facts: to reason, calculate the results of an action, postpone gratification, avoid danger—in short, to engage in rational actions. The ego mediates between the individual's biological demands and the demands of society. It integrates and controls the self.

Freud's superego is similar to Mead's "me." It stands for society and its demands, for the social norms that are the voice of conscience. The superego is also potentially harmful. The repression that is required for socialization to take place may cause too much guilt or may distort behavior in other ways.

Freud's theory of the superego helps explain how socialization can be harmful, leading the individual to self-punishing or self-destructive behavior.

> From the point of view of instinctual control, or morality, it may be said of the id that it is totally nonmoral, of the ego that it strives to be moral, and of the superego that it can be super-moral and then becomes cruel. . . . [Freud, 1923:44]

The autonomous ego

Freud emphasized the vulnerable ego, caught between a harsh superego and a demanding id. Since Freud's time, psychoanalysts have devoted much attention to the problems of the ego. Today many therapists concentrate less on exploring the unconscious and more on building up ego strength. The major goal of psychotherapy or of socialization is no longer simply to help the person adjust to society. Instead, it is to create a self that is able to control and direct its own behavior.

THE SITUATIONAL SELF

In one sense, the self is a unified, continuing entity. It persists through time as an unbroken chain of memories and a consistent identity. Yet the self is always situational.

Everyone has a core of uniqueness and identity. At the same time, everyone has a set of selves to match a variety of roles and audiences. Similarly, all individuals take on a series of selves as they pass from one stage of life to another. This point was made by William James (1842–1910) as follows:

> [The individual] has as many different social selves as there are distinct *groups* of persons about whose opinion he cares. Many a youth who is demure enough before his parents and teachers, swears and swaggers like a pirate among his ''tough'' friends. We do not show ourselves to our children as to our club-companions, to our customers as to the laborers we employ, to our own masters and employers as to our intimate friends. From this there results what practically is a division of the man into several selves. [1891:294]

To say that a situation can bring out the best or the worst in a person is to say that the self is fluid. But the self is situational in only a limited sense; the person is not formed or re-formed by situations.

The recognition of the situational self has led to new views of deviance, mental health, and the unity of the self. Deviance, once thought to be caused by a basic character defect, is now seen as situational. Many of the ''crazy'' responses of the mentally ill, for example, are interpreted as normal responses to crazy environments. In other words, more attention is being given to the social environment of the individual.

Lack of a unified self—a clear sense of identity —has long been considered a personal and social tragedy. This view is now being questioned on several grounds, including the following (Lifton, 1968; Berger, 1971):

1. Society will continue to undergo rapid change. During rapid change a person with a fixed identity risks unhappiness and maladjustment. Some people argue that the goal of socialization should be to create a flexible self.

2. Society is becoming more and more heterogeneous in terms of values and life-styles. A narrow identity limits a person's social interactions and personal development.

3. In modern society, a narrow identity may reflect a poverty of social experience. Each individual should be encouraged to play a variety of roles ranging from simple household tasks to community leadership.

Section Five
Deviance and the Failures of Socialization

Everyone is socialized, but there is a tendency to overemphasize the impact of socialization, to present an ''oversocialized conception of man'' (Wrong, 1961; Berger, 1963). In fact, the goals of socialization are seldom fully achieved. The goal of transmitting the society's culture is to some extent in conflict with the goal of creating unique human personalities.

Furthermore, in large and heterogeneous societies, several socializing agencies compete for influence. For example, the school may contradict what the child learns at home, or the values of the peer group may conflict with those of the school. This conflict is illustrated by the children of immigrants, who are exposed to two sets of values—one set held by the parents, the other by the host society. Because the values of the larger society are not supported at home or in the ethnic community, the child may understand them in an incomplete or superficial way. A person who is part of two cultures but is not completely socialized by either is said to be **marginal** (Stonequist, 1937; Golovensky, 1952).

Thus, people conform, but they conform in different degrees and various ways. Sociologists try to discover the different kinds of conformity and social control, how effective they are under varying conditions, and what differences they make to the personality and to society.

When social processes are studied in detail, it becomes clear that socialization is uneven and does not always succeed. Research on deviance, mental illness, inequality, and many other topics shows that socialization often fails, either from the standpoint of the individual or of society.

LABELING AND SOCIAL CONTROL

Agencies of social control—such as police, courts, and mental institutions—routinely screen, classify, and sort people according to official rules and categories. This process involves more than simply counting and recording deviant behaviors. The procedures of social-control agencies often determine whether any specific behavior will be classified as deviant. There are many steps between the commission of an offense and the official labeling of the offender, and many factors affect how the social-control agency responds.

Compared to boys from slum areas, middle-class boys who commit the same offenses have better prospects at each step of the way. If they are picked up by the police, they are less likely to be taken to the station. If they are taken to the station, they are less likely to be booked, and they are even less likely to be convicted and sentenced (Goldman, 1963; Terry, 1967). The key to this difference is the nature of the interaction between the officer and the youth. If the officer feels that the youth respects the authority of the police, favorable treatment is more likely (Piliavin and Briar, 1964). Middle-class families also have more social and economic resources that can be used to obtain legal counsel or to place their sons in private institutions such as boarding schools. All of these influences reduce the chances of conviction (Cicourel, 1968).

The comparatively severe social control of lower-class offenders results from "the fact . . . that the ideal of civil order, which is supposed to be maintained or at least defended by police officers, is primarily a middle-class ideal" (Sutherland and Cressey, 1978:393). The daily lives of poor people are inconsistent with this ideal order which stresses regular employment, nuclear family life, respectability, and an interest in "getting ahead." Consequently, lower-class offenders are likely to acquire official labels that identify them to others and to themselves as deviant persons.

Some sociologists consider the labeling process itself to be the key to understanding deviance.

> From this point of view, deviance is *not* a quality of the act a person commits, but rather a consequence of the application of rules and sanctions to an "offender." The deviant is one to whom that label has successfully been applied; deviant behavior is behavior that people so label. [Becker, 1963:9]

Labeling theory emphasizes the role of social-control agencies in assigning deviant labels and their lasting, stigmatizing effects on the individual.

STIGMA AND SELF

The Greek word *stigma* once referred to a mark cut or burnt into a person's body to show that the bearer was a slave, criminal, or traitor. The practice of physical marking has ended, but deviants are often stigmatized in other ways. As the term is now used, **stigma** labels an act or trait that is perceived as highly negative and sets the stigmatized person apart from ordinary people (Goffman, 1963b:Chapter 1).

A stigma generalizes from specific acts or traits to judgments about an individual's character. In many cases, a person who is convicted of a crime becomes a "criminal," a person who goes through a period of mental illness, a "mental case." What may have been a temporary condition or lapse is used to define a kind of person. As an ex-prostitute explained,

> I don't feel that I'm a whore now, but the social stigma attached to prostitution is a very powerful thing. It makes a kind of total state out of prostitution so that the whore is always a whore. It's as if—you do it once, you become it. [Millett, 1973:-65]

The stigma that attaches to the ex-convict—or even to a person who is accused of a crime and acquitted—often overrides the person's other qualities (Schwartz and Skolnick, 1962). The stigma may become the dominant characteristic of the self.

Primary and secondary deviance

When an offender is isolated and stigmatized for deviant behavior, the person's life and identity may become "organized around the facts of deviance" (Lemert, 1967:41). Primary deviance is the initial conduct that violated a norm and may be caused by any number of factors, such as peer group pressure; secondary deviance results from society's reaction to the original conduct. Besides defining the individual as deviant, thereby influencing his or her self-image, social responses are often experienced as unfair and demeaning. The outcome may be bitterness, withdrawal, and, in the end, acceptance of deviance as a way of life. In this way, society's attempts to control deviant behavior may backfire, leading to an increase in the stigmatized behavior.

SOCIALIZATION FOR DISADVANTAGE

Especially among those that are disadvantaged in the first place, socialization may impair human capacities. In the United States, socialization contributes to the subordination of nonwhites, the poor, and women relative to whites, the middle-class, and men. Marxist scholars refer to such perpetuation of inequality as the "reproduction" of structured relations.

Sometimes, parents simply accept their own and their children's disadvantage. In traditional societies, children are taught not to aspire above their station because doing so is unrealistic. In contemporary society, parents may "cool out" their children, getting them to accept their lot in life. Parents believe they are doing their best for a daughter when they prepare her for a good marriage rather than a good job; they do not see that they are limiting her options.

Until recently, cooling out children was a common practice in black families. In the 1940s, before the civil rights movement, 150 black children in New York and St. Louis were interviewed about their difficulties with whites. They reported a total of 487 incidents of "ridicule, physical ill-treatment, aggression, rude treatment, discrimination, and indirect

disparagement" (Goff, 1949:22). The children said they had reported 298 of these cases to their parents. "The instruction most frequently received [from the parents], appearing in 61 percent of the instances, was to withdraw" (Goff, 1949:57).

Since the civil rights movement and the emergence of more positive self-images among blacks, black parents are probably less prone to counsel withdrawal. Nevertheless, the legacy of poverty and racism leads to patterns of parent-child interaction that unintentionally lower the self-esteem and aspirations of the black child. Prolonged observation of inner-city children by two elementary school teachers dramatically illuminates the parents' dilemmas.

> Parents who expected the society to close many opportunities to their children and frustrate their aspirations because the children were black did what seemed necessary to them to prepare their children for a life of hardship. Many parents, by withdrawing individual attention somewhat abruptly while the children were still young, taught them a bitter but adaptive lesson—to be suspicious of the goodness of others, to anticipate disappointment. In low-income families with many children, these factors might be exacerbated by the need for young children to become able to care for themselves as quickly as possible so that the mothers could devote their attention to still younger children and infants. . . .
>
> Sullen withdrawal and avoidance behavior, marked by suppressed anger, became an increasingly typical response to adults as the children moved into the upper elementary school grades. This progression from open dependence and attention-seeking to increased separation from adults is partly a function of increasing maturation and has parallels in many communities. However, the intensity of the growing mistrust of adults, of ambivalent emotions, and of sullen, suppressed anger must be viewed in the context of coming up poor and black in an inner city in America. [Silverstein and Krate, 1975:17–18, 24]

Self-esteem

The fact that discrimination creates negative self-images among the disadvantaged contributed to the 1954 Supreme Court decision outlawing school segregation.

The decision recognized that school and other public facilities cannot be "separate and equal" because enforced and involuntary separateness . . . necessarily implies an inferior caste status, and thereby results in psychological degradation and injury to self-esteem. [Ausubel and Ausubel, 1963:109]

The decision referred to several studies showing that the prevalent negative evaluation of dark skin color was accepted by black children. A study in the 1940s presented 253 black children with four dolls that were identical except for color: Two were brown with black hair, the other two were white with yellow hair. The children were asked to give the experimenter the doll "that you like to play with best," the doll "that is a nice doll," the doll "that looks bad," the doll "that is a nice color." A majority of the black children showed a preference for the white doll (Clark and Clark, 1947:178).

Twenty years later, a white psychiatrist asked black and white southern children to draw pictures. Here are some of his comments on Ruby, a six-year-old black girl.

For four months . . . Ruby never used brown or black except to indicate soil or the ground. . . . She drew white people larger and more lifelike. Negroes were smaller, their bodies less intact. A white girl we both knew to be her own size appeared several times taller. While Ruby's own face lacked an eye in one drawing, an ear in another, the white girl never lacked any features. Moreover, Ruby drew the white girl's hands and legs carefully, always making sure that they had the proper number of fingers and toes. Not so with her own limbs, or those of any other Negro children she chose (or was asked) to picture. A thumb or forefinger might be missing, or a whole set of toes. The arms were shorter, even absent or truncated. [Coles, 1967:47]

More recent studies using dolls and drawings have shown a growing racial self-acceptance among black children. The original doll study was duplicated nearly a generation later in Lincoln, Nebraska, where blacks attend predominantly white schools. The later study found that both black and white children tended to prefer dolls of their own race. However, children of both races responded favorably to the different colored dolls and most had friends of the other race. (Hraba & Grant, 1970; Hraba, 1972).

Ruby's self-portrait.

Ruby's drawing of a white girl.

The slogan "black is beautiful" expresses the growing sense of pride among black Americans. That change is beginning to influence the image of blacks in television and movies where they are no longer confined to stereotyped roles of superstitious servants but appear in a wider range of more realistic characters. The presentation of competent black role models in the media enables black children to put themselves in the picture and hence helps them develop a more positive sense of self.

Chapter 4 **Summary**

Section 1/**The basis of socialization**

From the viewpoint of society, socialization is the process of fitting new individuals into an organized way of life and teaching them cultural traditions. From the viewpoint of the individual, it is the process of gaining a self. Socialization is based on several inborn qualities, including (1) the absence of instincts, (2) the long period of childhood dependency, (3) the ability to learn, (4) the capacity for language, and (5) the need for social contact.

Section 2/**Childhood socialization**

In modern societies, responsibility for the care of a young child is in the hands of one person, usually the mother. This makes great demands on the mother for self-control and resourcefulness, and the child is vulnerable to her personal limitations. The socialization of young children is a give and take between parent and child. Even infants interact socially, respond emotionally, and therefore participate in their own socialization. The human ability to express feelings and emotions is central to socialization, but learning to express feelings in acceptable ways is a primary goal of socialization.

There are two major patterns of socialization in American society: Repressive socialization stresses obedience and is adult-centered. Participatory socialization actively involves the child in the socialization process and is child-centered. Adaptation 4.1 describes societies that highly value personal independence, where punishment plays little or no part in childhood socialization.

Section 3/**Adult socialization**

Although socialization is a life-long process, adult socialization tends to be voluntary and takes place in connection with work or life-cycle changes. In homogeneous societies, the groups that socialize the individual have the same values, and a person's experiences fit into a single meaningful pattern. In heterogeneous societies, groups with different values compete with each other. As outlined in Adaptation 4.2, to be resocialized may require individuals to give up one way of life for another.

Section 4/**The social self**

Every culture gives its members a self—a unique, lasting identity. The content of the self may vary, but the process by which it is created is universal. According to Cooley, the self, built up through social interaction, is called the looking-glass self, which consists of the way we appear to others, the way we think they judge that picture, and a self-feeling.

G. H. Mead stressed the role of day-to-day socialization in shaping the self and the part that social others play in creating it. At first, the child's interactions are limited to specific individuals (*significant others*). In the second stage, the child responds to the collective attitudes of the larger community (the *generalized other*). The more conventional part of the self is the "me" and the more active part the "I."

Freud emphasized the struggles that go on within the self, which he divided into three parts: the id, which stands for gratification of impulses; the ego, for rational self-preservation; and the superego, for conformity with social norms. Freud considered the id the biological core of the self, which must be controlled, the ego a mediator between biological demands and the demands of society, and the superego, like Mead's "me," the voice of conscience.

Everyone has a core of uniqueness and identity as well as a set of selves to match a variety of roles and audiences. That is, the self is partly situational. Recognition of this fact has led to new views of the self, and more attention is being given to the social environment of the individual.

Section 5/**Deviance and the failures of socialization**

Especially in complex societies with sharply differing subcultures, socialization may be incomplete and unsuccessful. Individuals who are thought to conform to deviant subcultures become labeled as deviant by the official agencies. The stigma of such labels may become the dominant aspect of the self.

Socialization for disadvantage means channeling people into subordinate roles resulting in a loss of self-esteem and self-confidence. Both blacks and women have been socialized to have low aspirations. However, direct challenges to subordination and increased self-assertion are helping to break the pattern that socializes for disadvantage.

Suggested Readings

Brim, Orville G., Jr., and S. Wheeler
1966/1976 *Socialization After Childhood.* New York: Krieger.

Clausen, John A. (ed.)
1968/1969 *Socialization and Society.* Boston: Little, Brown.

Dreitzel, Hano Peter (ed.)
1973 *Childhood and Socialization.* New York: Macmillan.

Gove, Walter R. (ed.)
1980 *The Labeling of Deviance: Evaluating a Perspective.* Beverly Hills: Sage.

Kohn, Melvin L.
1977 *Class and Conformity.* Second edition. Chicago: University of Chicago Press.

Lamb, Michael E. (ed.)
1982 *Nontraditional Families: Parenting and Child Development.* Hillsdale, N.J.: Lawrence Erlbaum Associates.

Lynn, David B.
1974 *The Father: His Role in Child Development.* Monterey, Ca.: Brooks/Cole.

Mead, George H.
1934 *Mind, Self, and Society.* Chicago: University of Chicago Press.

Mussen, P. H., J. J. Conger, and J. Kagan
1979 *Child Development and Personality.* Fifth edition. New York: Harper & Row.

Piaget, Jean, and Barbel Inhelder
1969 *The Psychology of the Child.* New York: Basic Books.

Pilling, Doria, and Mia Kellmer Pringle
1978 *Controversial Issues in Child Development.* New York: Schocken Books.

Silverstein, Barry, and Ronald Krate
1975 *Children of the Dark Ghetto.* New York: Praeger.

Chapter 5

Interaction and Social Participation

Section One
Status and Role

This chapter and Chapter 6 discuss the main forms of social interaction and group participation from the intimacy of family life at one extreme to the complexity and impersonality of bureaucracies at the other. We begin by examining status and role, which are the building blocks of personal identity and social relations. In Section Two we discuss small groups and in Section Three primary groups and primary relations. Section Four reviews the characteristics and significance of communities. Section Five briefly outlines the idea of institution.

STATUS

A social **status** is a position in a social system: "mother," "student," and "doctor" are social statuses. These words locate people socially: mother in the family, student in the classroom, doctor in the clinic. Once we know someone's status, we know a good deal about what is expected of the person in the social setting to which that status applies.

A social **role** is the behavior that is associated with a given status. Since "professor" and "student" are statuses, there are professorial and student roles. The professorial role includes planning and teaching courses, giving lectures, grading students' work, serving on committees, doing research, attending the meetings of professional associations, and publishing scholarly books and articles.

The student role involves doing assignments, taking exams, and perhaps attending classes. It also includes taking part in extracurricular activities, which vary according to the student's other responsibilities, interests, and age. Thus, roles are the ways in which people meet the expectations and deal with the problems that go with statuses. Role and status are related to each other; role is "the dynamic aspect of status" (Linton, 1936:114).

Status and identity

Some statuses govern a person's social identity. When a status is so significant that it quickly comes to mind in answer to the "Who am I?" question, it is called a **salient status** or master status. A large part of a person's life is organized around such a status, which has a special symbolic meaning. Race, ethnicity, or religion are master statuses in many societies.

For many people, an occupation or profession is a master status. The professorial role fills much of the life of most professors. On the other hand, a temporary status—for example, a summer job—has little impact on a person's social identity.

Family status is salient for many people. For some men, the statuses of "husband" and "father" are as salient as their occupations. "Wife" and "mother" typically are salient statuses for women.

Traditional societies tended to have a limited number of stable, salient statuses. There was widespread belief in the rightness and permanence of one's "station." Occupational status was handed down from one generation to the next (that is, jobs were inherited). When people are born into a specific place in the social order, their status is ascribed. An **ascribed status** is acquired regardless of the person's actions or desires. Age, sex, and race are examples of ascribed statuses.

The opposite of an ascribed status is an **achieved status,** one that is acquired by choice and through personal effort. In Western society ascription has weakened, and statuses are more often achieved. Jobs are less often inherited than was the case in earlier times. Life is more fluid, and people occupy several different statuses at the same time and at different points in the life course.

Status and ranking

In everyday speech and much sociological discussion, the term *status* is used to refer to a position in a system of social ranks. "Professor" and "student" are ranked statuses. So are "sergeant" and "private." In fact, the whole set of military ranks may be called a status system. Because ranking is often associated with a system of statuses, it is easy to understand why the words *rank* and *status* are often used interchangeably. In strict terms, ranking should be thought of as one aspect of some statuses. For example, the status of "friend" does not imply higher or lower rank.

ROLE

As a theatrical term, a *role* is a part in a play that actors perform according to the playwright's instructions. The sociological meaning associated with a status or social position also suggests acting. The person does the things that are called for by the status. However, this acting is not just speaking lines that someone else has written but responding to social expectations. Learning what is expected in the more important social roles and how to respond in typical situations is a large part of the process of socialization.

Roles as patterns of behavior associated with social statuses can be looked at from three points of view: according to social expectations (the **prescribed role**), according to the way the role is seen (the **perceived role**), and according to how the role is acted out (the **performed role**).

The prescribed role tells what is expected of a person, to whom that person has responsibilities, and to whom she or he can turn for help.

The perceived role is likely to differ from the prescribed role because the way the person sees the role may not coincide with the ideal image of the role. The people with whom the person interacts may perceive the role in yet other ways.

How a person acts out the role—the performed role—depends on more than expectations and perceptions. Actual role behavior is always influenced by the pressures and opportunities of specific social situations.

Role dynamics

Prescribed roles are so numerous and important that they dominate social life. However, many roles emerge in the give-and-take of social interaction. In a small research team, for example, a spark plug may stimulate interaction and brainstorming, another person may help relieve tension, and an informal leader may keep the group working on the task at hand. Such roles are not based on clearly defined expectations; they take shape as the working group develops. They express personality traits and the dynamics of interpersonal relations that cut across prescribed roles.

Business executives take on roles that are usually well-defined. But as they settle into their jobs, their performed roles may diverge from their prescribed roles. They may find it necessary or desirable to concentrate on particular aspects of their roles: outside tasks, dealing with customers, buying raw materials, or negotiating with government agencies. Or their roles may concentrate on problems within the organization such as labor relations or production.

Role sets

Most roles and statuses are related to other roles and statuses and are, therefore, more complex than they appear at first glance. A mother is a mother in relation to her children, but being a mother is more than just one social relation. It is a bundle of relations to other family members and to the community as well as to children. Because she has children, her role set as mother includes relations with neighbors who have children and different relations with other neighbors who do not have children. Part of the role of mother may involve membership in a Parent-Teacher Association, just as part of the role of employer may involve membership in a Chamber of Commerce.

The concept of **role set** suggests that roles are complex and that each status generates more than one role. A single status, such as "husband," involves "an array of associated roles" (Merton, 1968:423). Someone who enters a new status usually acquires not a single role but a role set. A person who marries acquires not only a spouse but also other role partners. The new status of "husband" or "wife" creates a new role set in relation to the spouse and to the in-laws.

Role strain

Because of the many different demands contained in a role set, the person who occupies a status is subject to competing obligations and pressures. Demands on the husband or wife as companion and marital partner may at times conflict with breadwinner or parent obligations. The demands by one role partner—the husband or wife—may conflict with those of another role partner—the mother-in-law or child. Such strain is not just a clash of personalities. Rather, **role strain** is a natural, almost inevitable, consequence of the fact that role sets bind together people with different statuses, interests, and obligations.

A professor's role set includes relations to undergraduates, graduate students, teaching colleagues, research colleagues, administrators, publishers, and others. Luckily, not all of these role partners make conflicting demands at the same time, and with experience, the professor develops strategies for coping with the pressures of the system (Goode, 1960:486–490; Merton, 1968:425–433).

The strains and conflicts in role behavior are only partly due to the competing demands of role partners. Some strains arise because the role itself calls for inconsistent behaviors. For example, a role may call for friendship or intimacy but may also require impersonal judgment. Because professors often want to influence students deeply, they need to be on friendly terms with their students, treat them as unique persons, and develop a sense of mutual loyalty. But the professor must also judge the students' work and make decisions that may affect their careers. These conflicting demands can require painful adjustments on the part of both professor and student.

PATTERN VARIABLES

Contrasting terms often help to clarify abstract ideas, and sociology uses a number of such paired terms, such as caste-class, primary-secondary, ascription-achievement. Close study of social roles shows that a relatively few basic contrasting patterns, which have been called pattern variables, occur with high frequency. A **pattern variable** is a pair of contrasting terms that refer to ways of relating to oneself and to others. The contrasts point to social situations where tension between persons is likely to take place or where people may need to make difficult choices.

Four of the best understood and most widely cited pattern variables are: (1) universalism-particularism, (2) instrumentalism-expressiveness, (3) specificity-diffuseness, and (4) ascription-achievement (Parsons and Shils, 1951:76–91; Parsons, 1951:45–67).

Universalism-particularism

The entrance requirements of a state university are supposed to be applied uniformly to all who seek higher education, excluding no one who can pass the exams or meet grade standards. Such criteria are called **universalistic** because they are based on general rules or principles to be applied uniformly to all members of a given category, in this case, applicants for admission.

A **particularistic** criterion, on the other hand, recognizes the claim of an individual to be treated in a personal way. If you choose a physician or lawyer because he or she is a friend who needs the work, then you have made a particularistic choice. The classic example of particularism is nepotism, the hiring of relatives. Notice that there may be a norm of particularism: People may feel that it is right to be loyal to a friend or relative even though a stranger would do the job better.

Because universalism and particularism compete, the tension between them creates many difficulties in role behavior. It is usually assumed, probably correctly, that universalism is more fragile and needs to be protected. Most people have their deepest commitments to other persons who are committed to them in turn. It is hard to feel as committed to abstract ideas like justice as to a friend. For this reason roles based on universalistic principles are often protected against the intrusion of personal interests (particularism). For example, judges are expected to disqualify themselves if relatives or close associates appear before them or if they have financial interest in a case.

Instrumentalism-expressiveness

Many roles demand a rational, practical, cost-accounting approach to oneself, to other people, and to objects. Action is **instrumental** when it is governed by efficiency and effectiveness, when things are weighed for their worth as means to well-defined ends.

Students who go to college with definite jobs in mind have an instrumental orientation. On the other hand, those who have less definite plans and respond spontaneously to the new experiences and opportunities of college have an **expressive** orientation. The gratifications of expressiveness flow from action and response itself rather than from attaining a fixed goal. Individuals who act expressively invest their personalities in the acts. Consequently they are less efficient from the standpoint of achieving a specific objective.

A satisfactory balance of the expressive and the instrumental is essential for efficiency accompanied by personal satisfaction. The idea of meaningful work presumes such a balance: To be meaningful, work should offer opportunity for self-expression. When instrumentalism leaves no place for expression, the individual becomes a part of the machine or the office bureaucracy.

Specificity-diffuseness

The parties to a contract try to set down exactly what they will do and what they will be responsible for. Their obligations are defined and limited. Thus, it is said that contracts have **specificity:** they are limited and determined, not open-ended. As legal instruments, contracts are well adapted to the market economy. Business executives know what they are getting into and can calculate costs.

In enduring social relations, however, it is difficult to maintain a principle of limited commitment (Selznick, 1969:52–57). Executives may decide not to insist on the strict terms of a contract:

> Disputes are frequently settled without reference to the contract. . . There is a hesitance to speak of legal rights or to threaten to sue in these negotiations. Even where the parties have a detailed and carefully planned agreement which indicates what is to happen if, say, the seller fails to deliver on time, often they will never refer to the agreement but will negotiate a solution when the problem arises apparently as if there had never been any original contract. . . . [Macaulay, 1963:61, 64].

Diffuseness is the opposite of specificity: Diffuse social relations are open-ended and not sharply defined. Lasting associations tend to become more and more diffuse as time passes. It is easy to be specific about obligations and abide by an agreement when a single act is involved, such as the purchase of a house. But when buyer and seller expect to do business over a long period and depend on each other for cooperation, they cannot anticipate what might come up in the future and work out all details in advance.

Ascription-achievement

Ascription refers to the labeling process of ascribed status. It is a way of relating to others by classifying them and assigning them certain virtues, handicaps, rights, or limitations. Individuals are pigeon-holed and responded to not as individuals performing their roles but according to their labels (Foner, 1979).

Ascriptive labeling is common in role behavior because people tend to think of the role and the person together. A status label such as teacher or hard hat may automatically bring forth an image of personal characteristics. People respond to clues such as accent, dress, and manner that are associated with an ascribed status rather than to the personal competence of the individual.

Ascription contrasts with the principle of achievement. **Achievement** values persons according to performance. Every society requires some orientation to achievement, and it is a dominant cultural theme in Western industrial society, but it is not consistently applied. Rewards may not be fairly distributed, for example, when whites or men are more highly rewarded for their ascribed statuses—whiteness or masculinity.

Section Two
Interaction and the Micro-Order

The most meaningful human contacts occur in small-scale social settings. Through the process of acting in awareness of others and adjusting to the way they respond, a pattern emerges. The term **micro-order** refers to this pattern of interpersonal contact in small groups.

PATTERNS OF INTERACTION

Personal interaction is carried on partly according to the rules and norms of the culture. However, people are more than social puppets controlled by cultural norms. Real people with wants and preferences, strengths and weaknesses, live out their lives in social environments with practical opportunities and limits. Social interaction and the micro-order are the complex products of cultural norms, social expectations, and personal adaptations. They consist of both spontaneous responses and careful planning; they combine reactions to the present situation and memories of past experiences.

Definition of the situation

"If men define situations as real they are real in their consequences" (Thomas and Thomas, 1928:572). This much-quoted sentence means that, to a large extent, people create their own social reality. Human beings interact on the basis of their understanding of what a situation is and what it requires—for example, whether they should be serious or relaxed. Their **definition of the situation** interprets the situation and gives it social meaning.

When people share the same definition of a situation, social order exists. They know what to expect from each other and how to interact. Most of these shared definitions are learned without deliberate effort and are not given much thought. They make up "a world taken for granted" (Schutz, 1962:74).

The extent to which social life is taken for granted is revealed when people behave in unexpected ways, thereby challenging unconsciously accepted definitions of the situation. A sociologist made this point when he asked his students to spend an evening being as polite to their parents as if they had just been introduced, and to use formal terms of address like *Mr.* and *Mrs.* The students were to keep this up for the whole evening without explaining what they were doing. So strong were the reactions to this behavior that most of the students found it impossible to complete the assignment, and quite a few parental tempers had to be cooled (Garfinkel, 1967:Chapter 2). The exercise shows how the micro-order usually operates without the awareness of the actors and is exposed only when people are confronted with inappropriate behavior or when the taken-for-granted world is challenged.

The definition of the situation is not always taken for granted. In open and fluid situations, people work out their relationships while the interaction is going on. A new relationship evolves and becomes defined in the process of interaction. The meaning of the encounter for each of the parties depends on cues and hints, on maintaining distance or overcoming barriers to communication.

Even when they act according to accepted guidelines, people may compete to define some situations so as to serve their own interests. A person entering an interaction may try to give an impression of authority or sincerity, of being "with it" or "available." In doing so, she or he tries to control how others respond, that is, how they define the situation. The phrase "management of impressions" has been used to describe such strategies (Goffman, 1959:208–237).

If an individual's definition of the situation is too personal and peculiar, it causes trouble. For example, someone who treats a gathering as a party when everyone else is trying to hold a committee meeting creates problems. On the other hand, if enough people define the meeting as a party, the chances are it will become one.

This latter example illustrates what Thomas and Thomas meant by saying that a situation defined as real is real in its consequences. The definition of the situation becomes a self-fulfilling prophecy. An individual who is defined as insecure in interpersonal relations and is treated as insecure may find it impossible to relax and feel secure. Teachers who believe that ghetto children cannot learn and treat them as nonlearners help make their prediction come true.

The definition of situations is a subjective source of social order. Interactions are patterned by the beliefs and interpretations people bring to the situation and by the meanings they give to their own actions and those of others. This is a basic fact of social life. All groups and societies are held together by shared beliefs and interpretations.

BLUEPRINTS AND THE MICRO-ORDER

The "blueprint" view of social interaction assumes that people behave according to a set of cultural rules. In a given situation, the individual is supposed to follow the appropriate rule more or less automatically. And because others are assumed to have learned the same rules, the framework for orderly social behavior is ready made. A great deal of interaction is guided by such rules.

Civil inattention is an example of blueprint behavior. In Western society, there are informal rules that limit eye contact between persons who are not acquainted. When strangers meet in elevators, streets, and rest rooms, they are expected to glance at each other, but not long enough to suggest that the other is an object of special interest (Goffman, 1963a:84). Too much eye contact, or staring, may be embarrassing.

The limits of blueprints

Many sociologists are doubtful about the blueprint approach to interaction. They see it as a partial explanation that does not necessarily account for the most important aspects of the micro-order. Rules often provide only a general framework within which the actual terms of interaction are worked out (Blumer, 1969:Chapter 1; Wrong, 1961).

Another drawback of the blueprint approach is that it overestimates the amount of consensus about social rules. On formal occasions, such as public ceremonies and church rituals, the blueprint prevails. People know beforehand (or are shown then and there, sometimes by a printed program) exactly what is expected of them. On most other occasions, however, there is room for different interpretations of the situation.

Western societies are highly diverse, and their rules do not necessarily reflect the preferences, interests, or experiences of all of their members. Persons from varying backgrounds may have different ideas about how to behave—or no idea at all. For example, racial minorities and the dominant group, or youth and adult groups, may not share the same blueprints. But even people who usually accept the dominant values of the society and would like to live by its rules do not always do so.

The main limitation of the blueprint approach is that it does not account fully for the variety and uncertainty of social interaction. It cannot explain how a micro-order develops when people interpret the rules differently.

Ethnomethodology

The problem-solving nature of human interaction is emphasized by a school of thought called **ethnomethodology** (Garfinkel, 1967; Dreitzel, 1970). The Greek word *ethnos* means nation, people, tribe, or race. Hence, ethnomethodology refers to the methods and understandings people use in the course of their actions and interactions. People learn how to cope with the social world and how to relate to others as part of their everyday life. Ethnomethodologists claim that the understandings people gain in this way should be the starting point for studies of social organization. This is another way of stressing the importance of the definition of the situation.

(Text continued on p. 86)

Adaptation 5.1

Goffman/Interaction Rituals

Two themes are central to Goffman's studies of everyday life: (1) the fate of the self in social interaction, that is, how individuals are put at risk in their encounters with others and how they manage those risks, and (2) the fate of the micro-order, especially the devices that are used, often unconsciously, to maintain social life and interaction. Among the ideas that bear on these two themes are social life as episode, interaction as theater, the management of impressions, and the significance of ritual in human encounters.

SOCIAL LIFE AS EPISODE

The micro-order is made up of millions of minute, fleeting episodes. Even when people have long-standing relationships, they actually communicate in brief encounters. In this sense, "society" is not abstract—it is made up of specific activities and communications, many of which are transitory. To some degree, society as it is really lived is constantly coming into being and passing out of existence. "A sociology of occasions is here advocated. Social organization is the central theme, but what is organized is the co-mingling of persons and the temporary interactional enterprises that can arise therefrom. . . . A 'social gathering' . . . is a shifting entity . . . created by arrivals and killed by departures" (1967: 2).

Through an exchange of cues and gestures, participants indicate to each other their intended roles in the situation as well as what they expect the others' roles to be. This working consensus differs from one interaction to another. "Thus, between two friends at lunch, a reciprocal show of affection, respect, and concern for the other is maintained. In service occupations, on the other hand, the specialist often maintains an image of disinterested involvement in the client's problem, while the client responds with a show of respect for the competence and integrity of the specialist" (1959:10).

INTERACTION AS THEATER

Shakespeare's figure of speech, "all the world's a stage," can be developed into a model of the micro-

Source: A summary and interpretation of writings on the micro-order by Erving Goffman. His analyses appear in the following volumes: *The Presentation of Self in Everyday Life* (Garden City, N.Y.: Doubleday Anchor Books, 1959); *Encounters: Two Studies in the Sociology of Interaction* (Indianapolis: Bobbs-Merrill, 1961); *Behavior in Public Places: Notes on the Social Organization of Gatherings* (New York: Free Press, 1963); *Interaction Ritual: Essays on Face-to-Face Behavior* (Garden City, N.Y.: Doubleday Anchor Books, 1967); *Relations In Public: Microstudies of the Public Order* (New York: Harper Colophon Books, 1971). Quoted material, some of which is abridged, is used by permission of the author and copyright holder and Doubleday & Company, Inc. This adaption was prepared by Saul Geiser.

order showing how everyday life is pervaded by features of theatrical performance. Thus, many establishments are divided into "front stage" and "backstage" regions. In frontstage areas, such as livingrooms and food counters, decorum and cleanliness are displayed whenever outsiders are present; backstage, in bedrooms and kitchens, performers can relax in guarded secrecy. Social performances are often staged by teams, such as the husband and wife hosting a dinner party or the doctor and nurse acting with clinical efficiency in the presence of patients.

THE MANAGEMENT OF IMPRESSIONS

If interaction is like theater, then individuals must be like actors. The individual as an "actor" in social encounters must be skilled in the art of "impression management"—controlling his or her image so as to create a favorable definition of the situation. "For example, in American society we find that eight-year-old children claim lack of interest in the television programs that are directed to five- and six-year-olds, but sometimes surreptitiously watch them. We also find that middle-class housewives may leave *The Saturday Evening Post* on the living room end table but keep a copy of *True Romance* ('It's something the cleaning woman must have left around') concealed in the bedroom. . . . In their capacity as performers, individuals will be concerned with maintaining the impression that they are living up to the many standards by which they and their products are judged. But qua performers, individuals are concerned not with the moral issue of realizing these standards, but with the amoral issue of engineering a convincing impression that these standards are being realized" (1959:42, 251).

Hazards of impression management

Once the individual has projected an impression of himself or herself, others expect that impression to be maintained. However, a standardized performance is often difficult to sustain. The individual may make mistakes that give away the act; the audience may learn something about the individual's past that is not consistent with the character being portrayed; outsiders may accidentally enter backstage regions, catching a team in an activity that does not fit its frontstage image. A theme that runs through Goffman's work is the ever-present danger that someone will see through a performance or otherwise disrupt it. "When these disruptive events occur, the interaction itself may come to a confused and embarrassed halt. At such moments the individual whose presentation has been discredited may feel ashamed while the others present may feel hostile, and all the participants may come to feel ill at ease. . . . While the likelihood of disruption will vary widely from interaction to interaction, . . . there is no interaction in which the participants do not take an appreciable chance of being slightly embarrassed or a slight chance of being deeply humiliated. Life may not be much of a gamble, but interaction is" (1959:12, 243).

Intensity of face-to-face interaction

In the presence of others, the individual gives off information not only verbally but also by clothing, gestures, and posture. Therefore, face-to-face interaction increases both the emotional intensity and the hazards of social interaction. "Each individual can *see* that he is being experienced in some way, and he will guide at least some of his conduct according to the perceived identity and initial response of his audience. Further, he can be seen to be seeing this, and can see that he has been seen seeing this. Ordinarily, then, to use our naked senses is to use them nakedly and to be made naked by their use. Copresence renders persons uniquely accessible, available, and subject to one another" (1963a:16, 22).

People often try to avoid face-to-face interaction when they have something difficult to do, such as giving bad news or a scolding. On the other hand, face-to-face interaction offers opportunities to patch things up or to soften a blow by combining a threat with a smile or bad news with a hug.

INTERPERSONAL RITUALS

The foundation of social order lies in the interpersonal rituals—hellos, goodbys, courtesies, compliments, apologies, and handshakes—that punctuate everyday interaction. "The gestures which we sometimes call empty are perhaps in fact the fullest things of all" (1967:91).

In the context of religion, "ritual" is standardized conduct through which an individual shows respect and regard to an object of ultimate value (usually a supernatural being) or to its stand-in (for example, an idol or a priest). In other words, rituals have mostly ceremonial but little practical value. Yet as Durkheim—to whom Goffman owes a theoretical debt—pointed out, ritual and ceremony play a major role in holding society together; through worship of a common totem, some preliterate peoples reaffirm their solidarity as a group.

Religious rituals have become less important in modern secular societies, but many kinds of interpersonal rituals perform the same function. Four types of interpersonal ritual illustrate this point:

Presentation rituals show appreciation of the recipient. They include such acts as salutations, invitations, and compliments, "the length of the salutation depending upon the period that had elapsed since the last salutation and the period that seemed likely before the next" (1956/1967:71).

Avoidance rituals, on the other hand, show respect for the privacy of others through distancing behaviors such as limiting eye contact between persons who do not know each other. "In performing this courtesy the eyes of the looker may pass over the eyes of the other, but no 'recognition' is typically allowed. Where the courtesy is performed between two persons passing on the street, civil inattention may take the special form of eyeing the other up to eight feet, during which the sides of the street are apportioned by gesture, and then casting the eyes down as the other passes—a kind of dimming of the lights. In any case, we have here what is perhaps the slightest of interpersonal rituals, yet one that constantly regulates the social intercourse of persons in our society" (1963a:84).

Maintenance rituals reaffirm a relationship, for example, when persons with a long-standing relationship who have not seen each other for some time arrange to meet: "It is as if the strength of a bond slowly deteriorates if nothing is done to celebrate it, and so at least occasionally a little invigoration is called for" (1971:73).

A presentation ritual.

Ratification rituals, such as congratulations at marriage and condolences at the death of a spouse, mark the passage from one status to another.

Functions of interpersonal rituals

Different rituals serve different functions, but all have one thing in common: They are ceremonies in which the actor shows respect and regard for another person. Interpersonal rituals are important for three reasons: First, they are like traffic signs that keep the flow of interaction moving smoothly and direct it away from areas that could prove dangerous. Like "Do not enter" signs, avoidance rituals protect people from being approached in public places and leave them free to go about their business. Like a green light, invitations and greetings tell them when their presence is welcome and appropriate. Without the ritual of speaking and listening in turn, conversations would be reduced to chaotic babble.

A second function of interpersonal ritual is to ensure that individuals will escape unhurt when they enter interactional traffic. Each new episode poses a potential threat to the self-image of the individual.

The self is therefore a "ritually delicate object," ever alert to offenses that would reflect unfavorably upon it. Even having one's remarks ignored can be taken as a sign that one's self is somehow deficient; conversational etiquette requires that each person's remarks, however trivial, be acknowledged.

Third, the principle of reciprocity is built into the structure of interpersonal ritual. It typically involves a standardized set of moves and countermoves, or dialog, between two or more actors: "Hi, how are you?" "Fine, thanks. And you?" Together these moves make up a little ceremony in which both selves receive ritual support; it is like holding hands in a circle, in which each person gets back in the left hand what he or she gives with the right. Because such ritual exchanges occur so often in everyday interaction, they provide repeated opportunities for actors to sustain a workable, if idealized, definition of the situation. Though individuals are selfishly concerned with keeping up a favorable impression of themselves, their efforts must be expressed in the form of regard for the identities of others: "His aim is to save face; his effect is to save the situation" (1955/1967:39).

THE CONSERVATIVE NATURE OF THE MICRO-ORDER

Because of its episodic and fleeting character, the micro-order may seem flimsy and unstable. It depends mainly on informal sanctions to produce conformity, and anyone with enough self-assurance can override those sanctions simply by not becoming emotionally affected. Ethnomethodologists see the seeds of a "revolutionary" viewpoint in this analysis: The micro-order exists only because people *believe* it exists; social order is really quite unstable.

Yet Goffman's work has a conservative ring. He shows how interaction constrains people and why such constraints are needed if people are to create a shared and consistent definition of reality: "By entering a situation in which he is given a face to maintain, a person takes on the responsibility of standing guard over the flow of events as they pass before him. He must ensure that a particular *expressive order* is sustained—an order that regulates the flow of events, large or small, so that anything that appears to be expressed by them will be consistent with his face. . . . While his social face can be his most personal possession and the center of security

and pleasure, it is only on loan to him from society; it will be withdrawn unless he conducts himself in a way that is worthy of it. Approved attributes and their relation to face make of every man his own jailer; this is a fundamental social constraint even though each man may like his cell" (1955/1967: 9–10).

Perhaps the most conservative element in Goffman's account of the micro-order is his emphasis on shared values as the glue by which society is held together. Unlike more radical theorists who see society as marked by continual conflict and held together by force, he locates the basis of social order in the values that people hold in common. Ritual is important insofar as it is a means of reaffirming these values. Yet unlike earlier sociological theorists such as Durkheim, who stressed abstract values and ritual, Goffman shows that ritual performances permeate everyday life. "To the degree that a performance highlights the common official values of the society in which it occurs, we may look upon it . . . as a ceremony—as an expressive . . . reaffirmation of the moral values of the community. . . . The world, in truth, is a wedding" (1959:35–36).

Section Three
Primary Groups

The human need for emotional support is expressed in primary bonding or primary relations—sustained relationships that provide comfort and gratification of emotional needs. The many forms of primary bonding include parent-child relations, friendship, love, and membership in a tightly knit social group or community.

This section examines the nature of primary relations and their importance for the individual and society. It focuses on the **primary group**—the setting in which intimate, person-centered interactions take place. The term *primary group* was first used by Cooley to refer to groups characterized by

> intimate face-to-face association and cooperation. They are primary in several senses, but chiefly in

that they are fundamental in forming the social nature and ideas of the individual. The result of intimate association, psychologically, is a certain fusion of individualities in a common whole, so that one's very self, for many purposes at least, is the common life and purpose of the group. Perhaps the simplest way of describing this wholeness is by saying that it is a "we"; it involves the sort of sympathy and mutual identification for which "we" is the natural expression. One lives in the feeling of the whole and finds the chief aims of his will in that feeling [1909:-23].

PRIMARY RELATIONS

Primary groups differ from other groups in the nature of the ties between their members. A **primary relation** has three main features: (1) response to the

Primary relations and life-styles.

whole person, (2) communication in depth, and (3) personal satisfaction.

Response to the whole person

In a primary relation, the participants interact as unique, whole persons. Interactions are *unique* because response is to a particular person and cannot be transferred to others. Interactions are *whole* because each response is to many aspects of the other person's character and is freely given, permitting feelings to enter the relationship. The more complete the interaction, the more primary the relation.

Many human relations are not primary and are called **secondary** because they can easily be transferred to other persons and are limited in scope. For example, the relation between a clerk and a customer is transferable; each clerk and each customer acts in standardized ways that can be applied to other clerks and other customers. Also, the relation involves only those aspects of each person that are relevant to a business transaction. To relate as a person instead of as a clerk or a customer is to become aware of the other's personality and thus to approach a primary relation. In nonprimary relations, communication is more superficial. Nonprimary relations are not meant to reveal the deeper layers of personality and tend to be limited to public interaction.

Communication in depth

In a primary relation, few limits are placed on the scope and form of communication between participants. Communication often takes the form of nonverbal hints and cues as well as words, revealing feelings that would be hidden in public situations. This type of communication tends to influence the feelings and beliefs of the participants. Although intimate and extensive communication does not guarantee agreement, it does encourage similar attitudes and feelings to develop. In a primary relation, more and deeper communication means more opportunities for persons to influence each other.

Primary relations are not always affectionate and cordial. All relationships involve strains as well as positive responses, although they cannot survive very long on antagonism alone. When a personal relation is characterized by antagonism, communication is hampered and response is usually limited to a part of the participant's personality. A primary relation must entail a positive valuing of the other person, and the participants must have a sense of belonging together and of sharing a common identity in spite of strain.

Personal satisfactions

Primary relations contribute to personal development, security, and well-being. The individual is accepted as a unique person, not merely as a means to an end. To the extent that work is a source of satisfaction, primary relations tend to develop in work situations.

FROM SOCIABILITY TO KINSHIP

Once they are established, primary relations can survive without face-to-face interaction. Families, lovers, and friends maintain primary relations even when they are far apart. Obviously, many face-to-face settings (for instance, a courtroom) are impersonal. Face-to-face interaction is likely to occur in primary relations, but it is not essential to such relations.

Most primary relations, even between close friends, may deviate in some ways and at some times from the model described here. Primary relations can be placed on a continuum from sociability to kinship. (See Figure 5.1.) One end of this continuum—sociability—is interaction with casual acquaintances or neighbors. Fleeting encounters between strangers at a party or between a hitchhiker and a motorist (Mukerji, 1978) do not meet the conditions of primary relations: personality is involved only in a fragmentary way, communication is superficial and brief, and personal satisfaction is slight or nonexistent.

Farther to the right is the more enduring group of people who enjoy each other's company and maintain a friendship over a longer period. Yet their relationship may have little to support it beyond the satisfactions of companionship.

At the kinship end of the continuum are groups anchored in personality and social structure. Their relationships call for the greatest amount of psychic investment, and the participants' claims on each other are supported by law and custom. People who live together and depend on one another are more likely to know each other intimately and are thus better able to respond as whole persons. Their relationships are most likely to be fully realized primary relations.

Figure 5.1 places the congeniality group (a casual gathering) toward the low end of the continuum and the nuclear family toward the high end with a high degree of commitment and the expectation of personal fulfillment. This position suggests that commitment is a key variable influencing primary groups. If there is too little commitment, interaction is likely to be superficial.

Figure 5.2 adds another variable: intensity of interaction. The encounter group is marked by low

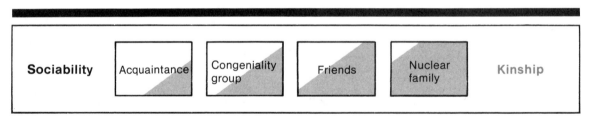

Figure 5.1 The Continuum of Commitment

		Commitment	
		Low	High
Intensity of Interaction	Low	Acquaintances	Kin (dispersed)
	High	Encounter groups Congeniality groups	Nuclear family Close friends

Figure 5.2   Commitment and Intensity of Interaction

commitment and high interaction. In the nuclear family, interaction and commitment are both high. Close kin who live apart may feel strong commitment to each other but engage in little interaction. When both interaction and commitment are low, there is almost no relationship at all.

PRIMARY GROUPS

A group is primary if it is based on primary relations. When people live or work closely together, **primary groups** usually emerge. Families, play groups, and neighborhood cliques encourage the formation of primary relations. However, small size alone does not guarantee primary-group formation. For example, a task force composed of people of varying backgrounds, ages, and ranks may not develop into a primary group.

On the other hand, large size does not necessarily prevent the formation of primary groups; sometimes whole communities can be based on primary relations. Primary communities are discussed later in this chapter.

Such diverse groups as families, soldier groups,

An extended family on their Minnesota farm in the late nineteenth century.

gangs, and factory cliques depend largely on primary relations and give their members emotional support—a function that is performed by a primary group. Obviously, not all of these groups protect or gratify their members in the same ways or to the same extent. A primary group in a factory can do some important things for its members and may affect the factory's organization, but it cannot do the job of the family. Thus, a primary group should be understood in the context in which it has developed and in which it performs its functions.

The primary group is the main link between the individual and society. Cooley emphasized the role of the primary group in the formation of character, for example, in the influence of parents on their children. Because it serves personal needs, the primary group can perform some functions for society —getting individuals to work or fight or show self-restraint. By providing emotional support, the primary group binds the individual to the group and, through the group, to the goals of the larger society.

The value of impersonality

Though love and friendship are found in primary relations, one should not therefore conclude that primary relations are always good and nonprimary relations are always bad. The fact that a relation is primary does not mean that it is desirable. Personal satisfaction is not the only social value.

In many situations it is better to maintain impersonal, or secondary, relations. Much business, military, educational, and legal experience suggests that it is best to keep things formal. For example, people are more likely to be treated equally and fairly if they are dealt with on an impersonal basis. Professional standards can then be maintained or individuals assigned to hazardous duties without reference to possible personal claims on those in authority.

Personal networks and the sociogram

Like all groups that are maintained for long periods, a primary group develops its own internal structure, that is, a pattern of fairly stable relations among its members. To some extent, the structure of a group reflects its members' feelings toward one

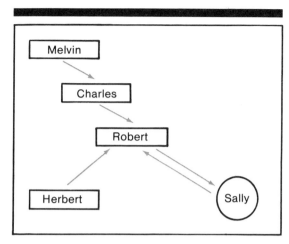

Figure 5.3 Sociogram of Best-Friend Choices in a Third Grade

another as persons. One can imagine lines of attraction and repulsion between various members, lines that hold the group together in some ways and pull it apart in others.

These attractions and repulsions can be uncovered by asking the members of a group whom they would choose to play or work with, or to serve as leader. On the basis of these responses, a sociometric diagram showing who chooses whom may be drawn. Such a diagram is called a **sociogram** (Moreno, 1953). See Figure 5.3 for a simple example. Researchers use such techniques when they observe and map the conversations, arguments, and clique behavior of a group. A similar but more complex approach is social-network analysis. (See Barnes, 1972.)

The group as haven

From the standpoint of the individual, primary groups have two functions: (1) They are havens where the individual can find comfort and security, and (2) they are the settings in which the main events of private life take place.

In primary relations, uniqueness counts. The participants believe they are accepted and wanted for what they are. Ideally, they do not feel that they need to be on guard, put forth their best efforts, or present a good appearance. Therefore, primary relations are a haven from the outside world, which measures people impersonally by what they achieve and how they appear. Primary relations are particularistic. What counts is who you are, not what you are.

Adaptation 1.1, which analyzed friendship on Tally's Corner, describes a hunger for lasting relationships that offer security and a sense of belonging. Friendships tend to be unreliable when people lack money, stable homes, steady jobs, and regular incomes. However, the people on Tally's Corner who do not have stable kin relations create imaginary kinship or "pseudo-kinship" ties that help meet their need for supportive relationships. Similarly, as a study of old people in a lower-class district in East London found, "people without relatives intensified other associations. They exchanged visits more often with neighbours and friends and, partly through mutual services, found a means of satisfying personal or social needs" (Townsend, 1957/1963:152).

Middle-class retirement communities where elderly people live in close contact with each other give the old a sense of psychological security among their age peers as well as an interesting and meaningful round of daily activities. A study of inheritance and disinheritance shows that primary relations among the residents of such communities can become so strong that the wills of the elderly leave their friends bequests that might otherwise be added to gifts to family members (Rosenfeld, 1979:77–82).

Section Four
The Quest for Community

The example just mentioned of primary relations in elderly communities shows that the impersonality of modern life is sometimes exaggerated. Many people, even in large cities, live out their lives within a stable circle of friends and relatives. But for many others there is enough openness, fluidity, and isolation to create a sense of loss—the loss of community. The quest for community is an effort to enlarge the primary group, to make affection, communication, and a sense of kinship part of the social environment.

GEMEINSCHAFT AND GESELLSCHAFT

The German sociologist Ferdinand Tönnies (1855–1896) contrasted two types of society, *Gemeinschaft* and *Gesellschaft*. *Gemeinschaft* may be roughly translated as "community," but the German word also suggests having roots, moral unity, intimacy, and kinship (1887/1963). Therefore, *Gemeinschaft* is often translated as "primary community." A *Gemeinschaft* is a society characterized by (1) assignment of status to the whole person so that work and the rest of social life are merged; (2) a high degree of group unity based on shared attitudes and aims; and (3) total commitment to the community, which is thought of as a large kin group.

In a *Gemeinschaft*, people feel that they belong together because they are of the same kind. Broadly speaking, they are kin, and their membership in the group, which has emotional meaning for the group as well as for the individual, cannot be freely renounced. People do not decide to join a *Gemeinschaft;* they are born into it or grow into it in the way friendships grow. This model of a communal society is typical of folk or preliterate societies. The decline of *Gemeinschaft* in the modern world is a decline in the sense of kinship with other members of the community.

The *Gemeinschaft* model does not fit all folk communities, however. A poor peasant village, for example, may not offer its people a sense of community. This was shown in a study of a village in southern Italy:

> The peasants of Franza [a pseudonym] are on the whole given to suspicion, quarrels, vituperation, violence, and conflicts of all sorts. . . . The land, which keeps them in the peasant state they intensely hate, is nevertheless a source of iniquitous quarrels between close relatives almost every time that it comes up for division or revision, which is indeed quite often. By their own standards and admission, the people of Franza are a wretched people. [Lopreato, 1967:103–104]

A study of another town in the same region found an ethos of "amoral familism": "Maximize the material, short-run advantage of the nuclear family; assume that all others will do likewise'' (Banfield, 1958:85).

At its best, *Gemeinschaft* evokes an image of communion and belonging. But the term also refers to a world of ascription, fixed status, extended kinship, and sacred belief. Such a society may be oppressive and may limit the expression and development of individual potential.

In contrast to a *Gemeinschaft*, a *Gesellschaft* is a voluntary, purposive association. (In German, *Gesellschaft* refers to a special-purpose organization such as a business association; the word can also be translated as ''society'' in the larger sense, but not as ''community.'') Tönnies used *Gesellschaft* to refer to a society in which the major social bonds are voluntary and based on rational self-interest. People enter into relations with one another not because they must or because it is natural, but as a practical way of achieving their goals. The typical relation in such a society is the contract, and the typical group is the voluntary special-purpose association, to be discussed in Chapter 6.

The historical trend toward large-scale, complex societies tends to create societies that fit the *Gesellschaft* model. More and more activities are governed by the voluntary actions of individuals who choose freely and keep their options open. Yet the *Gemeinschaft* model retains a strong appeal, and there are frequent efforts to create primary communities within societies characterized by voluntary association, mobility, and rational choice. Two such efforts are the modern communes and the intentional (utopian) communities of the 1800s.

COMMUNES

Beginning in the mid-1960s, groups of young people began forming communes, and by 1970, probably near the peak of the movement, there were about 1,000 rural and 2,000 urban communes in the United States (Zablocki, 1971:300). Communes were also formed in other countries. Many communes were small, with 6 to 8 or even fewer members sharing a house or farm; others with 25 or more members. Most communes included men and women, adults and children. The rural commune approached the ideal of communal living more closely than the urban

commune, whose members went to work or to school. The rural commune is in theory less dependent on the rest of society; for that reason, too, it is closer to the communal ideal.

Communes partly express alienation from society and partly experiments with different life-styles. Sharing is a chief characteristic of the commune (Fairfield, 1972). The impulse behind the formation of communes is the need for more satisfying primary relations. Thus communes may be seen as a response to the impersonality of modern life. They are part of a pattern that also includes the ideology of togetherness and the human potential movement. ''In this perspective, communes are not nearly so radical a phenomenon as they are commonly thought to be'' (Berger, Hackett, and Millar, 1972:-279). Still, forming a commune, or even joining one, is considered a radical step because the newcomer is not prepared by earlier experiences for such new commitments and psychic risks.

INTENTIONAL COMMUNITIES

Modern communes suggest comparison with the so-called utopian communities of an earlier time. During the nineteenth century, more than 100 such communities were founded in the United States (Webber, 1959:15). Some, such as the Shakers, the Amana Society, and the Hutterite Brethren, were small Christian sects seeking to establish ''godly societies'' in their own small communities. Others were secular experiments in communal living. An example is the socialist settlement founded in 1824 at New Harmony, Indiana, by the British industrialist-socialist Robert Owen, but like many such settlements, it soon failed (Briggs, 1968).

Although such communities are usually called utopian, it is more accurate to call them intentional. An intentional community is a voluntary association of people who live according to a specific plan of organization and code of conduct. An Israeli kibbutz is an intentional community, but it is not necessarily utopian. By contrast, a *natural community* grows without a plan or set of guiding principles.

The most striking difference between most communes and intentional communities is the latter are committed to a tight system of social control. Reli-

An Amish barn raising.
The community pitches in to help one of its own after a fire.

gious communities have the best chance of success because they can use doctrine to justify the subordination of the individual to the group. Every aspect of life can be given religious meaning and thus made subject to group control. The Shakers, for example, prescribed in painful detail the routines of daily life: how to get out of bed, how to get dressed, when to eat, when to speak (Webber, 1959:57–59).

The Society of Brothers (the Bruderhof) is a modern religious community with colonies in New York, Pennsylvania, and Connecticut. It supports itself by making children's toys to be sold to schools. The society's members—about 750 men, women, and children—live a highly organized life:

> A Bruderhof day is a patterned day, divided into small segments, each with its planned activity. Bells ring for lunch, for supper, for the evening activity, for the morning and afternoon sessions of work and school (Zablocki, 1971:45).

A study of 91 utopian communities founded in the United States between 1780 and 1860 reports that 11 lasted for at least 25 years and, by that measure, were successful (Kanter, 1968:503–516). Compared with the failures, the successful communities required more sacrifice, more financial investment, more participation, and allowed less personal autonomy. It appears that the benefits of community must often be purchased at the price of individual freedom.

Section Five
Institutions

In ordinary speech, *institution* implies something solid and lasting, something with a history and a future. Institutions often have their own buildings, so that specific structures come to mind when people think of religious institutions or political institutions. The sociological concept is built on the everyday meaning and contains two related ideas: An **institution** is (1) an established way of organizing social life and (2) a pattern that is valued by a group, community, or society. A list of American institutions would include Thanksgiving dinner, Congress, private enterprise, the family farm, the secret ballot, college football, and many others.

INSTITUTIONALIZATION

College football is an institution insofar as people care about it. They care, however, in different ways and for different reasons. Some care because they enjoy the game or identify it with college life; others care because football draws big crowds, makes money, and encourages the alumni and the community to support the college. Thus, football, or any other college sport, is valued for personal, social, or economic reasons. It is an established pattern that serves a number of goals and interests. The process of becoming valued and established is called **institutionalization.**

Being an institution is a matter of degree. Groups or practices are more or less institutionalized, that is, they are more or less firmly established and more or less highly valued. Consider, for example, a large corporation like General Motors or IBM. These organizations are firmly established. They involve many employees, investors, suppliers, and customers; large amounts of money, real estate, and technology; and numerous special interests, such as pensions and insurance. When big corporations run into financial trouble, as Lockheed and Chrysler did in the 1970s and 1980s, they may be "bailed out" by the government. Yet a large corporation is only partly institutionalized. It may be well established, but it is not always valued. If a financially weak corporation is reorganized or taken over by another company, most people probably do not care.

Institutionalization is strongest when the group or activity is valued for itself or for what it represents. This value is reinforced by practical concerns such as property ownership, participation in a network of activities, or widespread dependence on a given service or benefit. In addition to being valued for its traditions, the United States Military Academy (West Point) has a corps of influential alumni, a continuing claim on the United States budget, and a well-defined function in training officers. That is, it is both firmly established and highly valued.

Institutionalization goes on at all levels of social life, in small groups as well as in large organizations. A family may have its own institutions, such as playing cards on Saturday night. A chess club may meet regularly and be important to its members even though it is not important to the community. Throughout society, much effort is devoted to institution building. In business, for example, "institutional" advertising sells the company's identity rather than its products. Other devices, such as a company logo, a house organ, annual sales meetings, and established policies help create tradition and image. These forms of institutionalization have practical value because they encourage loyalty from members and respect from outsiders.

Major institutions

A few major institutions are recognized by the entire society as important to its welfare. These include kinship, marriage, religion, education, law, government, and the economic system. Institutions are established ways of organizing social life, but being established does not mean that they are always stable or secure. Institutions can be strong or weak, depending on whether they are trusted and respected and on how well they adapt to social change. In American society marriage is a weaker institution than it was in the past. Many more couples live together without marrying, and it is far easier to get a divorce. The roles of husband and wife have become less clear-cut, and there is less agreement about what they mean. Marriage is still highly valued—most people do marry (and some marry often)—but as a basic social institution marriage is less firmly established than it was only a few years ago.

ORGANIZATIONS AND INSTITUTIONS

An organization is a practical arrangement for getting a job done. It is a "lean, no-nonsense system of consciously coordinated activities" (Selznick, 1957:5). In theory, when an organization is no longer useful or has become inefficient, it is reorganized or allowed to die. Many organizations that are set up for specific purposes, such as political campaigns, are expected to have a short life. No one is upset when they are disbanded. Organizations become institutionalized as they develop traditions, values, and vested interests. Any organization (or part of one) can become institutionalized. For example, a course taught by a respected professor may become an institution. For many years, G. H. Mead's social psychology course was such an institution, at the institution called the University of Chicago, which is part of the major institution called education. As a matter of fact, Mead was a legend in his own lifetime—an institution at the University of Chicago and among social scientists. His contribution to sociology is drawn upon in Chapter 4 of this book.

Main areas of life such as education, religion, and government include both organizations and institutions. In the American system of government, for instance, the presidency is an institution, and so are many federal agencies—the National Park Service, the Internal Revenue Service, the Social Security Administration, the Marine Corps. But most agencies—and especially subunits within agencies—are expendable organizations, as is shown by the fact that they are often "reorganized." There is no strong commitment to their existence in a specific form. They are formed to get a job done, and when their tasks change, they are changed. However, they all have histories and they all are institutionalized to some extent. The study of bureaucracy (see Chapter 6) partly is concerned with the way organizations become institutions.

The institutional dilemma

Institutionalization poses a serious problem for various groups and for society as a whole. On the one hand, it brings stability and effectiveness to group life. On the other hand, it may produce fixed routines, rigid policies, and concern for the security of the group and group members. What began as an active, purposeful group may end up fat, secure, and useful but lacking in energy or idealism.

This dilemma may be seen most clearly in religion and politics. Whenever people organize in the name of ideals, they face a hard choice. If they want to maintain those ideals in their pure form, they may become isolated from the rest of society. If they want to become an effective institution, they may have to make compromises in the way the ideals are expressed. The formation of religious sects and the tension between sect and church are classic examples of this dilemma. The institutional dilemma can also be seen in politics when social idealism clashes with the practical necessities of party organization.

Chapter 5 **Summary**

Section 1/**Status and role**
A social status is a position in a social system. Statuses that govern a person's identity are salient statuses (mother, professor). A particular status acquired at birth that cannot be altered by choice or effort is called an ascribed status (sex, race). On the other hand, achieved statuses are gained through personal action. Rank may be an aspect of some but not all statuses.

Role, a pattern of behavior associated with a social status, can be examined from three points of view: prescribed, perceived, and performed. Since roles and statuses are related to other roles and statuses, they make up role sets. Such complex patterns impose conflicting demands on the person, thus creating role strain.

Pattern variables are pairs of contrasting terms that identify competing ideas and thus the location of tension in social situations. Four most often cited pattern variables are: universalism-particularism, referring to whether general rules are applied; instrumentalism-expressiveness, referring to the degree of efficiency or personal satisfaction; specificity-diffuseness, referring to the degree to which relations are sharply or vaguely defined; and ascription-achievement, referring to the degree to which individuals are identified by labels or performance.

Section 2/**Interaction and the micro-order**
The micro-order is the pattern of interpersonal contacts that emerges in small-scale situations. Definition of situations is a subjective source of social order. Objective conditions such as the environment in which an interaction takes place also influence the micro-order. The term *ecological*

patterning refers to the effects of environment on social life.

The ''blueprint'' view of social interaction assumes that people are bound by cultural rules which they follow more or less automatically. But blueprints only partly explain the micro-order and do not account for the variety and uncertainty of social interaction. Adaptation 5.1 examines how individuals deal with the risks involved in social encounters and maintain the flow of social interaction.

Section 3/**Primary groups**

The primary group is the setting in which intimate, person-centered interactions take place. A primary relation has three main features: (1) response to the whole person, (2) communication in depth, and (3) personal satisfaction. Primary relations range from sociability (more or less casual acquaintanceships and congeniality groups) to kinship (the nuclear family). Two variables defining primary relations are the strength of personal commitment and the intensity of interaction.

By providing emotional support, the primary group binds the individual to the group and, through the group, to the larger society. From the standpoint of the individual, primary groups are havens of comfort and security and are settings in which the main events of private life take place.

Section 4/**The quest for community**

According to Tönnies, two types of society are the *Gemeinschaft* and the *Gesellschaft*. A *Gemeinschaft* is characterized by assignment of status to the whole person, a high degree of group unity, and total commitment to a community, which is like an enlarged kin group. A *Gesellschaft* is a society in which people enter into relations by their own choice for practical, self-interested reasons.

A commune attempts to create a primary community within a society that fits the *Gesellschaft* model. Communes are partly an expression of alienation from society and partly a way of experimenting with different life-styles. Sharing is a chief characteristic of the commune.

The intentional communities of the nineteenth century were religious or secular experiments in communal living. They differed from most communes in their commitment to a tight system of social control.

Section 5/**Institutions**

As a sociological concept an institution is an established way of organizing social life and a pattern that is valued by a group, community, or society. The process of becoming valued is called *institutionalization*, which goes on at all levels of social life. A few major institutions (kinship, education, law, etc.) are recognized as important to the entire society. Organizations become institutionalized as they develop traditions, values, and vested interests.

Suggested Readings

Barnes, J. A.
1972 *Social Networks*. Reading, Mass.: Addison-Wesley.
Bell, Robert R.
1981 *Worlds of Friendship*. Beverly Hills, Calif.: Sage.
Cooley, Charles Horton
1909 *Social Organization*. New York: Scribner.
Hochschild, Arlie Russell
1978 *The Unexpected Community: Portrait of an Old Age Subculture*. Revised edition. Berkeley and Los Angeles: University of California Press.
Kanter, Rosabeth Moss
1972 *Commitment and Community: Communes and Utopias in Sociological Perspective*. Cambridge: Harvard University Press.
Mills, Theodore M. (ed.)
1970 *Readings on the Sociology of Small Groups*. Englewood Cliffs, N.J.: Prentice-Hall.
Zablocki, Benjamin David
1980 *Alienation and Charisma: A Study of Contemporary American Communes*. New York: Free Press.

Chapter 6

Bureaucracy and Its Alternatives

Section One
Formal Organizations

Because everyone needs to be treated as a unique individual, person-centered experience is a major theme in sociology. Much of everyday life and many of our most significant experiences involve the types of interaction and social participation described in the previous chapter. But most of our time is spent in large, complex organizations. Such organizations fulfill many individual and collective needs and at the same time create social and personal conflict.

These organizations provide the context and direction for work, education, government, national defense, health care, leisure, special interests, and, in many cases, even religious experiences. They are called formal organizations because they usually have explicit goals or purposes and a formal structure designed to achieve them. Thus, a **formal organization** is one deliberately established for a certain purpose. The goals to be achieved, the rules its members are expected to follow, and the status structure defining the relations among them have *not* spontaneously emerged in the course of social interaction. Rather, they have been consciously designed to anticipate and guide activities in order to achieve large-scale objectives.

STUDYING ORGANIZATIONS

The sociologist views an organization as if it were a little society. Specialized organizations have many of the features of societies, including the processes that hold them together or tear them apart. For example, stratification, socialization, and the formation of primary groups affect an organization's ability to achieve its goals.

Whatever its purpose, every organization tries to coordinate the activities of a group of people. Therefore, organizations have a number of characteristics in common. They all must:
1. give their members *incentives* to take part in their activities;
2. set up an internal system of *communication;*
3. exercise *control* so that their activities will be directed toward their goals.

A major task of the sociologist is to explore the ways in which incentive, communication, and control depend on relations among persons and groups within the organization. Figure 6.1 outlines how each of these elements is influenced by three sociological variables: socialization, primary relations, and stratification.

In addition, organizations must adapt to external conditions that may prevent them from achieving their goals or even threaten their survival. What goes on inside an organization is strongly affected by what goes on outside it, that is, by the environment in which it operates. A small store subject to intense competition from nearby stores has a very different environment from that of a large corporation operating in a national or international environment.

TYPES OF ORGANIZATIONS

Throughout this chapter, two major kinds of organization are treated. The first is "bureaucratic" or "administrative." It is made up of executives and subordinates who are brought together to do a job. The chief feature of the bureaucratic organization is its ability to mobilize human resources for the achievement of large-scale goals. People are hired to devote themselves to the organization's goals. Some writers call modern society "organizational society" because of the size, power, and variety of bureaucratic organizations (Presthus, 1962).

Bureaucratic organization

While popular depictions of bureaucracy express a negative image, social theorists show that it contributes to individuals and their societies. Writing before World War I, Max Weber claimed that bureaucratic organization was dominant because it is technically superior to other forms of organization: "The fully developed bureaucratic mechanism compares favorably with other organizations exactly as does the machine with the non-mechanical modes of production" (Weber in Gerth and Mills, 1946:214). Contemporary social scientists also stress the benefits of bureaucracy:

> Direct reports from citizens on their experiences with bureaucracy—as distinct from generalized conventional wisdom on the subject—indicate that they

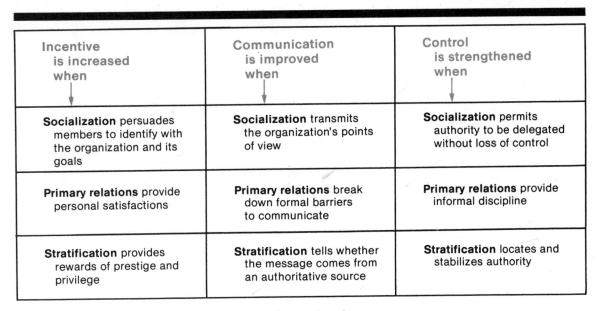

Incentive is increased when ↓	Communication is improved when ↓	Control is strengthened when ↓
Socialization persuades members to identify with the organization and its goals	**Socialization** transmits the organization's points of view	**Socialization** permits authority to be delegated without loss of control
Primary relations provide personal satisfactions	**Primary relations** break down formal barriers to communicate	**Primary relations** provide informal discipline
Stratification provides rewards of prestige and privilege	**Stratification** tells whether the message comes from an authoritative source	**Stratification** locates and stabilizes authority

Figure 6.1 Social Relations and the Organization

perceive far more good than bad in their daily interactions with it. Client polls, public opinion surveys, exit interviews, and mailed questionnaires all repeat the basic finding that the majority of encounters are perceived as satisfactory. Bureaucracy is reported as usually providing the services sought and expected. Most of the time it lives up to acceptable standards of efficiency, courtesy, and fairness. [Goodsell, 1983:139]

Although sociologists and other social scientists investigate both the contributions and the problems created by bureaucracy, they define the term (and other concepts) in a neutral manner: **bureaucracy** is the formal organization of administrative officials. Thus, a bureaucrat is simply an official.

Social scientists do not assume that all bureaucrats are rigid, insensitive, or power-hungry. The formal structure of a university includes regents (trustees), faculty, administrators, and students. The bureaucracy includes the administrators— president, vice-presidents, registrar, deans, department heads, and the like. Although students are not

part of this bureaucracy, they may have their own bureaucracy to run the student government and student activities.

Voluntary associations

The second major type of organization is the **voluntary association** (Sills, 1968). A voluntary association is formed by people who join together to pursue shared interests. An interest group, whether it is religious, economic, political, or recreational, is usually voluntary in that its members are free to withdraw or to contribute varying amounts of time or money to the group. How much one participates in a political party, club, or pressure group is usually a matter of choice.

Under certain conditions, the characteristics of both major types of organization may be combined. For example, the business corporation formed by selling stock may be seen as a voluntary association of investors. The stockholders are "members" of the corporation to whom the directors are responsible. However, the work of the company is done by employees who are not officially members of the corporation but are a vital part of its structure and operations. The modern large corporation has many thousands of stockholders who take little interest in the company beyond its earnings or the price of its stock. This raises the question: who are the real members of the enterprise? In one sense the stockholders who invest in the voluntary association, the corporation, are the members. In another sense the employees who do the company's work are the members.

A trade union is also more than a simple voluntary association—partly because membership may be required as a condition of employment, but also because, at least at the national level, the union has a large, permanent administrative staff. Many voluntary associations are formed in order to create an administrative organization for a special purpose, and the members "tax" themselves to support it. For example, members of the NAACP (National Association for the Advancement of Colored People) support a large headquarters, including a legal staff that has won major civil-rights victories. Such associations, however, tend to have relatively low member participation.

Membership in voluntary associations is characteristic of more than half of the adults in the United States. A national survey conducted in the late 1960s found that about 62 percent of adult Americans considered themselves to be members of at least one voluntary association and 39 percent reported membership in more than one group (Verba and Nie, 1972). These percentages include participation in labor unions and church-sponsored groups, but not churches themselves.

A 1981 Gallup survey reported slightly lower participation but dealt with a narrower range of voluntary activity. Defining volunteerism as "working in some way to help others for no monetary pay" (Gallup, 1981:1), this study did not include membership in a volunteer group if no work was actually done, and it excluded work in organizations which indirectly compensated volunteers through lower costs of services or materials. Thus, most labor union members were excluded as were members of cooperatives. Based on this definition,

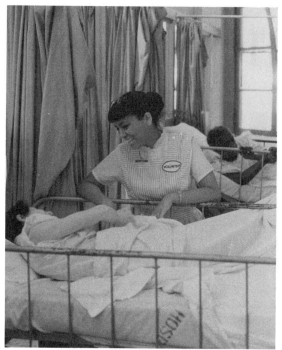

Candystriper. Teenage hospital volunteer.

half of the adults in the United States were involved in voluntary activity in relatively formal (associational) settings. These findings are based on cross-sectional (that is, one-time) research. If studies were done over the full life spans of individuals, it is quite possible they would find that virtually everyone in advanced industrial nations participates in voluntary associations at one time or another (Smith, 1975:250–51).

Some types of persons are more likely to engage in voluntary activities than others. The 1981 Gallup survey indicates that 75 percent of college graduates but only 26 percent of those with a grade school education participate in voluntary activities. "Volunteerism" is also characteristic of those with higher household incomes, women, persons under the age of 55, whites, people who are employed (particularly part-time workers), people with children under 18 in the home, suburban and rural residents, and those who live in larger households (Gallup, 1981:12).

Although membership in voluntary associations is fairly widespread, the intensity of member participation is much lower than in bureaucratic organizations. Only about 40 percent of those sampled by Verba and Nie reported being at least minimally active in such organizations, and the Gallup survey found that 55 percent of those who indicated they had volunteered during the previous year reported spending two hours or less per week in such activities during the three months prior to the survey.

All formal organizations, both bureaucratic and voluntary, have two main features: (1) **formal structure,** or the official rules, goals, powers, and procedures that determine how the organization's work is done, whether it is producing steel, winning votes, teaching children, or saving souls, and (2) **informal structure,** or the patterned interactions of persons and groups within the organization. Together, the formal and informal aspects make up the social structure of the organization. In every organization there is a tension between the impersonal, formal structure on the one hand and personal, informal interactions on the other. The next section discusses formal structure and Section Three analyzes informal structures.

Section Two
Formal Structure

The classic sociological analysis of the formal structure of bureaucracy was presented by Max Weber (1864–1920). Most contemporary studies use his definition as a point of departure and emphasize four major features: (1) division of labor, (2) hierarchy of authority, (3) rules and procedures, and (4) impersonality. The first two characteristics are often considered together and termed *complexity,* while the latter two are conceptualized as *formalization.* This may suggest why some researchers prefer the term *complex organizations,* while others use the term *formal organizations.* Essentially they refer to the same phenomenon but emphasize different aspects of it. Figure 6.2 shows the complexity—the division of labor and hierarchy of authority—of a large oil company.

DIVISION OF LABOR

Division of labor means the assignment of different functions or tasks to different parts or positions of the organization. The oil company shown in Figure 6.2 has five main divisions. The first explores for oil; the

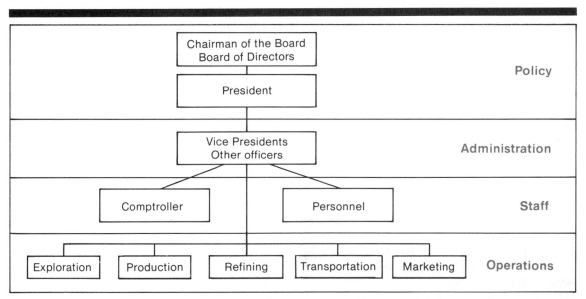

Figure 6.2   **Organization Chart of an Oil Company**

second produces it; the third refines it; the fourth handles transportation; and the fifth is in charge of marketing. The division of labor matches the division of company operations. Employees are chosen and jobs assigned according to the principle of specialization. In a very large organization, the assignment of jobs to specialists creates new groups, and the result is an organization of organizations.

There are several different bases for the division of labor within an organization. That shown in Figure 6.2, and probably the most widespread, is division of labor by function. Other bases for the differentiation of organizations are product, location, types of customers or other parties connected with the enterprise, process, and equipment.

Division of labor or specialization is characteristic of the structure of organizations as well as the positions within an organization. That is, some organizations are characterized by a more extensive division of labor than others, and some positions within a given organization are more specialized than others. In most organizations the positions at the bottom are more specialized than those at the top. Thus, while those who work at the policy and administrative levels may describe their jobs as offering variety, new experiences and challenges, those at the operations level may do the same few tasks in the same way every day. Assembly-line workers, for example, frequently describe their work as monotonous, routine, and nonchallenging.

HIERARCHY OF AUTHORITY

In a typical organization there is a **hierarchy,** or chain of command, in which some individuals and groups can give orders to others. The boxes and lines of Figure 6.2 show the chain of command within the oil company. Note that the five operating divisions are on the same level. The personnel department and the comptroller are a step higher, but neither has the right to give orders to the operating divisions. These departments are usually called **staff** groups. They receive orders from and make recommendations to the higher levels but do not directly supervise the lower levels. Most of the organization—that part involved in operations—is the **line.** It is made up of

supervisors who send instructions down the line to foreman, who in turn direct the daily activities of the workers.

Channeled communication

Some complex organizations, such as the military, insist that information or requests be sent through channels. If the oil company is a "tight ship," employees go through formal channels to give or receive advice and commands. A vice-president who wanted to talk to the chairman of the board would not bypass the president of the company. The vice-president might not make a big deal of it, but would probably mention to the president that "we ought to take up the problem with Ruud." Likewise, the head of the refining division would go through a vice-president to communicate with the president.

Rules of this sort are not followed rigidly because they can make it harder for subordinates to solve problems. But even in the most relaxed organization, a wise subordinate uses channels when dealing with important matters. Otherwise, the chief will not have the information he or she needs to make decisions or to defend the division when questioned by someone at a higher level.

Coordination

Division of labor is clearly necessary in a large organization. At the same time, the organization must make a united and coordinated effort to achieve its goals. This is the job of the higher levels (policy and administration), which review the activities of the various divisions, settle conflicts, and develop new policies. Top-level officials often act as judges, weighing the arguments of divisions that differ on company policy or have complaints against each other. Organizations vary in the extent to which top management initiates activity or simply reviews the work of the operating divisions.

The formal structure of an organization is not always written down, nor is it always fully understood by everyone involved. There may not be an organization chart. Sometimes the formal structure is so simple and well understood that it is not necessary to write it down. On the other hand, the relations may

A traditionally masculine board of directors.

be so complex that a chart of the whole system would be too complicated to be helpful. Many patterns gain (or are denied) official approval only when they are challenged and must be reviewed by top-level officials.

Bureaucratic authority

Weber and many of his followers view bureaucracy as a kind of legal system based on conformity to rules, correct procedure, and clearly defined procedure and jurisdictions. Therefore, Weber called bureaucratic authority **rational-legal,** in contrast to traditional or charismatic authority. In **traditional authority,** a leader's claim to obedience is backed by custom. **Charismatic authority** rests on belief in the special qualities of a particular person, such as a religious or political leader.

The contrast between traditional and **bureaucratic authority** may be seen in the shift from family-based management to professional (or bureaucratic) management in business and industry. Both types still exist, but professional management is much more common in modern society. Family (or patrimonial) management belongs to an earlier time.

Patrimonial management is a common first stage in a country's march toward economic development. In countries where the family is one of the dominating

Table 6.1   Prebureaucratic vs. Bureaucratic Management

	Prebureaucratic	Bureaucratic
Purpose	Ad hoc, reflecting personal goals of political or business leader	Definite and public; normally set by law or charter
Hierarchy	Weak and fluid; lower positions held at pleasure of chief; jurisdictions not definite	Clear jurisdictions; clear channels of communication and chains of command
Rules	Unsystematic, not always enforced, not binding on rule makers	Dependable, systematic
Authority	Traditional, charismatic	Rational-legal
Careers	Unstable, nonprofessional; positions for sale or granted as rewards for loyalty	Official is a full-time professional; no personal following; appointment based on merit
Decision making	Ad hoc, subject to whims of one-person rule	Systematic, routinized

Source: Based on Weber, 1922/1947:328 – 41; Gerth and Mills, 1946: chapter 8.

social institutions in the society, the family enterprise is a simple and logical instrument of business activity. Loyalty and trust within the hierarchy are assured. The forces of tradition and religion support the essential integrity of the family dynasty. The enterprise provides the means for safeguarding the security and the reputation of the family. [Harbison and Myers, 1959:69]

As a business grows, family management loses ground. Even an extended family is unable to supply enough money, ideas, or trained personnel to meet the needs of a growing business. For a while, the family can hire outsiders without losing control or changing the nature of the business. But in time the professionals begin to outnumber the family and take over more responsibility. At last the family may see that it will be better off if it turns over day-to-day operations and even some important decisions to professional managers.

Most of the time, family management means one-person rule. The boss makes as many decisions as possible and tries not to delegate any authority. Relations between boss and staff are personal, and the boss expects complete loyalty and obedience from the staff.

In a bureaucracy, authority is more impersonal, systematic, and limited, and is more often delegated. Authority is respected mainly for its competence. Officials have technical expertise, or at least administrative know-how. They have a claim to con-

tinuity in office, are appointed on the basis of merit, have definite duties, and are responsible for specific tasks.

All officials, including those at the top, accept the formal rules and procedures of the organization. In fact, their major duties include applying these rules or procedures to guide decision making in every phase of the enterprise. Employees are hired by a personnel department to fit specific job descriptions. They are trained, assigned, and supervised according to definite routines. If they are dismissed, it is almost always because, in the eyes of officials, they have not followed procedures or because they have violated the rules. In a bureaucracy, it is not enough to say that things have always been done a certain way, nor may an official make decisions outside the rules just because he or she is liked and admired by others.

Thus, bureaucratic or rational-legal authority is much more limited than traditional or charismatic authority. Deference is given to a position, not to an individual nor to generally defined traditions. The limits of the position and its authority are clearly defined and known to both the bureaucratic official and the official's subordinates. If the official attempts to go beyond these limits, there will usually be resistance among subordinates and frequently reprimands from superiors. Such limits are much more ambiguous in situations characterized by traditional authority, and a true charismatic leader may experience no such limits. Weber's conceptualization is displayed in Table 6.1 as a contrast between prebureaucratic and bureaucratic forms of organization.

RULES AND PROCEDURES

Some writers claim that the most important aspect of organizational structure is the degree of specificity of role prescription and the range of legitimate discretion (Hickson, 1966). Indeed, a central characteristic of bureaucratic organization is a set of procedures dictated by fixed rules which reduce decision making on the part of organizational members. Daily operations are governed simply by applying rules to particular cases. Such rules define not only the relationship of officials to their tasks, but also the relationship of one official to another. Anyone who has looked at the operations manual of a large organization or even an employee handbook is aware of how widespread rules can be.

The central function of rules and procedures is to control behavior. It is assumed that behavior is more likely to contribute to fulfilling organizational goals if it is specified in advance than if organizational members are permitted to elect from alternatives. Rules enable control to be exerted from a distance. They provide a substitute for the personal repetition of orders by a supervisor as well as an impersonal rationale for the supervisor. At the same time, they make explicit the subordinates' obligations, narrowing their areas of discretion. They also legitimize punishment in an organization because they make it possible for the offender to know in advance which behaviors are forbidden and what will happen if expectations are not fulfilled. If rules are objectively applied, they are usually perceived as fair. Finally, rules specify minimum levels of performance and may reduce emotional involvement and potential conflict (Gouldner, 1954:157–80).

Rules and authority

Obviously, there are parallels between an organization's hierarchy of authority and its system of rules and procedures. Both are created for control purposes and the nature of one is likely to influence the other. Bureaucratic authority, as mentioned above, is

Rules in school. The sex-segregated lineup.

indeed based on rules. These same rules may be modified by individuals holding positions vested with authority. Moreover, where rules have been fully developed, it is likely that personal surveillance by supervisors may be minimal.

A study of the relationship between these organizational characteristics in 40 industries found that as organizations increase in size, the cost of supervision increases for three reasons: (1) the number of potential social relationships to be controlled increases much faster than absolute size itself, (2) larger size usually lengthens the physical distance between members and those responsible for their performance, and (3) less direct personal contact between supervisors and subordinates heightens the likelihood of communication failures (Rushing, 1980). The study of 40 industries supports the following generalization:

[Rules] serve as substitutes for the exercise of personal influence and . . . are social inventions that accomplish more effectively what otherwise would require [face-to-face] influence. [Thibaut and Kelley, 1959:130,134]

IMPERSONALITY

Impersonality may be regarded as both a characteristic and a consequence of formal structure. **Impersonality** means the application of universalistic as opposed to particularistic standards (see the discussion of the pattern variables in Chapter 5). Thus, personal involvement is reduced on the part of both the organization and its members.

The benefits of impersonality

Impersonality is often painful, but it also has some advantages. Anyone who has tried to get service in a restaurant where the employees were too busy talking to each other to do their jobs can understand that a little impersonality in a work place might help keep the customers happy.

Where one person must make objective judgments about others, it is easier to do so impersonally. A professor who is too friendly with students may find it hard to make objective judgments about their work or may be accused of playing favorites. Rather than risk their objectivity in this way, many professors try not to be overfriendly with their students.

Keeping people at arm's length is even more important for judges and other government officials. The phrase ''government of laws, not of men'' reflects the social value of impersonality. Fairness and equal treatment may depend on an impersonal approach.

Thus, the norm of impersonality is usually incorporated as an element of bureaucratic structure for at least three reasons. First, it minimizes the potential for personal conflict. Second, it protects subordinates from arbitrariness on the part of supervisors. Finally, it helps to maintain vertical social distance between statuses so that very diverse and perhaps otherwise sharply incompatible persons can nevertheless cooperate sufficiently to get the job done.

Human costs of impersonality

Although impersonal decision making has many benefits, it can also cause dissatisfaction and even suffering. Sensible rules that protect people's rights are appreciated, but rules may turn into red tape, and decisions may ignore the fact that the customer, client, or employee is a person. People who make rules and apply them are often concerned with protecting ''the system''—and their own authority. Those to whom the rules are applied often feel that they are not treated fairly or with respect.

Many large companies meet the problem of impersonality by persuading middle- and higher-level employees to dedicate themselves to the organization. The ''organization man'' is expected to put the job and the company first. The only way the executive can protect his or her personal and family life is to

fight The Organization. Not stupidly, or selfishly. . . . But fight he must, for the demands of his surrender are constant and powerful, and the more he has come to like the life of organization the more difficult does he find it to resist these demands, or even to recognize them. [Whyte, 1956:404]

Some scholars believe that the greatest human cost of impersonality is the feeling of being anonymous and powerless, trapped in a machinelike system run by a distant, uncaring authority. That view may be overly pessimistic. Still, most students of organizations agree that something should be done to reduce the human costs of impersonality. Yet, it may be difficult to strike the appropriate balance between the costs and benefits of impersonality and those of personal relationships within organizations. The same personal ties may be rewarding for some but costly to others, as Adaptation 6.1 illustrates.

(Text continued on p. 109)

Adaptation 6.1

Kanter/The Bureaucratic "Marriage"

For decades, the study of organizations and organizational behavior was primarily a male enterprise. With few exceptions, male investigators researched and wrote about male employees in organizations. Although women were the subjects of one of the first series of studies credited with "discovering" the informal organization—the famous Hawthorne studies of the 1920s and early 1930s—they were neglected during the following four decades. This is reflected by the titles of major works during this period—William F. Whyte, Men at Work *(1961),* Robert Blauner, Alienation and Freedom: The Factory Worker and His Industry *(1964),* William H. Whyte, The Organization Man *(1956), and* Melville Dalton, Men Who Manage *(1959), to mention just a few. With the advent of the women's movement and the entry of larger numbers of women into the work force, including the profession of sociology, the masculine blinders are being removed.*

The purpose of this study is (1) to develop an understanding of how individual consciousness and behavior are formed by the individual's position within the organization, and (2) to document through an ethnographic study of one corporation—Indsco—the ways in which organizational structure forms people's sense of themselves and their possibilities within the organization. The investigation is concerned with men and women in both formal and informal contexts. It examines the roles of managers, secretaries, and managers' wives. The account that follows describes the relationship between secretaries and their bosses and illustrates how personal interests and private expectations lead organizational behavior away from its formal blueprints as well as how informal behavior may reintroduce aspects of prebureaucratic management.

As Weber saw it, bureaucracy vested authority in offices rather than in persons and rendered power impersonal, thereby undercutting personal privilege that stood in the way of efficient decisions.

Despite Weber's claims, not all relationships in modern organizations have been rationalized, depersonalized, and subjected to universal standards to the same degree. The secretary-boss relationship is the most striking instance of the retention of personal ties within the bureaucracy. Fewer bureaucratic "safe-

Source: Abridged and adapted from Rosabeth Moss Kanter, *Men and Women of the Corporation* (New York: Basic Books, Inc., 1977), pp. 73, 74 and 89–91. Reprinted as edited by permission of the author and Basic Books, Inc., Publishers.

guards" apply here than in any other part of the system. When bosses make arbitrary demands at their own discretion; choose secretaries on grounds that enhance their own personal status rather than meeting organizational efficiency tests; expect personal service with limits negotiated privately; exact loyalty; and make the secretary a part of their private retinue, moving when they move—then the relationship has elements of prebureaucratic organization.

There are three important aspects of the social organization of the relationship: *derived status* (the fact that the secretary primarily, and the boss secondarily, derives status in relation to the other); *arbitrariness* (the absence of limits on managerial discretion); and *fealty* (the demand of personal loyalty, generating a nonutilitarian aura around communication and rewards).

These three personal elements in secretarial role relations have led to the frequent use of the marriage metaphor to describe the relationship between secretaries and bosses. The metaphor aptly fits many elements of the position: reflected and derived status; greater privileges and lesser work for women attached to higher-status men; choice of a secretary on the basis of personal qualities like appearance, fusion of ''the couple'' in the eyes of others; a nonrationalized relationship with terms set by personal negotiation; expectations of personal service, including office ''housework''; special understandings that do not survive the particular relationship; expectations of personal loyalty and symbolic or emotional rewards; and an emotional division of labor in which the woman plays the emotional role and the man the providing role.

Indeed the progression from the secretarial pool and multiple bosses to a position working for just one manager resembles the progression from dating to marriage, echoed in managers' own comments about special feelings of responsibility toward a private secretary. Mary Kathleen Benet, in *The Secretarial Ghetto,* suggests that the more elevated the executive, the more closely the secretary's duties approximate that of a wife rather than of a stenographer-typist, including bill paying, sending Christmas cards, preparing refreshments, providing protection from subordinates/children, or making travel arrangements.

But the marriage metaphor is not just a catchy description used by critics. It is also implicit in the way many people at Indsco talk about the relationships between secretaries and bosses. Over time, a serious emotional bond could develop. One executive secretary promoted into management described leaving her old boss as a ''divorce.'' ''I worked with a really fine man before this slot opened, which is one of the hazards of a secretarial job. You work for truly fine people, and you get so identified with them that you really don't have a career that's your own. I'm sure I really felt a marriage was ending when we both talked about my moving. It

was almost as sad as getting a divorce. I was as emotionally involved in it. While in my explanations to myself I said it was fear of going to a new job, I think it was also fear of ending a relationship with a man I really enjoyed.'' For the first few months after her promotion, she stopped in to see him every morning, hanging her coat in her old office instead of the new one, and finding herself concerned if he had a cold or looked unhappy.

Some secretaries made the inevitable comparison between how *they* treated a boss and how wives did. As a secretary said: ''I think if I've been at all successful with men, it's because I'm a good listener and interested in their world. . . . Most of the ones I'm referring to are divorced. In looking through the years they were married, I can see . . . what probably happened. I know if I were the wife, I would be interested in their work. I feel the wife of an executive would be a better wife had she been a secretary first. As a secretary, you learn to adjust to the boss's moods. Many marriages would be happier if the wife would do that.'' On the other hand, there were also executive wives . . . who compared what *they* did for their husbands to the tasks of a good secretary. And, one manager suggested a *ménage à trois* in his remark to the real husband of a woman assisting him, ''You have her body; I have her head.''

If the marriage image had applicability, it also needed to be differentiated. There were *types* of office marriages at Indsco. Some were very traditional, perhaps among the remaining bastions of female submissiveness and deference. The traditional secretary, usually an older woman, knew her place, served with a smile, was willing to be scapegoated and take the blame for the boss's mistakes, and did not presume. For example, compare this description of former Senator Eugene McCarthy's secretary, Jean Stack, his ''protective alter ego,'' with the Victorian wife: ''She knew his reactions so well that his staff went to her for guidance. She paid family bills, scheduled his speaking dates and negotiated fees for him, protected him, anticipated his orders—and even took his clothes to the cleaner's. She was always careful to note, however, that she was not an adviser, and her favorite line was, 'When Mr. McCarthy hired me, he told me he wasn't hiring me to think.' She worked for him for eighteen years, and she never called him by his first name.''

At the other end of the continuum were the new ''liberated'' office marriages, generally involving younger women. Some secretaries refused to do ''housework'' and insisted on a contract that defined the relationship as they wanted it defined, indicating their needs and limits. The secretary to the manager of a field office, who proved herself intelligent and capable, made her job an administrative one. She demanded (and won) the title of assis-

tant to the manager and the right not to type unless absolutely necessary. (A special typist was hired part time). The manager, a casual, easygoing, and very liberal man, gave her highly desirable office space, taking less for himself, and tried to accommodate all of her wishes. But he wistfully mentioned that he sometimes longed for her to take more responsibility for seeing that the office stayed clean. And even this liberated secretary was still merely ''the wife,'' without a clear career territory of her own, but in a new kind of ''marriage'' in which she could demand privileges.

Section Three
Informal Structure

While the formal structure provides the major guidelines for the behavior of organizational members, it does not account for all of it. Understanding and explaining the ways in which members act in organizations requires knowledge of the informal structure as well as the formal blueprints for action.

SOURCES OF INFORMAL BEHAVIOR

Much of the patterned informal behavior that takes place in organizations develops when people face problems that cannot be handled by the formal system. Such problems have four major sources: impersonality, lag, generality, and personal interests.

Impersonality

The rules and roles of the formal structure are impersonal, and the individual is viewed as part of a technical, task-oriented system. In practice, however, it is often necessary to enlist personal loyalties if individuals are to give their best efforts to the organization. Interpersonal and group relations must be taken into account in addition to the formal patterns of communication and control. Personal contacts are important not only because individuals may benefit

from them but also because they help get the job done. Even in armies, friendship and pride in the outfit contribute to a unit's effectiveness.

Lag

As in any other code of rules or laws, changes in the formal system tend to lag behind changes in actual operations. Those who do the work run into unforeseen problems, some of which may not be recognized by officials. For example, a company's rules may have been developed before its workers joined a union. If the union is not recognized by the company, shop stewards may nevertheless represent the workers on day-to-day matters and the foreman may try to deal with the shop stewards even though the company and the union have not developed formal negotiation procedures. This informal pattern of consultation may continue for some time. If and when the company recognizes the union as representing the workers, the informal procedure may become part of the formal structure.

Generality

Rules have to be abstract and general. There cannot be a separate rule for every possible problem, and some problems cannot be foreseen. Thus, rules deal with *types* of problems rather than with every prob-

Values and Norms	**Informal group norms** within the organization; for example, "Don't be a rate-buster" **Basic attitudes** toward work, cooperation, loyalty, brought to the organization as a result of prior socialization **Social control devices;** for example, approval or ridicule
Group Structure	**Friendships,** either within the group or from outside, make claims on the individual **Cliques,** either friendship groups or alliances, show personal loyalty **Interest groups** have a stake in existing social arrangements (may be any group, including formal units)
Status System	**Informal privileges** attached to positions in the formal hierarchy **Power relations;** for example, the balance of power between local and headquarters units, depending on source of funds **Dependency patterns;** for example, dependence of staff on line

Figure 6.3   Elements of Informal Structure

lem that could possibly arise. A certain amount of authority must be given to the person who does the job or to a supervisor who can handle situations as they come up. The decisions they make tend to follow an informal pattern which may or may not be approved when reviewed by higher authority.

Personal interests

The sources of informal structure discussed so far are based on the idea that the members of an organization do their best to achieve its goals. However, that is not their only interest. Personal needs and concerns also enter the picture. For example, a new supervisor may cultivate the friendship of an experienced worker, thereby gaining valuable information about the job and the other employees. The worker may protect the supervisor when things go wrong. If this relationship continues, it becomes part of the plant's informal structure. Like the chain of command, it is an important fact that must not be overlooked by anyone who wants to understand the organization.

The individual may also bring to the job strongly held beliefs, such as negative attitudes toward minority groups or foreigners and loyalty to friends or kin. These beliefs become part of the organization's social reality. Figure 6.3 summarizes the ele-

ments of informal structure and their contributions to three aspects of organizational life: (1) values and norms, (2) group structure, and (3) its status system.

SMALL GROUPS IN LARGE ORGANIZATIONS

The development of primary relations, including friendships and cliques, is an important feature of informal structure. Many primary relations crisscross the formal structure and create new lines of influence and communication. Another kind of primary group is based on the formal structure. It includes task units, such as industrial work teams, office groups, or military combat teams.

The work unit as a primary group

Formal task units are part of the official division of labor, but they may also become centers of personal loyalty and support. The famous and controversial study of the Hawthorne plant in Chicago conducted between 1927 and 1932 included observation of the effects of interaction among members of the work group. A small group of men who wired telephone switchboards developed their own methods of social control and their own work norms, which did not match management's plans and incentives.

Among the informal work norms were the following: (1) You should not turn out too much work. If you do, you are a rate-buster. (2) You should not turn out too little work. If you do, you are a chiseler. (3) You should not tell a supervisor anything negative about a fellow worker. If you do, you are a squealer (Roethlisberger and Dickson, 1939: Part IV).

These and other norms limited the unit's productivity. Although the company had an incentive system to encourage high output, the employees believed they would be better off if their average hourly production showed little change from one week to the next. They felt that this would protect them from unreasonable expectations if their output went up, and from criticism if it went down. The Hawthorne wiremen stuck together informally to defend themselves against possible arbitrary action by management.

Groups of this kind are able to meet many of the individual's personal needs. The group will protect a worker who falls down on the job. On the other hand, the worker must conform to the group's norms.

In addition to observing the switchboard wiremen, the Hawthorne researchers studied production records, absenteeism, and labor turnover; talked with managers and workers; and made other on-the-spot observations. Since the results were published in the late 1930s, they have been the subject of much evaluation and criticism.

The mediating primary group

Primary groups cut two ways. They may either support or undermine formal patterns of communication and command. They may mobilize participants to achieve the organization's goals, or they may undermine those goals, as they did in the case of the Hawthorne wiremen, whose activities resulted in worker control of production.

Decisions in large organizations are often made

Individual	Mediating Group	Larger Organization
Wife	Family	Church
Employee	Work group	Company
Soldier	Squad	Army
Student	Living group	College

Figure 6.4 **Primary Groups as Mediators**

by committees or small task groups that are also affected by the dynamics of personal interaction. Small-group cohesion can influence the formation of policy. Even at the highest levels of government, policy making is often distorted by excessive conformity, game playing, protection of personal interests, and unrealistic wishful thinking.

An organization is more effective if its members belong to it through participation in a mediating primary group. Primary groups bind their members firmly into a larger social structure in much the same way that the family mediates between the individual and the larger society. (See Figure 6.4.) The stronger the mediating group, the firmer the bond between the organization and the individual.

The role of primary groups as mediators was given special attention in a study of the Nazi army (Shils and Janowitz, 1948). Although they were outnumbered and had inferior equipment, German soldiers were effective fighters even when they were being badly beaten. Their tenacity was often explained by strong Nazi political beliefs. However, the study showed that military solidarity was only in part based on political beliefs. For the ordinary soldier, the important fact was that he belonged to a squad or section. If he had the weapons, he was likely to go on fighting as long as he could feel a sense of identity with the group's leaders and give and receive affection from the other members of his squad. In other words, a strong primary group maintained its morale regardless of the political beliefs of its members.

The stability and effectiveness of the military group depended largely on the Nazi hard core, who accounted for 10 to 15 percent of the enlisted men, a higher percentage of noncommissioned officers, and a very much higher percentage of the junior officers. The presence of a few such men in the group provided a model for the less committed members. Threats by the hard core prevented divisive tendencies. The hard core thus provided a link between the ordinary soldier and the political leadership of the Nazi state.

Studies of morale among American soldiers during World War II and the Korean War also stressed solidarity at the squad and platoon level (Stouffer et al., 1949:105–91; Shils, 1950:16–39; Little, 1964). On the other hand, a study of combat soldiers in Vietnam concluded that the rotation system, in which each soldier served in Vietnam for twelve months, limited the formation of primary groups. The soldier was "essentially private and self-concerned," especially near the end of his tour of duty (Moskos, 1970:142–43). Nevertheless, primary-group solidarity might be a matter of life or death:

> If the individual soldier is realistically to improve his survival chances, he must necessarily develop and take part in primary-group relations. . . . In other words, under the extreme conditions of ground warfare, an individual's survival is directly related to the support—moral, physical, and technical—he can expect from his fellow soldiers. He gets such support largely to the degree that he reciprocates to the others in his group in general, and to his buddy in particular. [Moskos, 1970:145]

The solidarity of the combat group is a response to the urgent needs of a particular situation. Few lasting friendships are formed. When the soldier leaves his unit, the relationship ends.

(Text continued on p. 114)

Adaptation 6.2

Gardner and Moore/A Case of Jitters

Formal relations coordinate activities, not persons. The rules apply to foremen and machinists, clerks and vice-presidents. But no organization can restrict interaction to formal roles. In practice, employees interact as individuals, adjusting to daily experiences in ways that spill over the boundaries of their formal roles. The occupational role usually requires that the job be kept free from personal concerns. But every individual has private problems and interests. The tension between these problems and interests and the employee's occupational role is dramatized by the case of Bob.

DISTORTION UP THE LINE

Because of sensitivity to the boss and dependence on him, there is much distortion in communicating up the line of authority. Along with concern for giving the boss what he wants, there is a tendency to cover up, to keep the boss from knowing about the things that go wrong or the things that do not get done. No one wants to pass bad news up the line, because he feels that it reflects on him and that he should handle

Source: From B. B. Gardner and D. G. Moore, *Human Relations in Industry*, rev. ed. (Chicago: Richard D. Irwin, Inc., © 1950), pp. 37–38. Reprinted by permission.

his job so there is no bad news. Consequently, he does not tell the boss what a poor job he did or how stupid he was. That is, he does not do so unless he thinks someone else will get to the boss first. When he does have to break some bad news to the boss, he will probably have the problem fixed or have developed a good excuse.

Filtered information

Each individual in the line acts as a filter who sorts the information coming to him and selects what he will pass on to his boss. Because a boss responds most favorably to good news, good news goes up the line quite easily and rapidly. Information about improvements in output, quality, costs, and so on is transmitted readily from level to level. On the other hand, bad news moves more slowly; everyone is reluctant to communicate his mistakes or failures. The what-will-the-boss-think-of-me feeling encourages delays, excuses, and the development of tact in presenting bad news.

JITTERS

Take the case of Bob, foreman in the machine department, when he suddenly discovers that he does not have enough bronze rod on hand to complete the order of part number X37A22 for the end of the week and that it will keep two hand-screw machines going steadily to make delivery on time. So he talks to Charley, the machine operator who came to him asking for the rod:

Bob: "Are you sure there isn't any of that rod over in the rack? When we started on this job, I checked the storeroom records and there was plenty on hand."

Charley: "There sure isn't now. You remember when we first started on this order, somebody gave us the wrong specifications and we turned out a lot that had to be junked."

Bob: "That's right. Well, I'll call the stockroom and get some more over right away." (*Thinking*): I sure did slip on that. I completely forgot to order more rod.

(*He calls the stockroom.*) "I'll need two hundred

pounds of that ⅜ bronze rod for part number X37A22. We're in a rush for it, got to get the order out right away and a couple of machines are waiting. Can you get it right over?"

Stockman: "Sorry, we are out of that rod. Won't be able to get it in before Friday. Why didn't you call last week?"

Bob: "Can't you get hold of any before that? If I don't deliver those parts before Monday, the gadget assembly department will be tied up."

Stockman: "We'll do the best we can, but don't expect it before Friday. Why don't you guys give us a little more notice instead of waiting until your machines shut down and then expecting us to do miracles?"

Bob (*Thinking*): This is a terrible note! I slip up on ordering that rod the one time the stockroom is out of it. Why can't they keep some stock on hand instead of trying to work from hand to mouth? Just trying to make a good showing by keeping down inventory and they tie up production. They ought to realize that they are there to help the shop, not to give us all this trouble. Wonder what I can do now. The boss sure will give me hell when he hears this.

Maybe I ought to check with Joe in gadget assembly to see how many parts they have on hand and how long before he will need more. Maybe I better let him know what's happened so he will know what to expect. Maybe he can plan his work so the people on the assembly job can do something else for a few days.

But if I tell him what's happened, he will tell his boss, and his boss will jump on my boss and my boss will jump on me for letting this happen and not letting him know. So before I tell Joe anything I better tell my boss. Maybe if I tell him, he can tell Joe's boss, and I won't have to say anything to Joe. Joe's going to be plenty sore anyway. He got kind of hot the other day when I tried to get him to let me make some changes in the base plate for that Model N job. Seemed like he was just being stubborn. Wonder if he might have enough parts on hand so he could just go along and say nothing about this affair.

If I knew he had enough, I just wouldn't say anything and take a chance on getting some to him before he runs out. I'm afraid to risk it, though, without being pretty sure, because if he did have to shut down, my boss sure would raise Cain. Yeah, and Joe called the other day to know how we were coming on that lot we delivered yesterday, said he didn't want to get caught short. But Joe always does that. He starts crowding you for things long before he actually needs them. He seems to think no one will keep their promises unless he rides them. If I ask Joe how much he has on hand, he will suspect something and I will have to tell him.

Guess I better not take a chance on Joe. I will have to tell my boss first. But gee, how I hate to tell him! I know just what he will think. I know I should have remembered to order more when we spoiled the first run, but I was so busy getting caught up that I forgot. Anyway, you never would expect the stockroom to be out of a standard item like that. And if they ran this place right, they never would be. But my boss won't care about that. All he'll think is that I must be asleep on the job. He expects me to keep track of everything; and if I have to do the stockroom's job

for them to keep my job going, he expects me to do that. What will I tell him, anyway, that won't make me look like a fool who doesn't know his job? Maybe I better not tell him now. It won't hurt to wait till tomorrow, and maybe then the stockroom will know when I can expect the rod. Maybe they will do better than Friday, and I might squeeze by. When I do tell the boss, I want to be able to tell him just when we will be able to start on the job again, and maybe I can plan it so we won't hold up the assembly. Guess I will wait till tomorrow and see what I can figure out.

And Bob spends the rest of the day in a state of jitters trying to figure a way out of the predicament, or at least a partial solution which he can present to his boss when he finally is forced to tell him. He goes home that night with a terrible grouch, is cross to the children because they are so noisy, gets annoyed with his wife because she seems so cheerful, can hardly eat his supper, sleeps poorly, and hates to go to work the next morning. Such is the human element of communication up the line.

Section Four
Beyond Bureaucracy?

The distinctive characteristics of bureaucracy—a limited, but well-defined hierarchy of authority, defined spheres of competence, governance by rules and a career officialdom—create vested interests and a commitment to established routines. Bureaucracy emphasizes seniority and adherence to detailed regulations. The rigidities involved are acceptable and even necessary when the work of the organization is routine and depends on close supervision of unskilled personnel. Thus, bureaucracy was a valuable social invention for times that were characterized by a slow pace of social change, relatively simple technology and, in general, a more stable environment. These conditions are much less characteristic of today's organizational environment (Shariff, 1979).

Many contemporary organizations require more flexibility than the bureaucratic style allows, and

they are more concerned to stimulate initiative than regulate conduct. The following prophecy emphasizes the need for a postbureaucratic perspective:

> The key word will be "temporary." There will be adaptive, rapidly changing *temporary* systems. These will be task forces organized around problems to be solved by groups of relative strangers with diverse professional skills. The group will . . . evolve in response to a problem rather than to programmed role expectations. The executive thus becomes coordinator or "linking pin" between various task forces . . . [Bennis, 1968:73–74].

This vision of a flexible, problem-centered organization has begun to take shape especially in aerospace and other high-technology industries. Many scholars agree that the large organization, such as a business or government agency, need not have all the features of bureaucracy. An effective organization is more flexible, more responsible to leadership, and more open to initiative.

At the annual meeting, a stockholder speaks his piece.

It is not likely, however, that bureaucracy will disappear. Convincing evidence has been offered that it is alive and well today and that it is no less pervasive in the United States than it has been in the recent past (Shariff, 1979; Meyer, 1979).

Management will continue to depend on professionalism and will be required to offer job security. Authority will have to be delegated, thus creating spheres of competence and a continued need for coordination. Rules of some sort will be needed. If there is a postbureaucratic world, it will not be one without bureaucracy, but bureaucracy will be limited by nonbureaucratic approaches. Among these are new forms of improvisation, such as the temporary task force cutting across departmental lines. More attention will be given to what rules are intended to achieve, and techniques for enhancing initiative and morale will become more important.

This section discusses participation and control in large organizations, with emphasis on alternatives to bureaucratic management.

MODES OF PARTICIPATION

Participation varies in extent and in quality. Belonging to a book club requires relatively little attention, energy, or interest in its affairs. Such a membership is *segmental;* that is, it affects only a small part, or segment, of the member's life. Most members of most large organizations invest only a limited part of themselves in organizational activities. When participation is limited and segmental, the individual is likely to take little responsibility for the affairs of the group. This abdication is the basic social phenomenon that underlies Michels's theory of self-perpetuating leadership which is reviewed in Adaptation 6.3.

People who prefer not to participate may still be seriously affected by the organization's decisions.

Members of a trade union may not want to attend meetings or involve themselves in union affairs, but they have a substantial stake in what the leadership does. Students and faculty may be bored by administrative issues; yet, if they opt out they pay the price of losing control over rules and policies that affect them. Many people who are interested in the purposes of an organization and in its policies can not face up to the routine chores of participation. To be a member is one thing; to be an active participant is something else.

When segmental participation is accompanied by full freedom of movement from one organization to another, the cost of the individual is small. The organization may then be seen as selling a service or an opportunity. The person who can easily find another job need not depend on a specific employer. The employee is adequately protected by the job market. Ordinary stockholders simply sell their shares if the corporation does not do well. Similarly, members of political groups and other voluntary associations walk out when they no longer like what the organization is doing. They need not concern themselves with choosing new leaders (Hirschman, 1970: Chap. 2).

But freedom of choice and movement are not often available. Most people are dependent on their jobs. Many so-called voluntary organizations are really not so voluntary because they control access to jobs. Trade union membership is the most obvious example, but lawyers or physicians also may feel they must join a professional association in order to practice. It is not easy to quit a major organization if the alternatives are to join a group with little influence or to become a loner.

DEMOCRATIC AND AUTHORITARIAN FORMS

Some organizations encourage their members to participate in decision making, while others restrict this privilege. For example, Parent-Teacher Associations, the League of Women Voters, many political parties, and the United Automobile Workers union are organized to permit, at least formally, a degree of membership control. On the other hand, bank tellers, soldiers, elementary school students, and Boy Scouts are not expected to be actively involved in the control of their organizations.

Differences in organizational form may express the values people hold, but they also develop out of practical necessity. If a group only meets occasionally for discussions, democratic forms may be adequate, but groups that carry on extensive and continuous activities usually add **authoritarian** controls. They find it more effective to assign responsibility to a single individual or small group of executives who appoint junior officials to carry out assignments according to a plan. All large organizations follow this general procedure, although they vary in strictness of discipline and the extent to which employees and separate units are permitted to act independently.

The great variety of formal organizations cannot be neatly divided into democratic and authoritarian types. In fact, aspects of both democracy and authoritarianism are found in many large organizations. The charters of the United Steelworkers, the Farm Bureau Federation, the National Association of Manufacturers, and large corporations have rules that require meetings and elections to be held by members or stockholders so that at least basic democratic forms are preserved.

Not all organizations controlled from the top are equally authoritarian. Some corporations and agencies permit considerable decision making by committees and a wide degree of independence and initiative by subordinate officials. Organizations that encourage these patterns may be thought of as democratic in spirit and to some extent in form, even though final responsibility and authority remain at the top (McGregor, 1960; Likert, 1961).

Sometimes an executive is criticized as authoritarian because he shows a lack of regard for the opinions or feelings of his subordinates. Authoritarian behavior of this kind may be found in authoritarian organizations, but the two should not be confused. Some army commanders or corporation officials are authoritarian in their dealings with subordinates; others show tolerance and respect.

Some pride themselves on lone-wolf decisions; others consult with subordinates. But in all armies and in most businesses, authoritarian procedures predominate.

The word *authoritarian* has a negative connotation. Indeed, if the kind of discipline and decision making that prevail in an army or even a corporation were extended to the whole society, self-government could not survive. But authoritarian forms, when limited to specific activities and controlled by law and custom, do not necessarily challenge the cultural ideals of a democratic society. For example, administration is authoritarian within most democratic government agencies, but the head of each agency is responsible to an elected governor, prime minister, or president as well as to the elected legislature.

PARTICIPATION AND PRODUCTIVITY

Weber's model of top-down bureaucratic management is challenged in situations that demand high productivity and high quality standards. Many business firms get by without requiring their employees to do their best, show initiative, do careful work or contribute original ideas. But when companies encounter rough competition and realize they must improve to survive, managers worry about the human contribution. The drive for better human relations in industry has become more urgent because of the decline of American industry, especially compared with Germany and Japan.

In Japan there is much less emphasis on bureaucratic rules and hierarchy. The Japanese firm has a looser formal structure, fewer levels of authority, and less well-defined lines of communication. Instead, the informal structure is developed and a corporate culture is fostered, expressed in ritual and symbolism, such as participation in games, calisthenics, and social gatherings. Teamwork is stressed and employees are encouraged to contribute ideas on how to improve productivity and quality. The result is a pattern of organization that in many respects is strikingly different from the typical business organization in the United States.

Management consultants and researchers suggest, however, that the most effective American companies share many of the characteristics of the Japanese enterprise. One writer calls them "Type Z" organizations (Ouchi, 1981). In **Type Z** organizations decision-making is typically participative. Management understands that ordinary workers know a great deal about what goes wrong and how improvements can be made, and those actually involved in operations are drawn into the process. With workers participating, information about company activities and policies flows freely, and employees know they are valued and their needs and circumstances are taken into account. "Type Z companies generally show broad concern for the welfare of subordinates. . . . Relationships between people tend to be informal and to emphasize that whole people deal with one another at work, rather than just managers with workers and clerks with machinists" (Ouchi, 1981: 79).

Participative practices were used in Ford's effort to transform its truck production plant in Louisville, Kentucky, where quality, productivity, labor relations, and morale were notoriously poor. In 1979, in cooperation with the union, an employee-involvement program was organized:

> A joint steering committee of top plant and UAW officers started holding weekly meetings and "problem-solving work groups," made up mostly of hourly workers, began to spread through the plant. They took up matters ranging from piping music into the paint shop to improving the quality of parts supplied by vendors [*Fortune,* April 18, 1983:64].

Most important, Ford decided to involve the workers in the design of new models. In an unprecedented move, the designers sent their plans to the shop for comment. The hourly workers had plenty of ideas, many of which were accepted. In addition, workers were invited to participate in inspection procedures for quality control. According to *Fortune,* "the commitment to quality seems to have taken firm hold" and morale and productivity are high.

This approach is not really new. It is an application of well-established psychological and sociological principles, principles that emphasize informal interaction, primary groups, and socialization. These processes take the whole person into account and are the foundations of effective organization (see Fig. 6.1). The Japanese challenge has brought home to managers the importance of matters that have long been understood by human-relations specialists. Japanese methods have suggested some new ways of applying them.

The basic premise of the human-relations perspective is that people do their best when they are persuaded and supported, not when they are driven and coerced. This perspective has been adopted with enthusiasm in Japan in part because the culture encourages conformity and group participation. Americans have found it less congenial and therefore may take it seriously only when they must. However, the human-relations perspective was developed in this country. Its main practices, for example, policies that encourage consultation and protect job security, do not depend on a Japanese-style culture of conformity (see Argyris, 1957; Likert, 1961; McGregor, 1960).

Although group participation and informal structure are vital to good human relations, this does not mean the formal structure is unimportant. To change administrative organizations toward more participatory, less authoritarian management, the change must be strongly supported by top officials. Therefore authority and hierarchy do count. Furthermore, much of group participation is based on formal task units (See p. 110). Neither formal nor informal structure can be understood by itself; their interplay should be kept in mind.

(Text continued on p. 121)

Adaptation 6.3

Michels/The Iron Law of Oligarchy

"Who says organization says oligarchy." With these words the German political sociologist Robert Michels (1876–1936) summed up his famous "Iron law of oligarchy." Although his "law" is stated in unqualified form, his analysis supports more limited generalizations and shows that organization does not necessarily lead to **oligarchy,** *or self-perpetuating leadership. Michels' study, which was based mainly on the history of socialist and trade-union organizations in Europe before World War I, attempts to trace a connection between the basic necessities of organization and the evolution of self-perpetuating oligarchies. In summarizing his argument, we consider first the general need for organization and then the special circumstances that tend to produce oligarchy.*

THE NEED FOR LEADERSHIP

The importance of leadership depends on the size and complexity of the organization. In a small group, leadership may be only weakly developed; leaders arise spontaneously and serve temporarily and unofficially, without many rewards. The leaders remain members of the group, share its interests, and are influenced by the same social conditions as the other members. Since the group is small, most members may participate in decisions and actions.

On the other hand, no organization of any size or duration can exist without leaders. Someone has to organize meetings or evaluate the group's opinions and preferences, represent the group to other organizations or the public, and make many decisions that are necessary to carry out its aims.

These facts are not enough to justify the view that organization leads to oligarchy. The mere fact of organization, that is, the division of labor and delegation of tasks and powers to leaders, is not in itself undemocratic so long as the leadership cannot perpetuate itself. Something more is needed to give rise to oligarchy.

CONDITIONS MAKING FOR OLIGARCHY

The delegation of tasks and powers to leaders results in a concentration of skills and privileges in their hands. Not all members can perform the tasks of leadership in complex organizations. The jobs become specialized and require experience, knowledge, and individual aptitude.

Administrative skills are needed to keep the organization functioning and to get things done. Relations with the outside world, such as diplomacy, collective bargaining, or public relations, require technical knowledge. The leaders' skills set them apart from the rank and file. This specialization makes the members dependent on the leaders who can keep things going and get things done that further the aims of the group. The dependency of the rank and file—a central theme in Michels' work—makes the leaders indispensable and hence gives them increased power.

Leadership carries rights and privileges. In choosing the organization's staff, the leader can select people whose first loyalty is to him; thus, personal machines are built. Leaders also control the channels of information within an organization, and their control gives them special access to and influence over the opinions of the members. Concentration of skills and means of control place power in the hands of leaders and make leaders independent of the rank and file.

Adapted with permission of Macmillan Publishing Company from *Political Parties: A Sociological Study of the Oligarchical Tendencies of Modern Democracy* by Robert Michels, trans. by Eden and Cedar Paul. Copyright © 1962 by the Crowell-Collier Publishing Company.

The position of leaders is further strengthened by the members' political indifference and by their feelings of obligation to those who guide them and do the main work. Ordinary members do not have the inclination or time to participate in the tasks of an organization, and they are glad to have the work done by someone else. Moreover, they may recognize that they lack the skills of their leaders. The rank and file then submit willingly to the widening power of the officials.

Concentration of skills and privileges in the leaders' hands and the submission of the rank and file create opportunities for the self-perpetuation of the leaders. It is not surprising that they take advantage of the situation and try to stay in office. Michels held that leaders try to keep their power because it is inherent in human nature to seek power and retain it. "The desire to dominate, for good or evil, is universal" (1911/1949:206). This is a dubious and unnecessary assumption and is perhaps Michels' weakest point.

He gave other more defensible reasons for the self-perpetuation of leaders. Certainly leaders have a desire for personal security, and the benefits of leadership give them social status distinct from the ordinary members. They wish to retain their status and privileges, including their accustomed way of living and type of employment. The union official does not want to return to the assembly line. Leaders may also believe sincerely that they are serving the best interests of the organization and that a threat to them is a threat to the group as a whole.

Consequences of oligarchy

Self-perpetuation of leaders tends to subvert the aims of the organization. If leaders are independent of rank and file control, they may be tempted to use the organizational machinery and power for personal aims. With the divergence of interest between the leaders and the led, and in the absence of effective democratic control, leaders follow policies that may not serve the aims for which the group was organized. When Michels studied social reform movements, he was especially interested in the way a conservative leadership places stability and security for the organization (and for the leaders) above all other action aims. They are slow to introduce changes, they placate powerful enemies, and they strive for stability. For example, once they had achieved a larger membership, financial security, and discipline, there was a strong tendency among the trade unions of Europe to move from revolutionary to more conservative aims.

Oligarchy is inherent in democracy and cannot be eliminated. Michels held that the social differentiation between leaders and led is universal. This does not mean that tyranny always occurs, but that there is a tendency to oligarchy which requires definite social checks. "Nothing but a serene and frank examination of the oligarchical dangers of democracy will enable us to minimize these dangers, even though they can never be entirely avoided" (1911/1949:408).

Countervailing forces
To minimize the dangers of oligarchy, it is necessary to stimulate and strengthen the individual's aptitude for criticism and control.

> The predisposition towards free inquiry, in which we cannot fail to recognize one of the most precious factors of civilization, will gradually increase as the economic status of the masses improves and becomes more stable, and as they are admitted more effectively to the advantages of civilization. A wider education involves an increasing capacity of exercising control. Can we not observe every day that among the well-to-do the authority of the leaders over the led, extensive though it be, is never so unrestricted as in the case of the leaders of the poor? It is, consequently, the great task of social education to raise the intellectual level of the masses, so that they may be enabled, within the limits of what is possible, to counteract the oligarchical tendencies of the working-class movement (1911/1949:406f.).

Commentary
An argument similar to Michels' thesis was put forward in a study of the modern corporation (Berle and Means, 1933). In the very large company, there is wide dispersion of stock ownership. Spreading ownership and risk among many shareholders permits the massing of large quantities of capital for industrial development, but the individual stockholder has only a small voice in the company's affairs, and ownership is separated from control. Power is concentrated in the hands of management, which often becomes self-perpetuating.

Thus, self-perpetuating leadership is by no means restricted to the political organizations studied by Michels. The following points should be considered.

1. Members of many organizations surrender their formal right to make important decisions. They are willing for someone else to take over the task as long as their own special interests (for example, the continued flow of reasonable dividends) are not seriously affected. But when members abdicate their powers in normal periods, the leaders are able to consolidate their power and the members find it hard to assert themselves in times of crises.
2. The weakness of members can be ameliorated if they band together in organized factions. If alternative centers of power are created in the organization, the leaders may be called to account for their actions. This is what happens in the organization of pressure groups and parties in a political democracy. In special purpose organizations, however, the narrowness of member interests less readily sustains permanent opposition groups that can mobilize opinion and supply alternative leadership.*

*For a study of a deviant case—a trade union within which an institutionalized opposition developed—see Lipset, Trow, and Coleman, 1956.

Chapter 6 **Summary**

Section 1/**Formal organizations**

Formal organizations are those that have been deliberately established for a certain purpose. All such organizations must give their members incentives, set up a system of communications, and exercise control over their members. Bureaucratic organizations are made up of executives and subordinates who are brought together to do a job. Voluntary associations are formed by people who join together to pursue shared interests. Most adults in the United States spend a considerable amount of their time as members of bureaucracies. About half of them spend much less time as participants in voluntary associations.

Every organization has both a formal structure and an informal structure. The formal structure consists of the organization's official rules, goals, powers, and procedures. The informal structure consists of patterned interactions among persons and groups within the organization.

Section 2/**Formal structure**

Formal structure, especially bureaucracy, has four main elements: division of labor, hierarchy of authority, rules and procedures, and impersonality. These elements are usually more pronounced at lower levels in the organization than they are at upper levels. They are also more characteristic of bureaucracies than of voluntary associations. The authority exercised by bureaucratic officials is known as rational-legal authority and is much more limited than traditional or charismatic authority. Rules and procedures perform the same control functions as authority and are sometimes used as a substitute for it.

Section 3/**Informal structure**

Informal structure arises in response to a variety of factors including impersonality, lag (changes in the formal system lag behind changes in actual operations), generality (rules have to be abstract and general), and the personal needs and concerns of the organization's members. In addition, there is a "spillover" effect. Members of an organization interact not only in their formal roles but also as personalities.

Primary groups always develop within large organizations. These groups may become centers of personal loyalty and support, but their members must conform to group norms such as "Don't be a rate-buster." Primary groups are double-edged. They may support or undermine the formal system of communication and command. The primary group also mediates (stands between) the individual and the organization. If the primary group is effectively linked to the organization, participation is heightened; but if the link is broken, morale and discipline may suffer.

Section 4/**Beyond bureaucracy?**

Bureaucracy was especially effective when social change was slower and technology simpler. Organizations today require more flexibility and new forms of participation and control.

Because most participation in organizations affects only a small part of the member's life, many persons deliberately limit their participation. Consequently they may surrender control over the organization's rules and policies. Thus, more authoritarian forms may develop even when democratic procedures were originally intended. In structure and in practice, organizations vary from democratic to authoritarian, but most organizations are a mixture of both.

Social scientists and management consultants hold that employee participation and initiative are associated with both employee morale and productivity. Some United States firms have adapted ideas from Japanese management and have encouraged their workers to help change company policies and activities. The results are frequently greater worker commitment to quality and higher productivity. Most of these changes in the structure of authority and employee participation have their origins in established psychological and sociological principles.

Although the organization of the future will be characterized by more flexibility and employee initiative, the basic features of bureaucracy are likely to persist.

Suggested Readings

Drucker, Peter F.
1980 *Managing in Turbulent Times*. New York: Harper and Row.

Kanter, Rosabeth M.
1977 *Men and Women of the Corporation*. New York: Basic Books.

Katz, Daniel, and Robert L. Kahn
1978 *The Social Psychology of Organizations*. Second edition. New York: Wiley.

Ouchi, William
1981 *Theory Z: How American Business Can Meet the Japanese Challenge*. New York: Addison-Wesley.

Perrow, Charles
1979 *Complex Organizations: A Critical Essay*. Second edition. Glenview, Illinois: Scott Foresman.

Scott, W. Richard
1981 *Organizations: Rational, Natural and Open Systems*. Englewood Cliffs, N.J.: Prentice-Hall.

Selznick, Philip
1957 *Leadership in Administration*. New York: Harper and Row.

Thompson, James D.
1967 *Organizations in Action*. New York: McGraw-Hill.

Part Three

The Great Divides: Inequality and Discrimination

Chapter 7

Age and Sex

Part Three of this book, beginning with Chapter 7, analyzes age, sex, minorities, and class—the major structural cleavages in society, which we call "the great divides." The great divides based on age, sex, and race are biological in origin, but the social forms in which they are expressed are not biologically determined. They gain their significance from the ways differences between categories of people are socially interpreted and thus shape social relations.

In this chapter, we see how ages are defined and how they influence the experience of growing up and growing older. The chapter also considers how physical sex differences are interpreted and organize social life. The study of minorities is taken up in Chapter 8; social class and stratification are discussed in Chapter 9.

Section One
The Life Course

Statuses based on age, sex, and race are ascribed statuses. No amount of effort can make a 60-year-old into a 20-year-old. Similarly, sex and race cannot be changed except in rare cases and special conditions. Blacks do pass as white, but the personal costs are high. Sex change is even more rare and drastic.

In every society, several age categories are distinguished. But the number of categories recognized and the rights and responsibilities that go with them change over time and vary in different places. Similarly, everywhere certain activities are assigned to women and others to men; but male and female roles vary widely from one society to another.

In sum, both age and sex are biological characteristics that are socially recognized and socially defined. Social behavior is not determined biologically. The relationship between physical and social factors creates **biosocial** patterns of behavior.

AGE: EMERGENT AND ASCRIBED

Age differs from other ascribed statuses in that it is a process as well as a status. The status is **emergent** as well as ascribed. People who live long enough to

become old pass through all of the chronological ages and all of their society's age statuses in the course of a lifetime. A person who is born a white male normally remains white and male all his life. But if he survives to old age, he will pass through every age status—a sequence determined from the day of birth. Thus, unlike other ascribed statuses that are fixed throughout life, a person's age status changes as the years pass.

Role gain and role loss

Between birth and death, every organism experiences a predictable sequence of stages called the **life course,** which is defined by social and biological characteristics. It includes a series of transitions that involve taking on new roles or losing old ones. Becoming a spouse or a parent and starting a new job are **role gains.** Retirement and the death of a spouse or a parent involve **role loss.**

To some extent, role gain and role loss are two sides of the same coin. When a spouse dies, the survivor ceases to be a wife or husband and becomes a widow or widower. One role is exchanged for another. Upon becoming parents, men and women acquire the new roles of father and mother, and usually a new relationship to their own parents. In the eyes of their parents, they are no longer children. Thus, whether a change involves role gains or role losses, the individual must learn to perform new duties, adapt to new conditions, and readjust existing relationships.

The life course in modern societies is characterized by role gains during childhood, youth, and young adulthood, and by role losses in later life. From birth, when they have few social functions, individuals go through a series of role gains, each of which adds new functions. They become students, independent young people, employees, spouses, and parents. After reaching a peak in midlife, social functions thin out in a series of role losses. Children leave home; careers come to an end; friends and family members die.

Males and females follow parallel but distinct paths. Parenthood typically has a greater impact on the social functions of women, while employment tends to loom larger in men's lives. In the first three sections of this chapter, we explore how the life course is organized in North American society and how some other societies define life stages. The balance of the chapter examines the distinctive social experiences of females and males, how femininity and masculinity are constructed and learned, and some of the socioeconomic consequences of these patterns.

Rites of passage

The transition from one age category to another can be gradual or abrupt, formally observed or hardly noticed. When the transition from one social status to another is celebrated in a ceremony, it is referred to as a **rite of passage** (van Gennep, 1908/1960). Birth and puberty ceremonies, marriages, and funerals are the most common rites of passage. Becoming an elder may be formally observed in a retirement ceremony or in the handing over of responsibilities to a son or daughter. In traditional Japan, celebrations marked the transition from infancy, at about age 7, to preadolescence, the stage at which children were first "recognized as members of human society" and began to "perform traditional duties" (Norbeck, 1953:374).

All of these social markers call attention to persons who are undergoing a change of status. Rites of passage usually have three basic elements: (1) a *separation phase*, in which the person sheds the previous status, (2) a *transition phase*, and (3) an *incorporation phase* that confirms the new position (van Gennep, 1908/1960:Chap. 2). Separation may be symbolized in ceremonies that treat the individual's passage out of the prior status as ritual death and incorporation into the new status as ritual rebirth. The ritual makes clear which old rights and duties have been discarded and which new ones have been acquired.

Section Two
Childhood and Youth

For a time, human infants are completely dependent on adults for survival. Although they gradually become less dependent, children continue to need at least some adult attention for a number of years.

This section considers the period of partial dependence called childhood, the ways that societies define the nature and extent of childhood, and the transition to independence.

Normal babies have "a number of innate skills and reflexes, which—other things being equal—develop according to a predictable timetable" (Tucker, 1977:36). If a baby is reasonably well nourished and cared for, in due course he or she will smile, babble, reach for objects, sit upright, crawl, walk, and talk.

In addition, infants and children have identifiable psychological traits. The baby's need to become emotionally attached to a few significant adults was discussed in Chapter 4. Some fear of strange persons and novel situations may be inborn, along with curiosity and the urge to explore. All children investigate themselves and their surroundings. Whatever modes of socialization their society uses, almost all children learn to be competent adults. "Receptivity to a prevailing culture is in itself a constant characteristic of all childhood." (Tucker, 1977:99).

IMAGES OF CHILDHOOD

Despite the physical and psychological similarities of children, there have been many different images of childhood. Children have been viewed as little adults, as not yet human, as basically evil, or as pure innocents.

The little adult

Some historians believe that in Europe before 1700, childhood was not socially defined. Young people were infants until they were 7–10 years old and then passed directly from infancy to adulthood.

> In medieval society, the idea of childhood did not exist; this is not to suggest that children were neglected, forsaken, or despised. The idea of childhood corresponds to an awareness of the particular nature of childhood, that particular nature which distinguishes the child from the adult, even the young adult. In medieval society this awareness was lacking. That is why, as soon as the child could live without the constant solicitude of his mother, his nanny, his cradle-rocker, he belonged to adult society. [Ariès, 1960/1962:128].

Adults and children played together; leapfrog, tag, hide-and-seek, and blindman's bluff were played by everyone; nursery rhymes and riddles were for all ages; and scholars of 12 and 20 studied together. Children as young as 10 dressed like little adults, and they were encouraged to behave like adults. They visited taverns and probably became sexually active at a fairly early age. Much that is now called precocious was considered normal.

Children who committed crimes had the same legal standing as adults. "In England as late as the eighteenth century . . . a small girl aged seven was hanged . . . for stealing a petticoat." (Tucker, 1977: 93).

The little worker

The little adult worked at adult tasks with adults, and jobs were not always scaled down to their size or strength. Whether they did piecework at home or in the factories, helped on the farm or served a master, tended flocks or toiled in mines, children's hours were long and the work hard. A nineteenth-century account describes the exploitation of young miners.

> The child is obliged to pass on all fours, and the chain passes under what, in that posture, might be called the hind legs; and thus they have to pass through avenues not so good as a common sewer, quite as wet, and oftentimes more contracted. This kind of labor they have to continue during several hours, in a temperature described as perfectly intolerable. By the testimony of the people themselves, it appears that the labor is exceedingly severe; that the girdle blisters their sides and causes great pain. "Sir," says an old miner, "I can only say what the mothers say; it is barbarity; absolute barbarity." Robert North says, "I went into the pit at 7 years of age. When I drew by the girdle and chain, the skin was broken and the blood ran down. . . . If we said anything, they would beat us." [Cooper, 1842:49, cited in Skolnick, 1973:348]

Today the little adult has not disappeared. Children still work, and work hard, at adult-sized tasks. In 1973, the International Labor Organization of the United Nations set a minimum age of 15 for workers. This standard has been ratified by only 15 nations, and ILO research during 1979—the Year of the Child —showed that children are little more than slaves in the mines and factories of Asia, Africa, Latin America, and southern Europe (*Time,* September 10, 1979:23). Children who work long hours for little pay suffer the worst of both childhood and adulthood: the child's powerlessness and dependency and the adult's obligation to work for a living.

In developed nations, poor children take on adult duties earlier than middle-class children. For example, they may be kept home from school to look after younger siblings while the parents work. In spite of laws against child labor, the children of migrant laborers sometimes work in the field with their parents.

A little worker.

Varieties of childhood

Our ancestors probably varied as much in their child-rearing practices as we do. Some were strict; others were relaxed. Some enjoyed their children; others regretted being parents. They also had a variety of beliefs about the nature of children and the proper way to rear them.

The experience of childhood also differed according to the child's sex, social class, ethnicity, and region. Although less is known about the history of girlhood than of boyhood, girls traditionally were given less education than boys. Victorian writers warned against the "danger of education to women's health and morals" (Smith-Rosenberg, 1978:230). Girls were more closely supervised than boys, especially during their teens when sexual virtue became a concern. Women probably reached adulthood earlier and married younger than men.

Social class was another source of variation in the nature of childhood. Children from poor households had to start working much earlier than those who were better off. Rural children, working alongside their parents as soon as they were able, gained knowledge and skills on the job as they grew up. In towns and cities, poor children were apprenticed or became laborers or household servants. The relationships of apprentices with their masters' families were probably as varied as those of children with their parents.

Along with industrialization came new jobs for children in factories and mines. Poor and orphaned children were sent to workhouses or sold to factories (Stone, 1977:472). Until the twentieth century, the prolonged period of dependency that we think of as normal childhood was found only in the upper classes. For most people, childhood was shorter and harsher than it is today.

MODERN AMERICAN CHILDHOOD

In the past half-century, knowledge about the physical and intellectual development of children has increased to such an extent that it is no longer possible to think of children as little adults. Because children undergo rapid psychological change, conscientious parents try to give them a protected environment.

Specialists in child psychology, child psychiatry, pediatrics, and education make up what is almost an industry devoted to learning about and caring for children. In addition, institutions designed to meet the needs of children have become more numerous and more specialized. The most obvious and the most important of these institutions is the school. Others include children's libraries, summer camps, Sunday schools, the Boy Scouts and Girl Scouts. Whole hospitals are devoted to children, and when they are admitted to general hospitals, they are placed in children's wards. Young offenders are handled by a special system of laws and courts. Juveniles who are convicted are kept away from adult criminals, if possible, and sent to "reform" schools or assigned to special programs.

Children and schools

Universal education has probably done more than anything else to change the experience of childhood. Once available to only a small part of the population, education is now a major activity of all young people. Until the nineteenth century, only the children of the elite went to school. In the middle of the last century, fewer than half of all Americans aged 5 to 19 were enrolled in school, and even those who were enrolled went to small, one-teacher schools and attended only occasionally; most of the time they worked. Today more than 90 percent of those aged 5 to 19 are enrolled and school attendance is continuous (U.S. Bureau of the Census, 1975:369–70).

From about the age of 5 to their late teens, children spend more hours at school than they devote to any other activity except watching television. The child's year is the school year, and today it is twice as long, on average, as it was 100 years ago (Bane, 1976:15–16).

Universal, age-graded education reflects modern beliefs about children's special needs. Children are thought to benefit from activities tailored to their stage of physical, intellectual, and emotional development. They are relieved of outside duties so they can concentrate on learning, which society sees as the child's main duty and most important task. But while the school is supposed to serve children's needs, it restricts their interactions with older people and limits their opportunities to learn at first hand what life is like at other ages. Schools segregate schoolgoers from both infants and adults and divide pupils into small groups of age peers. Thus, children spend much of their time with other children of the same age and with one or two adults.

Taking children seriously

Separate environments and activities are intended to be responsive to the needs of children. But removing children from adult life encourages the idea that they are incompetent, that they cannot do what adults do.

> Childhood is conventionally seen as a time of carefree, disorganized bliss. . . . Children [are believed to] avoid work and serious pursuits at all costs. . . . In America, this belief lasts at least until the child enters the world of marriage and gainful employment. [Denzin, 1970:13]

The serious matters of childhood.

Because children are thought to be unable to organize their own lives, adults do it for them. Even very young children are placed in highly structured environments where their schedules are planned and their activities supervised. Many adults assume that without adult direction children would "waste" their time, doing and learning nothing. They would only play. Schools are therefore organized to prevent such waste and ensure that children acquire the disciplines, skills, and knowledge they will need as adults.

But in fact, many unsupervised childhood activities are neither trivial nor disorganized; rather, they are serious efforts to build an orderly and meaningful existence.

> Child's work involves such serious matters as developing languages for communication, [and] presenting and defending their social selves in difficult situations. [Denzin, 1970:14]

In school or outside of it, children act in an organized way, and they often engage in activities that require intense concentration and a great deal of effort. A similar degree of effort and commitment in an adult would be called work. Most of the motor skills that children master by the time they go to school are impossible for the baby: Using a spoon, drinking from a cup, standing and walking, fastening buckles and buttons, tying shoe laces—all involve coordination and, for the learner, sustained effort. Disabled adults who attempt to relearn such skills are taken seriously. But a child's earnest attempts to learn similar things are often viewed with amusement (Holt, 1974).

Just as some adults regard children's activities as unimportant, they look upon children's feelings as inferior to adult emotions. They assume that small size, innocence, and inexperience imply small emotions; they deny a child's pain by telling the child that what hurts does not hurt. However, therapists agree that children's pain and sadness must be taken seriously. Suicide attempts by children as young as 10 or 12 are evidence of the strength of children's emotions (*Time*, September 25, 1978:70).

TOWARD MODERN ADOLESCENCE

Some of the problems of adolescence are the inevitable result of growing up. Although youth is always a turbulent period, modern adolescence is complicated by the crosscurrents of a complex society. Changing from a child into an adult is not easy either for the person going through the change or for family, friends, and teachers.

Two nineteenth-century innovations changed the youth period from a gradual evolution toward independence to a period of frustrating dependence called adolescence. One of these innovations was universal compulsory education. The other was regulation of child labor (Kett, 1973). Both were part of the humanitarian movement of the late 1800s. Reformers opposed to the exploitation of young people in mines and factories introduced laws to protect them from heavy work, long hours, and unhealthy conditions. In the end, the young were barred from almost all paid work.

At first, only affluent families could support their children during a long period of schooling. The lower classes could not afford to keep their children out of the work force; they evaded or ignored laws that deprived them of needed income. Nevertheless, the changes brought on by the shift to an industrial economy could not be resisted. More and more jobs called for workers who could read, write, and keep accounts. The professions required long training. As children took jobs that did not even exist when their parents were young, parents could no longer fully prepare them for adult life. Modern adolescence evolved in response to these social changes, many of which postpone the social end of childhood.

The physiological end of childhood—puberty—is earlier than in previous generations. For American girls, average age of menarche (or first menstruation) was 16 or 17 in the mid 1800s; in the early 1900s it was around 15. Today it is about 12 (Coleman et al., 1974:94; Laslett, 1971). Boys also mature earlier than they did in the 1800s, and today's youth are bigger than their parents or grandparents (Gillis, 1974:187–88, Tanner, 1971:21–24).

The concept of adolescence

The term *adolescence* came into common use in the late 1800s (Hall, 1904). In the United States, adolescence is fairly brief with a definite beginning and end; it corresponds closely to the period of secondary schooling, which begins around age 12 and ends in the late teens. Children in the higher primary grades are "preteens," and high-school graduates are "young adults"—even if they go to college, are supported by their parents, and go home for holidays. The end of adolescence is marked by the right to stop attending school, to drive a car, to marry without parental consent, to vote, and to buy alcoholic beverages. Except for voting, the age at which these privileges and responsibilities begin varies between states, so that the legal signal of the end of adolescence is not one arbitrary age.

Modern adolescence is usually economically unproductive, and most of the real work of adolescents, like that of children, is learning. It is assumed that healthy psychological development requires steady concentration on the tasks of adolescence, and that young people must not be distracted from these tasks. Modern middle-class culture holds that young people should be protected during their teen years as they form coherent personalities and acquire skills and knowledge.

Becoming adult: new prospects

During the 1960s and 1970s, some observers questioned whether the school and the age-specific peer group prepare young people adequately for independence. The Report of the Panel on Youth of the President's Science Advisory Committee (Coleman et al., 1974) closely examined the problems of youth and offered a number of specific proposals.

The panel recommended major changes in school structure. Schools, they said, should not follow a standard curriculum but should provide more opportunities for self-motivated activity and specialization. At the same time, student roles should be diversified. Students should engage in part-time teaching and become involved in nonacademic activities.

The panel also recommended measures to diminish the separation of education from employment. If young people could move back and forth between school and work, they would have more contact with adults and some experience with the duties they will take on as adults. Adding education to the organization of work would allow persons of all ages to interact as teachers, learners, and co-workers.

A major strength of the adolescent peer group is the opportunity it offers for self-government. The panel felt that this should be recognized and promoted. Furthermore, youth should be encouraged—both as individuals and as groups—to become involved in community service for the needy, the handicapped, children, and old people.

Finally, the panel proposed an experiment with an educational voucher system. This would allow persons of age 16 and over who have finished high school to choose their own higher education or vocational training program. Vouchers issued for education could be redeemed at any time, even by adults, for many kinds of schooling. Thus, individuals would be responsible for their own education, rather than depending on their parents, school boards, or the state. A voucher system would also mean equal access to postsecondary schooling, since everyone would receive a voucher regardless of family income.

Section Three
Adulthood and Old Age

Independence and responsibility for oneself are the hallmarks of adulthood. Two steps that break the last bonds of dependency and signal the beginning of adulthood are marriage and setting up a separate household; most of adult life is shaped by the concerns of employment and family. Entering the work force, changing jobs and earning promotions, getting married, and rearing children are the major events and activities of adulthood.

CHANGES IN THE LIFE COURSE

Until fairly recently, most of married life was devoted to childbearing and child rearing. Few married couples lived out a long life together. People who survived beyond middle age were usually widowed and possibly remarried. Now, because of the long life expectancy in industrial countries, many people complete an entire life course from infancy to dependent (or unproductive) old age. Never before in human history have so many people lived so long. At birth, males in Anglo-American countries can expect to live 69 to 71 years; females 76 to 78 years.

In the late twentieth century childbearing is completed comparatively early, both husband and wife are likely to survive beyond middle age, and their child rearing stage ends when they are still fairly young.

These changes offer many couples a chance to broaden their relationships after the child-rearing years. The traditional family was geared to raising children, not to living in an "empty nest." Today, older couples often face the task of reassessing a relationship that began forty years earlier.

Historical changes in life expectancy, the timing and duration of childbearing, and the length of time that children remain at home are suggested in Figure 7.1. The figure shows average (median) ages and should be interpreted as follows: A woman who married for the first time in the early 1900s at a little over 20 years had her first child when she was about 23 and her last child when she was about 33. Her last child married when she was about 55 years old, and either she or her husband died soon afterwards.

A typical woman who married for the first time in the 1970s will complete her childbearing before age 30, more than three years earlier than did her grandmother. Her last child will be married when she is in her early fifties; then she can look forward with mixed feelings to about 15 years of married life before she or (more likely) her husband dies (Glick, 1977:5–13).

Other patterns

This typical adult life course is defined in terms of marriage and children. While it applies to most people, many individuals do not fit this pattern. Those who do not have children, who do not marry, or who have children outside of marriage are not represented in Figure 7.1. Also, the typical pattern

does not fully reflect the lives of those whose families are broken by divorce or premature death. Most people who lose a spouse before old age eventually remarry, and many have a second family, thereby prolonging the child rearing phase. Women who delay marriage and childbearing to concentrate on their careers also have a distinctive family cycle, but it is not yet clear whether the pattern will become widespread.

People who remain single throughout life have been less studied, and much less is known about how their lives differ from the majority who marry and become parents.

Prime time

Most adults experience the prime of life from the mid-thirties to the mid-fifties. In mid-life, they reach their highest levels of social competence, job security, and job satisfaction. More than at any other time, they are in command of themselves and their personal environments. Their physical capacities remain high, and their children are old enough so that child care is not a major burden. On the average, they have gained a degree of financial security through the purchase of a house and life insurance, and have managed to save some money.

Mid-life is the most fruitful period in professional and creative work. Social activities also reach their high point, "since this is the time of the most numerous personal relations and the greatest amount of social intercourse" (Frenkel-Brunswick, 1968:80). Scientists, artists, and scholars tend to be most productive in their middle years (Dennis, 1968:114).

Continuity and crisis

This picture represents mid-life as a relatively stable period, free of the dramatic role changes that characterize youth. During middle age, people often enjoy a period of consolidation; they have the advantages of experience and usually remain fairly vigorous, able to pursue their goals with purpose and energy. However, the middle years have their own tensions and transitions. Theorists disagree whether there is a predictable "mid-life crisis," when it occurs, and how it is defined.

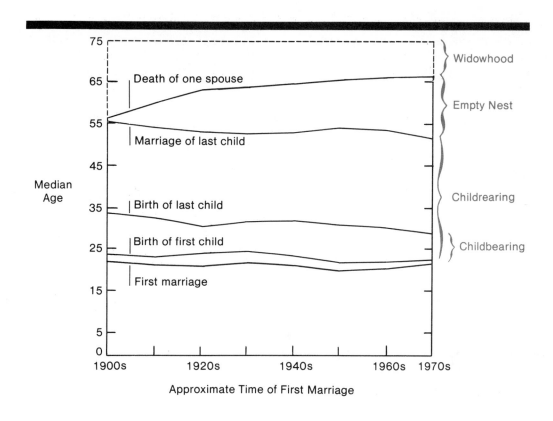

Figure 7.1 Median Age of Mothers at Beginning of Life Course Stages
Source: After Glick, 1977, Table 1 and Figure 1.

Certain physical changes are experienced by everyone. In addition people in mid-life go through significant role loss and role gain. Adults watch their children move through the first stages of the life course to become young adults themselves. Looking "up" the generations, they see their own parents age and die. While they give up their roles as active parents, middle-aged adults are likely to become grandparents, and they may acquire other new roles as care givers for the elderly. All of these changes are profound alterations of central, salient statuses that require individuals to reorganize their lives and adapt their personalities.

People in mid-life may have the sense that time is running short, that lifetime career goals must be met soon or not at all. Revising the ambitions of youth may be a sign of bitter disappointment and failure, or a step toward more realistic and potentially satisfying life aims. Whether it is resolved with a sense of frustration or accomplishment, reappraisal in middle age often feels like the last chance.

OLD AGE AND DEATH

The percentage of the United States population age 65 and over more than doubled between 1900 and 1980, from 4 percent to over 11 percent, and the elderly will be a large part of the population for the foreseeable future. The National Institute of Aging expects the number of Americans 75 and over to increase 53 percent by the year 2000 over the 1980 number—almost twice as fast as the total 65-and-over group. In other words, the proportion of the old who are very old will become statistically and socially more important.

Growing old

When a person becomes old depends on who is asking the question, and why. A healthy, involved elderly person may say that old age begins ten years later than his or her present age, whatever that may be. But people feel "old before their time" if their health is poor, if their spouses die, or if they are forced to retire when they are still healthy and still want to work.

There is much variation in the vigor, social involvement, and happiness of the elderly. Some people are active and optimistic well into their eighties or nineties, while others withdraw from most activities before they are 60. The most important single difference between the "young old" and the "old old" is health.

Older people have more health problems, especially chronic impairments and diseases, than younger people. They are more likely to suffer deterioration in hearing, vision, or balance, and to have trouble getting around. However, "only a small minority . . . are too handicapped to carry on their major activity, despite widespread chronic afflictions in old age." Healthy old people remain more active than those in poor health. They are also happier, more satisfied with life, and less likely to think of themselves as old (Riley and Foner, 1968, vol. 1: 345–47; 416; and Chap. 9; quotation at p. 292). In fact, good health is "the single best predictor of life satisfaction and morale among the elderly" (Myles, 1978:509).

Retirement

Employers usually retire workers at age 65, and at that age Americans become eligible for such old-age benefits as Social Security payments, Medicare, and some tax advantages. But not all workers retire at 65. In 1978, 21 percent of men and 8 percent of women past age 65 were still in the labor force (*CPR*, P-23, No. 85, August 1979:20). Retired

Crossing a great divide.
Because of increasing age segregation, the young and the old lose the pleasure and benefit of shared experience.

people are more likely to think of themselves as old than people of the same age who are still working (Blau, 1956:200).

Bereavement

In 1978, 37 percent of Americans aged 65 and over were widowed (*CPR*, P-23, No. 85, August 1979:7). Because women live longer on average than men and marry younger, they are much more likely to be widowed. More than half of women aged 65 and over are widows, compared with 14 percent of men. Among the population aged 75 and over, nearly 70 percent of the women and 23 percent of the men are widowed.

The stress of widowhood has at least three elements: (1) grief, (2) economic problems, and (3) loneliness (Barrett, 1977:857–59). For some time after the death of a spouse, emotional and even physical symptoms trouble the survivor. Many traditional cultures encourage formal ceremonies in which bereavement is acted out in the presence of the community. In the United States, however, expressive behavior has been removed from stage-managed funerals except among ethnic groups that retain their old-world customs. Limiting the expression of grief may retard or impair a bereaved person's adjustment to widowhood.

In addition to the burden of grief, the death of a spouse creates economic problems. Heavy hospital, medical, and funeral costs eat up savings. Often the survivor's income is insufficient to maintain the previous life-style.

In modern societies, the process of dying has been removed from everyday experience and taken into specialized places (hospitals or "nursing homes") to be supervised by specialized personnel and managed by specialized technologies. Doctors and nurses are often poorly prepared for this responsibility, and there is little socialization for death among either medical professionals or the general public. Older adults may approach the end of their own lives and that of their age peers with more fear and distress than in societies where people directly observe death and where dying is easily discussed.

Section Four
Gender Identity and Gender Roles

Like age differences, sexual characteristics are biological in origin and are socially interpreted. Biological differences between males and females are termed differences of **sex.** However, the social and psychological traits of males and females make up what is called **gender**—masculinity and femininity.

All babies are labeled girls or boys at birth and are socialized according to their labels. Early in life a person acquires a **gender identity**—the socially assigned label and personal self-definition as male or female. In almost all cases gender identity matches physical characteristics.

Once a child has gender identity, he or she begins to assemble **gender roles.** These are the socially defined rights and responsibilities that are assigned to males and females. Many authors use "sex

roles" loosely to cover both biological and social differences.

Identity is *what* a person is—male or female. Roles are *how* a person acts—what it means to be masculine or feminine. Gender roles give information on how to dress and behave, how to walk and talk, what to do, where to go, and with whom.

BECOMING BOYS AND GIRLS

Girls and boys are treated differently from the day they are born. The infant's sex is an important part of the birth announcement, and his or her clothes and furnishing are chosen on the basis of sex. Pink blankets or blue ones, frilly panties or sporty shirts symbolize society's differing expectations for girls and boys.

Mothers interact differently with their newborn sons and daughters. They are more likely to smile at and talk to baby girls and more likely to pick up and hold boys (Korner, 1974:110). The reasons for these differences are not clear, but they may include a socially based preference for boys as well as such biologically based traits as the inborn ability of infant girls to respond to verbal stimuli. Both parents are more likely to encourage sons to engage in physical activity and to punish them physically, and fathers are more likely to play more rough-and-tumble games with sons than with daughters. "The continuing theme appears to be that girls are treated as though they were more fragile than boys" (Maccoby and Jacklin, 1974:309).

Baby-sitters, other children, parents' friends, and later, teachers—all use gender labels to place children socially and to organize their relationships. There are different toys and games for boys and girls, different bathrooms to use at school; children's clothes are labeled "girls'" or "boys'" (though they may be identical except for the label). A child who was not labeled boy or girl would be a social blank.

GENDER ROLES AND STEREOTYPES

The norms of femininity stress delicacy, passivity, dependency, emotionality, weakness, nurturance, a "social" orientation, and verbal skill. When people are asked to identify behavior or characteristics that are feminine, they usually mention excitability, a need for approval and security, a tendency to cry readily, and being religious and domestic. On the other hand, masculinity in North American society means toughness, aggressiveness, independence, rationality, strength, competitiveness, a desire for achievement, and skill at mathematics. Typical men are characterized as aggressive, dominant, loud, and wanting to ''run the show'' (Spence et al., 1975).

Of course, real people do not match the stereotypes of macho men or helpless women. Some gender stereotypes probably have no basis in fact. An example is the idea that women are more patient and better suited to boring tasks than men. Others are exaggerations of observed differences. An example is the idea that women are more nurturant than men and that therefore men do not make good care givers. But a stereotype may create its own reality. People who are convinced of the truth of gender stereotypes may either lose or fail to develop traits that are believed to be unsuited to their sex. If children are repeatedly told that girls are not good at mathematics and science but that boys are, they begin to believe it, and the stereotype becomes reality.

Just as girls are taught to hide or suppress ''masculine'' traits, boys are taught that it is unmanly to express emotion, and they learn not to show their true feelings. Because boys are scolded and teased for crying, it is not surprising that as adults they express less tenderness or vulnerability. Neither the playboy nor the cowboy is allowed to express emotion (Balswick and Peek, 1971). High rates of heart disease, lung cancer, and accidental injury are the price that some men pay for trying to conform to the masculine stereotype of competence, confidence, and toughness (Waldron, 1976).

Evaluating gender traits

Masculine and feminine traits not only are different but are valued differently, and masculine traits usually rate higher. Feminine traits such as excitability, insecurity, and emotionality are seen as childlike, while masculine traits such as self-reliance and emotional control are seen as adult. ''Mature feminini-

ty,'' thus, is a contradiction in terms, and women are in a double bind: Since the standards of adult behavior are masculine, it is impossible to be both adult and feminine at the same time (Broverman et al., 1972). However, some of the traits associated with one sex are seen as ideals for both. For example, warmth, expressiveness, and kindness are womanly virtues that are ideal traits in both sexes. Similarly, independence and self-confidence are ideal characteristics for women as well as being typical of men (Spence et al., 1975).

Women who succeed in school and in their jobs may feel torn between the rewards of success and the cultural norm that devalues achievement for females. If they want a career, they may fear success because they think they will lose friends or be unable to marry (Horner, 1968; 1972). Fearing social rejection as a result of achievement, girls may not perform as well as they can and thus avoid dealing with the conflict.

Section Five
The Sexual Division of Labor

Most unpaid work at home is done by women. Although labor-saving devices have made the work physically easier, the housework week is still long and boring, and the houseworker* often lacks adult companionship. Until recently, paid work outside the home has been done mostly by men, but the balance is changing as more women enter the job market. Still, ''more'' is not the same as ''more equal.'' Women have more than their share of lower-status jobs, are paid less for equal work, and are still expected to do housework.

It is too soon to tell whether in the long run men and women will be equally rewarded equal participants in the world of work, both in the home and

---

*In this section, we use the term *houseworker* to refer to someone who performs regular household tasks. We choose this term because it avoids reference to the sex of the worker or to the relationship between the worker and other members of the household. Unless otherwise specified, the houseworker is unpaid. Usually the houseworker is also a wife and frequently a mother. We limit the use of *housewife* to those situations where the woman's status as wife is directly relevant to the discussion.

outside it. At present, employed women face many obstacles: interrupted employment, limited opportunities, slow advancement, and low pay.

GOING OUT TO WORK

The entry of women into paid work is among the most important economic and social transformations of the twentieth century. At the turn of the century, about one-fifth of American women, compared with about four-fifths of American men, were in the **labor force,** that is, working or looking for work. The percent of women in the labor force increased gradually until World War II. During the war many women filled jobs vacated by men serving in the armed forces, and over one-third of women had paying jobs. After the war there was a brief decline, but by the mid-1950s the percent of women in the labor market matched the wartime peak, and by 1982 it was 53 percent. (See Figure 7.2.)

Meanwhile the male labor force participation rate has declined, though not as much as the female rate has increased. In 1950, about 87 percent of males age 16 or older were in the labor force. In 1982, this figure had fallen to 76 percent.

Sex segregation in the labor force

Most women and men work at different kinds of jobs and in different industries. Men far outnumber women in craft, managerial and adminstrative, and farm work; women are more numerous in clerical and paid domestic work. Most employed women are concentrated in a few jobs: More than half are service or clerical workers. By contrast, men are found in a wider range of industries and in a wider range of jobs within those industries. The largest concentration of men is in craft work, which accounts for 21 percent of the male labor force (U.S. Bureau of Labor Statistics, June 1980: table A-22).

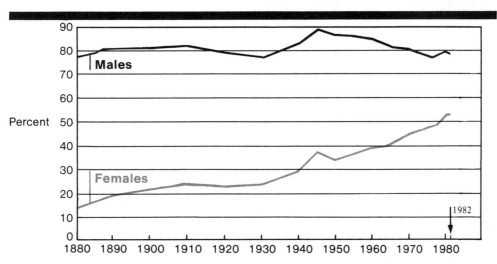

Figure 7.2 Labor-Force Participation Rates Over a Century by Sex, United States[a]

[a]Ages and definitions of the labor force vary: 1880-1930, gainfully employed age 10 and older; 1940-1960, persons in labor force age 14 and older; after 1960, persons in labor force age 16 and older.
Sources: Bureau of the Census, 1975: 127-128, 131-132; Statistical Abstract, 1979:392; Bureau of Labor Statistics, 1980: A8-A9; 1982: A4. Data for 1880-1930 from decennial censuses; data for 1940 and later years from sample surveys.

A closer look shows that women are concentrated in poorly paid, lower-status jobs. Since women make up about 40 percent of all professional and technical workers and over 40 percent of the labor force, it might seem that they have almost their fair share of the better jobs, but this is not so. Almost three-quarters of female professionals are nurses, other health workers, and teachers with relatively low income and prestige. The majority of male professionals are in high-status and high-paying positions such as doctors, lawyers, and engineers. Among sales workers, men sell expensive items like kitchen appliances and cars, on which they earn large commissions. Saleswomen, by contrast, are usually wage earners selling less expensive items over the counter.

> Even . . . where women outnumber men, for example, in library work . . . women are more commonly librarians than library administrators. In social work, they are case workers rather than supervisors; in education they are teachers rather than principals and instructors rather than associate or full professors. [Sassower, 1972:352–353]

Many female jobs are paid versions of the kinds of work women do as houseworkers: clothing manufacture, nursing, laundry, and other personal services. In the higher-status professions, women often specialize in work that fits female stereotypes. For example, female lawyers specialize in matrimonial law and female doctors in psychiatry and children's illnesses (Epstein, 1970:974; Nadelson and Notman, 1972:183). Surprisingly women doctors have not often specialized in the care of women.

Unequal pay

To compare the earned incomes of men and women, we must consider the number of hours and weeks worked. People who work only part time or only a few months a year cannot be lumped with full-time, year-round workers. These categories are important because only half of all employed females are employed full time, year round, compared with over two-thirds of all male workers. Therefore, Tables 7.1 and 7.2 are limited to men and women who work full time, year round. These tables show that whatever the type of work and whatever the educational background or experience of the worker, men are paid more than women. Even in public administration, where equal pay for equal work is official

Table 7.1   Median Income, by Occupation and Sex, United States, 1982[a]

Occupation group	Median income		Female income as % of male income (B ÷ A)
	Male col. A	Female col. B	
Administrators & managers	$28,820	$17,326	60
Professionals	$27,940	$18,423	66
Technical etc.	$22,260	$15,546	70
Sales	$21,901	$11,002	50
Clerical and kindred workers	$20,508	$12,693	62
Precision, production & craft	$20,913	$13,591	65
Machine operators etc.	$17,826	$10,876	61
Transportation	$18,508	$12,990	70
Laborers and helpers	$14,479	$11,369	80
Service workers, except private	$14,479	$ 8,831	61
All occupations	$21,077	$13,014	62

[a]Data were compiled in March 1983 for 1982 income and are for year-round full-time workers age 15 years and older.
Source: *CPR*, P-60, No. 140, July 1983: Table 7.

Table 7.2   Median Income by Education and Sex, United States, 1981[a]

| Years of school completed | Median income | | Female income as % of male income (B ÷ A) |
	Male col. A	Female col. B	
Less than 8	$12,386	$ 8,424	68
8	$16,376	$10,112	62
9 – 11	$17,496	$10,661	61
12	$21,344	$13,240	62
College, 1 – 3	$23,633	$15,594	66
College, 4	$28,030	$17,405	62
College, 5 or more	$32,325	$21,449	66
Total:	$22,857	$14,477	63

[a]Data are for full-time year-round workers age 25 and over.
Source: *CPR*, P-60, No. 140, July 1983: Table 7.

policy, the income of women is only two-thirds that of men (*CPR*, P-23, no. 58, April 1976:50).

Income, occupation, and education

Although on average men are paid more in every occupational group, the income gap is larger in some groups than in others. This is shown in Table 7.1. The income gap is smallest among professionals and technical workers and among transportation workers and laborers. In other words, women suffer less income inequality in jobs with high educational requirements and in jobs with few, if any, such requirements. The inequality is greatest among sales workers. Saleswomen are paid only half what salesmen earn, in part because of price differences in the things they sell.

With more education, both men and women earn more. However, men get a higher return on their educational investment. At every educational level, men are paid more than women with the same amount of schooling, as Table 7.2 shows. The number of years of school completed has surprisingly little effect on the difference between the median incomes of men and women. Female income as a percent of male income ranges from 68

percent for those with less than 8 years of school to 61 percent for those who attended but did not complete high school. Women must have four years of college before their median income reaches the level of men who did not complete high school. On average, a woman with postgraduate education earns less than a man who graduated from high school but never went to college.

Women often leave the labor force when they marry and have children. If they try to go back to work, as many do when their children start school, they find that their skills are rusty or perhaps obsolete because of technological changes such as the shift from typewriters to word processors. In addition, they must compete with young people just out of school. A woman who re-enters the labor force may well be faced with a choice between retraining herself or taking a lower-paying job. For the growing numbers in employment because of economic need, staying home is not an option. When they get a job they often go back to the bottom of the job ladder. They lose any seniority they had before leaving the labor force. Given these disadvantages, it is not surprising that women's wages are only a fraction of those received by men. However even women with uninterrupted careers are paid less than men.

Current trends

In the 1980s, fewer young women are leaving the labor force; more are returning to work; and they are returning sooner after giving birth than in former years.

The present status of women in the job market is the outcome of many factors: their childbearing and child rearing, the historical shift from agriculture and manufacturing to service industries, their weak political and legal status, and outright discrimination and segregation. Many of these factors are changing, but equality is not in sight.

One way to look at the problem is to ask how many women would have to change their jobs to make women's occupational picture match men's. The answer is not encouraging. Even in 1970,

> close to 70 percent of all women would have to change occupations in order for their proportion in each occupation to be the same as their proportion in the labor force as a whole. . . . At the turn of the century it may have been as high as 95 percent. . . . [A modest improvement] has occurred over the last 70 years, [but] it is clear that a great deal more change will be required if achievement is, in fact, to replace ascription. [Williams, 1979:86]

The myth of the male breadwinner

Although employed women have much lower average incomes than men, many women make major, often vital, contributions to family income (Laws, 1976:34–35). Employed wives' earnings contribute, on average, almost 30 percent of family income, and women in full-time employment supply about 40 percent of family income. Families living in poverty or close to the poverty line often depend on the wife's paycheck to make ends meet (Bell, 1976:241).

Several trends are increasing the number of women who bring in all or most of the family income. Separation and divorce rates are high; a larger percentage of women never marry; women are usually younger than their husbands and, on average, live longer than men. More than 40 percent of women are either single, divorced, widowed, or separated, and almost 70 percent of families with female heads have children under age 18 (*CPR*, P-23, no.

58, April 1976:17; Griffiths, 1976:9). Thus, an economic burden has shifted to those who are least able to carry it, namely, women with low earning power.

HOUSEWORK

Not too long ago, rural households produced most of the food, clothing, and other goods they needed. All family members contributed skills and labor; everyone worked. Adaptation 7.1 describes the work routines of rural women around the turn of the century.

The shift from an agricultural to an industrial economy moved work into new settings. At the same time, commercial production and mass marketing replaced home production of goods and services. As more people worked for wages in factories and shops, the meaning of work changed. Work came to be defined as paid employment, and housework was no longer thought of as real work because no money changed hands. Recently, however, there has been a reaction against this view of housework. Feminists do not take it for granted that only paid work is work. The slogan "Every mother is a working mother" demands that the value of housework be recognized, as it was in earlier times.

Housework is work

In the modern home, few material goods are produced. Much food is preprocessed, prepackaged, and precooked. The domestic jobs that remain are service activities like washing clothes and dishes and cleaning the house, that is, unskilled or semiskilled manual work. Housework is probably the most common form of manual labor, and houseworkers spend considerable amounts of time doing it. Indeed, for full-time houseworkers, the housework week was as long in the mid-1970s as it had been in the 1920s (Vanek, 1974; Oakley, 1974b; Robinson et al., 1972).

When households produced their own material goods, the production involved a lot of physical labor, but some of the work, such as spinning, weaving, and tool making and repair, was skilled. Both skilled work and heavy manual work have been removed from household routines. Craft skills such as carpentry, weaving, and dressmaking in the home survive as hobbies and do-it-yourself efforts rather than as essential functions. Nevertheless, some aspects of housework can be challenging and interesting. The houseworker who prepares attractive and nutritious meals on a tight budget is at once a bookkeeper, a comparative shopper, a dietician, and a chef.

Outside the industrial nations of the Americas and Western Europe, housework has not changed much since the nineteenth century. In some Eastern European countries, where most women are full-time members of the labor force, they also do the kinds of physically demanding housework that were characteristic of the last century in the Western world. A study of time use found that in Polish and Yugoslav cities, many households lacked running water and used wood or coal stoves and heaters. "Significant portions of time must be spent on work that amounts to 'hewing of wood and drawing of water' before other household chores can be undertaken" (Robinson et al., 1972:125).

In contrast to modern housework, much of the work of the preindustrial household was done in one room. The family relaxed and ate its meals in the room where the food was prepared and clothes were sewn (Oakley, 1974a:23–24). Thus, houseworkers were not long out of sight or out of mind. Housework was part of other household activities, and the houseworker was not isolated from the rest of the family.

Who does the housework?

All over the world, housework is women's work. Husbands do some household tasks, but a man is unlikely to be *responsible* for housework unless he lives alone and cannot afford a housekeeper. Husbands who have the skills do household repairs as well as some of the nonfood shopping, but wives, "whether employed or unemployed, shoulder almost all of the housework burden" (Robinson et al., 1972: 124).

On average, employed women spend 20 to 40 hours per week on housework, compared with 50 to 80 hours for full-time houseworkers. Employed men average only 3 to 4 hours per week doing housework. Both houseworkers and employed men spend less time doing housework on Sundays than on weekdays, but employed women do twice as much housework on their "days off" (Robinson et al., 1972:126).

Housewife and mother

Child care is generally the responsibility of the mother; when a father takes care of his child he is "babysitting," a job for adolescents. Men may help with a few tasks such as putting children to bed, but most fathers spend little time with their children, especially infants (Seiden, 1976:1112).

Many of the jobs of the housewife-mother are done at the same time. But some aspects of the two roles are not easily combined, and some women do not distinguish between housework and mothering. When they are asked whether they enjoy caring for their children, they talk about dressing the baby or washing bottles and diapers, not about interacting with the child. They find that the child's demands for care and attention interrupt their housework. Other women view housework as something that interferes with child care. These women believe mothering is more important, and often mention housework as the "worst thing" about being a housewife (Oakley, 1974b:43).

The cash value of housework

The economic value of a houseworker's services is painfully clear when a substitute must be hired or the work shared by the rest of the family. Estimates of the money value of women's unpaid work range from 10 to over 20 percent of the gross national product (GNP) of the United States and Canada. However, housework is not considered productive and therefore is not included in the GNP (Canadian Royal Commission, 1970:32). The economic value of housework is not taken into account in most income insurance, welfare benefits, and retirement plans.

The dependent housewife

Although the housewife "is just as much a producer of goods and services as the paid worker," unlike a paid worker she is economically dependent (Canadian Royal Commission, 1970:38). By doing housework and caring for children, she frees her husband to devote himself to his job, but her contributions to his earning power are not recognized even if she gives dinner parties for his business associates or types his reports. A wife has no direct legal claim on her husband's income other than his obligation to provide his family with food, clothing, and shelter. As long as the basic needs of the family are met, he does not have to give his wife or children any money. "There is no legal action that a wife can bring to require the husband to provide adequate support for herself and the children unless she is willing to leave him and set up a separate household" (Weitzman et al., 1978:308). Some laws make the wife less dependent, especially in "community property" states, in which property is owned jointly by the husband and the wife. In such states, a wife's share in the family homestead cannot be willed away by her husband or sold without her permission.

Few couples are aware of the "hidden clauses" in the marriage contract, and presumably the legal weakness of the wife does not affect the way most couples arrange their financial affairs. In some households, the wife gets a housekeeping allowance; in others, the husband gives his pay to his wife and she manages the money. In middle-class families, all income is usually deposited in a joint bank account to be drawn upon by either partner. Some wives are unhappy about not having any money to call their own, but this symbolic lack should not be confused with a husband's refusal to give his wife money. As far as is known, income is shared in the majority of households, although the wife's employment status may affect how equitably it is shared (Edwards, 1981).

The effects of dependency

The financial dependency of a housewife may reduce her security and that of her family if her husband is disabled or if she is deserted or divorced. When a woman is pushed into the labor force under such conditions, her chances of earning enough to support herself and her family are not very good, and the longer she is out of the labor force, the harder it is for her to become financially independent. A long interruption in a woman's career reduces her chances of getting a job and lowers her income if she finds one. Her years as a full-time housewife decrease her skills and bargaining power in the labor market, and her salary is almost sure to be lower than salaries of continuously employed workers of similar age.

A housewife's dependency may actually be increased by divorce, although alimony is awarded in less than 10 percent of divorces. Even when it is awarded, it may be hard to collect (ABA, 1965, cited in Steinem, 1973:38–39). In addition, if a marriage ends before the husband retires, the divorcee usually loses any share of his retirement income, to which she contributed indirectly by doing housework and sustaining him socially and emotionally during his career.

To reduce such dependency, the Canadian Royal Commission on the Status of Women recommended that houseworkers participate in the Canadian Pension Plan. The spouse who stays home would receive credit for "a portion of the contributions of the employed spouse and those contributions made by the employer on the employed spouse's behalf" (1970:40). This particular proposal has not been implemented but the idea is gaining recognition.

(Text continued on p. 145)

Adaptation 7.1

Smuts/Farm Women in the Nineteenth Century

Nearly half of all American women still lived on farms in 1890. Like farm women throughout history, they rose before the sun and spent their days as active partners in the family's common work. Just what they did depended on the kind of farm, its income, what other members of the family were able to do, the customs of the locality, and many other circumstances.

The work of one farm woman in Western Kansas during the last quarter of the century is described in the biography of a German immigrant (Ise, 1940). In the early years, when her home was a dugout with roof and front wall made of squares of prairie sod, she worked side by side with her husband, planting, harvesting, building, fighting grasshoppers and prairie fires, doing as much of whatever needed to be done as her great vitality permitted. Later, as more settlers moved in, as the farm prospered in good years, and as her sons grew older, the heavy field work was taken over by men—neighbors who helped in exchange for help in their own fields, hired hands, and finally her own sons. But this did not make the woman's work much easier, for the presence of male field workers brought a great increase in the work of processing and cooking food, making clothing, and keeping house.

Other farm tasks remained in her hands. These included the entire care of the kitchen garden and much of the work of caring for cattle, pigs, and poultry—herding cows to pasture and back, hauling well water for animals as well as for kitchen and laundry, feeding pigs, hens, and calves, milking and churning and doctoring. Most of what she needed for housekeeping she had to provide herself. She made brooms, mattresses, and floor mats from

straw and corn husks; soap, from lye and tallow; lye, from stove ashes. Lye was indispensable for softening water and hulling corn, as well as for soapmaking. She made almost all the clothing for a family that eventually included eleven children, at first by hand, later, most of the time, with a sewing machine.

The family's food supply depended largely on her efforts. Vegetables, fruits, berries, and melons she grew or gathered in spring and summer and preserved in fall for winter use. The butter she churned and the eggs she gathered served not only as food for the family but as currency to trade for cloth and the few foods and other necessities the farm did not produce. Instead of sugar, the family used molasses, which she made by pressing sorghum cane with her husband's help and boiling the juice. Vinegar, essential for pickling, was the product of molasses, rainwater, and yeast. For coffee she made a brew of browned rye grain.

On the rare occasions when members of the family went to town, or took longer trips to visit relatives, food and overnight lodging were always obtained without payment at houses en route. But this too was a charge on the labor of the wife, for she was expected to do as much for all who passed. Likewise, when the burden of sickness required more nursing than one family could provide, all of the women in the area were on call, and the calls were frequent.

She worked for money too. Aside from her contribution to the main cash crops of the farm, she brought in money by doing laundry for bachelors and widowers, by running the community's post office from her kitchen, by selling butter and eggs. As they grew older, her daughters helped in all of these tasks and then turned to school-teaching to add to the family's cash resources.

On a typical Kansas farm, in short, the work of

Source: Robert W. Smuts, *Women and Work in America* (New York: Schocken, 1959/1971). Abridged from pp. 6–12 by permission of Cambridge University Press and Schocken Books.

women provided almost all that was necessary for keeping house and for feeding, clothing, and otherwise sustaining the family. This meant that the income from the cash crops could be used to develop the farm, purchase machinery, improve stock, replace dugouts and sod huts with frame houses and outbuildings, put up fences, and still keep up with mortgage payments in years of drought, grasshoppers, or low prices. Without this division of work, few farmers could have survived the years of learning to cope with the unfamiliar soil and climate of the West.

Women's work often provided not only the necessities of the household but much of the cash for developing the farm as well. Willa Cather pointed out that the first prosperous, mortgage-free farms in Nebraska were owned by immigrant families whose daughters were not too proud to work as domestics in the nearest town, or even as paid hands on neighboring farms. "The girls I knew were always helping to pay for ploughs and reapers, brood-sows, or steers to fatten" (Cather, 1926:199–200).

Over much of the rural South, still impoverished a quarter-century after the Civil War, conditions were at least as primitive as in the West. On the frontier, women worked in the fields only during the first crucial years of establishing a farm, but on the poorer farms of the South both white and black women often performed heavy field work throughout their lives. As in the West, daughters could add to the family's cash income by teaching, but the mores of the South usually proscribed domestic employment for white women. For the daughters of the poor white farmers, the cotton mills, then springing up in the southern countryside, offered the main chance to earn money. Black women, both single and married, worked for pay as farm hands or as domestic servants. There were 2.7 million black girls and women over 10 years of age in 1890, the great majority of them in the rural South. At least 1 million of them were working, half in agriculture, half in domestic service.

Most farm women worked hard as part of a family enterprise, but a large group, perhaps a quarter of a million, ran farms on their own. The great majority were widows; some were married to men no longer able to work; and there were even a few thousand resolute never-married women among them.

LIFE IN THE CITY

When a family moved to the city, the man found a world of work unlike any he had known before. But the women continued to work in and around the home, and to do many of the same things she had done on the farm. There is no way of calculating how much of the goods and services enjoyed by urban families was provided by the labors of women about the home, but there is no doubt that it was a substantial part of the total.

Except in the crowded tenement districts of the large cities—which housed a small fraction of the total urban population—town and city dwellers often produced some of their own food. Especially in the coal and steel regions, the grounds around the urban and suburban house sometimes looked much like a rural farmyard. Many families kept chickens or rabbits, sometimes pigs or goats, and even a cow or two, and raised vegetables and fruits in their own garden plots.

Though only a few miles from the center of the greatest metropolis in the land, Queens County and much of Brooklyn were still semi-rural in 1890, and many families were as dependent on small-scale agriculture as on the industrial or commercial employment of the men of the family. North of what is now the midtown area, Manhattan itself was more bucolic than urban, and pigs and goats were often seen along the East River as far south as Forty-second Street (Schlesinger, 1933:84). At a time when men worked ten or twelve hours a day, six days a week, much of the care of urban livestock and gardens inevitably fell to women—quite apart from the fact that such tasks were theirs by tradition.

Chapter 7 **Summary**

Section 1/**The life course**

Ascribed statuses based on age and sex originate in biological characteristics but are not biologically determined. Age differs from other ascribed statuses because it changes throughout the life course, which includes a series of transitions that involve role gains and role losses. In modern societies, most role gains occur in childhood, youth, and young adulthood, while most role losses occur after mid-life.

Section 2/**Childhood and youth**

The duration of childhood has varied from one historical period to another. In Europe before 1700, children were treated as little adults, and many worked at adult tasks—a situation that still exists in some parts of the world.

Modern adolescence differs from traditional youth in that it begins later and ends earlier. Two innovations that led to the transformation of traditional youth were universal compulsory education and the regulation of child labor.

The school and the age-specific peer group have been criticized for not adequately preparing young people for adulthood. Among the reforms suggested are (1) providing for more self-motivated and varied activities in schools, (2) alternating school and work, (3) adding education to the organization of work, (4) supporting youth communities and organizations, (5) setting new age limits on employment, (6) experimenting with a voucher system for higher education, and (7) supporting programs that involve youth in public service.

Section 3/**Adulthood and old age**

The hallmarks of adulthood are independence and responsibility for oneself. For most people, adult life is shaped by the concerns of employment and family. Today many couples live beyond the childbearing and childrearing years and are faced with adjusting to an "empty nest."

People reach their highest levels of social competence, job security, and job satisfaction between the mid-thirties and the mid-fifties. Changes in relationships with their growing children and aging parents mark adulthood with a series of changes that may amount to a midlife crisis.

The most important difference between the "young old" and the "old old" is health, but only a minority are too handicapped to carry on their major activities. Retired people are more likely to think of themselves as old than are those of the same age who still work.

Widowhood has three main problems: grief, economic problems, and loneliness. Because the process of dying has been removed from everyday experience, there is little socialization for death. Older adults fear death more than members of societies in which people gradually grow familiar with death.

Section 4/**Gender identity and gender roles**

Biological differences between males and females are termed sex differences. Social and psychological traits make up gender, that is, masculinity and femininity. Early in life persons acquire gender identities based on stereotypes, which may have little or no basis in biological fact.

Section 5/**The sexual division of labor**

Most unpaid work is performed by women, but women are also active participants in the labor force. Over 50 percent of American women are now in the labor force, often in lower-paying, lower-status jobs than men. Even when only full-time, year-round workers are compared, women are paid less than men for the same work. At every educational level, men are paid more than women with the same amount of schooling. The shift from an agricultural to an industrial economy resulted in a change in attitudes, and housework was no longer thought of as work. However, estimates of the money value of women's unpaid work range from 10 to over 20 percent of GNP.

Suggested Readings

Age

Ariès, Philippe
1962 *Centuries of Childhood.* New York: Knopf.

Binstock, Robert H. and Ethel Shanas
1976 *The Handbook of Aging and the Social Sciences.* New York: Van Nostrand Reinhold.

de Mause, Lloyd (ed.)
1974 *The History of Childhood.* New York: Psychohistory Press.

Foner, Anne
1976 *Age in Society.* Contemporary Social Science Issues: Vol. 30. Beverly Hills, CA: Sage.

Haraven, Tamaro K.
1978 *Transitions: The Family and the Life Course in Historical Perspective.* New York: Academic Press.

Hess, Beth B. (ed.)
1980 *Growing Old in America.* Second edition. New Brunswick, N.J.: Transaction Books.

Levinson, Daniel J., et al.
1978 *Transitions: The Seasons of a Man's Life.* New York: Random House.

Riley, Matilda (ed.)
1979 *Aging From Birth to Death.* Boulder, Colorado: Westview Press.

Rosow, Irving
1974 *Socialization to Old Age.* Berkeley and Los Angeles: University of California Press.

U.S. Bureau of the Census
1982 *Characteristics of American Children and Youth: 1980.* Washington, D.C. CPR, P-23, No. 114.

Gender

Atkinson, Dorothy, Alexander Dallin, and Gail W. Lapidus (eds.)
1977 *Women in Russia.* Stanford: Stanford University Press.

Bernard, Jesse S.
1981 *The Female World.* New York: Free Press.

Oakley, Ann
1972 *Sex, Gender, and Society.* London: Maurice Temple Smith, Ltd.

Pilling, Doria and Mia K. Pringle
1978 *Controversial Issues in Child Development.* New York: Schocken Books. (Annotated bibliography.)

Teitelbaum, Michael S. (ed.)
1976 *Sex Differences: Social and Biological Perspectives.* Garden City, N.Y.: Anchor Books.

U.S. Bureau of the Census
1980 *A Statistical Portrait of Women in the United States: 1978.* Washington, D.C. CPR, P-23, No. 100.

Chapter 8

Section One
The Making of Minorities

Minority groups have existed all over the world for many centuries, but the expansion of European society is responsible for the existence of most present-day minorities. For more than four centuries, the European powers changed the map of the world through exploration, conquest, and massive migration. Whether they acted as colonial rulers or as settlers pushing aside native peoples, they created minorities.

This chapter analyzes minority groups in the United States and internationally. The first section introduces the influence of European colonialism, slavery, and labor markets on the creation of minorities. Section Two, which is also comparative, takes up the social definition of minorities in North America and Japan. Sections Three and Four concentrate on race relations and ethnic stratification in the United States. Section Five returns to an international comparative perspective, contrasts homogeneous and plural societies, and explores the ethnic situations in Canada, South Africa, and the USSR.

COLONIALISM

The period of European expansion set in motion the longest and most intense contacts between different peoples that the world has seen. When it was over, hardly anyone on the face of the earth escaped being affected in some way. Even the most isolated nomads had been exposed to the people or products of the West.

At the height of colonialism, the entire Western Hemisphere, Africa, Oceania, and much of Asia were carved up into European colonies or spheres of influence. Societies were established in which the dominance of one group by another was the basis of the social order.

By European standards, North America, the Pacific islands, Australia, and Cape Colony in South Africa were thinly settled with native peoples whose weapons were ineffective. Although all conquered peoples were treated badly, the most competent fighters were treated somewhat better than the rest. The Maoris of New Zealand and some native Africans, Americans, and Canadians were formidable foes. In New Zealand, Canada, and the United States, treaties were made with native "nations" that had legitimate governments and were recognized as occupying their land. Although American Indian and African farmers were seen as true owners of their land, they were paid only token amounts when they were forced off their property. In the eyes of Europeans, nomadic bands like the Australian Aborigines did not occupy their land. They were looked upon as a nuisance to be pushed out and often killed off.

European conquerors were on the whole ignorant of other cultures, disdained weaker peoples, and subjugated them by force. Given the greed, religious zeal, and self-confidence of the conquerors, it could not have been otherwise. The conquerors sometimes paid lip service to the law—European law—for the sake of keeping the record straight. But crimes by whites against natives were excused because the victims were not "civilized." Since natives were not Christians, they could not take oaths, and since they could not take oaths, they could not testify in court. Therefore, crimes by whites seldom came to trial unless they were observed by other whites who were willing to testify.

Although colonial governments often had good intentions toward native peoples, colonial administration was not easy. The colonizers were thousands of miles and months or years away from the restraining influence of the home government. The few explorers, traders, and settlers had to be brave and self-reliant—traits that tended to go along with brutality—and when their survival or the success of a mission hung in the balance, they were likely to view the natives as expendable.

Colonial mastery

The subordination of native peoples to their conquerors varied from time to time and from place to place, but the terms on which the Indians had to submit to the Spaniards are a good example of what went on almost everywhere for centuries.

> Columbus remarked of the Lucayans [the inhabitants of San Salvador]: "These people are very unskilled in arms . . . with fifty men they could all be subjected and made to do all that one wished." He and his

compatriots tricked and cheated the Indians at every turn. Before entering a new area, Spanish generals customarily read a *Requerimiento* (requirement) to the inhabitants. This long-winded document recited the history of mankind from the Creation to the division of the non-Christian world by Pope Alexander VI and then called upon the Indians to recognize the sovereignty of the reigning Spanish monarch. ("If you do so . . . we shall receive you in all love and charity.") If this demand was rejected, "we shall powerfully enter into your country, and . . . shall take you, your wives, and your children, and shall make slaves of them. . . . The death and losses which shall accrue from this are your fault." This arrogant harangue was read in *Spanish* and often out of earshot of the Indians. When they responded by fighting, the Spaniards decimated them, drove them from their lands, and held the broken survivors in contempt. As a priest among them said, the *conquistadores* behaved "like the most cruel Tygres, Wolves, and Lions, enrag'd with a sharp and tedious hunger." [Garraty, 1971:21]

Three centuries later, more legal niceties were observed. However, the later treaties were just as one-sided.

> The British Government acquired territory throughout Africa by hundreds of treaties with African chiefs. Indeed, at one time the Foreign Office provided printed treaty forms for the use of officials and explorers, . . . [but] all the treaties were in reality valueless. [Marquard, 1969:12]

Different ideas of what was meant by a contract or treaty led to confusion and more conflict. The Europeans thought they had bought the land. The natives often had no idea that land could be bought or sold; they thought they had let the Europeans use it. In North America, treaties giving Indian tribes control over part of their territory "forever" were soon overturned by later treaties. The experience of the Cherokees, the great tribe of the southern Appalachians, is a case in point. Between 1721 and 1783, ten treaties involving land cessions were made between Cherokee towns and southern colonies or states. Between 1785 and 1837, 12 treaties were concluded with the United States, and the Cherokees lost almost all of their holdings east of the Mississippi (Royce, 1887:131, 378). In some cases, contrary to Indian

custom, land was distributed among members of the tribes as personal holdings. This property was soon bought by whites.

In the United States, the conflict over ownership has not ended. Indian tribes are successfully challenging the government in the courts. Claims that amounts paid were too small, that force was used, or that legal procedures were not followed have enabled Indian tribes to receive some compensation for land that was taken generations earlier.

A similar sequence is occurring in Brazil. The rapidly growing Brazilian economy is exploiting the Amazon rain forests for timber and cattle. As a result, the small-scale tribal cultures are coming into collision with the agents of Brazilian economic expansion. The destruction of their environment is going on so fast that few tribal groups will survive long. At the beginning of this century, there were 1 million Brazilian Indians. Now there are fewer than 200,000 with weak control over their tribal lands.

SLAVERY

In Africa the only major European settlements south of the Sahara were in South Africa. Other parts of Africa were already densely occupied, and the Europeans wanted to exploit native labor rather than displace it. Africa was valued for its products, which were sold in the world market, and for a long time its most important product was slaves.

The slave trade from Africa to the New World extended over four centuries, ending in the late nineteenth century. It involved the transportation and suffering of perhaps 20 million persons as well as untold millions of deaths. All of the European nations took part in slavery and the slave trade in some way, but their practices varied. Differences in history, law, religion, and economic conditions led to at least three distinct slave systems. The British, Americans, Dutch, and Danes began with no slave tradition, no laws about slaves, and little religious concern for them. The Spanish and Portuguese system was based on prior experience with slavery, laws governing relations between slave and master, and recognition of the spiritual needs of the slave. The French system lacked a slave tradition and slave laws, but it shared the Catholic principles of the Spanish and Portuguese system.

Wherever it existed, the slave trade was extensive, profitable, and cruel. Human beings were treated as cargo, and slave traders at every stage of the transportation network developed callous attitudes toward human suffering.

Where slavery was practiced, it became the dominant social institution; in fact, it created slave societies. The slave society included blacks and whites, the law and the family, the labor system—the entire culture. Nothing escaped its influence, but there were some differences. In general, slavery was more severe in the northern nations and less so among the Spaniards and Portuguese. The Dutch were probably the most severe slave owners, the Portuguese the least. Three factors determined the severity of slavery: (1) attitudes and laws on manumission (granting freedom to slaves), (2) the religious definition of slaves, and (3) the social acceptance of freed slaves.

In Brazil, the law permitted manumission and the church encouraged it. The church regarded slave and master as equal in the sight of God. Slaves could compel their masters to free them by paying the original purchase price, in some cases in installments. Slaves who served in the armed forces were freed. A slave could marry a free woman, and the children of such a marriage would be free because the child's status followed that of the mother. For a small payment, a slave child could be freed at baptism. Slaves were freed on happy family occasions, and masters' wills often provided for manumission.

As a result of these policies, the number of freed slaves and their descendants became quite large in Brazil. As skilled and unskilled workers they were viewed as essential to the urban economy. When slavery was abolished—peacefully—in 1888, there were three times as many free blacks as slaves, and the former slaves quickly merged into the free community.

There were many more obstacles to freedom in the British colonies and the United States, where slaves were property. In the British West Indies, the Church of England did not consider slaves as baptizable

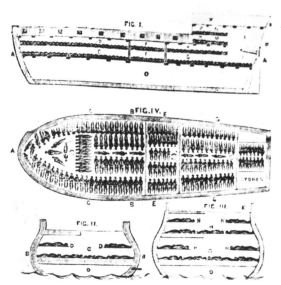

Human cargo in an eighteenth-century slave trader out of Liverpool, England.
These drawings were used in the antislavery movement.

human beings. In the United States, there was little opposition to teaching Christian doctrine to slaves, but blacks could not be preachers and literacy for blacks was opposed. The marriages of slaves often were not solemnized, and in any case, husband and wife or parents and children, could be separated in payment of their master's debts or simply as a business transaction.

An owner who wished to free a slave was taxed, and slaves could not buy their own freedom. In many states a freed slave was required to leave and never return. In Tennessee the master had to post a bond and secure the consent of the court before a slave could be freed. In Mississippi the master had to persuade the general assembly that the slave had done a worthy deed. Unlike the case in Brazil, children could not be freed at baptism and a slave could not buy a child's freedom. A master who freed a slave gave up the powers of a slave owner, but manumission did not give the freed slave all the rights of a freeborn person. Consequently, the population of free blacks was small and was unprepared to help the former slaves after emancipation.*

THE PLANTATION

Plantations were established to solve basic economic problems and exploit economic opportunities. Most slaves were plantation laborers, but plantations also existed in places where slavery was not practiced.

There were three main factors in the exploitation of undeveloped regions: ample land, labor, and demand for staple crops on the world market. It did not matter much whether the land was in Asia, Africa, or the Americas, or whether the crop was sugar, tobacco, cotton, or rubber; similar economic problems led to similar interracial situations. With land so easily available, free workers could not be kept on the plantations, and planters had to find a supply of field laborers they could control. Slavery was one obvious solution (Nieboer, 1900). Other forms of forced labor were convicts and workers brought in under contract for a fixed period, often seven years.

During the nineteenth century, when the developers of the Hawaiian plantations found that the Polynesian islanders could not and would not fill the demand for workers in the expanding agricultural economy, they imported contract laborers from Asia. Asian immigrants included 45,000 Chinese who arrived in the last quarter of the nineteenth century, 140,000 Japanese who entered between 1890 and 1919, and 125,000 Filipinos between 1909 and 1934.

None of these workers was willing to remain on the plantations any longer than they had to. As soon as their contracts ran out—sometimes sooner—each immigrant group left plantation work for better jobs. The job vacancies on the plantations were filled by still newer immigrants (Lind, 1938). The

*Modern research on slavery in the New World was stimulated by Tannenbaum's *Slave and Citizen* (1947). Later research has blunted Tannenbaum's contrasts between Anglo America and Latin America (see, for example, Davis, 1966; Foner and Genovese, 1969: esp. bibliography, 262–68; Genovese, 1972). But regardless of how slavery and the slave trade are interpreted, they are essential parts of the study of race relations.

racial and ethnic composition of present-day Hawaii is thus partly a result of opportunities to produce crops for the world market and recurring labor shortages on the plantations.

MIGRATION

Any large population movement, whether forced or voluntary, brings peoples with different backgrounds into contact and creates minorities. The phrase "a nation of immigrants" is a fairly accurate description of the United States only if the descendants of slaves are counted as immigrants.

Refugees from Southeast Asia driven by political turmoil in Indochina are becoming minorities in many countries. Cuba has forced some of its citizens out of their country as an act of national policy and international politics. Migration from many countries of people seeking to better themselves economically has been going on for centuries. When migration is sudden and involves large numbers of people or when it seems to be disorderly, especially during economically troubled times, the problems are seen as minorities problems.

Minorities are "created" when at least two conditions exist: first, people with different backgrounds are brought into contact, and, second, one group is able to dominate the other. Colonialism, slavery, and the plantations are historical situations in which minorities were created (Thompson, 1958:506–7). Mass migration continues to bring diverse peoples into dominant and subordinate relations, and thus to create racial and ethnic minorities in many parts of the world.

The dominant/subordinate relationship may be far less threatening than slavery, political control, or forced migration. Minority problems can also arise when people feel they are not in command of their own cultural destiny, for instance when they fear for the survival of their ancestral language. Countries with relatively few ethnic tensions and cultural minorities that are not politically or economically repressed are finding that the identity of quite small ethnic groups must be taken into account: The language movements in Wales and Brittany are examples.

Section Two
Awareness and Antagonism

MINORITIES ARE SOCIALLY DEFINED

Minority group is commonly used to identify a racial or ethnic population, but it is an imprecise term. In the United States, Indians, Africans, and European immigrants from many different countries are called minorities, although in some places they make up a majority of the population. In South Africa, the dominant European population is less than one-fourth the size of the black African "minority." **Minority,** thus, refers to a separate identity and often a condition of subordination, not necessarily a smaller number.

The definition of race

Race and ethnicity are often used interchangeably, but they are not the same. **Race** refers to differences based on biologically inherited traits such as skin color. **Ethnic group** refers to differences in social characteristics such as language, religion, birthplace, and culture.

Physical appearance and the genetics of race are less important than how race is interpreted and socially evaluated. People can be "color blind," but they can also see racial differences where none exist.

The absence of visible racial differences does not prevent one group from defining another as a different race. For example, French Canadians and Anglo Canadians were once called races. In traditional Asia, outcaste groups are erroneously thought to have different racial origins from those of the dominant population. (See Adaptation 8.1.) Throughout the history of the United States, European immigrants from one country after another were called races and were considered inferior to earlier settlers. At differing rates they learned the language and adopted the culture of their new country—they became more or less **assimilated.** As the children or grandchildren of those immigrants were fully assimilated into American society, they were redefined as "white"—which is what they always were.

Prejudice and stereotypes

Racial prejudice is based on oversimplified beliefs called **stereotypes.** A person who holds a stereotype accepts a few characteristics as a full description of all members of a minority, even though the group may be composed of millions of people with a wide variety of characteristics. Stereotypes are sometimes favorable, especially when applied to one's own group, but most outgroup stereotypes are negative. Even positive traits can be given negative weight: The Jew is shrewd, the Yankee provident; the Jew is stingy, but the Calvinist frugal (Merton, 1948/1968:-482–84).

THE VOCABULARY OF RACE

Every group has its own vocabulary for members of outgroups, and the terms used are often stereotypes. Understandably, minorities object to such terms. For example, some Italian Americans insist that the word *Mafia* should not be used in the mass media because it links a criminal organization with persons of Italian background. And, as the name implies, the Anti-Defamation League of B'nai B'rith works to counter prejudice and discrimination against Jews and other minorities.

Minorities have begun to be clear about what they want to be called, although the terms they prefer often change. Increasing self-confidence leads them to choose terms that reject stereotypes and convey a sense of pride and political activism. Examples are *black, Chicano,* and *Québecois* (or Quebecer). *Québecois* points to the geographic base of the French Canadians and their hopes for self-determination. *Chicano* is a symbol of political assertiveness for Americans of Mexican origin who reject their subordinate status. The change from *Negro* to *black* is another example of growing racial identity.

Negro into black

Before World War II, Robert E. Park observed that

> Negroes . . . are more and more disposed to reject any terms or any racial distinctions that reflect and tend to preserve the memories of an earlier inferior status.

There is, finally, one small but significant change in the ritual of race relations that, it seems to me, needs to be specially noted. The great majority of Negroes now, after a good deal of discussion and differences of opinion, have adopted the term "Negro" as a racial designation in preference to another and more logical but less familiar expression like "Afro-American." Having adopted it, however, they spell it with a capital N. [Park, 1937:xxiv]

Thirty years later, however, the word *Negro,* which derives from the Spanish word for black, became unacceptable to many blacks. No doubt *black* was adopted more quickly because of its use by the mass media. However, the thrust toward rapid change was the growing self-awareness and self-confidence of blacks. *Black* is emphatic and simple. It does not carry the historical connotations of inferiority that are attached to "Negro" or its corruption, "nigger." *Black* implies greater separation between the races, at least for the time being, but it also implies a sense of identity and self-pride.

Thus, the terms used by minorities to refer to themselves both signal and contribute to social change. In half a century, the term *Negro* changed from polite to general to unacceptable usage. As an American sociologist put it, "I was born colored, I grew up Negro, I became black, and now I am Third World."

(Text continued on p. 155)

Adaptation 8.1

Donoghue/Racism in Japan

In Tibet, Korea, and Japan, outcaste populations are called races even when the members of such minorities cannot be identified by their physical traits. In cultural terms also, they are similar to the majority in all ways except those connected with their outcaste status. However, the popular belief is "that the outcastes are so different from oneself that they must *be a different race" (Passin, 1955:40). These beliefs are surprisingly similar to the beliefs about racial minorities found in Western countries.*

The Japanese outcastes, who account for only 2 percent of the population, are biologically the same as other Japanese but are assumed to be a separate race (Price, 1966:6–33). The Japanese word Eta *means "outcaste" and is an insult.* Buraku *refers to places where Eta live. Therefore, the word* Burakumin, *"the people of the Buraku," is commonly used to identify the outcaste group.*

A great deal of misunderstanding concerning the Eta exists in Toyoda.* Most citizens prefer to avoid the subject of the Burakumin even in conversation. Few city residents have ever been to the outcaste district, and most have never knowingly met an outcaste. Buraku dwellers do not affect the lives of the Toyoda people and do not constitute a recognized social problem. This lack of concern, however, in no way diminishes the attitudes of prejudice and hostility; rather, it propagates ignorance, obscurity, and even mystery. Four of the most general attitudes held by Toyoda informants toward the pariah caste are offered below.

Source: John Donoghue, "An Eta Community in Japan: The Social Persistence of Outcaste Groups," *American Anthropologist.* Reproduced by permission of the American Anthropological Association from *American Anthropologist* 59(6):1000–1017, 1957. Not for further reproduction.

*Toyoda is a fictional name chosen to protect the privacy of persons in the real community.

IGNORANCE AND PREJUDICE

Disgust is the most widely held and commonly verbalized attitude. Individuals who are unwilling even to discuss the outcastes distort their faces and exclaim, *kitanai* (dirty). These feelings are sometimes manifested more directly. For example, after one of the customers in a small wine shop noticed blood on the hands and shirt-sleeves of a young outcaste, he shouted disparagingly at him and was joined by several others: "You are dirty, you animal killer! Look at the blood all over you! You are a filthy *yaban* [barbarian, savage]!"

Fear is another common attitude of the Toyoda people. Outcastes are considered dangerous and capable of inflicting bodily harm. There are exaggerated stories of their physical prowess and fighting skill, and they are likened to the gangsters and hoodlums portrayed in American films. There is also the fear that surrounds the unknown. Burakumin are believed by some to be sinister characters with evil powers, and mothers sometimes frighten their children with gruesome tales of the Eta bogeyman. It is said, too, that the outcastes are afflicted with such contagious diseases as syphilis, gonorrhea, tuberculosis, and leprosy.

Because the Burakumin and their village are forbidden, the attitude of *erotic curiosity* prompts such questions as: Do the Eta look different? Are the women really beautiful? Are they rough, like gangsters? Do they actually speak a different language? What kind of food do they eat? Many wonder if Buraku girls are "better" than ordinary women; some young males have erotic desires for outcaste women; and restaurant hostesses often joke about an imputed enlargement or distortion of the genitals of the male Eta.

The spread of the final attitude, which might be termed *objectivity*, seems to be increasing steadily among the younger generation, but it has the fewest adherents in Toyoda. This attitude is not widespread because it depends primarily on observation. "Look at the Eta and their houses—they are dirty, they have dirty occupations, and they are diseased." "The Eta always marry each other, so their strain is weak. They are an exclusive, intimate group that rejects outsiders and any form of aid." "I feel sorry for the Eta because of their lowly position, but I will have nothing to do with them until they learn to live like other Japanese, that is, give up their occupations, marry outside their small community, clean up their villages, homes, and themselves, and drop their hostile clannish attitudes." Such beliefs are based less on legend than others but, as with race relations in the United States, they operate as a self-fulfilling prophecy in maintaining the outcaste status.

MYTHS AND MORES

The beliefs and myths of the Toyoda citizenry preserve majority group exclusiveness by associating the Burakumin with violations of some of the most fundamental and sacred Japanese values—those centering on purity, lineage, and health. The following are two of many popular legends heard in the city.

A young man met a beautiful girl in a restaurant. After a short courtship they were married, against the wishes of the boy's parents. They lived happily for a while, but when their children were born idiots with spotted complexions, it was discovered that the girl was a Burakumin.

This is probably the most widespread myth, as it is employed by parents to discourage children from affairs that might result in a love marriage. Even the most informed Japanese balk at the thought of marriage to an outcaste because of the popular notion of their weak strain from long inbreeding.

It was customary prior to the turn of the century for Burakumin to wash the bodies of deceased commoners in return for an offering of *sake*, but after the outcastes began to realize their emancipation, they frequently requested money for their services. Sometimes the demands were exorbitant. When the sum was refused, the Burakumin would threaten the family by vowing to drink the water used in bathing the body. The people were usually frightened into accepting the Burakumin demands.

The legend illustrates the supposed barbaric quality of the Burakumin; not only were they mercenary, but they profaned the sacred, defiled the dead, and imbibed the impure and dirty.

Section Three
Accommodation and Protest

Slavery was the most important influence on American race relations. It created the largest minority and built a pattern of domination into American life. Long before the days of organized militant protest, blacks with outstanding personal qualities spoke against oppression and made an impact on American society. Two such individuals, both of whom were born into slavery, were Sojourner Truth (1790–1883) (see Adaptation 8.2) and Frederick Douglass (1817–1895) (see Douglass, 1960; Foner, 1950–1955). But most slaves struggled simply to protect themselves and their families from abuse and to live out their lives in a semblance of peace.

LIVING WITH JIM CROW

When federal troops were withdrawn from the South in 1877, the status of the freed slaves fell rapidly. The race relations that developed at this time were in some ways as harsh and oppressive as slavery itself. Blacks were isolated and dominated, first by informal rules and then by local and state laws. Segregation and discrimination regulated contacts between blacks and whites and controlled the lives of blacks from the cradle to the grave.

Jim Crow was a new style of repression that differed from slavery in important ways (Doyle, 1937; Woodward, 1966).

> The Jim Crow laws put the authority of the state or city in the voice of the street-car conductor, the railway brakeman, the bus driver, the theater usher, and also into the voice of the hoodlum of the public parks and playgrounds. They gave free rein and the majesty of the law to mass aggressions that might otherwise have been curbed, blunted or deflected.
>
> The Jim Crow laws, unlike feudal laws, did not assign the subordinate group a fixed status in society. They were constantly pushing the Negro farther down. [Woodward, 1966:107–8]

Because whites could legally control the actions of blacks in some situations, white bullies were encouraged and "nigger baiting" was a safe game. Daily life became less and less secure for blacks, who "put on" a style of etiquette that burlesqued true courtesy. Exaggerated subservience and pretended ignorance thinly covered resentment. For example,

> A Negro who lived in Atlanta, where Negroes board streetcars at the rear, went to Birmingham, where Negroes board streetcars at the front. Hence, on one occasion, when he stopped a streetcar, he got on at the wrong end. He said, however, that he apologized to the conductor by saying that he thought the car was going the other way. [Doyle, 1937:235]

So many laws governing blacks were passed by so many legislative bodies that confusion was a part of everyday life. Black travelers were especially vulnerable because customs and laws varied so much from one place to another. Even within the same city, the rules might be inconsistent:

> At the Union Station in Atlanta, Negroes may leave the waiting room provided for them and patronize the newsstand and lunch counter in the white waiting room. At the Terminal Station in the same city, they cannot enter the white waiting room for any purpose. [Johnson, 1943:46]

Public transportation has always been a focal point in the struggle against discrimination. Around the end of the nineteenth century, there was a flood of laws segregating railways and, later, streetcars. In 1906, Montgomery became the first city in the United States to require separate streetcars for the two races. In 1955 and 1956, it was the scene of the bus boycott that gave impetus to the movement led by Martin Luther King, Jr.

Even in the worst days of Jim Crow, it would not have been accurate to sum up race relations as domination on one side and submission on the other. Most whites did not abuse blacks, nor did they favor abuse, but not many openly challenged those who did. Some whites viewed the new rules as long-standing, natural, and necessary laws. For the most part, the blacks were quiet, but there were outbursts of defiance, individual acts of desperate courage, and occasional boycotts. Many behaviors that were misunderstood and called "Uncle Tomism" were really disguised defiance. Uncle Tom behavior was often put on in order to reduce tension, avoid abuse, and survive.

ORGANIZED PROTEST

The first major protest movement was the all-black Niagara group, founded in 1905 and led by W.E.B. Du Bois. This was an important shift from the conservative policy of black self-improvement proposed in the public speeches of Booker T. Washington. The demands and militancy of the Niagara group were startling in the early 1900s. In style and content, they were similar to the protests of the 1960s. The leaders called for integration, equality, and the vote. They blamed whites for the problems of blacks and for the tension between the races.

Under the leadership of Du Bois, the National Association for the Advancement of Colored People (NAACP) was formed in 1909. The grass-roots membership of the NAACP was largely black, but a small group of white progressives contributed money, influence, and talent, especially legal knowledge. In fact, Du Bois, who served as director of research and editor of the NAACP journal, *The Crisis,* was the only black member of the national staff until James Weldon Johnson became secretary in 1921 (see Meier and Rudwick, 1971:Introduction).

Legal action

The NAACP took overt action at a time when action was considered radical. Its strategies included lobbying and suits against residential segregation and disfranchisement laws. For example, in a 1915 case brought by the NAACP, the Supreme Court declared the "grandfather clause" unconstitutional. This clause had been added to southern state constitutions after emancipation, denying the vote to anyone whose ancestors would not have been eligible to vote in 1860. Slaves, of course, never had voting rights. In 1944, the NAACP won a Supreme Court decision that ended all-white primaries and expanded the political participation of blacks.

The basic goal of the NAACP was to destroy segregation, and its main target was the school system. It attacked obvious inequalities—the lower salaries of black teachers and the lack of graduate and professional schools for blacks in southern states—hoping that truly equal facilities would be so expensive that segregation

W.E.B. Du Bois (1868-1963), American historian, sociologist, and activist. Early works include *The Suppression of the African Slave-Trade to the United States of America* (1896), *The Philadelphia Negro* (1899), and pioneering community studies at Atlanta University using questionnaire and survey techniques (1897-1910). Long a leader in the pan-African movement, he became a citizen of Ghana just before his death.

would fall of its own weight. Not until about 1950 did the Association decide to attack directly the principle of segregation in the schools, on the grounds that segregated facilities were inherently unequal. [Meier and Rudwick, 1971:35]

This strategy was finally rewarded by the Supreme Court in 1954. The landmark decision—*Brown* v. *Board of Education of Topeka*—established the principle that segregation in public schools is unconstitutional.

By the mid-1960s, the civil rights movement had become national in scope, resources, and goals. The school desegregation case was a truly national event, and other events such as the Montgomery bus boycott, the desegregation of the armed forces

(Fahy Committee, 1950; Moskos, 1966), the desegregation of professional baseball (Broom and Selznick, 1963:528–32), and the de-stereotyping of radio, television, and film characters (Cripps, 1967) proved that change was possible. They helped set the scene for further change.

Pressure politics and demonstrations

The NAACP was criticized from both sides. Conservatives claimed that it was dangerously militant, while radicals called it a mouthpiece of the black middle class and a captive of the few but active white members. In fact, many black business leaders supported the NAACP.

The difference in tactics between the NAACP and other organizations resulted in an informal division of labor. Of the activist organizations, the most important for several years after World War II was the Congress of Racial Equality (CORE). The NAACP continued its court actions against discrimination in housing and segregation on railroads, buses, and other public facilities. At the same time, CORE used sit-ins to attack discrimination in restaurants, hotels, and theaters in the northern and border states. The NAACP won the court cases and CORE implemented them. In the famous ''freedom rides,'' for example, CORE tested the Supreme Court's ruling that desegregated interstate transportation.

Martin Luther King, Jr., and nonviolent protest

The Montgomery bus boycott of 1955–1956 was important not only because it was successful but also because it brought the Rev. Martin Luther King, Jr.,

Dr. Martin Luther King, Jr. leading a Freedom March from Selma to Montgomery, Alabama, in 1965.

to national attention. King applied Mahatma Gandhi's principles of nonviolence to the civil-rights movement. He also mobilized the growing self-confidence of blacks. In 1957, he established the Southern Christian Leadership Conference (SCLC), which encouraged acts of passive resistance and efforts to register blacks to vote.

THE RIOT AS PROTEST

Martin Luther King's calls for nonviolence and reconciliation were made during the most turbulent decade of modern American history. Besides demonstrations against the Vietnam War, there were violent outbursts in black ghettos across the country. A few developed into riots. In Harlem (1964) and Watts (1965), for example, looting and arson (mostly against businesses), stoning, shooting, and personal assaults caused injury and death. However, despite widespread gunfire and the large number of people involved, there was less loss of life during the long, hot summer of 1964 than in the Chicago riots of 1919, when blacks were attacked by white mobs (Broom and Glenn, 1967:185–86).

Compared with the nonviolent protests of CORE and the SCLC, which had clear and attainable goals, the riots of the 1960s seemed pointless and ineffective. However, they had a point: They directed white attention to the poverty of blacks and to their feelings of resentment and despair.

Types of riots

The race riots of the early 1900s were mostly attacks on persons. The conflicts centered on relations between blacks and whites, with whites insisting that blacks show respect and keep their distance. The violence took the form of beatings and killings.

The race riots of the 1960s showed a different pattern: (1) They tended to be started by blacks, often in response to what they saw as provocation by white police. (2) The riots were more frequently directed against property than against persons. (3) The grievances of blacks centered on poverty and discrimination as well as repressive police action. "While the civil disorders of 1967 were racial in

character, they were not *inter*racial'' (Kerner Report, 1968:110). Insofar as there was group conflict, it involved clashes between black citizens and white police.

The 1980 riots in Miami appear to be a third type. Again provocations by police and a feeling that the courts did not deal fairly with blacks led to violence. The precipitating incident in May 1980 was the acquittal by an all-white jury of four police officers who had been charged with beating to death a black Miami businessman. There was also underlying resentment against the favorable treatment of Cubans. It was not that blacks wanted Cubans to be treated poorly. Rather they wanted their own long-standing needs to be given priority.

During a television interview, a black social scientist in Miami pointed out that the riot was directed against persons as well as property.

> This riot is different. It's different from what we saw in the '60s. We have seen horrible things in this community, the bodies in the streets, I've seen and others have seen, the mutilations, and what have you. This riot involves the intentional attempt to kill. In the riots of the '60s, people—white people were killed because they got in the way, black people were killed because they got in the way. But in this situation, the anger is so intense, the feelings are so rampant now, that the attacks as I've seen them have been aimed at white people with intent to do great bodily harm to people. . . . There may be other areas in which black people will compromise, economic areas, social or political areas, but when it comes to the question of justice, there is no room to give. And people feel intensely wounded by the sense that justice has been denied in such an atrocious case as this. [Dunn, 1980:3]

EQUAL OPPORTUNITY AND AFFIRMATIVE ACTION

The struggle of blacks and other minorities to overcome the heritage of slavery and discrimination has largely centered on equality of opportunity. Until the middle of the twentieth century it was taken for granted that blacks, women, and others would be denied equal access to political influence, good education, good housing, and good jobs.

In 1941, during World War II, President Roosevelt established a Fair Employment Practices Committee to eliminate discrimination in government and in private employment related to the war effort. Gradually, "fair employment" and "equal opportunity" were accepted as public policy. But acceptance was often tentative and uncertain; and it varied greatly from one state or community to another. Little real progress was made until the civil rights movement of the late 1950s and 1960s gathered strength.

The Civil Rights Act of 1964 was a major political breakthrough. It barred discrimination in any program receiving Federal assistance and also stated:

> It shall be an unlawful employment practice for an employer . . . to discriminate against any individual . . . because of such individual's race, color, religion, sex or national origin; or to limit, segregate or classify his employees in any way which would deprive or tend to deprive any individual of employment opportunities or otherwise adversely affect his status as an employee, because of such individual's race, color, sex, religion or national origin.

The following year (1965) President Johnson issued an executive order requiring all government contractors to "take affirmative action" to eliminate discrimination in employment.

The idea of **affirmative action** brought about a significant change in policy. At first, affirmative action meant only that employers should take positive steps to see that no discrimination occurred in the way employees were hired, promoted, trained, laid off, or paid. That was consistent with the goal of breaking down barriers to equal opportunity.

Soon, however, affirmative action came to mean that steps should be taken to make the composition of a work force, at all levels, reflect the racial, ethnic, and gender composition of available workers. The effects of past discrimination against minorities and women would be corrected by giving them preference, and specific timetables were called for. Thus affirmative action emphasized not merely equality of *opportunity* but equality of *result*. This has become a source of major controversy for two reasons: (1) in a particular competition, preferential treatment means that nonminority individuals are denied equal opportunity, and (2) the principle of merit—that a job or other opportunity should be given to the best qualified person available—may be slighted.

Affirmative action as preferential treatment was challenged in the case of Alan Bakke, a white who claimed that reverse discrimination denied him admission to the University of California medical school. In 1978 the U.S. Supreme Court upheld his contention and ordered the university to admit him. However, the Court did approve more flexible affirmative action programs.

(Text continued on p. 161)

Adaptation 8.2

Sojourner Truth, Free Woman

Slavery in the United States was an institutional assault on the personality, but some slaves found the strength to surmount the degradations of slavery and to strive for freedom, not only for themselves but also for others. Accounts of such persons are rare, partly because most slaves were illiterate. Documents that survive reveal figures of heroic dimensions, one of whom was Sojourner Truth, born in the 1790s in Ulster County, New York. She was illiterate, but she left her mark on her time and in history.

For the first half of her life Sojourner Truth was known by her slave name, Isabella. Separated from her parents before she was 10, she had three owners before she was 13. The last was a man named Dumont, who owned her for 18 years and chose a slave to "marry" her. Dumont promised to free her a year before all the slaves in New York were to be freed, but when she asked for her papers, he decided to keep her the additional year because he had suffered losses due to the birth of one of her children. To repay the losses, she stayed until the wool was spun and the heavy fall work done, but then she ran away with her youngest child. When Dumont came after her the next day, the abolitionist family that had sheltered her for the night paid him $20 for her services for the remainder of the year and $5 for her infant, and set them free.

Just out of bondage herself, she resorted to the law to free another son from an Alabama plantation; and later, as a domestic servant in New York, she was the first black to win a suit for slander against prominent whites. The case, involving a much-talked-about religious scandal, had occasioned two books—one grossly abusive—the other championing her and incidentally giving the full employment record of her first years in freedom (Pauli, 1962:11).

Religion dominated her life, and taking the name Sojourner Truth, she spent her later years traveling around the country, lecturing and preaching. She addressed her audiences as "children" because, she said, they were all the children of God, and she was old enough to be their mother anyhow. Before the Civil War, her audiences were mostly white, and she spoke often for abolition. After emancipation, she urged freed persons to grasp what the war had won for them.

Abolitionism absorbed much of her attention, but she also campaigned for feminism and was the only black woman to attend the first national women's rights convention in 1850. In 1851, at a women's convention in Akron, Ohio, she gave one of the most

Source: Based on Hertha Pauli, *Her Name Was Sojourner Truth* (New York: Avon, 1962), and Miriam Schnier, ed., *Feminism: The Essential Historical Writings* (New York: Random House, 1972).

Sojourner Truth in her 70s.

eloquent speeches in feminist literature, part of which follows:

Well, children, where there is so much racket there must be something out of kilter. I think that 'twixt the Negroes of the South and the women of the North, all talking about rights, the white men will be in a fix pretty soon. But what's all this here talking about?

That man over there says that women need to be helped into carriages, and lifted over ditches, and to have the best place everywhere. Nobody ever helps me into carriages, or over mud-puddles, or gives me any best place! And ain't I a woman? Look at me! I have ploughed and planted, and gathered into barns, and no man could head me! And ain't I a woman? I could work as much and eat as much as a man— when I could get it and bear the lash as well! And ain't I a woman? I have borne thirteen children, and seen the most all sold off to slavery, and when I cried out with my mother's grief, none but Jesus heard me! And ain't I a woman? [Schnier, 1972:94–95]

About 15 years later, when the major issue was Negro suffrage, she said:

> I hear so much about colored men getting their rights but, not a word about the colored women. . . . I want women to have their rights, and while the water is stirring I'll step into the pool. Now that there's a stir about colored men's rights is the time for women to get theirs. . . . You never lose anything by asking everything. If you bait this suffrage hook with a woman, you'll surely catch a black man. [Pauli, 1962:220–21]

After emancipation she devoted herself to the welfare of freed persons and campaigned for the grant of government land in the West so they could become economically independent. She taught housekeeping skills to ex-slaves who had been field hands. When their children were kidnaped and taken to Maryland (where abolition was still being argued in the courts), she persuaded frightened mothers to swear out warrants for the return of their children, as she herself had done many years before.

After the Civil War, public transportation in Washington, D.C., was desegregated, but few ex-slaves were willing to test their legal rights. Sojourner Truth took up the challenge and on her visits to the city seized every chance to ride. On one occasion her shoulder was dislocated when a conductor tried to push her off a streetcar.

Even in her old age Sojourner Truth campaigned for desegregation. She always insisted on her rights. Throughout her life this most modern of nineteenth-century women, slave or free, worked to change the system.

Section Four

Ethnic Stratification

Each ethnic minority in the United States has come upon a different scene, a different pattern of opportunities and hardships with a different set of competitors. History can tell how the Irish, Italians, and other ethnic groups progressed, but their experience contains little advice for blacks, Hispanics, and Native Americans facing radically different conditions.

In the nineteenth and early twentieth centuries, many poorly educated European immigrants and their children achieved quick success because they arrived when labor was in short supply and industry was expanding. Greek, Italian, Jewish, and other European immigrants moved up the socioeconomic ladder farther and faster than expected when they arrived. The children of those immigrants achieved much higher educational, occupational, and income levels than their parents.

On the average, second-generation Jews and Greeks reached higher levels than native-born white Americans with native-born parents. Second-generation Italians also surpassed the latter group in occupation and income, and nearly equaled them in education. By all three measures, these immigrant groups have been successful (Broom, Martin, and Maynard, 1971; Sowell, 1978:part 2).

In the late twentieth century, blacks, Hispanics, and Haitians are not likely to progress as rapidly as Italian, Jewish, and Greek immigrants did. Machines have replaced manual labor; small businesses can no longer compete with big ones; and it takes a lot of education to go even a short way up the job scale.

THE NONWHITE LABOR FORCE

The nonwhite labor force, which is more than 90 percent black, differs from the white labor force in unemployment rate and in occupational and educational characteristics. Over the past two decades, the nonwhite unemployment rate has been double that of whites. In 1983, the unemployment rate for whites was about 10 percent, for Hispanics 17 percent, and for blacks 21 percent (U.S. Bureau of Labor Statistics 30 [April] 1983:Table A57). Most nonwhites work in industries and occupations that are vulnerable to changes in the economy, although the growing number in government employment have greater job security. Nonwhites are overrepresented in most lower-paid occupations and underrepresented in higher-paid ones. About two-fifths of nonwhites, compared with over half of white workers, have white-collar jobs. This occupational inferiority of nonwhites extends throughout the economic structure of the United States.

In Table 8.1 we can see how nonwhite representation in various occupational groups has changed. The table states the extent to which the actual distribution of nonwhites among these groups differs from what would be ''expected'' if the nonwhites had their share of jobs in each group. Clearly, the situation has improved. In 1940, the professional

category contained only about one-third (.36) of the ''expected'' nonwhite share. By 1980, this figure had reached .78. During the same period, the ratios for farming occupations and private household work fell sharply.

Progress toward improved nonwhite status may be seen in both manual and white-collar jobs but is relatively slow at the managerial level, in sales, and in top-level blue-collar work. The slow progress in blue-collar jobs can be explained by the small percentage of blacks in craft unions (largely owing to a history of union discrimination). Because blacks have less seniority, they are the first to lose such jobs.

Within the major occupational groups, nonwhites

Table 8.1 Ratio of Actual to Expected Percentage of Nonwhites, by Occupation, 1940–1980

Explanation: The ''expected'' percentage of nonwhites in any occupational group is the same as the percentage of all workers in that group. For instance, in 1980 6.3 percent of all employed workers in the United States were sales workers, and therefore one would ''expect'' 6.3 percent of employed nonwhites to be in that occupational group. In fact, only 2.8 percent of employed nonwhites were so employed. Thus, the ratio of actual to expected is 2.8 ÷ 6.3 = .44. If nonwhites were represented proportionately, the ratio would be 1.00. A ratio of more than 1.00 indicates overrepresentation; a ratio of less than 1.00, underrepresentation.

Occupational Group	1940	1950	1960	1970	1980[a]
White collar					
Professional and technical	.36	.40	.49	.64	.78
Managers and administrators (nonfarm)	.17	.22	.23	.33	.44
Clerical workers	.12	.29	.46	.76	.99
Sales workers		.18	.23	.34	.44
Blue collar					
Craft and kindred workers	.27	.38	.49	.64	.75
Operatives and kindred workers	.57	.94	1.08	1.34	1.34
Nonfarm laborers	2.06	2.56	2.59	2.18	1.52
Service					
Private household workers	4.66	5.92	5.46	3.89	3.00
Other service workers	1.53	2.00	2.02	1.77	1.64
Farm					
Farmers and farm managers	1.31	1.22	.78	.45	.20
Farm laborers and supervisors	2.57	2.28	2.46	1.68	1.36

[a]Because of changes in the occupational classification and the form of questioning, data for 1980 are not strictly comparable with earlier years.

Source: For 1940–1960, Glenn, 1963:Table 1. Ratios for 1970 and 1980 are computed from basic data in *Monthly Labor Review* and U.S. Department of Labor Statistics 27 (May) 1980:table A22.

tend to be concentrated in the lower-paid jobs. Most of the nonwhites in the professional and technical category are clergymen and teachers rather than doctors, lawyers, engineers, or other highly paid professionals (Broom and Glenn, 1967:111–13). The decline in nonwhite representation in farm labor and private household service indicates an important shift of nonwhites out of jobs that offer little or no chance of advancement. While it is still unfavorable, the occupational status of nonwhites has improved markedly.

Ethnicity and family income

Inferior occupation inevitably leads to lower incomes. Figure 8.1 compares black, Spanish-origin, and white family incomes. Spanish origin includes persons of Mexican origin, Puerto Ricans, and others with Spanish background who may be of any race. In 1982, 29 percent of white families had incomes of $35,000 and over, compared with 10 percent of black families and 14 percent of Spanish-origin families. Only 9 percent of white family incomes fell below $7,500, but 21 percent of Spanish-origin and 29 percent of black family incomes were below that level. The income picture of Hispanic families is somewhat better than that for blacks, but both are far below the white income profile.

Differences between the races in income inevitably lead to differences in accumulated wealth. Analysis of data from a Bureau of the Census survey shows that in 1979 the average personal wealth of black households ($24,600) was about one-third that of white households ($68,900). (Pearl and Frankel, 1982, Table 6). "Although black households make up 12 percent of all households, they hold only 4

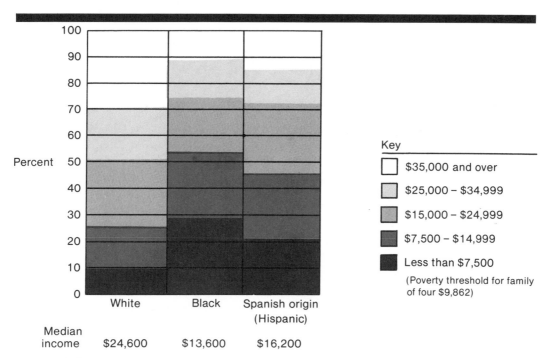

Figure 8.1   Family Income in 1982 by Racial/Ethnic Background, United States (in percent)[a]

[a]Families are classified by origin of householder. Persons of Spanish origin (Hispanic) may be of any race. Double counting of these families slightly affects the percents reported for whites and blacks.
Source: CPR, P-60, No. 140, July 1983: Table 3.

percent of the combined wealth of blacks and whites. In 1979 blacks held approximately $211 billion in personal wealth compared to $4.875 trillion held by whites.'' (OHare, 1983:3)

ETHNIC POLITICAL POWER

Forty years ago Gunnar Myrdal observed that ''from the actual power situation in America *the beliefs held by white people rather than those held by Negroes are of primary importance*'' (1944:110). In the 1980s, this statement retains considerable truth, but white beliefs have changed greatly and blacks have much more control over their own fate, especially in politics. A 1983 Gallup poll reported that 68 percent of Southern adults and 77 percent of the national total would vote for a ''generally qualified black man'' if he was nominated by their party. The national figure was double that for 1958.*

In 1960 in the 11 southern states, 56 percent of whites, but only 29 percent of blacks, were registered to vote. Registration drives have added many blacks to the voting rolls, and in 1982 black registration was around 56 percent compared with 66 percent for whites (*Statistical Abstract, 1982–83:488*). The mayoral elections of 1983 mobilized more voters, both black and white, and the registration gap was narrowed. Black voters are eagerly courted by white politicians, some of whom were hardline segregationists only a few years ago. Where blacks are highly concentrated, sophisticated and highly organized, voter mobilization has propelled them into leadership positions.

Office holding is the most direct measure of political power. Since the voter registration drives of the 1960s, black officials have been elected in greater numbers in the urban North as well as in the South. Between 1970 and 1981 the number of black office holders increased from 1,500 to over 5,000.

*Gallup used the phrase black *man* to make the figures comparable with earlier polls. In a parallel Gallup question about willingness to vote for a woman, 80 percent of the national sample responded ''yes.'' When the question was first asked in 1937 only 31 percent said ''yes.'' The trends in responses may imply a general shift in public attitudes toward candidates in terms of their qualifications and away from historically powerful ascriptive criteria.

In the southern states alone, there were more than 3,000 black elected officials in 1981, a fact of profound importance both for its practical effects and its impact on black morale.

Although there have been no black senators since 1979 and the defeat of Senator Edward Brook (Republican, Massachusetts) who held office for 12 years, in 1983 there were 20 blacks in the U.S. House of Representatives, all Democrats. In 1977 there were 16 and in 1962, only 4. However, the growth in black office holding at the national level still falls far short of parity. Blacks comprise about 12 percent of the population but less than 4 percent of the members of Congress.

In the 1980s three of the four largest cities in the United States have black mayors: Los Angeles, Chicago, and Philadelphia. Such black mobilization has generated anxiety and resentment, especially among working-class European ethnics. In Chicago, for example, they crossed traditional party lines to vote for a white Republican against a black mayoral candidate, but in both Chicago and Philadelphia, which are approximately 40 percent black, black Democratic candidates for mayor defeated their white opponents.

There are fewer Hispanics—15 million, compared with about 25 million blacks—but the fact that a large percentage of Mexican Americans live in the Southwest makes them a political force in that region. In 1982 there were 5 Hispanics in the House of Representatives; in 1983 there were 9, and 8 of them were Democrats. Similarly, the concentration of Puerto Ricans in the Northeast gives them regional political power. Well before the end of the century Hispanics will be more numerous than blacks.

The first and most rural of minorities—Native Americans—total fewer than 1 million and are scattered among many small settlements. Their wide dispersion hampers political organization, but they have a growing sense of Indian identity that goes beyond tribal membership (Wax, 1971:144–51). In the past they were politically quiet, or at least no one listened. Today they are actively pressing land claims and calling for recognition of their cultural identities. The larger tribes are working toward a revival of communal organization and common ownership of their reclaimed lands.

Section Five
Ethnic Pluralism

Countries can be arranged on a continuum, or series of steps, from ethnically homogeneous societies to ethnically heterogeneous, or plural societies. At one extreme are those with a single language, religion, culture, and race; at the other extreme are countries of great diversity.

HOMOGENEOUS AND PLURAL SOCIETIES

Before World War II, Australia was a good example of a homogeneous nation-state. It was an English-speaking Christian country with one culture and one ethnic population. Except for a small subordinate population of Aborigines, most Australians were migrants or descendants of migrants from the British Isles and Ireland, and English was their mother tongue, the language learned at home in childhood. There was some tension between Protestants and Roman Catholics, the latter mostly of Irish descent, but on the whole the Australians were a unified people with a clear sense of national identity.

Present-day Australia is much more cosmopolitan. Since World War II, the arrival of immigrants from many countries has moved Australia along the continuum away from the homogeneous end and toward the plural end.

Norway and Japan are especially homogeneous. Almost all of Norway's inhabitants are Norwegian-speaking Lutherans. The only ethnic minority in Norway is a very small population of Lapps. Japan has three minorities: a small number of Koreans, the Burakumin (Eta) discussed in Adaptation 8.1, and the Ainu, the few survivors of a tribal people. However, for the most part the country is racially, linguistically, and culturally homogeneous. Furthermore, Japan seems determined to keep Japan for the Japanese. Japanese people have migrated to other countries, especially Canada, the United States, Peru, and Brazil, and Japanese governments have long criticized countries that discriminate against Japanese immigrants. But foreigners who might want to settle in Japan—including refugees—face almost insurmountable barriers.

Plural societies

Countries as homogeneous as present-day Norway and Japan are exceptions rather than the rule. Plural societies are more common. The idea of plural societies grew out of observations of the complex, multiethnic colonies of Southeast Asia:

> Probably the first thing that strikes the visitor is the medley of peoples—European, Chinese, Indian, and native. It is in the strictest sense a medley, for they mix but do not combine. Each group holds by its own religion, its own culture and language, its own ideas and ways. As individuals they meet, but only in the marketplace, in buying and selling. There is a plural society, with different sections of the community living side by side, but separately, within the same political unit. Even in the economic sphere, there is a division of labour along racial lines. [Furnivall, 1948:304]

Plural societies are composed of different peoples who live side by side, but remain separate (see Smith, 1960; Kuper and Smith, 1969).

Plural societies are formed by historical forces such as conquest and colonialism. They may lose their plural character through assimilation, in which the various ethnic groups within the society become less culturally distinct. Homogeneity can also occur by ethnic "purification," as in Hitler's eradication of German Jews or Vietnam's expulsion of ethnic Chinese. On the other hand, a plural society may split up into smaller, ethnically unified nations, as occurred in the Balkans after World War I—hence the term *balkanization*.

A MULTITUDE OF PEOPLES

Most countries live with strangers in their midst, but the variety within a single nation is often ignored by outsiders unless a political struggle brings it to world attention. Consider these examples: At least 6 percent of China's population consists of non-Chinese, many of whom live in frontier areas just across national borders from members of the same ethnic group. Iran has large Turkish, Kurdish, and Arabic-speaking minorities concentrated in well-defined regions. Belgium is split between Dutch-speaking Flemings in the north and French-speaking Walloons in the south. Switzerland is divided among German, French, Italian, and Romansch speakers. The large west African country of Nigeria contains Yoruba, Ibo, Hausa-Fulani, and other tribal-linguistic groups that live in specific regions. The population is also split by religion into Muslims, Christians, and others. The Welsh in Britain, the Bretons in France, the Basques in Spain are all separatist elements, and the foregoing are but a small sample of plural societies.

In this section we choose for closer comparative analysis three heterogeneous societies—Canada, South Africa, and the USSR—which are very different from each other in historical origins, in the ways pluralism is expressed, and in the impact of ethnic diversity on national solidarity.

Canada: division without race

Canada has been defined as "a collection of North American territories whose major problem is not the Black problem" (Rioux, 1971:123). Some Canadians call the tension between French and English speakers a racial problem, and until 1941 the Canadian census incorrectly used the word race in referring to these two European peoples.

Cultural dualism: Official terminology now makes the distinction on the basis of language: French speakers (Francophones) and English speakers (Anglophones). In the 1976 census, about 26 percent of Canadians claimed French as their tongue, and the province of Quebec is over 80 percent French. Although the Canadian population of British ancestry has declined during the past century from 60 percent to about 40 percent, immigrants from other countries have adopted English so that it is still the dominant language and is spoken in two-thirds of Canadian homes (*Canada Year Book,* 1978–1979:160). Canadian Indians and Eskimos (Inuit) account for only about 1 percent of the population.

Quebec is set off from the rest of Canada by religion as well as language. French has constitutional protection as an official language, and the Roman Catholic religion and parochial education are similarly protected. These guarantees encourage French Canadians to remain in Quebec where they have a strong political base.

Inequality: An element of class conflict is also added to ethnic cleavage. Although they are not a suppressed minority, French Canadians are economically inferior to the "British." The fact that they are subordinate even where they are the numerical majority has long been a source of resentment (Hughes, 1943; Porter, 1968; Canadian Royal Commission, 1967–1970, esp. 1969, vols. 3A, 3B; Roseborough and Breton, 1968). The Québecois blame their economic inferiority on discrimination by British and American capitalists, but they were not as well prepared as the British and the European immigrants to take advantage of economic opportunities. In Quebec, the family, the church, and the parochial schools were not geared to an industrial economy (Porter, 1968). However, in recent years the French have become more urban and better prepared to compete in a technological society.

The French have successfully resisted assimilation, and the possibility of separating Quebec from the rest of Canada is a source of continuing political strain. For more than two decades, Canadian leaders have searched for a way to reduce the tension between Quebec and the other provinces. Greater autonomy for Quebec and clearer separation of powers between the national and provincial governments did not satisfy the Québecois. More drastic constitutional proposals have been considered, such as granting Quebec special status as a province "not like the others" and the formation of a confederation in which Quebec would be one state and the rest of the provinces another.

Canada is trying to resolve by political means the strains of cultural division, economic inequality, and historically based tension where two kinds of values are in conflict: (1) the ideal of a culturally homogeneous nation-state, and (2) the ideal of a plural society that is flexible enough to allow separate religious and linguistic identities to co-exist in a single political community.

South Africa: separate and subordinate

South Africa has abundant natural resources, which it exploits with cheap black labor and modern technology. It is a rich country and would be far richer if its human resources were fully developed. In South Africa, skin color governs every aspect of life for all members of society. Out of a population of 30 million, 5 million whites are at the top of the social ladder no matter what their talents or level of education may be. There are two main elements of the white population: persons of British background —mostly urban—and the more numerous Boers (meaning farmers). Descendants of early Dutch settlers, Boers consider Africa to be their home. They call themselves *Afrikaners* (Africans) and their language, an offshoot of Dutch, *Afrikaans*. Educationally and economically they are somewhat inferior to English South Africans, but they are politically dominant and are becoming urbanized.

Race and caste: Ranked below the whites are about 3 million persons of mixed ancestry called Coloured (or Cape Coloured), most of whom speak Afrikaans. Culturally they are closer to the Boers than to black Africans, but politically and socially their status is weak and ambiguous. Also at an intermediate social level are nearly a million Asians— descendants of contract laborers from India. Just as the Coloureds tend to be concentrated in one province, the Cape, the Asians are concentrated in Natal province.

At the bottom of the socioeconomic scale are over 21 million undereducated, underemployed, and underpaid black Africans. They have been called *Bantu* (the name of the largest linguistic family), but they prefer to be called *black*.

Apartheid: Racial subordination has long been a way of life in South Africa, but apartheid is fairly new. **Apartheid** (officially, separate development) is a system of rigid racial separation governed by strict regulations. It consists of three types of separation between the races—the ''color bar,'' residential segregation, and territorial apartheid (Davenport, 1977:chap. 19; van den Berghe, 1966; Lever, 1978: chap. 11).

1. The color bar regulates the daily lives of nonwhites and limits contacts between nonwhites and whites. In some respects, it resembles the Jim Crow practices of the southern United States in the early 1900s. Nonwhites are assigned to segregated and inferior facilities, both public and private. They are required to carry passbooks, and their movements are controlled. In the mid-1970s, the government began to moderate some features of the color bar, but it is not clear how far this trend will go because hard-line whites resist any relaxation in the control of blacks.

2. Residential segregation has actually increased since Afrikaner nationalists gained power in 1948. Racially mixed neighborhoods have been turned into homogeneous ghettos through massive shifting of racial groups. For the most part, nonwhites are restricted to their own sections except during working hours.

New housing has slightly improved the physical environment of many blacks who used to live in shacks in decaying slums. However, blacks, Asians, and Coloureds have also been displaced from adequate housing in established communities. In South Africa, as elsewhere, urban renewal is urban removal. Neighborhoods are broken up to satisfy plans of the group with political power. As the urban work force grows to meet industrial demands, more segregated townships are built. They are new and orderly, but bleak, cramped, fenced in, and far from the city center and the work places of their residents. These densely settled ghettos concentrate both people and discontent. The 1976 riots in the black townships drew international attention to South Africa and dramatized for South African whites the resentment felt by the million residents of Soweto and other townships.

3. Territorial apartheid plans for a future in which blacks will be settled in separate territories according to language and tribal origin. This part of the apartheid system is the most controversial. It would turn South Africa into a multinational state in which each black people would have its own ''homeland,'' but only limited self-government.

Strains and dilemmas: Although South Africa is over 70 percent black, blacks will occupy only about 13 percent of the country if the homeland policy is carried out. As planned, the homelands are inadequate to house the rapidly growing black population and do not provide a base for viable separate economies. Furthermore, a single homeland may not be a single geographic unit, but might consist of scattered fragments of land completely surrounded by other political units, making the homeland hard to administer and impossible to exploit efficiently.

According to the homeland plan, those blacks who are not needed to work in the white economy will be moved to homelands no matter where they were born or live. Even blacks who were born in white areas and have permission to live and work in white areas are legally defined as residents of the homelands. Since most families live in the homeland territories, those blacks who work in white areas must live apart from their families and be deprived of a normal family life. By the end of the century, blacks will compose three-fourths of South Africa's population. As originally planned, there is no provision for increasing the amount of land assigned to them, but this is now a subject of heated debate.

Some whites oppose the stricter forms of apartheid and a minority of whites oppose the entire apartheid policy. Apartheid is most costly for nonwhites, but it is a highly inefficient, expensive, and fundamentally unproductive form of social administration. The taxes and human effort that might otherwise be devoted to social and economic advancement are spent on imposing controls that frustrate personal development and degrade relations between the races.

Many apartheid rules are unworkable in a modern industrial state, and some rules are bent because the South African economy needs a competent black workforce to keep its industry and services going. A shortage of skilled workers has resulted in improving the range of opportunities for blacks, who have thus gained access to better paying jobs.

Apartheid in action.
Police inspecting passbooks.

Blacks refer to the passbook as *dompas,* which in Afrikaans means stupid pass.

However, equal pay for equal work is ruled out, and to place blacks in supervisory positions over whites would violate basic South African principles.

Citizens of Western countries, especially church groups, have urged a boycott on South African goods and a ban on investments in South African companies. They argue that if South Africa is isolated, it will change its social system and put an end to apartheid. However, some observers feel that isolation would only serve to strengthen South African extremists (Kennan, 1971).

The police in South Africa have the power to put down dissent. They can detain dissidents without trial. To Westerners, such controls seem not very different from what goes on in communist countries. Yet there is a vocal political opposition in South Africa, and the press criticizes the government. Academics speak out against government policies, but they do so at risk of being "banned" and having their publications removed from circulation.

South Africa is experiencing growing pressure from increasingly militant blacks, Coloureds, and Asians, as well as tension between hard-line and moderate whites. The stability of a repressive system is clearly at risk but the determination of the regime should not be underestimated.

The USSR: internal colonialism

The USSR (Union of Soviet Socialist Republics) is made up of more than 100 diverse ethnic groups. These include Slavs (Russians, Ukrainians, Belorussians); non-Slavic Europeans (Moldavians, Estonians, Latvians, Lithuanians, Germans); non-European Christians (Georgians, Armenians); and non-European Muslims (Azeri, Kazakhs, Uzbeks, Tadzhiks). According to Soviet ideology, these various subnations will merge and their cultural differences will disappear. But there is no sign that they will assimilate. For example, the German nationality, deported from its Volga and Black Sea areas during World War II to localities in Asia, resists assimilation (Koch, 1977). In the future the USSR will probably be even more a patchwork of ethnic regions than it is today.

The Slavic peoples (Russians, or "Great Russians"; Belorussians; and Ukrainians) make up about three-quarters of the total population. They are mostly European and have declining birthrates like other Europeans. The most important of the Soviet republics, the Russian Republic (RSFSR), contains a little more than half of the total population of the USSR. By the end of this century the population of the Russian Republic will be less than half of the total population, and all the Slavic peoples combined will amount to less than two-thirds of the total (Feshbach, 1978:tables 1,2).

All Soviet citizens must carry passports stating their "nationality" (as Armenian, Georgian, or the like). Nationality is based on parentage, regardless of birthplace or place of residence. A child born in Lithuania to Uzbek parents is an Uzbek, not a Lithuanian. However, passports do not entitle Soviet citizens to move and settle freely within the USSR or even within their own subnation. People must live where the military allows them to live (Hollander, 1973:346).

> With the exception of the Jews, each large group has its own homeland: this might be one of the Soviet Union's fifteen union republics, or one of the twenty "autonomous republics" and eight "autonomous regions" that are located within the union Republics. [Meyer, 1978:156]

The present Jewish population of the USSR is estimated at under 3 million—far below the prewar figure—and of all the ethnic groups in the USSR, they are in the most hazardous position. Russian anti-Semitism has a long history. The Soviet campaign against religion, when applied to Jews, is compounded by the fact that Jews are defined as a nationality as well as a religious group. Unlike other nationalities, however, they do not have an officially recognized language or educational system. But the greatest barrier to the preservation of Jewish identity is the lack of a territorial base (Hollander, 1973:347–48).

Russian colonialism: The USSR of today is a survival from the Russian empire of a century earlier, and colonialism did not stop with the Russian Revolution. Ethnic Russian migrants are the top officials in all but one of the Soviet republics, and Russians hold privileged positions in the non-Russian republics. Russians and other Slavs predominate in the military command, in the highly mechanized military units, in the industrial bureaucracy, and at the upper levels of government throughout the country. Russian migrants are also the most highly educated people in the less developed republics (Andrews, 1978:447,450). Except where there are resources to be exploited, industrial investment and production are concentrated in the western (Slavic) part of the country.

Muslim population growth: In 1970, 1 in 7 Soviet citizens was Muslim, but the Muslims of Soviet Central Asia are growing much more rapidly than the Slavic population. By the year 2000, 1 in 3 Soviets will be Muslim (Feshbach, 1978:86). These Muslims are divided among many language and ethnic groups and are so strongly attached to their villages that they are unwilling to migrate or marry anyone of a different nationality. They prefer to send their children to non-Russian schools and ''are remarkably ignorant of the Russian language. . . . They even prefer higher education in their own language although a fluent knowledge of Russian is essential to a good Soviet career'' (Frankland, 1979).

Despite official opposition, Muslim leaders have kept the Islamic community alive. They have done so partly by making the practice of Islam easier, by replacing the pilgrimage to Mecca with pilgrimages to the tombs of local saints, and by stressing the fact that Muslim life cycle ceremonies are as much national/ethnic as religious in nature.

> It is not an Ayatollah Khomeini that Moscow has to worry about but a steadily growing Muslim community which by its existence challenges the Soviet State's ideals of centralisation and proletarian homogeneity. [Frankland, 1979]

Thus, religion, language, geography, and demography combine to create growing minority problems in the USSR.

Conclusion

This section has described three plural societies, all of which are products of colonialism. Canada is a free Western democracy divided by ethnicity and religion as well as geography, and where ethnic na-

tionalism has led to an open political struggle in which all can take part.

South Africa is a racially complex country controlled by a white minority, but white political leaders realize they must take into account the new militant mood of blacks. They recognize that internal political adjustments are necessary both to maintain economic development and to restrain black discontent. In the meantime, the heavy hand of police control enforces apartheid.

The USSR is also an ethnically complex society. Its fastest-growing ethnic minorities live in well-defined but underdeveloped territories of Central Asia. Compared with those of Canada and South Africa, Soviet minorities are relatively isolated from the worldwide growth of ethnic nationalism. The USSR of the next century will be strongly influenced by how the Soviet government deals with its ethnic minorities and by the way ethnic awareness is translated into political action.

Chapter 8   **Summary**

Section 1/**The making of minorities**

The existence of minority groups in the modern world is mainly the result of European exploration, conquest, and migration. Colonialism brought even the most remote regions into contact with Western culture and created societies based on the domination of one group over another.

Slavery is another major factor in the creation of minorities. All of the European nations took part in the slave trade, but some were more severe toward slaves than others. The severity of a slave system depended on laws permitting manumission, the religious definition of slaves, and the social acceptance of freed slaves.

Section 2/**Awareness and antagonism**

''Minority'' is a condition of subordination, not a quantity. Race refers to inherited traits, ethnicity to social and cultural characteristics.

A stereotype is a simplified belief about members of a particular group that ignores the group's wide variety of characteristics. Recently minorities have begun to select terms like Chicano and black, which imply a positive self-definition.

Section 3/**Accommodation and protest**

Even during slavery, blacks struggled against slavery and oppression, and the struggle continued after the Civil War. Organized protest began in the early 1900s with the Niagara group, which called for integration, equality, and the vote. The NAACP engaged in lobbying and court action. Its outstanding victory was in *Brown v. Board of Education of Topeka,* in which the Supreme Court ruled that segregation in public schools is unconstitutional.

The Rev. Martin Luther King, Jr., came to national attention during the Montgomery bus boycott of 1955–1956. He applied Gandhi's principles of nonviolence to the civil rights movement and established the SCLC to encourage passive resistance and voter registration of blacks. During the 1960s, violent protest was widespread. Riots in black ghettos called attention to the poverty and despair of blacks. Among the outcomes of black protest was affirmative action, governmental policies designed to improve the condition of blacks, other minorities, and women.

Section 4/**Ethnic stratification**

In the nineteenth and early twentieth centuries, immigrant groups were able to move up the social ladder relatively quickly. Today, however, machines have replaced manual labor; small businesses cannot compete with big ones; and it takes a lot of education to go even a short way. Blacks and Chicanos are not able to progress as rapidly as earlier immigrant groups did.

Nonwhites have a higher unemployment rate and less job security than whites, and are overrepresented in low-paid jobs. Nonwhite family incomes are well below white family incomes.

Since the voter registration drive of the 1960s, black officials have been elected in greater numbers in both the South and the North. There has also been an increase in the number of Chicanos holding national office. Native Americans are less effective politically because of their small numbers.

Section 5/**Ethnic pluralism**

In the modern world, homogeneous societies like Japan and Norway are the exception rather than the rule. Plural societies, composed of people who live side by side but remain separate are much more common. Conquest and colonialism are responsible for such plural societies as Canada, South Africa, and the USSR.

The province of Quebec is set off from the rest of Canada by the fact that its population is largely French speaking and Roman Catholic. French Canadians are at an economic disadvantage because their culture was not well geared to an industrial economy. Tensions between British and French Canadians continue, and the political solution is in doubt.

Relations between the races in South Africa are governed by apartheid, a system of racial separation that consists of the "color bar," residential segregation, and territorial apartheid. Territorial apartheid is highly controversial because it restricts many blacks to "homelands" that are not economically self-sufficient and cover only a small fraction of South Africa.

All South African minorities, Asians and Coloureds as well as blacks, are becoming increasingly militant. The system makes it hard to operate a modern industrial state efficiently. The dominant white regime is under internal strain as well as external pressure.

The USSR contains over 100 different ethnic groups of which the Slavic peoples are dominant. They hold privileged positions in the non-Russian as well as the Russian republics of the USSR and occupy higher positions in government, industry, and the military. The Jews are in a doubtful position because they are defined both as a nationality and as a religious group, but they have no territorial base.

The most rapidly growing populations in the USSR are the Muslim peoples, and by the year 2000, 1 in 3 Soviets will be Muslim. The future of the USSR will be strongly influenced by how the Soviet government deals with its increasing Muslim population as well as with its other ethnic minorities.

Suggested Readings

Bahr, Howard M., Bruce A. Chadwick, and Robert C. Day (eds.)

1972 *Native Americans Today: Sociological Perspectives.* New York: Harper & Row.

Foner, Laura, and Eugene D. Genovese (eds.)

1969 *Slavery in the New World: A Reader in Comparative History.* Englewood Cliffs, N.J.: Prentice-Hall.

Genovese, Eugene D.

1972 *Roll, Jordan, Roll: The World the Slaves Made.* New York: Random House.

Gordon, Milton M.

1978 *Human Nature, Class and Ethnicity.* New York: Oxford University Press.

Grebler, Leo, Joan W. Moore, and Ralph C. Guzman with Jeffrey L. Berlant, Thomas P. Carter, Walter Fogel, C. Wayne Gordon, Patrick H. McNamara, Frank G. Mittelbach, and Samuel J. Surace

1970 *The Mexican-American People: The Nation's Second Largest Minority.* New York: Free Press.

Myrdal, Gunnar, with the assistance of Richard Sterner and Arnold Rose

1944 *An American Dilemma: The Negro Problem and Modern Democracy.* New York: Harper & Row.

U.S. Bureau of the Census

1979 *The Social and Economic Status of the Black Population in the United States: An Historical View, 1790–1978.* CPR, P-23. No. 80. Washington, D.C.: GPO.

Williams, Robin M.

1977 *Mutual Accommodation: Ethnic Conflict and Cooperation.* Minneapolis: University of Minnesota Press.

Wilson, William J.

1978 *The Declining Significance of Race.* Chicago: University of Chicago Press.

Chapter 9

Strata and Classes

Section One
Method and Theory

This last chapter on the Great Divides deals with how people are ranked and how society is shaped by inequality and social class. Popular awareness of differences in life chances and life-styles is not new. More than a half century ago, English children read this fantasy about social class among mermaids:

> Suddenly, before she had time to realise it, the boat dived, and Effie found herself in a kingdom under the sea.
> It was the land of the mermaids!
> There they were, hundreds and hundreds of them in their silvery city.
> There were well-to-do mermaids with golden tails. There were the middle-class mermaids with silver tails, who spent a good deal of time trying to imitate the ways of the well-to-do mermaids. And there were the common mermaids, who were very noisy indeed, and swallowed their fish whole, and went about in swarms and shoals. [*Bo-Peep*, 1917].

It does not take a sociologist or a merperson to be sensitive to striking differences in life-styles and income. People often identify themselves as members of one class or another and, when asked, can accurately place themselves in a list of social ranks. Ideas about class may be influenced by popularized reports of sociological research, but they are mainly the result of people trying to make sense of significant aspects of their own lives.

Inequality, social rank, and social class are important concerns of sociology because they affect so many areas of personal and social life. Child rearing, relations between wives and husbands, political power, longevity, and industrial organization—these and many other aspects of social life bear the imprint of social class.

STUDYING SOCIAL STRATIFICATION

There are both objective and subjective approaches to the study of social stratification.

The objective approach

The objective approach uses such indicators as income, number of years of school completed, occupation, or formal positions of authority. These indicators are called objective because they are based on readily observable facts rather than on what people think or feel. They allow for more precise measurement than is possible in the other approaches and are often used in sample surveys of large populations and as a supplement to community studies.

Individuals or families that are located at the same level on an aspect of social rank, such as power, prestige, or income, make up a **social stratum.** Thus, all families whose incomes fall within a certain range are an income stratum, and all people who have completed a certain number of years of school are an education stratum. After studying income distribution statistics, a sociologist might divide a population into strata by dollar amounts (for example, $5,000 income brackets) or by percentages (for example, each 20 percent of families from highest to lowest income). For educational strata, the researcher might decide to group individuals by number of years of school completed or by diplomas received.

Ranking people by income or occupation tells only part of the story. All persons whose incomes fall within the same stratum do not think of the same amount of money in the same way, and the social effects of similar incomes may be quite different. An income of $25,000 a year means one thing to a middle-aged blue-collar worker near the peak of earning power, but it means something else to a young professional just beginning a career. The importance of a certain amount of money also depends on such factors as past income and savings, incomes of friends and relatives, income security, and the rate of inflation, both present and expected.

The subjective approach

With experience, individuals develop fairly clear ideas about what classes are like, what kinds of people belong to each class, and how the class system works. These ideas are sometimes termed *images of social class,* and they vary according to the social rank of the individual (Davies, 1967; Jackman, 1979; Svalastoga, 1959).

The subjective or self-rating approach tries to find out where individuals place themselves on the social ladder. The researcher may ask them whether their income is below average, average, or above average for their community. Or they may be asked more precisely how they would rank themselves in terms of economic standing, prestige, and the like.

Where people place themselves in the class system depends largely on their **reference groups,** that is, the groups with which they compare themselves. A foreman who lives in a blue-collar suburb may rate himself fairly high because he earns more than most of his co-workers, friends, and neighbors. However, if he begins to associate with well-paid professionals, his income will seem low. His objective economic standing does not change, but the way he thinks about it changes. Therefore, self-rating studies often try to identify the reference groups of the individuals in the study.

A common subjective technique is to ask people the name of the social class to which they belong or ask them to pick it from a list of social classes: upper, middle, working, or lower (Center, 1949: 77; Jackman, 1979). This technique is useful when the class labels are familiar to a large part of the population and there is general agreement about what they mean: only 2 percent of respondents in the Jackman study said they could not answer the class questions.

Subjective versus objective

In this discussion, the self-rating approach is described as subjective and some other techniques as objective. As used here, these terms refer to types of information and not to standards of evidence. Findings based on objective measures are not always superior to findings based on attitudes and opinions. Moreover, subjective data (self-ratings

At an official gathering, the British upper crust display their finery.

and ratings of others) can serve as a basis for conclusions that are objective in the sense that they are unbiased.

SOCIAL CLASSES: THE MARXIST MODEL

The words *strata* and *classes* are often used interchangeably to describe different social ranks or levels. However, when Marxist scholars speak of **class,** they are concerned not with social rank or statistically defined strata, but with problems of social organization and change.

Marx's theory of class*

From the historical standpoint, social classes are more than ranks in a hierarchy. According to Marx, classes are the basic building blocks of society, groupings of people—for example, industrial wage earners—who perform similar roles in the economic system.

The Marxist theory of class is summarized briefly in the following paragraphs.

The origin of classes. Social classes arise from the "relations of production," that is, the way work is organized. Some people own land; others are tenant farmers. Some work for wages; others are employers. However, Marx did not think of social strata such as occupation or income levels as classes. He believed that social class was rooted in key economic roles, such as the roles of employer and employee, that cut across industries and occupations.

Polarization. According to Marx, the major social classes of the modern era were the class of landowners and capitalists and the class of wage earners. Marx was aware that the class system was more complex than this, but he foresaw a polarization of society into two major camps: the capitalists or **bourgeoisie,** including commercial farmers, opposed to the workers or **proletariat,** who owned nothing but their labor power. Small farmers, small-business owners, and professionals would become employees of large businesses owned by a few wealthy capitalists and would be forced into the proletariat.

*For further discussion see Bendix and Lipset, 1966:6–11; Bottomore and Rubel, 1956; Dahrendorf, 1959, and Feuer, 1959.

Objective class and subjective class. The objective conditions of work and power define the individual's class level and interests. The employer's interests are opposed to those of the employees, no matter how sympathetic the employer or how friendly the employees. A worker does not become a member of the bourgeoisie simply by identifying with it.

Marx believed that in the course of time classes would become subjective, or self-aware, as well as objective. For example, manual workers were bound to become an organized, self-conscious class because life in a factory brings workers together in ways that make them aware of their common interests and strength.

Class rule and class struggle. In almost all societies, a few people have ruled the rest. But ruling must be understood in economic as well as political terms. A dominant economic class controls the society, including the government—the government is bourgeois when it serves the interests of the capitalist class. Thus, politics is shaped by economics, and political struggles are conflicts between economic classes.

Progressive versus reactionary classes. Changes in technology and social organization create new classes that challenge older ones. The capitalist class was "progressive" in that it created the conditions that led to the rise of a new class—the proletariat. The capitalists became reactionary, as did the feudal lords before them, when they tried to obstruct social development.

The end of the class system. The proletariat includes most of the society and has the widest aspirations. Therefore, the victory of the proletariat will be final, and classes will be replaced by a classless society.

Critique of Marxism

Criticisms of Marx's theories cluster around four main points:

Marx overemphasized the significance of economic class, both as a factor in individual behavior and as an explanation of historical events. Other sources of personal and group behavior are often more important than class. For example, nationalism and ethnic loyalty may overshadow class divisions. In addition, other aspects of social stratification, such as prestige, may have a greater influence on thought and action than do economic aspects. While economic class sometimes has a decisive effect on politics, politics can be independent of class influences and interests (Dahrendorf, 1959:chapters 7, 8).

Marx did not anticipate the forces that might reduce the polarization of classes. He thought that universal male suffrage would lead to the victory of the working class in England. He assumed that the workers, motivated by their common interests, would vote as a single group. But this did not happen. Nor did Marx anticipate the importance of more widespread participation in politics and the expansion of government programs to improve working and living conditions (Marshall, 1950/1964).

The prediction that workers would develop class consciousness and revolutionary aspirations was only partly correct. The polarization of society that he expected has not happened, although concentration of great wealth and power in the hands of a small number of corporations has the potential to polarize. Tendencies to split the society along class lines are counterbalanced by the multiplication of social strata based on occupation, education, and prestige. The American version of the class struggle is a conflict over wages, fringe benefits, job security, and working conditions—a far cry from the proletarian revolution predicted by Marx.

Marx thought the victory of the proletariat would end exploitation and that government would be replaced by an "administration of things." He hoped for a humane socialism and did not foresee the rise of totalitarianism as a threat to capitalism and democracy.

Despite these criticisms, Marxism has made a major contribution to sociology, especially social history. Although most sociologists do not accept all the elements of Marx's model, his ideas have made them aware of the role of class in history. To some extent they follow lines of thought that began with Marx and pursue the research problems he played a major part in defining.

THE FUNCTIONAL MODEL

Functional theorists reason that as society evolves in response to changing circumstances, successful adaptations survive and unsuccessful adaptations fall by the wayside. Stated in crude form, the necessity to make society work largely determines the broad pattern of social relationships and the types of persons that fill social positions.

The attempt to account for the persistence of inequality is one of the most challenging and challenged expressions of functionalism. The functional theory of inequality can be summarized as follows: Important, difficult, and dangerous tasks must be performed if the society is to survive. Talented people must be found and trained to do such tasks and to do them well. For some scarce skills, selecting the best candidates and training them involves a large commitment of time and effort. The ablest people can be persuaded to make the necessary effort to prepare for and to perform the tasks only if they are rewarded with high prestige and other advantages. Inequality is thus the result of getting the best-qualified people into important positions where they make valuable contributions to society (Davis and Moore, 1945).

Critique

The idea that only high rewards induce people to do these important duties has been repeatedly challenged (Tumin, 1953; Lopreato and Lewis, 1963; Stinchcombe, 1963; Goode, 1967; Alves and Rossi, 1978). Several questions are often raised:

Could people who have the potential to become doctors, engineers, scientists, and executives be socialized so they would feel obliged to enter these fields even if they anticipated only the same rewards as blue-collar workers?

Would the pleasure of doing highly skilled work be enough to motivate them to train for such jobs and do them well?

Is the long training necessary for highly rewarded occupations a sacrifice, or is the training itself rewarding?

Are people in responsible positions paid more than those in positions with less responsibility?

Do high rewards ensure the best performance of responsible tasks?

A study of more than 700 of the largest American businesses provides an answer to the last two questions. From the standpoint of functional theory, the amount that chief executives received was not related to how well they were doing their jobs or to the societal importance of the company's product. Executives of corporations producing steel, drugs, food, and clothing were not paid more than those producing cigarettes, cosmetics, or soft drinks. Instead, the compensation received by a chief executive was related to the size of the company (Broom and Cushing, 1977).

Most sociologists agree on the following general reservations about the functional theory:

1. Although some inequality in rewards may be necessary for society to function well, extreme inequality is not. The salaries and fringe benefits of executives in large corporations are many times larger than those of their low-paid employees. Top executives of some large corporations receive millions of dollars in salaries, plus stock options worth more millions in capital gains that are taxed at a low rate, plus interest-free loans, plus such expensive perquisites as the use of company cars, planes, and club memberships, plus "golden parachute" deals to protect the executive if the company is taken over by another corporation. These rich rewards are not necessarily richly deserved but are granted by the executives to themselves because they control the voting process on the board and in the annual stockholders' meetings.

2. The difference between top and low salaries is much smaller in publicly controlled organizations where executives perform tasks equal in difficulty and importance to the tasks of business executives. This comparison suggests that extremely large rewards are not necessary to ensure that important work is well done. Indeed, prestige and other nonfinancial rewards are often substituted for money. People give up sizable incomes to accept important government positions or to do more interesting or challenging work. The financial rewards of a job are not necessarily determined by the worker's contribution to society. Teachers rate above the average on a standard occupational prestige score (See Table 9.2, p. 184). However, they are rarely paid as much as their training and responsibility

suggest. On the other hand, athletes earn vast sums for brief performances and although they may be very talented, they do not contribute to improving the society.

3. Many people make a lot of money even though they do not have important positions or do socially useful work. Criminals are an obvious example. Noncriminal jobs such as those in the tobacco and liquor industries may be well paid even though the products are harmful.

4. The functionalist model does not take into account inherited wealth and ascribed status. Some inequality may be necessary to help identify, develop, and reward unusual talent, but no such claim can be made for inequality that is passed from one generation to the next. Inherited inequality is dysfunctional rather than functional because it tends to obstruct rather than encourage the discovery and employment of talent.

Section Two
Inequality

We now turn to specific forms of inequality: income, wealth, power, and prestige, all of which are interrelated. Income above the level required to maintain a given spending style leads to the accumulation of wealth. Wealth feeds on itself, generating further income from interest, dividends, and rents. Wealth and high income command services and deference, and they contain the seeds of power. They secure access to expert advisers and to persons who control investment opportunities. They permit entrée to places where the action is—financial and otherwise—and the chance to exercise power. In the language of the real estate dealer, high-income people are "qualified" buyers. Wealth, especially "old" wealth (earned by ancestors), is a source of prestige. Keep these interrelations among the kinds of inequality in mind while considering the separate measures.

INCOME

Of the objective measures of inequality, data on income are the most systematically compiled and the most widely available. Therefore, the distribution of income is often used as a test of inequality, especially when comparing countries, regions, or the same country at different times.

Nations differ in how they keep their records, in the accuracy and completeness of their statistics, in what they define as income, and in the way they estimate or ignore the money value of fringe benefits. A major complication is the impact of different taxation systems, which alter pretax income in diverse ways. It is therefore difficult to compare incomes earned in different countries, but it is interesting and important to try. However income is measured, there is no country in which all citizens receive even approximately the same income.

One of the most ambitious efforts to rate countries on income based on wages and salaries before taxes grouped a sample of 25 countries on a scale from most equal (group 1) to most unequal (group 5). The countries within each group were also ranked from most equal to most unequal:

1. Czechoslovakia, New Zealand, Hungary, Australia
2. Denmark, the United Kingdom, Sweden, Yugoslavia, Poland, West Germany, Canada, Belgium, the United States, Austria
3. The Netherlands, Argentina, Spain
4. Finland, France, Japan
5. Brazil, Chile, India, Sri Lanka, Mexico

Among the noncommunist countries, those that are most highly developed tend to be more equal. Australia and New Zealand are especially equal, but France, a highly developed country, is very unequal. In comparing countries of similar economic development, most communist countries are more equal than noncommunist countries.

As in capitalist countries, the more industrialized communist countries seem to be more equal than the less industrialized ones (Lydall, 1968:156–57). China was not included in the study, but it probably runs contrary to this generalization. It is a very poor developing country, but it may not be extremely unequal. Reliable income data for the Soviet Union are also hard to come by. There is a heavy concentration at the bottom of the income distribution (Kennan Institute, 1978:Appendix Table 1). However, if we take the value of subsidized rents and staple foods into account, the Soviet Union is likely to be more equal than capitalist countries at a similar development level.

The most extreme inequality is found among the very poor and industrially backward countries of Africa, Asia, and Latin America. In Indonesia, the income of the top 0.5 percent of population averages $2,000 per person, while the income of the bottom 50 percent averages $67. Other very poor countries such as Pakistan, India, and Bangladesh, whose annual per capita incomes average about $100, are also very unequal. They contain a number of families with comfortable incomes and a few with great wealth, but the prospects of reducing poverty and inequality in these countries are not good because of their rapid population growth (Uphoff, 1977).

Income inequality in the United States

Table 9.1 is a snapshot of the income distribution at one point in time. It shows the wide disparity of income in the United States during a period of inflation and high unemployment. The table shows family incomes because most people live in families and the family group is the economic unit for the majority of Americans. Clearly, most American families have comfortable incomes. However, 12 percent of all families and 23 percent of persons living outside families are below the poverty line. In all, more than 34 million persons live in poverty, and even more are barely above the poverty line.

Another way to study inequality is to look at how the pattern has changed. Figure 9.1 (see p. 181)

Table 9.1 Income Pyramid of United States Families, 1982

Income levels	Percent of families
$60,000 and over	6.2
50,000 – 59,999	4.7
40,000 – 49,999	9.1
30,000 – 39,999	15.8
20,000 – 29,999	23.0
10,000 – 19,999	24.5
Under $10,000	16.6
	N = 61,393,000

Source: *CPR*, P-60, no. 140, July 1983:Table 11.

The slum as playground.

shows the trend in the distribution of United States incomes over a generation stated in constant dollars. The term *constant dollars* means that the decline in the dollar's purchasing power is taken into account. If the data were reported in *current dollars* —the number of dollars actually earned each year— the figures would be hard to interpret because of the effects of inflation. For example, in personal buying power, the 1982 dollar was worth roughly one-third as much as the 1963 dollar.

The median income of American families, expressed in 1982 dollars and rounded to the nearest hundred, was $13,000 in 1947. It reached a high of $26,100 in 1978 and in 1982 had fallen to $23,-400. The percent of families with low incomes de-

clined until around 1968, remained stable for several years, but began to climb again during the 1980s recession.

Expressed in 1982 dollars, about 12 percent of families had incomes over $25,000 in 1952. In 1960 the number had reached 28 percent, in 1970 48 percent, and in 1978 52 percent. But in 1982 47 percent of families had incomes over $25,000, not quite as many as twelve years earlier.

Following World War II the economic status and the consumption styles of a very large part of the American population significantly improved. But the 1980s recession began to bite into the incomes even of those families above the median level. From the perspective of 1947 when the median family income was about $13,000, most Americans in 1982 seemed to be very well off with a median income of over $23,000. From the perspective of 1982, there had been enough erosion of income to cause concern among those accustomed to an increasingly liberal pattern of expenditure.

WEALTH

Because people with large incomes spend only a small fraction of their resources, wealth is more highly concentrated than income. Studies of the concentration of wealth depend mostly on estate (inheritance) tax returns. In the United States such returns must be filed within a year of a person's death if the value of the estate exceeds a specified level, but there is a lag of several years before tax information is analyzed statistically. Information is never gathered on the lower range of estates that are not subject to tax.

There is evidence that the concentration of personal wealth at the very tip of the pyramid has diminished in the past half century.* In the 1920s the net worth of the top one-half of one percent (0.5 percent) of the population was about one-third of all personal wealth in the United States. In 1976 the net assets of the richest 0.5 percent had declined to

*Wealth is measured by net worth: assets minus liabilities. Assets consist of cash, real estate, stocks, bonds, insurance, partnership shares, and other property. Liabilities are debts, taxes owed, interest payments due, etc.

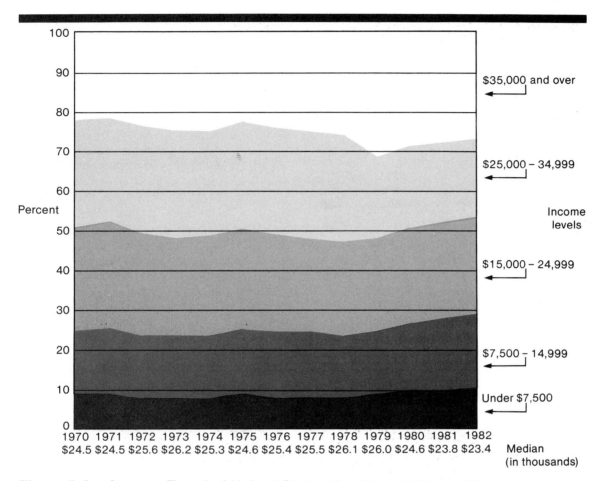

Figure 9.1   Income Trend of United States Families, 1970 – 1982
(in constant 1982 dollars)
Source: CPR, P-60, No. 140, July 1983: Table 3.

about 15 percent of total wealth *(Statistical Abstract, 1982–83:*Table 743; Smith, 1982:14 and Table 1).

> Where has the share of the wealth previously owned by the very rich gone? Has it been scattered broadly across the entire distribution? Our best guess is that it has merely shifted downward a few percentiles. This kind of redistribution from the super rich to the nearly super rich is redistribution to be sure, but it is hardly of social or economic significance (Smith, 1982:5).

The "redistribution" is not of social or economic significance because it had little impact on social and

economic equality. If the share held by the richest people had been spread broadly, then there would have been increased equality instead of a shifted concentration.

What has happened since 1976? The stock market boom of the early 1980s was combined with high rates of unemployment, mortgage foreclosures, and business failures. We estimate that as a result the nation experienced increased concentration of wealth, a pumping up rather than a filtering down of personally held assets.

In the United Kingdom, the trend toward reduced concentration of wealth resembled the United States pattern. The top 1 percent of wealth holders owned about one-fourth of personal wealth in 1975—a little more than the amount owned by the bottom 80 percent of the population (Burghes, 1979).

Most data on wealth holders are for individuals. However, from the standpoint of inequality and social stratification, family wealth is more meaningful. The rich spread their wealth and its benefits among family members. Reports based on individual wealth therefore understate the impact of wealth concentration on the whole society. Accumulated wealth passed from generation to generation perpetuates inequality and "reproduces" a moneyed class.

Billionaires and centimillionaires

Much of the 15 percent of total personal wealth held by the one-half of one percent of the U.S. population is concentrated in the hands of a very few billionaires and centimillionaires whose wealth is measured in hundreds of millions of dollars. Studies of persons of great wealth are fraught with difficulties and perhaps legal hazards. With rare exceptions the wealthy would rather not talk about their wealth, and they can make it difficult for anyone to find out the details. Their holdings are numerous and complicated, and they are often not in publicly held companies. Thus a special kind of detective work in interpreting financial records is required to study the very rich, and this is rarely tried in a systematic way.

Under the auspices of the financial magazine, *Forbes,* three specialist interpreters of financial records attempted to identify the 400 richest people in the United States, whom they call "The Forbes Four Hundred" (Seneker et al., 1982). The authors suggest that they intend to repeat the study from time to time, and their success or failure in doing so will be an indication of how far rich people can frustrate what to sociologists seems a legitimate effort in financial journalism.

The investigators identified 13 billionaires and 387 centimillionaires. All but three of the billionaires gained their riches from oil, either by their own efforts or by inheritance. Five of the billionaires and five centimillionaires are children of oilman H. L. Hunt, who is invariably referred to,

and with some reason, as "legendary." Twenty-three centimillionaires won their wealth through oil ventures and even more through oil combined with other activities such as real estate. In all 45 inherited their wealth from oil related enterprises. Twenty-nine others were heirs of the duPont fortune. These do not include numerous other members of duPont families whose individual shares are large but do not reach the $100 million benchmark.

The investigators say the extraordinarily rich use their money to create jobs, goods, and services (Seneker et al., 1982:100). However, examination of their evidence suggests that this is not always the case. The billionaires seem to manage their money, or have it managed for them, with more attention to investment in resources and real estate than to applying their assets directly to productive purpose. This is probably owing to the fact that so many of the "400" derive their wealth from oil. In 1980 several of the Hunt heirs were involved in a massive speculation in silver commodity futures, which was only resolved by a bail-out loan in excess of $1 billion arranged by the Federal Reserve Board, presumably to prevent chaos in the world commodity markets. The restraints imposed by the Federal Reserve as a condition to the bail out did not demote the speculators below the billionaire class.

Two of the centimillionaires are identified with outright criminal activities. No doubt there are others whose wealth represents money well "laundered" in this or past generations.

Several of the billionaires, however, turned their talents to inventing and developing new products. In doing so they made a lot of money and created many jobs through their enterpreneurship and technical skills, for example: Steven Jobs of Apple Computer, David Packard of Hewlett Packard, Kenneth Olsen of Digital Equipment, An Wang of Wang Labs, and Edwin Whitehead, who developed medical instruments.

PRESTIGE

Stratification by prestige is part of daily life. It is a source of pain for some people and of satisfaction for others. In contrast to economic inequality, which draws on objective data, prestige is more subjective and personal. In evaluating a friend, we think of personal characteristics such as kindliness and honesty, but these may have little or no connection with prestige. Prestige is more likely to be assessed by such social characteristics as family status, neighborhood status, organization memberships, college attended, and occupation. Of these, occupational status has proved to be the most satisfactory way to estimate the prestige of categories of people.

Occupational prestige

Studies conducted in the United States since 1927 show a high degree of consistency in the prestige of various occupations. In the two best-known studies, those conducted by the National Opinion Research Center (NORC) in 1947 and 1963, 90 occupations were rated by national samples of respondents. The prestige scores from the two studies are highly correlated, although during the 16 years most scientific occupations gained prestige and most artistic occupations lost prestige (Hodge, Siegel, and Rossi, 1964). (See Table 9.2, pg. 184.)

The prestige scores contain few surprises. In general, white-collar work has higher prestige than blue-collar work: Supreme Court justice stands at the top and shoe shiner at the bottom. Nuclear physicist is at the top of the academic heap. Sociologist is several points above economist but several points below psychologist. Viewed as a whole, the prestige scores are highly correlated with the income and educational levels of workers in each occupation (Broom and Maynard, 1969), but there are some interesting exceptions. Minister and school teacher rank higher in prestige than in income, but undertaker and nightclub singer have less prestige than would be estimated from their income. A farm owner-operator ranks higher than might be predicted from either income or education.

Obviously, the prestige of occupations reflects more than economic rewards and educational requirements. Responsibility, independence, working conditions, and place of work may also influence the ratings (Garbin and Bates, 1961). The reality of ranks is not questioned, but they can be interpreted in different ways. More complex ratings suggest that what is being measured is not prestige as such but the more general values attached to jobs (Gold-

thorpe and Hope, 1972:31). Comparisons of occupational prestige in different countries show a striking similarity in overall ratings (Hodge, Treiman, and Rossi, 1966; Treiman, 1977).

The most interesting variations in occupational rankings occur among blue-collar jobs. Some kinds of manual work that require technical skills are becoming more important and commanding higher wages. Perhaps this changed ranking foreshadows further changes in attitudes toward manual labor and shifts in the relative prestige of some blue-collar and white-collar jobs.

A sample survey that related 12 occupation groups to 5 social classes found a high consensus in class assignment at the upper and lower levels. However, jobs in the middle of the range, especially skilled blue-collar and lower white-collar workers evoked less agreement. Such blue-collar categories as ''plumbers and carpenters'' and ''foremen in factories'' and also white-collar groupings of ''school teachers and social workers,'' ''small businessmen,'' and ''supervisors in offices and stores'' were more widely spread among class categories (Jackman, 1979:449–451).

Highly skilled jobs generated by new high technology occupations no doubt have correspondingly high status. However, low-skilled clerical jobs that merely involve entering numbers in a computer instead of in a ledger are still clerical jobs and have relatively low prestige. The glamour of the computer rubs off fast.

In the socialist countries of eastern Europe, manual work is highly regarded. Manual workers, especially miners, earn higher wages than clerical workers, and their prestige ratings are also high (Treiman, 1977:144–48). In Poland technicians are rated above office workers in certain rewards and life-styles, and this ranking may be the case in other socialist countries as well (Wesolowski and Slomczynski, 1968:210).

POWER

Power is harder to study than prestige. With only a little exaggeration, Benjamin Disraeli, Queen Victoria's prime minister, observed that ''the most powerful men are not public men. The public man is responsible and the responsible man is a slave. It is

Table 9.2   Prestige Ratings of Occupations

Occupation	NORC Score	Rank	Occupation	NORC Score	Rank	Occupation	NORC Score	Rank
U.S. Supreme Court justice	94	1	Artist who paints pictures that are exhibited in galleries	78	34.5	Plumber	65	59
Physician	93	2				Automobile repairman	64	60
Nuclear physicist	92	3.5	Musician in a symphony orchestra	78	34.5	Playground director	63	62.5
Scientist	92	3.5				Barber	63	62.5
Government scientist	91	5.5	Author of novels	78	34.5	Machine operator in a factory	63	62.5
State governor	91	5.5	Economist	78	34.5	Owner-operator of a lunch stand	63	62.5
Cabinet member in the federal government	90	8	Official of an international labor union	77	37	Corporal in the regular army	62	65.5
College professor	90	8	Railroad engineer	76	39	Garage mechanic	62	65.5
U.S. representative in Congress	90	8	Electrician	76	39	Truck driver	59	67
Chemist	89	11	County agricultural agent	76	39	Fisherman who owns his own boat	58	68
Lawyer	89	11	Owner-operator of a printing shop	75	41.5	Clerk in a store	56	70
Diplomat in the U.S. foreign service	89	11	Trained machinist	75	41.5	Milk route man	56	70
Dentist	88	14	Farm owner and operator	74	44	Streetcar motorman	56	70
Architect	88	14	Undertaker	74	44	Lumberjack	55	72.5
County judge	88	14	Welfare worker for a city government	74	44	Restaurant cook	55	72.5
Psychologist	87	17.5	Newspaper columnist	73	46	Singer in a nightclub	54	74
Minister	87	17.5	Policeman	72	47	Filling station attendant	51	75
Member of a board of directors of a large corporation	87	17.5	Reporter on a daily newspaper	71	48	Dockworker	50	77.5
Mayor of a large city	87	17.5	Radio announcer	70	49.5	Railroad section hand	50	77.5
Priest	86	21.5	Bookkeeper	70	49.5	Night watchman	50	77.5
Head of a department in a state government	86	21.5	Tenant farmer (one who owns live- stock and machinery and manages the farm)	69	51.5	Coal miner	50	77.5
Civil engineer	86	21.5				Restaurant waiter	49	80.5
Airline pilot	86	21.5	Insurance agent	69	51.5	Taxi driver	49	80.5
Banker	85	24.5	Carpenter	68	53	Farm hand	48	83
Biologist	85	24.5	Manager of a small store in a city	67	54.5	Janitor	48	83
Sociologist	83	26	A local official of a labor union	67	54.5	Bartender	48	83
Instructor in public schools	82	27.5	Mail carrier	66	57	Clothes presser in a laundry	45	85
Captain in the regular army	82	27.5	Railroad conductor	66	57	Soda fountain clerk	44	86
Accountant for a large business	81	29.5	Traveling salesman for a wholesale concern	66	57	Sharecropper— one who owns no livestock or equipment and does not manage farm	42	87
Public school teacher	81	29.5				Garbage collector	39	88
Owner of a factory that employs about 100 people	80	31.5				Street sweeper	36	89
Building contractor	80	31.5				Shoe shiner	34	90

Source: Robert W. Hodge, Paul M. Siegal, and Peter H. Rossi, "Occupational Prestige in the United States, 1925-63," *American Journal of Sociology,* 70 (1964), Table 1, pp. 290-92. (By permission of the University of Chicago Press, copyright 1964.)

private life that governs the world." Private people who are also powerful tend to guard their privacy, and their doing so makes it difficult to study the distribution and use of power at the national level. The exercise of power in organizations has already been discussed in Chapter 6.

Elites have been defined as "the few who get the most of any value . . . the rest are the rank and file" (Lasswell, 1934/1950:3). Thus, there are many kinds of elites—business elites, prestige elites, cultural elites, intellectual elites, and power elites. Sometimes, as in Britain, elites consolidate and form an *establishment*.

Power elites

One view of the power structure in the United States holds that it is a cohesive *power elite* consisting of (1) a corporate elite made up of executives of large companies, (2) a military elite made up of senior officers, and (3) a small political elite consisting of the president and top officials in the executive branch (Mills, 1956:chap. 12). This power elite makes the most important decisions at the national level. And because its members have similar social backgrounds, values, and interests, they tend to form similar judgments and to act in unison. In this view, different interests and concerns are not balanced off against each other (cf. Domhoff, 1967).

At the end of his presidency, Dwight D. Eisenhower spoke of a "conjunction of an immense military establishment and a large arms industry" and warned "against the acquisition of unwarranted influence, whether sought or unsought, by the military-industrial complex" (Farewell Address, January 17, 1961). It has been argued that the relationship between large corporations and the government has a strong effect on national policies that overrides the traditional separation of public and private sectors (Galbraith, 1967).

A competing view of the power structure in the United States is the *pluralist* or *balance thesis,* which holds that major decisions tend to be compromises among several interest groups, each of which has a veto that it can use to thwart decisions that threaten its interests (Riesman et al., 1950:242–55). In this view, power has become more widely dispersed as

a result of the growing number of interest groups as well as certain changes in the capitalist system.

The two views stress contrasting aspects of reality: Various groups make their influence felt in different ways at different levels of the power structure. Though local labor unions are a major force in a few communities, business interests tend to dominate at the community level. On the other hand, national labor leaders are a powerful force in national politics and in the making of broad economic decisions. At the national level, labor organizations act as lobby groups usually competing but sometimes cooperating with corporate and special interest lobbies when their objectives coincide.

Section Three
Poverty

The persistence of poverty in rich countries is a matter of widespread concern to politicians and informed citizens. But daily contact with the poor and awareness of the impact of poverty is limited mainly to the poor themselves and to those who run welfare programs.

Poverty in less developed countries with average annual incomes of around $100 per person is very different from poverty in countries like the United States, where the poverty line is far above that level. In the poorest countries, poverty is a way of life. If absolute poverty is defined as a deficiency in the diet, as many as 700 million people live in absolute poverty (M. Williams, 1977:8–9). If absolute poverty is defined by a simple thing like an unsafe water supply, half of the people in developing countries, perhaps 1.5 billion, live in absolute poverty.

Mass poverty in the Third World was once a rural phenomenon, but it is now engulfing the fast-growing cities of the poorest countries. Poverty in such countries as Bangladesh and Somalia is conspicuous evidence of the consequences of uncontrolled population growth and economic failure. In despair, some demographers and economists call them "basket cases."

Many of America's poor live in circumstances that would be envied by those starving on the streets of Calcutta. However, there is no reason for the urban

A poor child in Brooklyn is statistically much better off than a poor child in Pakistan. But should he consider himself fortunate?

poor of New York to compare themselves with the urban poor of Calcutta. Nor is there any reason for them to compare themselves with their great-grandparents, although the goods and services that are now considered to be a subsistence budget would have been classified as "comfortable" at the beginning of the century (Rainwater, 1974:48). Inevitably the urban poor compare their living conditions with the well-off people they see around them. "Our desires and pleasures spring from society, we measure them, therefore, by society. . . . Because they are of a social nature they are of a relative nature" (Marx, quoted in Rainwater, 1974:22).

THE EXTENT OF POVERTY

In 1959, when systematic data on poverty were first compiled for the United States, there were 39.5 million poor persons and nearly one-fourth of the population was poor. During the 1960s, the number of the poor fell to a low of 23 million in 1973. In the mid-1970s the number of poor began to rise again, and there was a sharp increase in the 1980s recession. In 1982 when the poverty line for a family of four was an income of $9,826, over 34 million persons (15 percent of the total population) were in poverty. Broken down by ethnicity, the figures are: 12 percent of whites, 36 percent of blacks, and 30 percent of Spanish origin (Bureau of the Census press release, August 1983). The long-term trend in ethnic poverty is shown in Adaptation 2.2, p. 23.

The poverty rate for old persons is higher than for those under 65. Middle-class people who have worked all their lives and saved through retirement plans often find their security destroyed by inflation. Because they value self-reliance, they are caught in a bind created by their own values. They have lost the security they earned with their savings but are reluctant to accept the welfare aid to which they may be entitled.

A large fraction of the poor are "hard-core" poor: many old persons, those who lack skills that are in demand on the job market, women with children but without husbands, and those with severe mental and physical handicaps. The chances of falling below the poverty line are closely related to family size. For families in which the householder is female with no husband present, the numbers are especially ominous. For example, in 1981 four out of ten white six-person families with female heads and almost eight out of ten such black families were below the poverty line (*CPR,* P-60, no. 138, March 1983: Tables 17, 18).

The income of the hard-core poor cannot be raised by increasing their productivity. Only by changing the norm that links the right to consume with the individual's contribution to the economy can such poverty be eliminated. With almost 32 million persons in poverty, what would it take to raise the income of all poor families and individuals above the poverty line? A rough calculation suggests that the total deficit of the poor in 1981 was about $37 billion, which was over 1 percent of the United States GNP ($3,291 billion). Depending on personal values and priorities, some pointed comparisons can be made between the amount needed to eliminate poverty and the amount spent on tobacco, alcohol, pot, cosmetics, pet food, a type of military hardware, or some other goods and services. The total expenditure on tobacco in 1981 was about $23 billion and on alcoholic beverages over $46 billion.

UNEMPLOYMENT

The largest single cause of poverty in the United States, Canada, and Great Britain is chronic unemployment and underemployment. Since 1970, the number unemployed in the United States has not fallen below 4 million and has gone above 11 million. Even under favorable economic conditions, the unemployment rate in the United States and Canada has rarely been below 6 percent although Sweden, Japan, and West Germany maintain much lower unemployment rates.

International comparisons are necessarily crude because countries vary in how they define unemployment. The United States definition includes those who did not work during the week the survey was conducted and who had looked for work during the preceding four weeks. Persons who gave up the job search are called *discouraged workers* and are not included with the unemployed even though they are willing to work. If they were added to the statistics, the number unemployed in 1982 and 1983 would have been increased by some 2 million.

Young people just entering the labor force are more than twice as likely to be unemployed as the average worker. In the past women had a higher unemployment rate than men, but this may be changing. Women with children but without husbands have a higher rate than married women living with their husbands. Blacks suffer from double the unemployment of whites, and the rate for young blacks can be twice the black average. Such selective unemployment eats away at family stability, the aspirations of the young, and the security of children.

Prolonged unemployment clearly is more damaging than brief periods out of work. From 1970 to 1979, when the overall United States unemployment rate ranged between 5 and 8.5 percent, one-third to one-half of the unemployed had been without work for a month or less. The average time they were out of work was between 9 and 16 weeks, and the percent out of work for half a year or longer ranged from 6 percent of the unemployed in 1970 to a high of over 18 percent in 1976 (*Statistical Abstract,* 1978:408;

1979:394). In 1982 over one-third of those classified as unemployed had been out of work for over four months. According to a Conference Board survey, 24 percent of all wage earners were unemployed at least once during 1982.

For older people who remember the depression of the 1930s, mass unemployment conjures up pictures of millions of jobless, bread lines, and soup kitchens. The voice of Bing Crosby singing the plaintive ''Brother, Can You Spare a Dime?'' brings back desperate years before widespread unemployment insurance when the unemployed had to fall back on public or private charity (Angell, 1936/1965; Bakke, 1935/1940; Ginzberg et al., 1943).

Unemployment now affects a smaller percentage of the labor force than it did in the depths of the great depression; *on the average* it does not last as long; and the unemployed are cushioned by unemployment insurance. Major dislocations such as the 1980s recession caused a high unemployment rate although still far below the 1930s depression level. Especially hard hit were building construction and automobile manufacturing. Workers in localities where such industries were concentrated experienced exceedingly high unemployment rates for extended periods, in many cases long enough to exhaust their unemployment insurance.

A study of the effects of unemployment shows that joblessness is linked with high levels of discontent and great personal cost. Compared with the employed, the unemployed are less satisfied with their family life, their achievements, and especially their income, and those who are out of work for longer periods are more likely to be dissatisfied. Not many choose to be unemployed (Schlozman and Verba, 1978).

The under class

Although they stand on the lower rungs of the status ladder, lower-level blue-collar workers and most poor people are integrated into the social order. They can hope to improve the lot of their children, if not their own, and a majority of the poor will not remain poor.

Below the lower blue-collar workers is a submerged population, an **under class** almost out of reach of the larger society. They are the chronically unemployed or underemployed. Their children often work at odd jobs to supplement the family income. Illness is common; savings are unknown; possessions are often pawned. What little money they have is badly managed.

The disorderly misery in which the under class live might suggest that they should be promising recruits for revolutionary movements. However, Marx did not think so and classified them as outside the boundaries of social labor. They are, in Marxist terms, the *lumpenproletariat* who do not perform productive work and are not available for revolution. To be available for revolutionary activity implies an awareness of the social system and a degree of political involvement. Far from being potential political activists, many members of the under class are not sufficiently aware of how the system works even to claim their welfare entitlements. Without a permanent address, many of the under class fall through the so-called safety net and are not counted in the statistics.

Section Four
Contrasting Life-Styles

Section Three examined the magnitude and persistence of poverty and some of the effects of impoverishment. The first part of this section contrasts a few correlates of stratification revealing how socioeconomic status affects everyday life. Next, brief sketches of elite life-styles are given, which throw those of poverty into stark relief. It concludes by discussing a gray area of the socioeconomic order —the large and growing underground economy that seems to involve persons at almost every social level.

CORRELATES OF STRATIFICATION

Stratification affects everyday life in many ways and at all levels. Table 9.3 illustrates some of the differences among three broad social strata in terms of life

Table 9.3   Stratification Correlates: United States

Characteristic	Education stratum		
	Lower	**Middle**	**Upper**
Median household income, 1981 [a]	$9,700	$20,600	$31,200
Children ever born per 1000 women [b]	4,247	3,598	2,389
Voted in 1980 election [c]	43%	59%	80%
Think extramarital sex relations are always or almost always wrong [d]	90%	86%	79%
Think homosexual relations are always or almost always wrong [d]	90%	82%	62%
Used seat belt during last ride in car [e]	9%	13%	28%
Believe in literal interpretation of the Bible (Christians only) [e]	56%	40%	21%
Favor stricter handgun laws [e]	51%	58%	67%

Characteristic	Income Stratum		
	Lower	**Middle**	**Upper**
Victims of burglary per 1,000 households [f]	101	81	87
Overweight women [g]	52%	43%	9%
Own a dishwasher [h]	6%	23%	64%
Say they are "very happy" [i]	29%	38%	56%
Consider themselves Democrats [j]	55%	43%	36%
Don't belong to a voluntary association [k]	69%	58%	45%
Travel less than 5 miles to work [l]	57%	44%	29%

[a] *CPR*, P-60, no.137, March 1983:31.
[b] *Statistical Abstract*, 1975:table 75 (women ever married, aged 35-40).
[c] *Statistical Abstract*, 1982-83:493.
[d] NORC surveys (1973, 1974, 1976).
[e] Gallup survey (1982).
[f] *Statistical Abstract*, 1978:181.
[g] Burnight and Marden, 1967:75-92.
[h] *Statistical Abstract*, 1975 (table 665).
[i] Gallup survey (1971).
[j] Gallup survey (1975).
[k] Hyman and Wright, 1971:table 4.
[l] *CPR*, P-23, no. 99, July 1979:12.

chances, advantages, attitudes, and behavior. These differences are *correlates* of stratification, that is, they occur more often in some strata and less often in others. You will not be surprised to see in the table that people with more income are more likely to own dishwashers and that people with less education are more likely to have low incomes.

In the dishwasher example, the connection between the stratification variable (income) and the correlate (owning dishwashers) is clearly cause and effect. Similarly, more education is likely to result in higher income. In other cases, the connection

between cause and effect cannot be definitely established. Take, for example, the fact that a higher proportion of lower-income women than of higher-income women are overweight. We cannot prove that a low income causes people to be overweight, but it is easy to think of reasons why being overweight might be linked to a low income. Poor people must buy cheap, filling foods to satisfy their hunger. Better-off people eat a diet high in protein, and their diet contains fewer empty calories. Because poor people tend to be less well educated and less informed shoppers, they do not get the best food value for their dollars. Thus, a statistical example leads to a consideration of how low income might be connected to a physical condition.

"Lower," "middle," and "upper" are broad categories, and each one contains many kinds of people with a wide range of attitudes and behavior. Nevertheless, the table is a useful summary of relationships between social rank and how people live, act, and think. The following discussion suggests how combinations of social characteristics result in distinctive life-styles.

ELITE LIFE-STYLES

At the top of the social hierarchy, people have enough wealth so they do not need to work unless they want to, but many of them nevertheless work diligently all their lives. Others relax and enjoy the fruits of their ancestors' labors. There is an old New England saying that those who are really rich can live on the interest of the interest on their investments. In other words, without invading the principal of their wealth, indeed while their wealth continues to grow, rich people can live as lavishly as they please.

However, wealth does not create instant prestige. "The Forbes Four Hundred," especially the billionaires, are very different from a "Society" Four Hundred (Amory, 1960). The following brief historical account of an American elite reveals the mechanisms that led to the growth and decline of a cohesive, privileged, mostly affluent group that were part of "Society" or had close ties with it. Their common life-style and values made them a **status group** as well as part of an economic class (Weber, in Gerth and Mills, 1945:180–195).

American elite

The most important institutions that contributed to the growth of a traditional American elite were the New England boarding schools and fashionable eastern colleges. Children of the elite met at school, intermarried, and formed ties that endured after they returned home. The Episcopal church, which developed into a national upper-class institution, also encouraged and benefited from the solidarity of the elite. In addition, the growth of large corporations

and easy travel helped local-community social elites form a national upper class (Mills, 1956; Baltzell, 1958; 1966).

The rise and decline of a WASP (White Anglo-Saxon Protestant) elite spanned four generations. The founding generation, the "robber barons," made their fortunes during the second half of the 1800s and left large inheritances to their families. They endowed the elite private schools, Ivy League colleges, museums, libraries, and other civic facilities.

Their sons, the second generation, went to the colleges their fathers had endowed, but few of these schools had places for women. After college, the sons found jobs in banking and business through family connections. They maintained large estates, summer homes, household servants, and an affluent life-style that was closely tied to communities. "In many ways it was the generation that produced the last exclusive and still authoritative upper class in America" (Baltzell, 1976:505).

The third generation came of age during the depression of the 1930s, when many families lost their fortunes. However, the sons still went to private schools, sometimes on scholarships. This generation served in World War II, which has been described as "the most leveling and homogenizing war in our history." After the war, those at the top lived "almost anonymously in unostentatious houses without full-time live-in servants, traveling by air to ski in New England, Colorado, or Europe or to sail the Caribbean or the Mediterranean" (Baltzell, 1976:508). Their life-style today is no longer tied to specific communities, but it is still clearly an affluent life-style.

Unlike earlier generations who were admitted on the basis of family background, members of the fourth generation are not guaranteed places in elite colleges. Even so, the quality of their schooling and their home environment give these students an advantage in competing for places in Ivy League colleges and in the world of work.

In recent years, marriage outside WASP circles has become more common while class awareness and solidarity declined. The rich are not less rich than they used to be, but they come from more varied backgrounds. They lack the group and class solidarity of an earlier day. Findings from The American Leadership Study show that WASPS are numerically dominant in all leadership sectors except business and Congress, and even in business and Congress they are overrepresented. The achievement of leadership status by ethnic groups is impeded at entry but ethnicity is not an absolute obstacle to a leadership career (Alba and Moore, 1982: 380–81).

Soviet elite*

An old Soviet joke says that capitalism is the exploitation of man by man, and socialism is the reverse. However, in terms of basic reported income the USSR is more egalitarian than capitalist countries. In the Soviet Union, private ownership of land, natural resources, and productive machinery is banned, making it hard to accumulate wealth. Small valuables are also hard to get, and consumer durables and vehicles, so common in Western economies, are still scarce or restricted. Basic housing (meager), health care (probably adequate), and food (monotonous but adequate) are available to all.

The USSR does not pretend to be strictly egalitarian, and it is probably less equal than it pretends to be. It is an industrial state, and its workers have a range of skills and talents that are rewarded at different rates. Members of the bureaucracy also receive rewards according to their authority and power.

Russia is a closed society, and its inequalities are not public knowledge. If anyone knows how much of the nation's wealth or income or luxuries is held by those at the top, no one is telling. The public is aware of differences in life-style, but not of the extent of those differences and how they are maintained.

Many goods and services are scarce in the USSR, but elite life-styles are possible for those in privileged positions: party officials, government officials, recipients of state honors, members of the intelligentsia, and academicians. They are rewarded for their high status with higher or untaxed incomes, bonuses or special pensions, and payment in special

*Based on Connor, 1979; Hollander, 1973:chap. 6; and Matthews, 1978.

currency to be spent in shops that are not open to the general public. They enjoy subsidized vacations and foreign travel, the use of holiday homes (whose luxury varies according to their status), larger dwellings at reduced cost, better health services, and better schooling for their children.

In Russia, elite life-styles are not governed by the ability to pay. They are part of a separate economic sector with its own rules. Privileged persons can use their contacts, influence, and bribery, or *blat*, to get goods and services that are in limited supply. Like most of humanity, members of the Soviet elite prefer a comfortable life-style to an austere one.

THE UNDERGROUND ECONOMY

The total amount of economic activity in a country is much larger than reported GNP because every country has an **underground economy** beyond the reach of tax collectors or the police. But it is not clear where legal transactions end and the underground economy begins. This problem in Britain has been described as follows:

> Suppose Mrs. Jones knits her husband a sweater in return for the housekeeping allowance. She pays no income tax, he pays no value-added tax [a kind of sales tax]. Yet no one would dream of accusing her of tax-dodging. But what if she knits for a neighbour in return for babysitting? Or for the electrician who mends her washing machine? Or for a shop that pays her in cash?
>
> Most would place the boundaries of the black [underground] economy somewhere between the second and third example, if only for practical reasons. Small transactions between neighbours are nearly as undetectable as the quite untaxable give and take of family life. Even when that cut-off point is decided, the black economy is a neat label for a very untidy collection of activities. [*The Economist*, September 22, 1979:106]

Underground workers

The participants in the underground economy are of three types: (1) poor people, the unemployed, and those on Social Security; (2) systematic tax evaders, mostly self-employed people who also work in the regular economy, and (3) criminals. The least organized of these are unemployed and underemployed people who work to bridge their period of unemployment or to supplement their income, but are paid in cash with no tax withheld and thereby become part of the underground economy. Sometimes a cash payment is a matter of convenience, but more often it is intended to keep the transaction secret, at least from the tax collector.

The dangers in this type of transaction are often overlooked: The worker loses the protection of accident insurance and Social Security credits. Furthermore, organized crime creeps into the cracks in the system of informal economic transactions. Stolen property or defective goods are sold by more or less innocent vendors to more or less innocent buyers, who choose to ignore the source of the bargain. Petty bribery and threats to reveal matters to the police can turn into extortion.

The second group of participants in the underground economy are part-time tax evaders, usually self-employed persons with legal businesses, some of which are quite lucrative. They pay tax on the visible part of their income, but in the underground economy they accept payment in cash or in kind, or swap goods or services. (Note that the exchange of services may be legal tax avoidance rather than illegal tax evasion.) It is hard for salaried employees or wage earners to participate in the underground economy, but self-employed professionals, shopkeepers, and blue-collar workers can do so fairly easily. Some lawyers and doctors reduce their taxable income by offering their services on the underground market; mechanics or construction workers can also do jobs on the side for extra pay that is not reported as income. When a shop owner fails to ring up a sale on the cash register, the practice, to evade paying tax, is called "skimming." If an employee does not ring up a sale and pockets the cash, it is theft.

The third and most highly organized groups of participants in the underground economy are criminals. Law enforcement agencies sometimes penalize criminals for tax evasion when they cannot make a case directly against their criminal activities —theft, prostitution, drug pushing, and extortion. The underground economic transactions of the poor and unemployed do little harm to the economy

as a whole and are probably helpful to the workers themselves if they are short-run activities and do not become a way of life. The underground activities of the self-employed and of criminals, however, distort the working of the market and shift the tax burden onto those whose jobs are entirely in the regular economy *(Time,* September 17, 1979:57). Underground activities are never included in official statistics, but many people are involved. Estimates for the United States suggest that between one-tenth and one-quarter of the GNP falls in the underground economy (Malabre, 1980).

Underground economies are not solely capitalist pathologies. Unreported moonlighting, bribery, and engaging in prohibited forms of trade exist in socialist countries and are called economic crime (Connor, 1972; 1979:248).

Section Five
Social Mobility

In modern societies, much of the population is constantly on the move: from place to place, job to job, and school to work. Geographical mobility becomes social mobility when a residence change results in new jobs, new life-styles, and new personal ties. A job shift may involve changes in income, opportunities, working conditions, and work mates. Improved education may lead to new credentials and new job prospects. Occupational change contributes to **social mobility**—significant change in social position, life chances, and life-styles.

VERTICAL AND HORIZONTAL MOBILITY

The study of social mobility emphasizes major alterations in the way of life of large numbers of people. Most attention is given to **vertical mobility**—an upward or downward change in the rank of an individual or group. A promotion or demotion, a change in income, marriage to a person of higher or lower status, a move to a better or worse neighborhood—these are all examples of vertical social mobility. A change that does not involve a major movement up or down the stratification ladder is called **horizontal mobility.**

	FUNCTIONAL CATEGORIES (SITUSES)		
STRATA	**Finance and Records**	**Manufacturing**	**Transportation**
High	Bank manager H ←	Industrial engineer → H	Railroad president
	Accountant	Lithographer	Airline pilot
Middle	Bookkeeper	Bookbinder	Railroad conductor
	Bank teller V ↑	Tool and die maker	Mail carrier
Low	File clerk ↓ V	Forge worker	Bus driver
	Bank messenger	Factory laborer	Section hand

V ←——→ V Vertical mobility, from stratum to stratum
H ←——→ H Horizontal mobility, from situs to situs

Figure 9.2 Types of Mobility

Vertical mobility is usually measured by occupational change. In modern industrial societies, a person's job tells more about that person's position in the pattern of inequality than any other fact. Fortunately, it is easy to find out people's job histories. They talk freely about their work, and data about occupations are fairly straightforward.

Vertical and horizontal occupational mobility are illustrated in Figure 9.2. A bank messenger who is promoted to bank teller experiences vertical mobility. If an accountant in a bank moves to a credit union to do similar tasks at about the same salary and with the same prestige and authority, neither horizontal nor vertical movement takes place. The accountant remains at the same occupational level and in the same sector of the economy.

Suppose the bank accountant goes to work at the same pay for an airline in a department that deals with cost controls on passenger services. This mobility is horizontal, from the finance sector to the transportation sector. On the other hand, some moves are both horizontal and vertical, for instance, when a junior bank executive joins a manufacturing company in an administrative post with more responsibility and a higher salary (Morris and Murphy, 1959).

CAREER MOBILITY

Social mobility can be studied from the standpoint of changes over the life span of an individual or from the standpoint of changes within a family over two or more generations. As the term implies, **career mobility** refers to changes in social rank that occur during an individual's life, especially during his or her working life. To find out about career mobility, people are asked about the jobs they held at various points in their lives: for example, first job, job at the time of interview, and last job if they are no longer in the labor force. A person's chances of moving up the occupational ladder are strongly influenced by (1) amount of education (Blau and Duncan, 1967:152–61), (2) the nature of the first job, and (3) father's occupation. (See Figure 9.3.)

A detailed analysis of Wisconsin high school students of the class of 1957, who were restudied over an extended period, concludes that higher education is crucial to high-status jobs. Being well off is the best guarantee of going to college and, thereby, of getting a good job. Affluent families encourage higher education, provide a stimulating home environment, and often help their children enter a specific occupation (Sewell and Hauser, 1975:100, 105–7).

Less obvious factors also play a part in occupational attainment. Small families can give each child more resources, attention, and encouragement. Those who postpone marriage are more likely to succeed than those who marry early. In Denmark, males who married before age 25 tended to be downwardly mobile, while those who married between the ages of 25 and 29 tended to be stable and those who married at age 30 or older to be upwardly mobile (Svalastoga, 1957). There is evidence of a similar pattern in the United States. Ambitious males may postpone marriage in order to complete their education and begin their careers. Willingness to postpone marriage may be a sign of an underlying personality trait: ability to forego present gratification in order to attain a future goal (Rosen and D'Andrade, 1959: 185–217. McClelland, 1961; Straus, 1962:326–35).

INTERGENERATIONAL MOBILITY

The study of career mobility, which deals with changes during a person's working life, covers a rather short period and does not throw much light on how class is inherited. To study mobility over a longer period, it is better to compare the positions of parents and children (traditionally in terms of the occupations of fathers and their sons) at similar points in their careers or at similar ages. This is

called **intergenerational mobility.** For example, the jobs held by a father could be compared with the jobs of his son at the ages of 21, 41, and 61, that is, when they had just entered the labor force, when they were near mid-career, and when they were near retirement.

Mobility among women

Because most men work for pay much of their lives, the study of father/son occupational mobility is fairly straightforward. The same has not been true of the study of intergenerational mobility among women. The mothers of many working women were never in the labor force, or worked outside the home for only a short time. Although homemaking has both social and economic value, researchers did not take it into account, possibly because domestic work, whether paid or unpaid, has low prestige and is taken for granted. (This topic was discussed in Chapter 7.) Therefore, the intergenerational mobility of women was often studied by comparing the occupations of their fathers and husbands, if any (Rossi, 1971). Thus, if the daughter of a skilled worker married a professional she was said to be upwardly mobile. This is indeed a kind of vertical social mobility, but it is not the same as father/son occupational mobility, and it tells nothing about women who do not marry.

The fact that until recently researchers used the status difference between two men as a measure of a woman's intergenerational mobility is ironic evidence of the socioeconomic subordination of women. Occupational studies of women are complicated by the fact that women's careers are often interrupted, and some women never join the labor force. However, over half of American women are now in the labor force, and the number is rising rapidly. As more women are employed and employed for longer periods, it is possible to apply the same methods to study the occupational mobility of women and men.

STATUS ATTAINMENT

Of the many forces and events that affect mobility, a few are particularly important. To study them, it is

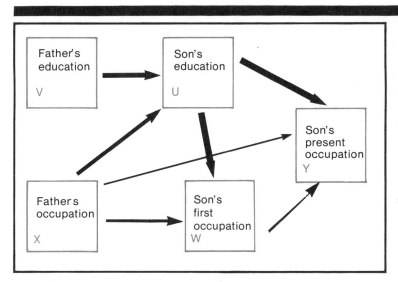

The direction of the influence is shown by the arrows, and the importance of the influence is shown by the weight of the arrow lines. For simplicity, path coefficients and external influences are omitted. One weak link, V→Y, is not shown. Another link, V→X, is also left out because it does not influence the son's occupational attainment. Caution: The diagram does not include all of the variables that affect mobility.

Source: After Blau and Duncan, 1967:170.

Figure 9.3   The Status Attainment Model

necessary to sift out accidental and personal events and concentrate on broad trends. Life histories can throw light on human experience in a way that statistical analysis cannot. But the experience of individuals can be best understood when it is interpreted within an explicit framework. Such a framework is shown in Figure 9.3, a simplified path diagram based on a landmark study of what is called the *status attainment* process (Blau and Duncan, 1967:170).

The figure shows that the process by which occupational status is inherited is more complicated than the term "inheritance" suggests. The father's condition affects the son's but not directly. In fact, that direct link (X → Y) between father's job and son's job is the weakest of all the paths shown in the diagram. The path from the father's job to son's first job (X → W) is also fairly weak. The father's influence comes from his occupation and education, which together affect the son's education (X → U and V → U). In turn, the son's education strongly influences his first job (U → W) and his later job U → Y).

The status attainment model has been applied, elaborated, and qualified in a large number of studies (Colclough and Horan, 1983). As shown in Figure 9.3, the original model focused on the occupational prestige achieved by men and for the most part, white men. Later studies showed that the basic model does not fit the achievement of blacks as well as it does of whites because race is a powerful ascriptive mechanism (Porter, 1974). The original research, however, did not ignore blacks (Blau and Duncan, 1967:chap. 6).

In its broad outlines the status attainment process can be applied to women, but again, important qualifications are necessary. Mother's occupation significantly influences the occupational achievement of women, and the influence of education does not come entirely from the father. In fact, the education link is stronger between mother and daughter than between father and daughter. Furthermore, general family background seems to be more important for women than for men (Treiman and Terrell, 1975; McClendon, 1976; Rosenfeld, 1978).

The entire approach has been criticized for emphasizing individual characteristics over structural influences such as the organization of the labor market. No doubt the model will receive further application, elaboration and criticism, which is the way science advances.

MOBILITY AND SOCIAL STRUCTURE

Industrialization creates social mobility by reshaping opportunity patterns, reducing the number of jobs in agriculture, and creating a demand for workers in new industries and services. Thus, industrial and technological change plus urbanization cause **structural mobility** by pushing workers off the land and pulling them into urban industrial jobs. During period of rapid change, much of the work force is in flux as it responds to the pressures and opportunities of the labor market.

A different kind of mobility, called **circulation mobility,** occurs when persons move into higher or lower occupational levels than their parents, displacing children of other parents and reducing the ''inheritance'' of occupational status.

International comparisons

A generalization that links economic development and social mobility holds that once a given level of economic development is reached, as is the case in most Western countries, their ''overall pattern of social mobility appears to be much the same'' (Lipset and Zetterberg, 1959:13). According to this reasoning, whatever the starting points may be, there is a strong tendency for mobility patterns to become similar. At first the convergence idea was generally accepted, but more rigorous research shows a wide variation in the speed, amount and type of mobility among industrial and post-industrial societies.

A comparative study of father-to-son mobility in three countries—Australia, Italy, and the United States—found that they differed on the major dimensions of mobility but the basic pattern in all three countries was out of farming into manual jobs and out of manual into service, white-collar jobs. Of the three, the United States had the highest rate of mobility and the most movement out of agriculture. In other words, much U.S. mobility was structural—caused by industrial change, the result of shrinking farm employment. Australia had less occupational mobility than the United States but more than Italy. Australian mobility was of the circulation type rather than the structural type. Thus Australia had more equality of opportunity. Of the three countries, Italy had the lowest overall rate of mobility, and Italian mobility was more structural than circulation. Italy offered less equality of opportunity than either Australia or the United States (Broom and Jones, 1969).

A second comparative study also found significant differences in the mobility patterns of three countries —England, France, and Sweden. England, which was the first country to industrialize from the mid-eighteenth to the mid-nineteenth centuries, was closest to the convergence model. Sweden industrialized late but fast. Its high overall mobility was caused by rapid industrial change and a social democratic policy that strongly emphasized equality of educational and occupational opportunities over a long period. France differed from England and Sweden and, indeed, from all other countries discussed in this section. France modernized slowly, and its traditional classes based on agriculture and small business remained stable. Relatively few manual workers opened shops or went into service occupations (Erikson et al., 1979; 1982).

A third study compared Finland and Hungary, both of which industrialized after World War II but under different political systems. Before the war, they were primarily agrarian societies at similar levels of industrial development. After the war, they developed rapidly along different paths. In Hungary the socialist government decided to emphasize manufacturing, and workers from agricultural families entered jobs in heavy industry. The Finnish government did not direct the country's economic development. Finland experienced very high occupational mobility, especially into the service sector rather than into manufacturing (Pöntinen et al., 1983). In general, countries that industrialized recently tend to have high worker productivity, a rapid decline in agricultural jobs, and many workers shifting to service-type nonmanual rather than to manual jobs (Singelmann, 1978:114).

The evidence in these three studies shows that the convergence idea oversimplifies reality. The amount and pattern of occupational mobility vary from time to time and place to place owing to differences in natural resources, educational standards, capital, population pressure, social traditions, industrialization, and the speed of economic growth. Countries that manage their economies, as Hungary does, are a special case because they can and do deliberately alter job opportunities and mobility patterns.

Dual labor market

The structure of the labor market is an important influence in determining who gets which job opportunities and how much mobility is achieved. Stimulated in part by research on the plight of racial minorities, the concept of a **dual labor market** has been developed. The labor market is considered to be not a single-opportunity structure but at least two major sectors called primary and secondary. The primary labor market pays relatively high wages, provides good working conditions, job stability, chances for promotion, and fair worker discipline. Firms that offer such jobs are in the center of the economy. The secondary labor market has lower paying jobs, inferior working conditions, little chance for advancement, harsh job discipline, and high labor turnover. Firms in the secondary sector are on the periphery or fringe of the economy (Baron and Bielby, 1980; Harrison, 1977; Piore, 1977; Lord and Falk, 1982). The primary/secondary division suggests that when workers successfully enter the primary sector in normal times, they can plan their careers with reasonable expectation of tenure and promotion. Disproportionate numbers of ethnic and racial minority persons and women find their way into the secondary labor market. Their careers are likely to be characterized by short tenure in a series of jobs with poor rewards, little security, and small cause for job satisfaction.

Open and closed systems

Societies may be classified according to the extent to which they resemble an open model with relatively unhampered mobility, or a castelike (closed) model with tight restrictions on mobility. In the closed model, status is ascribed; that is, it is based on characteristics over which the individual has little or no control—race, sex, and ethnic and family background. Ascriptive societies are often called castelike, but no society has a pure caste system with absolutely closed social categories. At the opposite extreme is the open class society, in which status is achieved rather than ascribed. In the open class society people earn their positions by exercising their skills, knowledge, education, and effort. This type of society is achievement oriented rather than ascription oriented.

All societies, however, are mixtures of ascription and achievement. Industrial societies tend to demote highly born incompetents and promote capable, ambitious persons from lower levels. Yet even the most advanced countries allocate rewards and grant opportunities on the basis of ascribed characteristics. Soft jobs are found for mildly incompetent people with the right connections. Family background, sex, race, and ethnicity still count.

Societies that have subordinate racial groups are a mixture of open and closed characteristics. Color may place castelike restrictions on mobility and limit the operation of achievement criteria. The United States is such a society, and color is an ascriptive mechanism. If sex is considered as a basis for ascription, most societies could be classified as mixed, castelike societies.

Caste in India

Traditional India has been considered a closed caste system. It was a complex arrangement of thousands of separate groups governed by rules of descent and marriage, occupation, ritual, and ideas about purity and pollution. Especially in southern India, there were rules against touching, approaching, or even exchanging glances with a member of the lowest caste. If members of higher castes did so, they would become polluted and would have to be purified. The lowest groupings (so-called untouchables or Harijans) were excluded from temples and schools used by higher-caste groups and were required to use separate paths and wells and to live in isolated villages (Leach, 1960; Srinivas, 1962; 1966; Silverberg, 1968).

Contrary to popular belief, the numerous Indian castes were not and are not social strata. They vary widely on all dimensions of stratification, and several castes may be located at the same economic level. Despite the complex rules of the caste system, castes can move up and down in prestige, power, and privilege. Members of a caste may improve their collective standing over time by following standards of behavior that apply to high-ranking castes. Furthermore, there is a range of prestige and influence within each caste, and individuals and families can occupy higher or lower positions within their caste.

Although many traditional occupations are linked to specific castes, the castes are not strictly occupational categories. Members of certain castes have the right to engage in certain occupations, and some very large categories of occupations, such as agriculture, trade, and military service, are open to members of any caste.

> On the one hand, older caste groups such as the barbers and washermen are breaking down into smaller units because so many of their members no longer follow the traditional occupation and tend to despise those who do. On the other hand, new caste groups are being formed around new occupational specialisms—skilled mechanical work, semiskilled dock and plantation work and so on—because caste affiliations are used, all over India, to facilitate labour recruitment. Once a caste group has attached itself to a particular kind of work it soon increases its hold by bringing into it only fellow members of the same group. [Stevenson, 1967:29a]

The caste system in India has been put under stress by modernization. Public transportation, urbanization, and industrial development have broken down many caste rules and interfered with residential and food taboos. In 1949 the Indian government made untouchability illegal, but this reform was resisted. In fact, the bitterness that followed the new law may have played a part in the assassination of Mahatma Gandhi. Thus, although there is strong pressure to reform caste practices, many aspects of the system persist throughout Indian society (Srinivas, 1966).

Survivals of the Indian caste system are of interest to the student of stratification because caste influences the way the labor market is organized, and because in such a system mobility is likely to take place by groups rather than individuals. Efforts of Indian caste groups to monopolize certain jobs bring to mind attempts by families and ethnic groups in Western societies to monopolize jobs through the control of labor unions. Favoritism and individual effort, ascription and striving are at work in all kinds of societies.

Chapter 9   **Summary**

Section 1/**Method and theory**

The objective approach to the study of social stratification uses such indicators as income, education, and occupation. In the subjective approach, people are asked where they would place themselves in a list of social classes. The words *strata* and *class* commonly refer to social levels. *Class* is also used in a strong sense, especially by Marxist scholars, to identify groups such as industrial wage earners who perform similar roles in the economic system. Marx believed that classes arise from the way work is organized; that society would be increasingly polarized into two classes, the bourgeoisie and the proletariat; that in the course of time classes would become subjective or self-aware as well as objective, and that eventually the proletariat would prevail.

Marx overemphasized the importance of economic forces. Other factors such as nationalism and ethnic identity cut across class divisions, and the polarization he predicted has not come to pass.

The functional theory of stratification states that inequality in complex societies is necessary to ensure that important tasks will be done by qualified people. This theory is questioned on the grounds that it does not explain extreme inequality, inherited inequality, or high rewards for socially wasteful or destructive behavior.

Section 2/**Inequality**

A comparison of earned incomes in different countries shows that there are no equalitarian countries, either communist or noncommunist. Communist countries appear to be more equal than noncommunist countries at the same stage of industrial development, and the greatest income inequality is found in the poorest and least industrialized countries.

In the past 35 years, the median income of American families has nearly doubled while the percent of families with very low incomes has declined. However, the United States is still far from equal. Canada may be somewhat more equalitarian.

Wealth is more highly concentrated than income. As measured by individual wealth holding, the degree of concentration may have diminished somewhat in both the United Kingdom and the United States. Family wealth holding is probably a more meaningful measure of inequality, and there is a higher degree of family than individual wealth concentration.

The ranking of occupations reflects responsibility and independence as well as income and education. The prestige of different occupations tends to remain fairly constant and to be similar in various countries except that manual workers in eastern Europe have high standing.

One view of the American power structure holds that a cohesive power elite whose members have similar backgrounds makes the important decisions at the national level. A contrasting view—the pluralist or balance thesis—holds that major decisions are compromises among several interest groups.

Section 3/**Poverty**

Poverty may be measured in absolute or relative terms. If poverty is defined as a shortage of food and clean water, there are hundreds of millions of absolutely poor people in the least developed countries. The poor in Western countries do not experience such deprivation. However, people compare their economic position with others in the same society rather than against some distant standard.

Although the poverty rate in the United States has declined, about 14 percent of the population are still below the poverty line. The poverty rate for blacks and persons of Spanish origin is higher than the rate for whites in general. Older persons and

families headed by women also have higher poverty rates.

A fairly high rate of unemployment has become chronic in the United States, Canada, and Great Britain. Young people and blacks have the highest unemployment rates.

Section 4/**Contrasting life-styles**

Position in the stratification system is related to attitudes, health, and many other aspects of daily life.

The WASP elite began with the ''robber barons'' of the 1800s, who maintained large estates and sent their sons to private schools and elite colleges. Today, four generations later, the life-style of this class has changed, but these families still have clear advantages.

The Soviet elite also has a distinct life-style. Party officials and other high-status individuals are rewarded with untaxed income and privileges that enable them to enjoy a much more affluent life-style than ordinary Soviet citizens.

In the underground economy goods and services are exchanged in kind or paid for in cash so that transactions fall outside the tax system. People in all strata seem to be touched by the underground economy even though some transactions are violations of the criminal law.

Section 5/**Social mobility**

Most studies of social mobility focus on vertical mobility—an upward or downward change in the rank of an individual or group. Career mobility refers to changes during a person's lifetime, and is influenced by amount of education, nature of previous jobs, and father's occupation. Other factors affecting career mobility are family size and age at marriage.

Intergenerational mobility has been measured by comparing the occupations of fathers and their sons. In the past the social mobility of women has often been measured by comparing the occupations of their fathers and husbands.

In the status attainment process, father's occupation and education influence son's education, which in turn strongly affects the son's occupational career. A daughter's career is influenced by these factors plus her mother's occupation and education, as well as general family background. The status attainment model has been criticized as emphasizing individual characteristics over such structural influences as the organization of the labor market.

Technological change and urbanization cause structural mobility by pushing workers off the land and pulling them into industrial jobs. Circulation mobility occurs when persons who move into occupations at different levels from their parents displace the children of other parents. The amount and pattern of mobility differ from one country to another according to differences in resources, finances, demography, traditions, and the speed of economic growth. Managed economies alter job opportunities and mobility.

The labor market is not a single whole but is divided into at least two major segments. One segment contains most of the desirable jobs; the other is made up of the less pleasant and poorly rewarded jobs, which are filled largely by disprivileged persons.

In a closed or castelike society, status is ascribed. In an open society, status is achieved, that is, status is won through skill, knowledge, and effort. All societies are somewhere between these two extremes.

Some caste regulations in India have broken down under the strain of modernization, but caste still powerfully influences daily life. Many traditional occupations are linked to specific castes, but the Indian caste system is not a hierarchy of occupational strata.

Suggested Readings

Baltzell, E. Digby
1964/1966 *The Protestant Establishment: Aristocracy and Caste in America.* New York: Vintage Books.

Bendix, R., and S. M. Lipset (eds.)
1966 *Class, Status and Power: Social Stratification in Comparative Perspective.* Second Edition. New York: Free Press.

Brittain, John A.
1977 *The Inheritance of Economic Status.* Washington: The Brookings Institution.

Coleman, Richard, and Lee Rainwater
1978 *Social Standing in America.* New York: Free Press.

Kahl, Joseph A. (ed.)
1968 *Comparative Perspectives on Stratification: Mexico, Great Britain, Japan.* Boston: Little, Brown.

Kerbo, Harold R.
1983 *Social Stratification and Inequality: Class Conflict in the United States.* New York: McGraw-Hill.

Marshall, T. H.
1963 *Class, Citizenship and Social Development.* Garden City, N.Y.: Doubleday.

Rainwater, Lee
1974 *What Money Buys: Inequality and the Social Meanings of Income.* New York: Basic Books.

Srinivas, M. N.
1966 *Social Change in Modern India.* Berkeley and Los Angeles: University of California Press.

Wright, Erik Olin
1978 *Class, Crisis and the State.* London: NLB.

Wrong, Dennis H.
1980 *Power: Its Forms, Bases and Uses.* New York: Harper Colophon Books.

Part Four

Population Perspectives

Chapter 10

Demographic Analysis

SCHEDULE *of the whole Number of* PERSO[NS] *several Districts of the* UNITED STATES, *ta[ken] to* "An Act providing for the Enumeration [of inha]bitants of the United States;" *passed March* 1[...]

DISTRICTS.	Free white Males of sixteen years and upwards, including heads of families.	Free white Males under sixteen years.	Free white Females including heads of families.	All other free persons.	Slaves.
* Vermont	22,135	22,328	40,505	255	16
New-Hampshire	36,086	34,851	70,160	630	158
{ Maine	24,384	24,748	46,870	538	NONE
{ Massachusetts	95,453	87,289	190,582	5,463	NONE
Rhode-Island	16,019	15,799	32,652	3,407	948
Connecticut	60,523	54,403	117,448	2,808	2,764
New-York	83,700	78,122	152,320	4,654	21,324
New-Jersey	45,251	41,416	83,287	2,762	11,423
Pennsylvania	110,788	106,948	206,363	6,537	3,737
Delaware	11,783	12,143	22,384	3,899	8,887
Maryland	55,915	51,339	101,395	8,043	103,036
{ Virginia	110,936	116,135	215,046	12,866	292,627
{ Kentucky	15,154	17,057	28,922	114	12,430
North-Carolina	69,988	77,506	140,710	4,975	100,572
South-Carolina	-				
Georgia	13,103	14,044	25,739	398	29,264

	Free white Males of twenty-one years and upwards, including heads of families.	Free Males under twenty-one years of age.	Free white Females, including heads of families.	All other Persons.	Slaves.	Total.
S. Western Territory	6,271	10,277	15,365	361	3,417	35,691
N. Do.	-					

Truly stated from the original Returns deposited in the Office [of] the Secretary of State.

TH: JEFFERSON.

October 24, 1791.

* This return was not signed by the marshal, but was enclosed and referred to in [a] letter written and signed by him.

In Part Four, the two final chapters, we present two perspectives on population studies. Chapter 10 outlines the elementary sources and methods of demographic study with concrete examples from the United States and other countries. Chapter 11 applies the methods and evidence from demographic research to the two major aspects of population dynamics: migration and population growth, one of the great problems of our age.

The first section of Chapter 10 introduces the census. Section Two discusses age and sex composition, and the social implications of varying age and sex ratios. The last section reviews the measurement of fertility, mortality, and life expectancy. In each case the social significance of differing rates is assessed.

Section One
The Uses of Demography

People everywhere—especially government officials—are increasingly aware of the need for accurate knowledge about population. Environmental protection and other ecological concerns are affected by population growth and migration. The planning of schools, hospitals, and other civic facilities calls for data on the size and age distribution of populations, both now and in the future. Federal funding for states and state funding for cities depend on population size and composition. Evaluation of health services requires precise measures of birth, death, and illness rates. And analyses of trends in the economic and social conditions of women and ethnic minorities can tell us whether efforts to achieve equality are working.

Experts on population, called *demographers,* focus on these and related problems, but demography is too important to be left only to experts. Ordinary citizens do not need to become demographers, but they need to be well informed if they are to have a say in social policy. Business leaders also have a practical interest in the future of the population. They use the demographic skills to plot the growth or decline in communities, age groups, and ethnic groups that make up their markets. Armed with such information, they are more likely to predict shifts in demand for their products before changes occur. Otherwise they may learn their demographic lessons the hard way when profits collapse because company plans are based on faulty population statistics.

The study of human populations, or **demography** (from the Greek word *demos,* meaning "people"), depends on statistics taken from official records of births, deaths, marriages, and migration, or from censuses and sample surveys. It is simple enough to add up the number of births and deaths recorded in a country. It is a bit harder but more important to relate maternal and infant mortality rates to the age, income, and race of the mother. This kind of information guides social policy by identifying the groups that are in greatest need and by suggesting new public measures that may become necessary.

THE CENSUS AS FACTFINDER

The word *census* comes from the Latin *censere,* meaning to value or to tax. Since ancient times census taking has often had a practical reason, such as raising money or troops. Early censuses are recorded in the Bible, the most famous of which is the Roman imperial decree that required Mary and Joseph to be in Bethlehem to be counted (Luke 2:1–5). Although women and children were not usually counted, men had to be in their hometowns in order to reduce the chance that they would be missed.

The most important source of population data in most countries is the census. In the United States, the Bureau of the Census conducts year-round fact-finding activities as well as the ten-year census. The size and diversity of the United States makes census taking more difficult than in countries with small, homogeneous populations. As a result the U.S. census may not be as precise as, say, Norway's. Adaptation 10.1 outlines the history and workings of the U.S. census.

(Text continued on p. 208)

Adaptation 10.1

The United States Census

The United States was the first modern nation to require a regular census in its Constitution:

> Representatives and direct Taxes shall be apportioned among the several States . . . according to their respective Numbers, which shall be determined by adding to the whole Number of free Persons, including those bound to Service for a Term of Years, and excluding Indians not taxed, three fifths of all other Persons. The actual Enumeration shall be made within three Years after the first Meeting of the Congress of the United States, and within every subsequent Term of ten Years. . . . [Constitution of the United States, Article I, Section 2]

From the start, the census gathered more information than the Constitution required. In planning for the first (1790) census, James Madison recognized the potential value of the census and urged Congress to extend its information gathering beyond bare enumeration.

The name of the head of each family was recorded and the total number of persons in the family, classified as free or slave. Free persons were further classified as white or other, free whites as male or female, and free white males as over or under 16 years of age. Slaves were "other Persons" in the Constitution, and 60 percent of their total was counted for purposes of apportionment and taxes. Figure 10.1 is from the report of the first census, a pamphlet of 56 pages.

The evolution of the census is a product of growth in population, industrial development, technological advances, and sophistication in coping with large quantities of facts. Printed census sched-

Source: Based in part on *Bureau of the Census, Factfinder for the Nation, 1948; The Story of the Census, 1790–1916; U.S. Census of Population and Housing, 1960, Principal Data-Collection Forms and Procedures* (1961); *1970 Census User's Guide; Census '80: Continuing the Factfinder Tradition;* and other publications of the Bureau of the Census, Washington, D.C.

ules were first used in the fifth census (1830). In the seventh census (1850), the individual instead of the family became the unit of enumeration, and individual data on age, sex, race, and occupation were recorded. As a result more detailed tabulations and cross-tabulations were possible.

SCHEDULE *of the whole Number of* PERSONS *within the several Districts of the* UNITED STATES, *taken according to* "An Act providing for the Enumeration of the Inhabitants of the United States;" *passed March the 1st,* 1790.

DISTRICTS.	Free white Males of sixteen years and upwards, including heads of families.	Free white Males under sixteen years.	Free white Females including heads of families.	All other free persons.	Slaves.	Total.
• Vermont	22,135	22,328	40,505	255	16	85,539
New-Hampshire	36,086	34,851	70,160	630	158	141,885
Maine	24,384	24,748	46,870	538	NONE	96,540
Maffachufetts	95,453	87,289	190,582	5,463	NONE	378,787
Rhode-Island	16,019	15,799	32,652	3,407	948	68,825
Connecticut	60,523	54,403	117,448	2,808	2,764	237,946
New-York	83,700	78,122	152,320	4,654	21,324	340,120
New-Jerfey	45,251	41,416	83,287	2,762	11,423	184,139
Pennfylvania	110,788	106,948	206,363	6,537	3,787	434,373
Delaware	11,783	12,143	22,384	3,899	8,887	59,094
Maryland	55,915	51,339	101,395	8,043	103,036	319,728
Virginia	110,936	116,135	215,046	12,866	292,627	747,610
Kentucky	15,154	17,057	28,922	114	12,430	73,677
North-Carolina	69,988	77,506	140,710	4,975	100,572	393,751
South-Carolina	-	-	-	-	-	-
Georgia	13,103	14,044	25,739	398	29,264	82,548
	Free white Males of twenty-one years and upwards, including heads of families.	Free Males under twenty-one years of age.	Free white Females, including heads of families.	All other Perfons.	Slaves.	Total.
S. Weftern Territory N. Do.	6,271	10,277	15,365	361	3,417	35,691

Truly ftated from the original Returns depofited in the Office of the Secretary of State.

TH: JEFFERSON.

October 24, 1791.

• This return was not figned by the marfhal, but was enclofed and referred to in a letter written and figned by him.

Figure 10.1   Summary Page, The First Census of the United States

Despite the growing complexity of census taking, there was no continuing census organization during the nineteenth century. A temporary organization was set up every ten years until 1902, when the Bureau of the Census was established as a permanent part of the national bureaucracy.

The census has long been a leader in the field of statistical processing. Machine tabulations were first used in the ninth census (1870). The 1890 census introduced a punch-card tabulating machine devised by a bureau employee, Herman Hollerith, who later became one of the founders of International Business Machines Corporation (IBM).

By 1960, high-speed electronic equipment had been introduced, and questionnaires were designed so that the information could be "read" by FOSDIC (Film Optical Sensing Device for Input to Computers). FOSDIC scanned microfilms of completed schedules and converted the information into magnetic impressions on tape. This did away with the card-punching operation—a major source of clerical error. The tape was then processed by computers, making editing and coding more uniform.

An operation as large as the United States Census is inevitably expensive. From the planning stage through publication, the 1980 census cost about $1 billion, a price that brought forth widespread protests. Stated another way, it cost approximately $4.50 a head, the price of a small pizza, to collect, summarize, and analyze information about 226 million people. Whether the taxpayers get their money's worth can be debated, but there is no way a modern country can do without a census.

TRUSTING THE CENSUS

A national fact-finding agency has public-relations problems as well as technical problems. Many countries have difficulty taking censuses because the people avoid the census takers, or give incomplete or false information. The U.S. census has been fairly free of this kind of problem. A survey of public reaction to the 1970 census found that a sample of Wisconsin respondents had positive attitudes toward the census in general and the use of mailed forms in particular (Sharp and Schnore, 1971). This favorable attitude is contrary to the impression in the popular press, which gives the Census Bureau a hard time at least once every ten years.

In attempting to hold onto federal funds distributed on the basis of population, city officials have protested census figures that show central cities losing population to the suburbs. Follow-up surveys usually show that there was an actual decline in the central cities. However, all censuses probably undercount the population. Thomas Jefferson thought that the first census, which recorded 3,929,326, was an undercount and that the actual population was well over 4 million. Modern censuses are likely to miss young, old, mobile, poor, and racial minorities, who tend to be concentrated in central cities. Since the undercounted groups include many people who need social services, the errors can cause those groups to be shortchanged.

SAMPLING IN THE CENSUS

Extensive use of sampling techniques is an economical way for the Census Bureau to gather a large amount of data on a wide range of topics. Sampling was used for some items in 1940, and since 1950 much information has been based on samples, which are identified as such in the census reports. The basic 1980 questionnaire for the whole population is given in Figure 10.2. Figure 10.3 shows some questions asked of a 21 percent sample of the population.

Estimating overall figures from sample figures is a matter of probability. For example, suppose a previous census found that 17.6 percent of males aged 25 years and over *in a 20 percent sample* had completed four years of high school. On the basis of this sample, it would estimate that 7.5 million males, or 17.6 percent of all males *in the total population* aged 25 years and over, had completed high school, but it does not mean that the national figure was *exactly* 7.5 million. That number is the midpoint of a fairly narrow range and is used with the understanding that the chances are about two out of three that the total population lies between 7.5 million plus 5440 and 7.5 million minus 5440. (The degree of probability and range of accuracy are derived from the mathematics of statistics.)

In one sense, figures based on samples are never precise. They must be used with the understanding

Here are the QUESTIONS — These are the columns for ANSWERS. *Please fill one column for each person listed in Question 1.*	PERSON in column 1 Last name First name — Middle initial	PERSON in column 2 Last name First name — Middle initial
QUESTIONS ASKED OF ALL HOUSEHOLDS		
2. How is this person related to the person in column 1? *Fill one circle.* *If "Other relative" of person in column 1, give exact relationship, such as mother-in-law, niece, grandson, etc.*	*START in this column with the household member (or one of the members) in whose name the home is owned or rented. If there is no such person, start in this column with any adult household member.*	If relative of person in column 1: Husband/wife; Son/daughter; Brother/sister; Father/mother; Other relative If not related to person in column 1: Roomer, boarder; Partner, roommate; Paid employee; Other nonrelative
3. Sex *Fill one circle.*	Male; Female	Male; Female
4. Is this person — *Fill one circle.*	White; Black or Negro; Japanese; Chinese; Filipino; Korean; Vietnamese; Indian (Amer.) *Print tribe*; Asian Indian; Hawaiian; Guamanian; Samoan; Eskimo; Aleut; Other — *Specify*	White; Black or Negro; Japanese; Chinese; Filipino; Korean; Vietnamese; Indian (Amer.) *Print tribe*; Asian Indian; Hawaiian; Guamanian; Samoan; Eskimo; Aleut; Other — *Specify*
5. Age, and month and year of birth *a. Print age at last birthday.* *b. Print month and fill one circle.* *c. Print year in the spaces, and fill one circle below each number.*	a. Age at last birthday b. Month of birth: Jan—Mar; Apr—June; July—Sept; Oct—Dec c. Year of birth: 1 ● 8 9; 0 1 2 3 4 5 6 7 8 9; 0 1 2 3 4 5 6 7 8 9	a. Age at last birthday b. Month of birth: Jan—Mar; Apr—June; July—Sept; Oct—Dec c. Year of birth: 1 ● 8 9; 0 1 2 3 4 5 6 7 8 9; 0 1 2 3 4 5 6 7 8 9
6. Marital status *Fill one circle.*	Now married; Widowed; Divorced; Separated; Never married	Now married; Widowed; Divorced; Separated; Never married
7. Is this person of Spanish/Hispanic origin or descent? *Fill one circle.*	No (not Spanish/Hispanic); Yes, Mexican, Mexican-Amer., Chicano; Yes, Puerto Rican; Yes, Cuban; Yes, other Spanish/Hispanic	No (not Spanish/Hispanic); Yes, Mexican, Mexican-Amer., Chicano; Yes, Puerto Rican; Yes, Cuban; Yes, other Spanish/Hispanic
QUESTIONS ASKED OF SAMPLE HOUSEHOLDS		
8. Since February 1, 1980, has this person attended regular school or college at any time? *Fill one circle. Count nursery school, kindergarten, elementary school, and schooling which leads to a high school diploma or college degree.*	No, has not attended since February 1; Yes, public school, public college; Yes, private, church-related; Yes, private, not church-related	No, has not attended since February 1; Yes, public school, public college; Yes, private, church-related; Yes, private, not church-related
9. What is the highest grade (or year) of regular school this person has ever attended? *Fill one circle.* *If now attending school, mark grade person is in. If high school was finished by equivalency test (GED), mark "12."*	**Highest grade attended:** Nursery school; Kindergarten Elementary through high school *(grade or year)* 1 2 3 4 5 6 7 8 9 10 11 12 College *(academic year)* 1 2 3 4 5 6 7 8 or more Never attended school — *Skip question 10*	**Highest grade attended:** Nursery school; Kindergarten Elementary through high school *(grade or year)* 1 2 3 4 5 6 7 8 9 10 11 12 College *(academic year)* 1 2 3 4 5 6 7 8 or more Never attended school — *Skip question 10*
10. Did this person finish the highest grade (or year) attended? *Fill one circle.*	Now attending this grade *(or year)*; Finished this grade *(or year)*; Did not finish this grade *(or year)*	Now attending this grade *(or year)*; Finished this grade *(or year)*; Did not finish this grade *(or year)*
	CENSUS USE ONLY A. I N	*CENSUS USE ONLY* A. I N

Figure 10.2 1980 Census Questionnaire

QUESTIONS ASKED OF SAMPLE HOUSEHOLDS

Name of
Person 1
on page 2:

Last name   First name   Middle initial

11. In what State or foreign country was this person born?
*Print the State where this person's mother was living
when this person was born. Do not give the location of
the hospital unless the mother's home and the hospital
were in the same State.*

Name of State or foreign country; or Puerto Rico, Guam, etc.

12. If this person was born in a foreign country –
a. **Is this person a naturalized citizen of the United States?**
  - ○ Yes, a naturalized citizen
  - ○ No, not a citizen
  - ○ Born abroad of American parents

b. **When did this person come to the United States to stay?**
  - ○ 1975 to 1980   ○ 1965 to 1969   ○ 1950 to 1959
  - ○ 1970 to 1974   ○ 1960 to 1964   ○ Before 1950

13a. Does this person speak a language other than English at home?
  - ○ Yes   ○ No, only speaks English – *Skip to 14*

b. **What is this language?**

(For example – Chinese, Italian, Spanish, etc.)

c. **How well does this person speak English?**
  - ○ Very well   ○ Not well
  - ○ Well   ○ Not at all

14. What is this person's ancestry? *If uncertain about
how to report ancestry, see instruction guide.*

*(For example: Afro-Amer., English, French, German, Honduran,
Hungarian, Irish, Italian, Jamaican, Korean, Lebanese, Mexican,
Nigerian, Polish, Ukrainian, Venezuelan, etc.)*

15a. Did this person live in this house five years ago (April 1, 1975)?
*If in college or Armed Forces in April 1975, report place
of residence there.*
  - ○ Born April 1975 or later – *Turn to next page for next person*
  - ○ Yes, this house – *Skip to 16*
  - ○ No, different house

b. **Where did this person live five years ago (April 1, 1975)?**
  (1) State, foreign country,
      Puerto Rico,
      Guam, etc.:
  (2) County:
  (3) City, town,
      village, etc.:
  (4) **Inside the incorporated (legal) limits of that city, town, village, etc.?**
  - ○ Yes   ○ No, in unincorporated area

16. When was this person born?
  - ○ Born before April 1965 –
       Please go on with questions 17-33
  - ○ Born April 1965 or later –
       Turn to next page for next person

17. In April 1975 (five years ago) was this person –
a. **On active duty in the Armed Forces?**
  - ○ Yes   ○ No

b. **Attending college?**
  - ○ Yes   ○ No

c. **Working at a job or business?**
  - ○ Yes, full time   ○ No
  - ○ Yes, part time

20. If this person is a female –   None 1 2 3 4 5 6
**How many babies has she ever
had, not counting stillbirths?**
*Do not count her stepchildren
or children she has adopted.*   7 8 9 10 11 12 or more

21. If this person has ever been married –
a. **Has this person been married more than once?**
  - ○ Once   ○ More than once

b. **Month and year
of marriage**

**Month and year
of first marriage**

(Month)   (Year)   (Month)   (Year)

c. **If married more than once – Did the first marriage
end because of the death of the husband (or wife)?**
  - ○ Yes   ○ No

22a. Did this person work at any time last week?
  - ○ Yes – *Fill this circle if this
    person worked full
    time or part time.
    (Count part-time work
    such as delivering papers,
    or helping without pay in
    a family business or farm.
    Also count active duty
    in the Armed Forces.)*
  - ○ No – *Fill this circle
    if this person
    did not work,
    or did only own
    housework,
    school work,
    or volunteer
    work.*

                              Skip to 25

b. **How many hours did this person work last week
(at all jobs)?**
Subtract any time off; add overtime or extra hours worked.

                              Hours

26a. Has this person been looking for work during the last 4 weeks?
  - ○ Yes   ○ No – *Skip to 27*

b. **Could this person have taken a job last week?**
  - ○ No, already has a job
  - ○ No, temporarily ill
  - ○ No, other reasons *(in school, etc.)*
  - ○ Yes, could have taken a job

27. When did this person last work, even for a few days?
  - ○ 1980   ○ 1978   ○ 1970 to 1974 ⎫
  - ○ 1979   ○ 1975 to 1977   ○ 1969 or earlier ⎬ *Skip to 31d*
  - ○ Never worked ⎭

28 – 30. Current or most recent job activity
*Describe clearly this person's chief job activity or business last week.
If this person had more than one job, describe the one at which
this person worked the most hours.
If this person had no job or business last week, give information for
last job or business since 1975.*

28. Industry
a. **For whom did this person work?** *If now on active duty in the
Armed Forces, print "AF" and skip to question 31.*

(Name of company, business, organization, or other employer)

b. **What kind of business or industry was this?**
Describe the activity at location where employed.

*(For example: Hospital, newspaper publishing, mail order house,
auto engine manufacturing, breakfast cereal manufacturing)*

c. **Is this mainly –** *(Fill one circle)*
  - ○ Manufacturing   ○ Retail trade
  - ○ Wholesale trade   ○ Other – *(agriculture, construction,
                                    service, government, etc.)*

29. Occupation
a. **What kind of work was this person doing?**

*(For example: Registered nurse, personnel manager, supervisor of
order department, gasoline engine assembler, grinder operator)*

b. **What were this person's most important activities or duties?**

*(For example: Patient care, directing hiring policies, supervising
order clerks, assembling engines, operating grinding mill)*

30. Was this person – *(Fill one circle)*
  Employee of private company, business, or
    individual, for wages, salary, or commissions
  Federal government employee
  State government employee
  Local government employee *(city, county, etc.)*
  Self-employed in own business,
    professional practice, or farm –
      Own business not incorporated
      Own business incorporated
  Working without pay in family business or farm

33. What was this person's total income in 1979?
*Add entries in questions 32a
through g; subtract any losses.* $ 00
If total amount was a loss,   *(Annual amount – Dollars)*
write "Loss" above amount.   OR ○ None

Figure 10.3   1980 Census Questionnaire: Some Sample Population Questions

that the actual figures are probably close to the computed figures. In another sense, however, they are very precise, because once the range of accuracy has been specified, the degree of probability (for example, odds of 2:1) can also be specified. Sample statistics for the United States as a whole are very close to the results that would be obtained from a complete population count because the samples are well designed and both the samples and the total population are quite large.

Section Two
Population Composition

The term *composition* refers to the biological or social makeup of a population according to sex, age, race, birthplace, occupation, education, dependency, and other characteristics. The composition of a population at a given time contains clues to what happened in the past and hints about what is to come.

THE SEX RATIO

The proportion of males to females in a population is called the **sex ratio (SR).** It is stated as the number of males per 100 females. A sex ratio of 100 means that the population is evenly divided between males and females; a figure greater than 100 means that there are more males than females; a figure less than 100 means that there are fewer males than females. At birth, the sex ratio for whites in the United States is about 106, but from that age on the ratio of males to females decreases. The sex ratio declines with increasing age because in developed countries females live longer than males. In less developed countries they do not, and they did not in the United States at some times in the past.

Unbalanced ratios

A sex ratio that deviates very far from 100 is considered out of balance. Through much of North American history there was a high sex ratio because of heavy male immigration. The large number of males of marriageable age among immigrants created competition for wives and some family disorganization, especially in the early stages of immigrant communities. Many men remained single, others married late, and still others sent to the home country for brides or married outside their ethnic group. In contrast to "new" countries like Canada and the United States, which had prolonged male immigration and a high sex ratio, Great Britain, an "old" country, was a net exporter of males for many decades. For this reason, as well as many war deaths, Britain has had a low sex ratio, in the middle and low 90s, for over a century.

Until the 1940s the number of males in the United States was always higher than the number of females in the country as a whole, and a high sex ratio of 106 was reached in 1910. The overall sex ratio of the United States is now 94, an all-time low. The sex ratio of Canada is also at a low point —about 100. It too has varied widely, reaching a peak of 113 at the census of 1911 (Norland [Yam], 1974:Table 3:1; 1979 UN *Demographic Yearbook,* Supp.: Table 3).

The sex ratio for blacks in the United States has been lower than that for whites, but the reasons for this difference are not clear. Allowing for the fact that many young black men are missed by the census, there is still a significant difference between the black and white sex ratios. In 1980 the overall black sex ratio was 90; the white ratio was 95. Under age 15, the ratios were about 101 for blacks and 105 for whites.* The most important difference was in the age bracket 25 to 44, where the black ratio was 85 and the white ratio 99. (*Statistical Abstract of the U.S.,* 1981:25). Whatever the cause, low sex ratios at ages when most men are in the work force and families are being formed add to the personal and family problems faced by many blacks.

An unbalanced ratio can have alarming implications. For example, in traditional China sons were a

_____

*The ratios for the Spanish-origin population, which according to the United States Census classification can be of any race, were almost identical with those for whites.

form of old-age insurance and were needed to continue the family line and perform religious rituals for the family ancestors. Daughters, on the other hand, did not continue the family line or take part in ancestor worship. Furthermore, they were a financial burden because they had to have dowries. One ''solution'' was female infanticide, which lasted into the twentieth century and was widespread enough to produce a high sex ratio (Orleans, 1972:36–37). Preference for male children still influences the Chinese birth rate, particularly among rural families that feel they must have a son.

CHANGING AGE COMPOSITION

Long-term trends in birth and death rates as well as sudden disasters such as war, famine, and epidemics, all leave their marks on the age composition of a population—the percent of the population in each age group. A special kind of graph, the population pyramid, and the concept of the cohort will help to clarify the nature and significance of changes in age composition.

Cohorts

All individuals born in a given year are an *age cohort;* all who began working in a given year are an *occupational cohort;* and all students who entered college in the same year make up an *educational cohort.* The idea of **cohort** therefore focuses on a number of people exposed to similar experiences at the same time (Glenn, 1977). Researchers use cohort analysis to trace a group over time.

The 1984 college educational cohort (the class of 1988) would be studied in this way: A sociologist would note how many drop out each year, when they go to work and what jobs they take, how many marry, how many children they have, and so forth. The 1984 cohort would then be compared with earlier and later cohorts. *When* something happens to people can be as important as *what* happens to them. A depression that occurred just when a cohort was entering the work force would be more damaging to that cohort's job chances than a depression that occurred five years earlier, when they were in high school, or ten years later, when they would already have jobs.

Population pyramids

Sometimes called the tree of ages, the **population pyramid** shows both the age and sex composition of a given place at a given time (see Figure 10.4). A vertical line divides the number (or percents) of males on the left from females on the right. Usually the figures are grouped by age categories, for instance, the population under five, between five and nine, and so on. Sometimes detailed figures are presented in single years of age. In a traditional rural population with high birthrates and high death rates, such as a developing country or the United States during the 1800s, the diagram looks like a true pyramid with a very broad base and a pointed top. The diagrams for present-day populations in industrial countries only faintly resemble true pyramids as shown in Figure 10.4 on pg. 210.

Once a major change occurs in its age structure, a population will continue to reflect that change as the affected group grows older. Figure 10.4 shows four age-sex pyramids for the United States beginning in 1960 and projected to 1990. Observe the changing overall shape of these diagrams. Note also how specific birth cohorts move up the tree of ages: the depression cohort, a product of the low birthrates of the 1930s, appears as a narrow band in each pyramid; the baby boom cohort as a wide band. At the bottom of the 1990 diagram is an echo of the baby boom, the children of the baby boom cohort. The parents of students reading this book were probably born late in the 1930s depression or early in the 1940s during World War II, and you were probably born after the end of the baby boom but not as recently as the baby bust. Trace your parents' cohort through the four pyramids and locate your own cohort. Look back and look ahead.

The four diagrams taken together show how major changes continue to influence the composition of a population and suggest the problems and opportunities of a society. The baby boom is followed by a boom in an older age group in each successive pyramid as the babies become school-age children, then young adults entering the work force and starting families, then middle-aged adults at the peak of their earning power, and finally old people living on savings, Social Security, and retirement income.

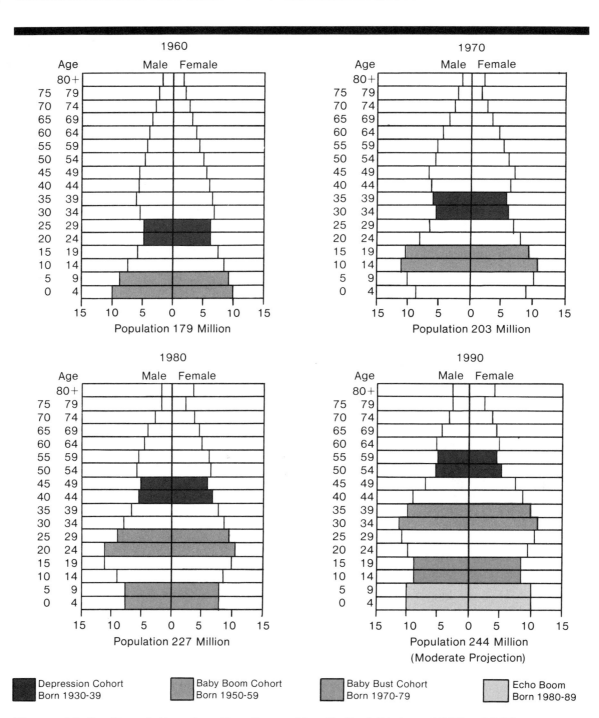

Figure 10.4 Population Age-Sex Pyramids, United States: 1960 – 1990

Sources: 1960-1980 U.S. Bureau of the Census; 1990: unpublished tabulations prepared by Leon Bouvier for the Select Commission on Immigration and Refugee Policy, 1980.

The dependency ratio

Despite the echo of the baby boom that appears at the bottom of the 1990 pyramid, the United States and other Western countries will have aging populations until well into the twenty-first century. When the population includes a large percent of very young or very old people, there is a high *dependency ratio*. That is, the number of people too old or too young to work is large compared with the working-age population. Assume that working-age population includes everyone from age 15 to age 64. A **dependency ratio** would be calculated by adding the number of people under 15 to the number aged 65 or over and dividing that total by the number aged 15 to 64. This calculation assumes that persons enter the work force at age 15 and leave it at 65, that everyone aged 15 to 64 works, and that everyone outside that bracket does not work.

The retirement age of 65, which is institutionalized in the Social Security system, is hard to justify on demographic grounds. It is a historical accident created in the nineteenth century by the German chancellor Otto von Bismarck. To win the support of the working class, he established a number of welfare policies, including a pension system. At that time few people survived into old age, and by setting retirement at age 65, he could be sure that the state would not need to pay out much in pensions. The present problem of funding old-age pensions is the result of lower birthrates, improved longevity, and premature retirement of many persons who are still capable of working productively.

For industrialized countries, a dependency ratio based on true dependency status would set the cutoff point for childhood dependency at 18 or later and for people leaving the work force at 67 or later. More realistic retirement ages would recognize differences according to type of job. A manual worker engaged in heavy labor obviously wears out sooner than an office worker. However, the 15 to 64 age bracket is usually used as the yardstick to compare nations. By this measure, the dependency ratios of the United States and Canada were about 52 in 1980, higher than Japan's 48 but much lower than India's 83 (1979 *UN Demographic Yearbook*, Supp.:Table 3). The much larger dependency ratio of India signals differ-

ent as well as more difficult problems for Indian society compared with the industrialized countries. About one-fourth of the dependent population in Canada, and the United States is made up of persons over 64, but in India the figure is less than one-tenth. India is burdened with a very large number of dependent young.

Section Three
Fertility and Mortality

The term **fertility** refers to actual reproduction and **fecundity** to potential reproduction, that is, the biological maximum number of births possible. In industrial nations fertility is only a fraction of fecundity. Even in developing countries with high birthrates fertility does not approach the biological maximum (Bongaarts, 1975).

MEASURING FERTILITY

A simple way to measure fertility is to compare the number of births with the size of the population. This **crude birthrate (CBR)** is expressed as a rate per 1,000 population and is calculated as follows:

$$\frac{\text{births in a year}}{\text{midyear population}} \times 1000 = \text{CBR}.$$

Substituting 1980 figures for the resident United States population in this equation gives:

$$\frac{3,610,000}{226,505,000} \times 1000 = 15.95,$$

the crude birthrate for the United States. The crude birthrate is commonly used in writing about population problems (See Table 10.1). It is useful and easy to calculate but it is important to know its limitations. Adaptation 10.2 shows how misleading the crude birthrate can be.

A country could have a low crude birthrate because it contained large numbers of males or old people but few women of childbearing age. But if the number of births is taken in relation to the small number of women of childbearing age, a high fertility rate might be revealed. Whether a given birthrate should be considered high or low depends on the number of women of childbearing age in the population. In fact, the fertility of American women is lower than the crude birthrate suggests because a large proportion of the U.S. population is made up of women of childbearing age. In earlier times, relatively more of the population was below childbearing age, as is the case in developing countries today.

The population at risk

To analyze differences in age and sex composition, demographers use more refined measures based on the "population at risk." With respect to fertility, the population at risk consists of women of childbearing age—about 15 to 44. The number of births per 1,000 women in that age bracket is called the **general fertility rate.** For the United States, the general fertility rate was 68 in 1980, compared with 118 in 1955.

Because a large fraction of births, especially in Western countries, occurs to women in a fairly narrow age band, say 20 to 29, demographers calculate **age-specific birthrates.** These rates are calculated by dividing the number of births to mothers in a specific age group by the total number of women in that age group and multiplying by 1,000. Age-specific birthrates for U.S. and Canadian women are as follows:

	United States		Canada	
Ages	**1955**	**1980**	**1959**	**1976**
15–19	90	53	60	33
20–24	242	115	234	108
25–29	190	113	227	128
30–34	116	62	148	65
35–39	59	20	87	21
40–44	16	4	28	4

Source: *Statistical Abstract of the United States,* 1975: Table 70; 1981: George, 1974:Table 2.4; 1979 *UN Demographic Yearbook,* Supp.:Table 6.

The table shows, for example, that in 1955 there were 16 births in the United States per 1,000 women aged 40 to 44, but in 1980 there were only 4 births for that age group.

Net reproduction rate

The rate at which a group of women are replacing themselves with daughters is the **net reproduction rate (NRR),** the total number of female children born per woman to a cohort of women passing through the childbearing period. Using this measure, it is possible to tell quickly whether true fertility is high or low. The statement that NRR equals 1.0 means that on the average each woman is producing one daughter to replace herself (and each couple an average of two children living to childbearing age). In developed countries with low death rates, the "average" woman would have to produce slightly more than one daughter to make up for the few women who die before menopause, the end of their childbearing years. In earlier times, when many women died before menopause, the average woman might have to produce two or more daughters to replace herself.

In the early 1980s the NRR for the whole world was about 1.7. Figures for Canada, West Germany, Japan, the United Kingdom, and the United States were 1.0 or lower. By contrast, China's NRR was 1.4, India's 1.9, and Mexico's a very high 2.8.

Differences in fertility

Groups within a population have children at different rates, although the gaps seem to be narrowing. Here are some of the more important differences in the United States:

1. Rural areas have higher fertility than urban areas.
2. The larger the city, the lower the fertility.
3. Fertility of blue-collar families tends to be higher than that of white-collar families.
4. Catholic fertility is higher than Protestant fertility, but Catholic fertility is also declining and the Catholic-Protestant difference is decreasing.
5. Black fertility is higher than white fertility, but it follows white trends.
6. People who are poor and poorly educated have higher birthrates than those who are better off and better educated.

MORTALITY

Death rates are calculated like fertility rates. The most commonly used death rate, the **crude death rate (CDR),** is the number of deaths per 1,000 population and is calculated as follows:

Table 10.1   Crude Birth and Death Rates, Natural Increase, and Years to Double Population, Selected Countries, About 1980

Country	Rates per 1000 of population			Years to double population[b]
	Births	Deaths	Natural increase[a]	
World	30	12	18	39
Australia	15	7	8	84
Brazil	37	9	28	26
Canada	15	7	8	84
China	31	11	20	35
Egypt	39	13	26	27
West Germany	10	12	−2	—
India	36	15	21	33
Indonesia	38	17	21	33
Ireland	22	8	14	64
Israel	24	7	17	33
Italy	11	10	1	200
Japan	14	6	8	84
Mexico	34	6	28	20
New Zealand	16	8	8	84
Nigeria	49	23	26	27
Poland	20	10	10	66
Spain	15	8	7	66
USSR	18	10	8	84
United Kingdom	13	12	1	200
United States	16	9	7	100

[a]Natural increase is crude birthrate minus crude death rate.
[b]Estimated number of years to double the population, assuming that natural increase continues at the rate reported.
Source: Basic data from United States Bureau of the Census, 1978, *United Nations Monthly Bulletin of Statistics*, 1983 (January):6 – 9, and country reports.

$$\frac{\text{deaths in a year}}{\text{midyear population}} \times 1000 = \text{CDR}$$

Thus,

$$\frac{1,986,000}{226,505,000} \times 1000 = 8.8,$$

the crude death rate for the resident population of the United States in 1980. This was roughly half the average CDR of 17.2 recorded for 1900. If the crude death rate of 8.8 is subtracted from the crude birthrate of 15.95, the result is a natural increase of 7.15 per 1,000 of population in 1980. Table 10.1 presents estimated crude death rates for several countries.

As in the case of fertility rates, it is necessary to take age into account when analyzing crude death rates. If countries with large percentages of old people (such as the United States, Canada, and Britain) are compared with countries that have low percentages of old people (such as India and Egypt), one would expect the countries with more old people to have high death rates. As it turns out, India and Egypt have higher crude death rates despite their young populations.

The infant mortality rate

The **infant mortality rate,** which is considered to be a definitive test of a country's standard of welfare, is the number of infants who die in their first year per 1,000 live births. Infant mortality ranges from rates in excess of 150 in some developing countries of

Poverty and infant mortality in Peru. A father carries his child's coffin.

Latin America, Africa, and Asia to rates as low as 9 in Scandinavia and the Netherlands. The USSR infant mortality is a surprisingly high 31, perhaps because of inferior health care for mothers, over-crowding, and pollution (Feshbach, cited in Murphy, 1983:38). Canada, Australia, New Zealand, and most Western European countries have rates of less than 15. In 1980 the United States rate was 12.5, about one-fifth of the 1935 rate of 58. Both black and white infant mortality have been halved in the last 40 years, but the black rate is still 40 percent higher than the white rate. Native peoples such as American Indians and Australian Aborigines have infant mor-tality rates notoriously higher than the national aver-ages.

The maternal mortality rate

The overall **maternal mortality rate** in the United States is about 11 maternal deaths per 100,000 live births, an impressive decline from 582 in 1935 (U.S. PHS 79-1222, 1978:8; *Vital Statistics of the U.S.*). White maternal mortality is about 6.4. The rate for blacks is about 25, which is about the same as for whites in the late 1960s. The lag in the improvement of the black rate reflects the lower income and poorer living conditions of blacks.

Statistics support the popular belief that, holding age constant, the first birth is the most dangerous for the mother. By age, the risks connected with childbirth are greatest for older mothers, and the most favorable age for childbearing is the early twenties.

LIFE EXPECTANCY

Where and when you were born largely determines how long you can expect to live. Life expectancy is an estimate of the average number of years of life remaining. It is based on life-table statistics such as those prepared by life insurance companies. Life expectancies can be calculated from any age, but estimates from birth are usually used to study trends or compare countries. The figures are averages: Many people do not achieve the average life duration and others beat the odds.

Persons born in prehistoric times could expect to live 18 to 25 years, and at the time of the Roman Empire this figure had risen only to 20 to 30 years. By 1880 the life expectancy for people born in northern and western Europe was in the mid-forties; for those born in southern and eastern Europe it was in the mid-thirties, but in much of the world it was still in the mid-twenties. Since the late 1800s the gains in life expectancy have been greater than all

the gains combined since prehistoric times (Preston, 1977:163–65).

At present western Europe (especially the Scandinavian countries), Canada, and the United States have favorable life expectancy figures. Sweden scores high (75 years), and so do Japan (76), Canada (73), and the United States (73). Mexico and Brazil (60) have made much progress toward improving life expectancy in recent years. However, China (53) and India (47) lag far behind.

Life expectancy is higher for females in industrial countries, and the gap between the sexes has increased from about 2 to 3 years in the 1800s to 7 to 8 years today. Typical are the following: Canada, 69 years for males versus 76 years for females; the

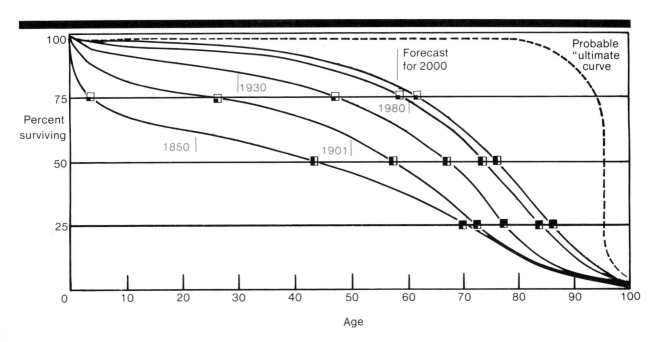

Age at which survivors are reduced by
☐ ¼   ▮ ½   ◼ ¾

Figure 10.5 Percent of All Persons Born Surviving to Successive Ages, United States, 1950 – 2000, and a Hypothetical Ultimate Survival Curve

Source: For 1850, 1901, and 1930, Metrololitan Life Insurance Company, Statistical Bulletin, March 1952. The current curve is compiled from Monthly Vital Statistics Reports. That for 2000 is compiled and computed from unpublished data supplied by the U.S. Bureau of Census, National Population Estimates and Projections Branch. The "ultimate" hypothetical curve is from Hayflick, 1980:60.

United States, 70 versus 77; United Kingdom, 70 versus 76; Australia, 71 versus 78. But Indian expectancy is 48 years for males versus 47 for females (*Statistical Abstract of the United States, 1982–83:* 862).

Survival trends

The dramatic improvement in life expectancy between 1850 and the present is shown in Figure 10.5, but little improvement is forecast for the year 2000. In 1850 three-fourths of the newborn in the United States only reached the age of 5; in 1901 three-fourths reached age 24; and now the same proportion live more than 60 years. The age to which half of the newborn survived increased from 45 years in 1850 to more than 74 years at present. These changes are due to advances in medical care, public-health practice, nutrition, and life-style. Some consequences are:

1. Many more people live through their working years, thus adding to potential economic productivity.
2. More people reach old age, thus adding to old-age dependency.
3. Fewer deaths among the young means that fewer births are needed to maintain the population.

Life span

"Premature" deaths may be further reduced, but it is unlikely that the limits of human existence will be extended by very much. To assume that they will is to mistake higher life expectancy for an increase in the total human life span. Note in Figure 10.5 that the gain in survivors at the three-fourths point and beyond is not nearly so great as the gains at the one-half and one-fourth points. Beyond the one-half point, the current curve is close to that for 2000, suggesting little improvement. A hypothetical ultimate curve for human survival, given in Figure 10.5, describes the limits of survival for which humanity is programmed.

"Three score and ten" (Psalms 90:10) was an unduly optimistic life expectancy in biblical times, but it was a realistic estimate of the human life span. The proportion of people surviving to old age may not increase drastically in developed countries where the objective is to improve the quality of health rather than simply to prolong life. In less developed countries, the immediate task is to prevent premature deaths by better food, sanitation, and protection against contagious disease.

(Text continued on p. 218)

Adaptation 10.2

The Case of the G.E. Babies

All statistical measures are based on assumptions. The demographer must make sure the measures used are the right ones for the population being studied. It is also necessary that they be calculated accurately. The reader's task is to understand the assumptions behind the statistics as well as the arithmetic applied to them.

When the wrong measure is used or a measure is applied to the wrong population, the results will be wrong no matter how accurate the arithmetic. The following account is a classic example of how to get wrong answers and how to avoid them.

On January 14, 1953, General Electric announced that it would award five shares of its common stock to any employee who had a baby on October 15—the company's seventy-fifth anniversary. Originally the company said it expected about 13 winners. It arrived at this figure by applying a daily U.S. birthrate to its own 226,000 employees. This computation actually yielded a prediction of 15 births; but a G.E. public relations man thought it might be nice to trim the figure to 13, the number of original G.E. investors. The mathematics suffered from more than public relations, however. G.E. employees, since they include no children and no one over 65, are obviously a much more fertile group than the population as a whole. When this fact sank in, a company statistician made a new assault on the problem. He estimated that the size of an average G.E. family was 4.2. This meant that the total number of people in the G.E. families was close to a million. Applying the crude annual birthrate to this group and dividing by 365, he came up with a new prediction of 72 births on the big day.

As it turned out, there were not 13, 15, or 72 babies born to G.E. employees on October 15. There were 189.

Subtracting the company's highest expectations of 72 from 189 gives 117 "extra" babies. Where did G.E. go wrong? Well, among other things, the company made no allowance for the incentive provided by its own stock. This oversight, remarkable in a company that has had a lot to say about capitalist incentives, was apparently rectified by the employees. The latter not only enjoy having children, but, it appears, they rather enjoy the idea of becoming capitalists. And they seem to have known a good thing. In a generally declining stock market, G.E. common stock rose during the pregnant months from 69 to 78 7/8.*

*Reprinted from "Sixty Six Million Americans." Based on an excerpt from *Fortune Magazine*. © 1954 Time Inc. All rights reserved.

HOW G.E. WENT WRONG

G.E.'s statisticians applied the wrong rate to the wrong group. They applied the United States crude birthrate to G.E. employees, assuming that G.E. employees were a true sample of the United States population. If the crude birthrate was to be used, it should have been applied to the whole population of G.E. family members, not just to the workers.

G.E. finally included family members in its calculation of the crude birthrate. But even the population of G.E. family members was not representative of the total population of the United States. For example, G.E. families contain a large proportion of individuals in their productive (and reproductive) years and few old persons.

The G.E. statisticians also failed to take into account several other factors that affect the birthrate: (1) the section of the country, (2) the size of the communities where the employees lived, (3) their income, (4) their education, and (5) their race.

How G.E. could have done better

G.E. could have applied age-specific birthrates to the women of childbearing ages in G.E. employees' families. This number could have been corrected for seasonal fluctuations in births. Corrections for other characteristics would be harder to make and probably pointless, for the following reasons.

Because we do not know all the characteristics of the G.E. population, we cannot make a more refined estimate. Possibly (as *Fortune* assumed) the offer was an incentive to some G.E. families to try to have a baby on the right day. Families that intended to have a child anyway might have tried to take advantage of the offer, but it seems unlikely that a couple who did not intend to have a baby would change their minds because of a chance to win stock worth around $350. The influence of incentive could have been estimated and the prediction improved if the company had interviewed a sample of G.E. wives and female employees about whether or not they intended to have a baby soon.

Of course, G.E. could have ducked this issue by announcing the award eight months instead of nine months before October 15. Instead, the announcement was made about 273 days before the anniversary date. Since a full-term pregnancy lasts about 280 days, some of the births that occurred on that date may have been induced (hastened) by the women's doctors.

There is at least one more complication. Any estimate of a daily birthrate, even for a rather large population like the G.E. families, is subject to error because daily birthrates vary even more widely than seasonal or monthly birthrates. In 1950, the United States crude birthrate ranged from 20.9 for April to 25.5 for September. The shorter the period, the greater the range of variation (and the smaller the population, the greater the range of variation). The chances of making a correct prediction for any particular day and any particular group are, therefore, not very good.

Chapter 10 **Summary**

Section 1/**The uses of demography**
The scientific study of population, called demography, is becoming ever more important as the dangers of population pressures increase. Business and civic leaders are also discovering the usefulness of demographic knowledge.

The most important single source of population data is the census. The U.S. Constitution provides for the census to apportion the members of Congress every ten years. Censuses usually undercut the population, especially the young, old, mobile, poor, and minorities.

Section 2/**Population composition**
The composition of a population is its makeup in terms of age, sex, race, occupation, and the like. The sex ratio is stated as the number of males per 100 females. An unbalanced ratio—one that deviates very far from 100—can be caused by heavy migration of one sex, infanticide of one sex, war, or other disasters.

Age composition is determined by the birth and death rates of specific age groups. The population pyramid is a convenient way to picture the age and sex composition of a population. Future population pyramids will also reveal the progressive effects of a major change such as a depression decline in births or a post-war baby boom. Cohort analysis is used to trace what happens to a particular group that has been exposed to a set of experiences at the same time. The dependency ratio measures the proportion of young and old people in the population.

Section 3/**Fertility and mortality**
A population's fertility, or actual reproduction, never reaches its fecundity, or biological ability to reproduce. The most common measure of fertility, the crude birthrate, states the number of births in a year per 1000 of population. Whether a crude birthrate should be considered high or low depends on the number of women of childbearing age in the population, that is, the "population at risk." A measure focusing on women of childbearing age is the general fertility rate, which is the number of births per 1000 women aged 15 to 44 in a given year. Net reproduction rate (NRR) is the rate at which a group of women are replacing themselves with daughters. This measure indicates whether the true fertility of a nation is high or low.

The crude death rate is the number of deaths in a year per 1000 population. The infant mortality rate, which is an indicator of a country's welfare standing, states the number of infants who die in their first year per 1000 live births.

A person's life expectancy—the number of years of life remaining—greatly depends on where and when he or she was born. Females born in industrial countries have higher life expectancies than males. While life expectancy has improved dramatically since the industrial revolution, the human life span has hardly changed.

Suggested Readings

Commission on Population Growth and the American Future
1972 *Population and the American Future*. Washington, D.C.: GPO. (See also the detailed Commission Research Reports in seven volumes, especially Vol. 1, Demographic and Social Aspects of Population Growth.)

Heer, David M.
1975 *Society and Population*. Second edition. Englewood Cliffs, N.J.: Prentice-Hall.

Kalbach, Warren E., and Wayne W. McVey
1971 *The Demographic Bases of Canadian Society*. Toronto: McGraw-Hill of Canada.

Ross, John A. (ed.)
1982 *International Encyclopedia of Population*. New York: Macmillan.

Thomlinson, Ralph
1976 *Population Dynamics*. Second edition. New York: Random House.

U.S. Bureau of the Census
1980 *Population Profile of the United States: 1979*. CPR, series P-20, no. 350, May 1980.

Westoff, Charles F. et al.
1973 *Toward the End of Growth: Population in America*. Englewood Cliffs, N.J.: Prentice-Hall.

Statistical sources

Demographic Yearbook of the United Nations.
(Compiled from statistics supplied by member countries of the United Nations.)

United States Bureau of the Census
1975 *Historical Statistics of the United States: Colonial Times to 1970*. Washington, D.C.: GPO.

United States Bureau of the Census
The Statistical Abstract of the United States. Published annually.

(Many countries publish similar handbooks or yearbooks, which include a wide range of statistical data and references to both official and nongovernmental sources.)

Chapter 11

Population Change

This chapter begins with a discussion of migration, both international and within the nation, leading logically to conclusions about the nature and significance of population redistribution. In the last section we discuss major world populations trends. The situation in advanced industrialized countries like the United States is compared with less developed countries like India and China, where rapid growth threatens the environment, the quality of life, and social stability.

Section One
Migration

INTERNATIONAL MIGRATION

Before 1800 the largest migration between continents was the transportation of between 10 and 20 million slaves from Africa, mainly to the New World (Curtin, 1969). The number of European migrants to the Americas before 1800 was probably less than half the number of slaves brought from Africa.

After 1800 a massive flow from Europe to the Western Hemisphere took place. Perhaps as many as 75 million migrants entered the Americas. This, the largest intercontinental migration in history, re-

lieved population pressure in Europe during a period of rapid increase. Even countries that did not suffer from population pressure also participated in colonial expansion. Small Portugal sent much of its population across the oceans to explore and establish colonies from Asia to Brazil.

Table 11.1 presents the origins and destinations of migrants during this peak intercontinental migration so far as the data can be secured from historical sources. All but 2 million of the 53 million migrants between 1846 and 1932 came from Europe. More than three-quarters of the migrants came from only five sources: the British Isles, Italy, Austria-Hungary, Germany, and Spain.

Figures for immigrants in the table exceed those for emigrants by about 6 million because of the different time spans covered—111 years for immigration and 86 years for emigration—and because the immigration records are more complete. The chief sending countries were European, the chief receiving countries, the Americas; the United States alone received three-fifths of the total. Of those entering the United States between 1821 and 1924 about 30 percent returned to their homelands; of those entering Argentina, about 47 percent went home (Carr-Saunders, 1936:49).

Migration to the United States has been long,

Table 11.1   The Great Intercontinental Migration

Country of origin	Percent of emigrants[a]	Country of destination	Percent of immigrants[b]
British Isles	34	United States	58
Italy	19	Argentina	11
Austria-Hungary	10	Canada and Newfoundland	9
Germany	9	Brazil	7
Spain	9	Other America	6
Scandinavia	5	Australia and New Zealand	6
Russia	4	Other Non-America	3
Portugal	3	Total number immigrants	59,167,000
Other Europe	4		
Non-Europe	3		
Total number emigrants	53,450,000		

[a]Emigrants for the period 1846–1932.
[b]Immigrants to the United States, Canada, and Brazil for the period 1821–1932. Various dates apply for all other countries.
Source: Computed from Carr-Saunders, 1936:49.

large, and diverse. The country gained a population to match its resources and a work force for its farms and industries. Numerous migrants have made lasting contributions to the nation's culture and economy. The United States still is by far the major destination for migrants.

After the foreign-born population peaked at 14 million in 1930, the ratio of foreign-born to total population declined. The 1970 census counted about 11 million foreign-born in the 50 states—about the same number as the 1900 total for 45 states. From 1860 to 1920 the number of foreign-born in the United States ranged between 13 and 15 percent of the total; in 1980 it was about 5 percent of the total, but of a much bigger total. Restrictive immigration policies partly account for the decline in the percent foreign-born (Keely and Kraly, 1974). Immigration is now much larger than the low rates of the 1930s and 1940s. The "mix" of immigrants includes large numbers from the Caribbean, Latin America, and Asia—a decided shift from the earlier European-born immigration.

Refugees

The "boat people" whose plight captured the imagination of many in 1980 are only a fraction of the total number of refugees from Indochina. Since 1975 more than 1 million have been expelled or have fled from Indochina, and uncounted others died while attempting to flee. Many thousands in camps in Southeast Asia, mainly Thailand, and Malaysia, still await resettlement; others have been taken in by several countries. China and the United States have accepted the largest numbers. If refugees are calculated as a proportion of the population of the host country, Hong Kong, Australia, the United States, France, and Canada have been the most hospitable. Japan, Sweden, Holland, and Britain have been among the least welcoming. In the United States and Canada the Indochinese refugees are just another element in populations that are already ethnically diverse. In small, homogeneous countries, the refugees are highly visible additions.

During the early 1980s, the United States again experienced a sudden flood of migrants who strained the capacity of understaffed immigration authorities, this time from Cuba. In less troubled economic times

these refugees from the Caribbean would not have attracted so much attention after the first few months. But wherever they go, there is high unemployment. Particularly in Florida, Cubans are seen by blacks as competitors for scarce jobs and as an ethnic minority that has jumped ahead of its place in a long waiting line. To complicate matters even more, included in the 1980s Cuban immigrants were criminals and other "undesirables" expelled by Cuba to test the U.S. open-door policy. Such expulsion is a sinister element in international relations: using forced migration to embarrass and burden a neighboring country.

But just what is a refugee? This question was dramatized by the Haitian "boat people"; some of their boats were turned back before they reached Florida, and some were lost at sea. Unless they had family already in the United States or other special immigration privileges, many of the Haitians were deported or interned. An argument raged over whether they should be considered political refugees who can be admitted fairly readily or economic refugees for whom there is no special provision. Because Haitians are black, their treatment also became a racial issue. Race and ethnicity no longer loom so large in U.S. immigration policy as they once did, but they still lie beneath the surface of public debate.

How many illegals?

The inability of the United States to control immigration is a continuing source of concern. The present level of immigration is not even accurately known because cheap air travel and long, poorly patrolled borders allow hundreds of thousands of "undocumented" migrants to enter the United States from Mexico, Central America, and the Caribbean. Once in the United States, these "illegals" live in crowded ethnic communities where, because of their illegal entry, they can easily be exploited by employers or landlords. To stem the flow of illegal aliens and prevent their exploitation is probably beyond the present resources of the immigration services and law-enforcement agencies.

Mexicans make up a large part of all illegal immigrants, and newspaper stories give estimates as high as 2 or 3 million a year. Careful study throws

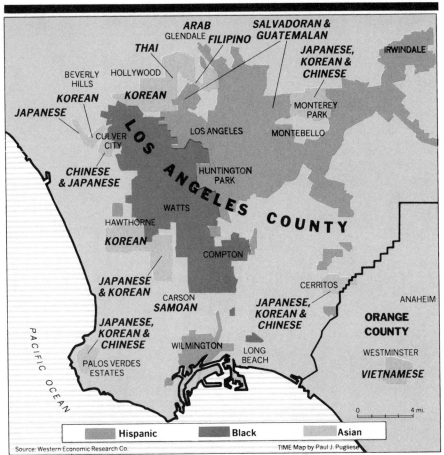

Figure 11.1   Ethnic Los Angeles

The new "Ellis Island," is not merely an entry point for processing immigrants who move on to other regions. Perhaps 2 million immigrants have settled in the Los Angeles area since 1970. Some of the ethnic groupings shown in the map, such as Hispanics, blacks, Japanese, and Chinese, are long-established residents, but their numbers have grown in recent years. Others represent the recent migration waves: Arabs, Vietnamese, Thai, and Central Americans. These new ethnic communities have altered the demographic nature of a subregion in constant change.

doubt on such figures. One clue to the number who enter illegally is the number who are caught, which is about 700,000. It is claimed that for every undocumented immigrant who is caught two or three are not caught and that almost all stay in the United States. However, both statements are doubtful. Many immigrants, both legal and illegal, return to their native countries, especially when the countries like the United States and Mexico share a border. Thus, there is a considerable difference between *gross* in-flow, the total number entering a country, and *net* in-flow, the total remaining.

Furthermore, many Mexican illegal immigrants enter and leave several times. Studies that consider the two-way border traffic and carefully examine the age and ethnic characteristics of the U.S. population suggest that the net annual increase in the U.S. population from Mexican illegal immigration

Mexican "illegals" in 1948. Three of a cargo of forty arrested in Chicago after traveling from Texas in a false-bottomed truck.

may range between 82,000 and 234,000 rather than 2 or 3 million (Heer, 1979:422. See also Hewlett, 1981–82; Keely, 1977; Keely and Kraly, 1978).

Demographic analysis estimates that no more than 4 million illegal migrants of Mexican origin lived in the United States in 1980 (Bean et al., 1983). A total of 4 million residents is a far cry from 2 to 3 million illegal immigrants per year. This does not mean that illegal immigration is unimportant. The entire problem of immigration control undergoes close examination by Congress and the nation at large, particularly during periods of economic downturn. But

because population problems are long-term problems, immigration as well as fertility must be regularly examined for its effects in future decades.

IMMIGRATION POLICY

Refugees and illegal border crossing are sensitive and conspicuous aspects of immigration policy in turmoil. In response to population and political pressures, the rich industrial countries seem to be entering a new and uncertain migration era. Individuals from developing countries with very high birthrates will seek out the apparent opportunities in industrialized countries where friends and relatives live and work. Governments of developing countries prefer a fraction of their population to emigrate for two reasons. First, a small part of their rapid growth is exported. Second, migrants send money back to their families, thus raising living standards and creating a pool of capital for economic activity in the home country.

Opponents of immigration claim that added population puts strains on the society and imposes economic penalties. If there are more people, there must be more schools, more roads, more public utilities, more housing—and all of these must be paid for. The costs are a burden to taxpayers and a strain on land and resources. They were not so important in thinly settled rural economies, but advanced urban societies must make a much larger investment per person to maintain a high standard of living.

Some countries have very restrictive migration policies. It is not hard to get into Japan as a visitor, and the Japanese travel freely. However, Japan does not encourage foreigners to become residents; it has not taken in many refugees; and the half million or so persons of Korean descent have a hard time in Japan. Other countries such as Canada and the United States have declared more open policies. Although they may attempt to limit immigration and make it more orderly, it is not likely that they can or will try to clamp a lid on future immigration.

INTERNAL MIGRATION

Americans have a reputation for geographic mobility, and statistics support that impression. Since the Current Population Survey first studied internal migration in 1948, about 20 percent of the population were found to change residence each year. Fully two-thirds of the movers stay in the same county, but about one-fifth move to other states.

Redistribution

Such geographical mobility is not random. The selectivity of origin and destination reshapes the demographic landscape. In general the central states and the industrial Northeast have lost population in

recent years, and this trend was apparent in some states as early as the 1960s. The West and especially the South have gained population (Kasarda, 1980:374–80). Between 1975 and 1980 the Northeast and North Central regions lost over 2.5 million, the South gained nearly 1.8 million and the West 0.9 million. Both blacks and whites participated in the interregional migration, and the migration of blacks to the South seems to be gaining speed (1981 *Statistical Abstract:*13).

Analysis of data from three surveys conducted in the mid-1970s shows that over half of interstate migrants moved for job-related reasons. Contrary to popular impression, only 5 percent of interstate movers gave change of climate as the main reason. About 7 percent moved to be closer to relatives, and other family-related reasons account for an additional 10 percent (Long and Hansen, 1979:6).

Redistribution has involved shifts in type of settlement as well as region. The United States is highly urban in terms of residence, industry, and life-style. But not until 1920 was the country urbanized in the sense that more than half the population lived in cities. Today three-fourths of Americans are urban dwellers. That does not mean progressive concentration in the central cities. In fact, the urban core has increased very little in recent years while metropolitan growth outside the central city has been quite rapid.

There are now signs of significant population growth beyond the metropolitan area, and the 1980 census shows that the rural population actually increased in the 1970s (Long and DeAre, 1982). People have always been obliged to go where the jobs are, and since the country became urban, jobs have concentrated in urban centers. Recent shifts in economic activity away from smokestack industry into services and high technology to a great extent reduce the need for metropolitan concentration. This change will permit more families to live in less densely settled areas (Chalmers and Greenwood, 1980).

To call the trend toward dispersion a rural migration suggests an image of scattered self-sufficient farming communities. It would be more accurate to think of the thinly settled areas as merging urban and rural styles—a promise of new ways of living and working. The future distribution of population in both regional and rural-urban terms will thus be conditioned by two main factors—competition in the job market and the ability of people to choose a less crowded environment that affords easy access to urban facilities. While those processes are going on, the face of the city itself is undergoing change (Long and DeAre, 1983).

Section Two
World Population Trends

THE POPULATION PROBLEM

While modern industrial countries are growing slowly or not at all, less developed countries will continue to grow rapidly for many years. The threatening term ''population explosion'' is not mere doomsday talk: The problem will not just go away. A very large, rapidly increasing world population is pressing on a limited land area and using up resources that cannot be replaced. The social problems created by these changes have never occurred before on a worldwide scale. One result is rising tension between rich and poor countries over who gets what resources at what price and how they are used.

Some people believe that the population problem has been solved by improved birth control, but contraception is only part of the answer. The future population of the world—perhaps the future of humanity—will be determined by whether people, especially in the Third World, decide to limit births. And their decisions depend on social factors such as traditions favoring large families in many poor countries and among the poor in rich countries.

Components of change

Four factors determine total population—births, deaths, immigration, and emigration. They are presented in Figure 11.2 which shows the **components of change** as rates (persons per 1,000 of population) for the United States over the past half century. Births minus deaths gives the net natural increase (or decrease). Immigrants minus emigrants gives the net immigration (or emigration). Net natural increase plus net immigration gives the net growth.

Separate curves for immigration and emigration are not presented. The curve showing the net change from births and deaths is also left out because it looks like the net growth rate, which combines the results of all four components. Note how closely the net growth rate has been governed by changes in the birthrate. The death rate has drifted down to a fairly stable level. In developed countries it varies little except when there is a war or other major disaster.

SOCIAL CONTROL

Each component of population change means different things in terms of social policy and individual freedom. Governments try to control immigration, and in some cases emigration, with passports, visas, and border checks. The death rate depends to a large extent on governments rather than individuals. Deaths can be greatly reduced by improving water quality and waste disposal, controlling contagious diseases, and supplying adequate food.

The birthrate, on the other hand, is determined largely by the personal decisions of hundreds of millions of people. Efficient birth control methods, widely available in industrial countries, enable individuals to decide when they will have children, and in these countries people choose small families. In developing countries, reliable birth control methods are not so easily available, and family planning often clashes with traditional values that favor large families. Nonetheless, governments do not always allow the birthrate to depend on individual decisions. They can intervene for or against fertility. Nazi Germany and Fascist Italy favored high birthrates, but China, India, and other countries have used pressure to limit reproduction.

China

In the early years of the People's Republic of China (after 1949), the leaders were not worried about population growth even though the birthrate was about 43 per 1,000.

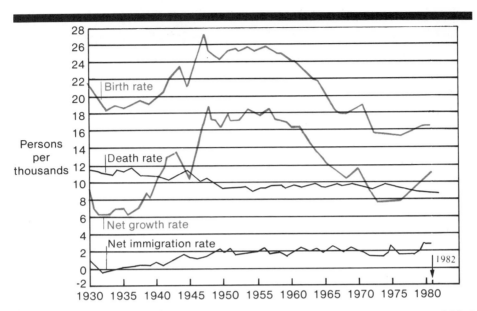

Figure 11.2 Annual Rates of Net Growth, Births, Deaths, and Net Immigration, United States, 1930 – 1982

Source: CPR, P-25, no. 545, 1975, no. 706, 1977, and monthly estimates.

Marxist ideology attributed human misery not to excessive population growth but to the maldistribution of income and other supposed defects in the existing social order. Since under the new society the productivity of the people was supposed to increase more rapidly than their number, the Communist leaders were reluctant to admit that the size of China's population could, in any sense, present a problem. . . . As late as April 1952, the *People's Daily* denounced birth control as ''a means of killing off the Chinese people without shedding blood'' and as quite unnecessary since China was a country with vast unsettled lands and unexploited natural resources, and people were ''the most precious of all categories of capital.''

In pre-Communist China, premarital sexual intercourse was regarded as extremely reprehensible, and chastity held a high place on the list of womanly virtues. This is one of the traditions of old China accepted and nurtured by the Communists and the ''liberation'' of Chinese women does not extend to the endorsement of free love. All evidence suggests that China's youth continue to pursue the puritanical

sexual mores of the past. There was truly little need for the slogan: ''Making love is a mental disease which wastes time and energy.'' [Orleans, 1972:39, 49–50]

As a basic policy of its modernization program, the government has acted to limit population growth by urging birth control, postponed marriages, and small families. Contraception, sterilization, and abortion are widely available and free, and China's family planning program is among the most extensive in the world. It is estimated that by 1970 the crude birthrate had been reduced from a high of 43 to about 32. The birthrate target is 17 or 18, which would result in an annual population growth of about 1 percent (Jaffe and Oakley, 1978:103, 107). The Chinese family planning program is closely watched by Third World countries with similar problems. In the longer term, China's policy is to strive to *reduce* the population. Toward that end, the government rewards the one-child family with financial subsidy

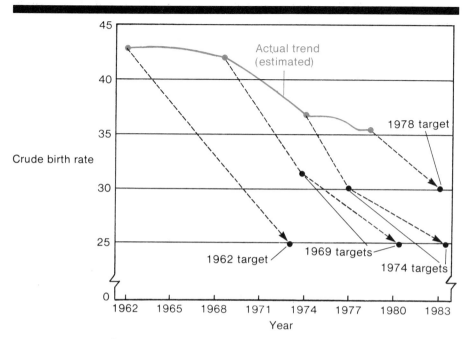

Figure 11.3 Birthrate Targets Adopted by India
Compared with Actual Trend, 1962 – 1983

Source: Nortman, 1978: 281. Adapted with the permission of the Population Council

and better living quarters and the single child with nutritional, educational, and job preferences (Chen, 1979). Negative sanctions are imposed on families with more than two children.

Mother India

It has been clear for many years that Indians with large-family values, especially in rural areas, would not respond quickly to the gradual spread of birth control information and small-family propaganda. Sterilization campaigns made progress in some areas, but they had little impact on the country as a whole.

For more than 25 years Indian governments have set birthrate targets, as shown in Figure 11.3. All of them missed badly. The top continuous curve shows actual crude birthrates, and the arrows mark the decreases that the governments hoped to achieve. For instance, the target adopted in 1962 when the birthrate was 43 hoped for a birthrate of

25 by 1973. The actual 1973 birthrate was over 37. In 1978 when the birthrate was 36, the target for 1983 was a birthrate of 30. Obviously, none of the goals was realistic. Even the relatively modest decrease hoped for between 1978 and 1983 was not achieved.

In the mid-1970s India Gandhi's government directly attacked the large-family system. In some Indian states a standard of three children was set, and a major propaganda campaign was launched, including compulsory sterilization, financial rewards, and job preference to people with small families. For the first time, the country's health and propaganda resources—national, state, and local—were mobilized on a scale that matched India's population problem. Propaganda and economic incentives, as well as pressure, brought to birth control clinics millions of people who otherwise would not have been reached.

The drama of the birth control campaign made the population problem a personal matter to many

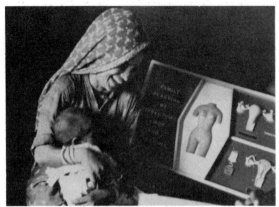

(Left) Education for infertility: The woman.
(Right) Education for infertility: The men.

Indians. Millions of undereducated rural Indians became familiar with the idea of sterilization and many were sterilized. However, an American demographer predicted that "efforts at coercion would be more likely to bring down the government than the birthrate" (Notestein, quoted in Landman, 1977:103). In fact, the Gandhi government was defeated in 1977 partly because of the birth control campaign, which was engineered by Prime Minister Gandhi's son Sanjay. A less authoritarian and more patient government strategy with more respect for individual dignity might have achieved its goals at less political cost.

The Desai government, which replaced Gandhi's in 1977, turned to a low-key, less effective policy encouraging personal choice. Although the government was concerned about the size of the population and its rapid growth, economic sanctions and overt compulsion were not used. Gandhi's return to power in 1980 reverted to a more activist strategy but one that is not so aggressive as that of the 1970s. At the current growth rate of 2 percent per year, India will have a population of 1 billion by the year 2000 (Nortman, 1978:277–78, 281). By comparison, the total population of the world in the mid-1800s was 1 billion.

FERTILITY TRENDS IN THE WEST

In rich countries, where most people can control the timing and number of children, fertility is largely self-controlled and responds quickly to historical events, prosperity or depression, and shifting social values (Dorn, 1950:332). The "baby boom" that occurred in the United States after World War II had a number of causes: births postponed by the war, an increase in the marriage rate, and a fall in the number of childless and one-child marriages (see Westoff, 1978:37). The decline in the birthrate that followed the boom was a return to a long-term trend, and after the early 1960s, fertility fell rapidly (*CPR,* P-20, no. 308, June 1977; P-20, no. 336, April 1979).

The contraceptive revolution
National surveys in the United States show a desire for small families and increased use of more effective birth control techniques (Ryder and Westoff, 1971; Westoff and Ryder, 1977; Westoff and Jones, 1977a).* The percentage of women who never used

*Findings of the 1975 study, on which the 1977 publications are based, are strictly applicable only to continuously married women.

birth control has decreased steadily, and by 1975 almost all recently married women had used some form of birth control. In addition, highly effective techniques (the pill, sterilization, and the intrauterine device, or IUD) have come into more general use. The "contraceptive revolution" is a fact of life in the developed countries.

Between 1965 and 1975 the pill was the most common method of birth control, but sterilization was increasingly used and by 1975 nearly equaled the pill in acceptance. For couples who intended to have no more children, sterilization of either the husband or the wife was preferred by nearly 2 to 1.

Shrinking differences

Since 1965 the differences have been shrinking between whites and blacks and between Catholics and non-Catholics both in the number of children wanted and in the number of actual births in these groups (Ryder, 1973; on Canada, see Long, 1970; Henripin and Légaré, 1971). Both conforming and less conforming Catholics have shown declining fertility (Jones and Westoff, 1979:215). The fertility of the American Jewish population has paralleled the trends for the American population in general, but Jewish fertility has been consistently lower (DellaPergola, 1980).

Fertility differences between high- and low-income families are also narrowing, but women of lower socioeconomic status still have more children. The difference is especially large among young unwed mothers, who often leave school to take care of their children. Low education is thus both a cause and an effect of high fertility: Women with little education are likely to have little knowledge about birth control, and single women with small children are unlikely to stay in school (*CPR, P-20*, no. 308, 1977).

Pro-growth policies

Most population policies are concerned with how to limit growth. However, some countries with falling birthrates have expressed anxiety that their populations will be too small. Austria and both Germanys have more deaths than births; Britain is at the balance point; and if current trends continue, the population of Europe as a whole will begin to decline by the end of the century. There is no good reason why the present population size should be taken as a minimum, but many political and business leaders assume that any population decline is a bad thing.

Concern over declining population has been expressed from Japan to Romania, and steps have been taken to reverse the trend. In France, where national prestige is linked to population size, pro-growth policies include cash allowances, tax relief, a guaranteed minimum income for unwed mothers, a two-year maternity leave for government employees, and in some cases draft exemption for young fathers. East Germany succeeded in raising its crude birthrate from 10.6 in 1975 to 13.3 in 1977 by introducing several pro-growth measures in mid-1976. The financial incentives to have children included an interest-free loan for as much as $10,-000 to buy a house or furniture. "The debt is reduced by $1,000 for the birth of a child within eight years and by another $1,500 for a second child, and is excused entirely on the birth of a third child. . . . According to one report, 90,000 women . . . have accepted the government's invitation to go into baby production" (Westoff, 1978:40).

Concern about low birthrates must appear a luxury to political leaders in India, China, and other rapidly growing countries. But in worldwide terms it does not matter much whether the populations of France, Germany, and other industrial countries increase a little or decrease for a while.

WORLD POPULATION GROWTH

In 1650 the population of the world was about 500 million. Two centuries later it had more than doubled to over 1 billion. In the 80 years between 1850 and 1930 it doubled again, and in less than 50 years it doubled yet again, so that it is now over 4 billion. Present estimates place the doubling time at 39 years, which means a world population of 8 billion by the year 2010, when most of the readers of this book will be the late middle-aged (Carr-Saunders, 1936:43; Ehrlich et al., 1977:182–83). See Figure 11.4, p. 232.

The demographic transition model

The population changes that occurred during the industrial and urban development of Europe may be summarized as three stages of a model of **demographic transition:**

Stage 1, covering almost all of human existence, has a high birthrate balanced by a high death rate, especially high infant mortality.

Stage 2 is a period of explosive growth, which began in Europe around 1650. The death rate gradually falls, but the birthrate remains high.

Stage 3 occurs when birth control takes effect. The birthrate declines; the age composition of the population changes with a decrease in the percentage of children; and there is a trend toward a balance between births and deaths. A complete demographic transition, with the birthrate reduced to a level close to the death rate, has taken place only in recent years and only in technologically advanced, literate societies.

Limits of the model

Demographic transition is a *model* based on what has happened in developed countries. It is not inevitable and the sequence of events is not a rule. Japan experienced a different form of demographic transition: Birth and death rates began to decline together about 1920; that is, the decline in the birthrate did not lag behind the death rate (Muramatsu, 1971:1).

There are three reasons why the pattern may not occur in the least developed countries today. First, their birthrates are higher than European birthrates were during stage two. For example, the estimated birthrate in Britain in the early 1800s was less than 35 per 1,000, but in such countries as Tanzania and Iran it is over 45, and in some countries it may be over 50 per 1,000 (Teitelbaum, 1975). Second, death rates in the poorest countries have declined faster than did European death rates. The sharp declines in death rates have been brought about largely by health and sanitation measures introduced from industrial countries. Third, in some of the poorest countries the population is young and birthrates remain exceedingly high. Therefore, a very high rate of population increase cannot be avoided and may be prolonged far beyond what the transition model would suggest.

Prospects for population control

The steps to population control are the same in all societies:

1. Willingness to have small families.
2. Availability of effective birth control methods.
3. Awareness and acceptance of birth control methods as a way to achieve small families.

All of these steps must occur if population growth is to be controlled. The only alternative to self-controlled fertility is large-scale governmental action.

Some demographers believe effective population control may be within reach (for example, Bogue, 1967; Kirk, 1971). However, it is early for such claims. Although stationary populations are realistic in North America, Europe, and Japan, the prospects are dim for most developing countries. Stationary populations are not in view even for Taiwan, South Korea, and Hong Kong, where fertility rates have fallen to fairly low levels and where rising education and living standards began to reduce fertility even before family planning programs were started.

Slowly developing countries like those in Africa, Central America, and Southeast Asia present a more discouraging picture, family planning has not produced a quick decline in fertility ''in a population still mired in illiteracy and poverty and characterized by traditional behavior'' (Hauser, 1971:453). Outside of the developed countries, the population bomb is ticking, and most projections of the world population for the end of this century are around 6 billion (Demeny, 1979).

ZERO POPULATION GROWTH

The term **zero population growth (ZPG)** has become a slogan for those who favor population control. However, it is a mistake to think that the population will stop growing as soon as there is an average of two children per family. A population with a large percentage of women of childbearing age, even with a fairly low net reproduction rate (NRR), could produce a high crude birthrate and continued population growth for many years. Remember that NRR = 1 when the average mother bears on the average one daughter.

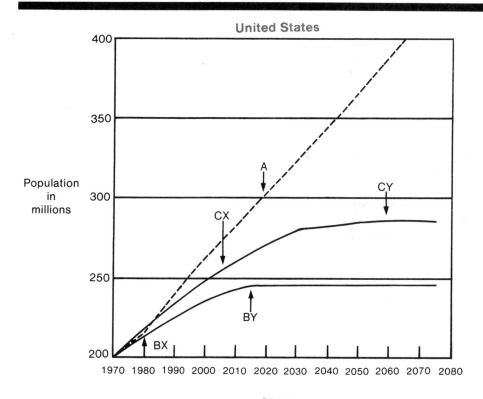

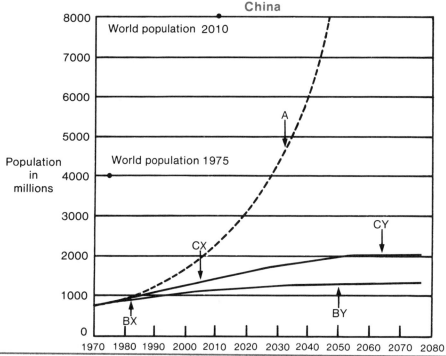

Figure 11.4
Projected Population Under Varying Fertility Assumptions
Constant fertility (A)
NRR = 1.0 in 1980 (BX)
NRR = 1.0 in 2000-2005 (CX)
X to Y = Lag in reaching stationary population
Source: U.S. Bureau of the Census, 1971: Table 2, and current census projections for the United States

The arithmetic of ZPG

To illustrate how the population continues to grow after NRR = 1, three projections of the populations of the United States and China are shown in Figure 11.4. Each curve is based on different assumptions. Curve A assumes that fertility rates will remain constant at the levels of the late 1960s, and will continue to grow indefinitely. Curve B assumes that NRR = 1 in the United States about 1980 and in China in 1980–1985. Curve C assumes that NRR will equal 1 in 2000–2005. The labels BX and CX mark the points on the B and C curves at which NRR = 1. The labels BY and CY mark the corresponding points at which the population will stop growing. According to the low projections of the Census Bureau, BY in the United States would be reached in the year 2015, with a stationary population of 250 million. CY would be reached in 2055, with a population of 288 million.

These statistical projections are not predictions. They do not take into account possible changes in birth control practice, age-specific death rates, migration, or natural disasters. But they do give a realistic picture of the lag between NRR = 1 when the average mother bears only one daughter) and a no-growth population.

The graph for China shows the enormous difference in growth that will occur if NRR = 1 is delayed from early in the 1980s (BX) to about 2005 (CX) or if NRR does not fall to 1. BX would produce a Chinese population of roughly 1.4 billion in 2050. CX would produce a population of 2 billion about 2065.

The numbers involved in the constant-fertility curve (projection A) can be grasped if we start with the population of the world in the mid-1970s—about 4 billion. The population of China was then over 800 million, or about 20 percent of the world total. If China's population continues to grow at the constant rate represented by curve A, it will reach the 1975 world total of 4 billion by the year 2025. By comparison, at constant 1960s fertility (curve A), it would take the U.S. population 100 years to reach 400 million, or half the 1975 population of China.

However, the population of China is not growing as fast as that of Mexico, India, and several other large countries. Although India has a population of about 650 million, it has a higher rate of natural increase than China. Thus, at constant fertility India's population would reach 4 billion in roughly 50 years, and soon after that it would have the largest population in the world. Mexico's population at constant fertility would equal the present population of the United States in 35 to 40 years and the present population of China in about 75 years.

Comparisons like these are facts that all political leaders must face, including those who fear that population control would benefit the rich countries and not the poor ones (Stycos, 1968). Moreover, emigration cannot do much to relieve population pressure. Even if the less densely populated parts of the world, such as the USSR, North America, and Australia, were willing to lower their standards of living and accept large numbers of immigrants from countries with fast-growing populations, only temporary relief would result. Clearly, the population problem must be solved within the borders of all but the smallest countries.

Chapter 11 **Summary**

Section 1/**Migration**

Before 1800 the largest intercontinental migration was the transportation of slaves from Africa to the New World. After 1800 a much larger number migrated from Europe to the Western Hemisphere. More than half of the European migrants settled in the United States. Growing population pressures, economic depressions, and political disturbances generate migration flows that create international strains, particularly on the United States with its tradition of offering haven to refugees. Large numbers of unauthorized migrants enter the United States from Mexico, Central America, and the Caribbean, but there is evidence that illegal immigration has been exaggerated.

The American reputation for geographical mobility is well founded. About 20 percent of the population change residence each year. Although two-thirds of movers stay in the same county, about one-fifth move to other states. Geographic migration is selective and reshapes the national demography. The Central States and the industrial

Northeast have lost population while the South and West have gained. Both blacks and whites participate in the interregional migration. Job-related reasons are the most important influence on interstate migration. The era of metropolitan concentration may be passing, and a trend toward population dispersion may be under way.

Section 2/**World population trends**

The four components of population change are births, deaths, immigration, and emigration. Immigration, emigration, and to some extent deaths can be controlled by governmental actions, but the birthrate is determined more by individual decisions. China has lowered its birthrate by economic and social pressure, providing free birth control facilities, and encouraging later marriage. India has been less successful, and its policy has not followed a consistent strategy. In Western countries, the ''contraceptive revolution,'' the widespread use of effective contraceptive methods, has resulted in a rapid decrease in fertility in all sectors of the population. Population control depends on the wish to have small families, available birth control methods, and acceptance of those controls, either voluntarily or under pressure.

The demographic transition model describes a sequence of changes that took place in Europe: (1) high birth and high death rates followed by (2) declining death rates and explosive population growth, and (3) declining birthrates and a trend toward a balance between births and deaths. The sequence is not a demographic law and it is not likely to occur in the least developed countries.

A population may continue to increase even when it has a net reproduction rate equal to 1 (that is, the average mother ''replaces'' herself with one daughter). The population will continue to grow until the percentage of women of childbearing age falls to a level that balances the number born and the number dying. This lag points to the crux of the population problem.

Suggested Readings

Borrie, W. D.
1970 *The Growth and Control of World Population*. London: Weidenfeld and Nicolson.

Brown, David L., and John M. Wardwell (eds.)
1980 *New Directions in Urban-Rural Migration: The Population Turnaround in Rural America*. New York: Academic Press.

Keely, Charles B.
1979 *U.S. Immigration: A Policy Analysis*. New York: The Population Council.

Keyfitz, Nathan
1983 *Population Change and Social Policy*. Cambridge, Mass.: Abt Books.

Orleans, Leo A.
1972 *Every Fifth Child: The Population of China*. London: Eyre Methuen.

Piotrow, Phyllis T.
1980 *World Population: The Present and Future Crisis*. Headline Series 251. New York: Foreign Policy Association.

Spengler, Joseph J.
1978 *Facing Zero Population Growth: Reactions and Interpretations, Past and Present*. Durham, N.C.: Duke University Press.

Key Terms*

acculturation (3) The adoption of new traits or patterns as a result of contact with another culture.

achieved status (5) Status acquired by using skills, knowledge, and other qualities over which one has some control. Compare **ascribed status**.

achievement (5) As a pattern variable, valuing persons according to their role performance. Compare **ascription**.

affirmative action (8) Efforts by government to improve the condition of minorities and women, especially by preferential treatment in employment or education.

age-specific birthrate (10) The number of births per 1,000 women in an age group in a given year.

apartheid (8) In South Africa, a strictly enforced system of racial segregation and subordination.

ascribed status (5) Status, such as race, based on characteristics over which one has little or no control. Compare **achieved status**.

ascription (5) The labeling process that values people according to how they are classified rather than as persons performing roles. Compare **achievement**.

assimilation (8) The process by which ethnic groups lose their separate identity and become part of the larger community.

authoritarian forms (6) In organizations, assignment of responsibilities to executives.

biological drive (4) A physical tension, such as hunger.

biosocial (7) Referring to patterns of behavior that result from the interaction of physical and social factors.

bourgeoisie (9) According to Marx, the property-owning class, including commercial farmers, that controls capital and the means of production in capitalist society. Compare **proletariat**.

bureaucracy (6) The formal organization of administrative officials.

bureaucratic authority (6) See **rational-legal authority**.

career mobility (9) Changes in social rank that occur during an individual's life.

charismatic authority (6) Authority based on belief in the special qualities of a particular person.

circulation mobility (9) Vertical mobility between generations not caused by industrial change and resulting in a reduction in direct occupational ''inheritance.'' Compare **structural mobility**.

class (9) A social grouping based on a distinctive role in the economic system, for example, manufacturers, small merchants, or industrial workers. Often used as a synonym for **social stratum**.

cohort (10) Any group of people exposed to the same influence or situation at the same time.

community (5) A comprehensive group within which the most important activities of a person's life can be carried on.

components of population change (11) The four factors—births, deaths, immigration, and emigration—that determine total population.

conflict approach (1) A sociological perspective that emphasizes the divisions within society and the domination of some groups over others.

consensus model (1) A perspective that emphasizes social stability and the persistence of shared ideas.

content analysis (2) Systematic coding of written material.

control (2) A research procedure designed to prevent external or irrelevant variables from influencing the findings of a study.

*Numbers in parentheses refer to the chapter in which the term first appears.

crude birthrate (CBR) (10) The number of births per 1,000 population in a given year.

crude death rate (CDR) (10) The number of deaths per 1,000 population in a given year.

cultural relativism (3) The understanding that each culture must be judged on its own terms and that the worth of a custom can be judged only by its contribution to the total culture.

cultural universal (3) An element that is common to all cultures.

cultural value (3) A widely held belief or feeling about what is important to the community's identity or well-being.

culture (3) The shared ways of thinking and believing that grow out of group experience and are passed from one generation to the next.

culture shock (3) The disorientation and frustration that result when one is among people who do not share one's basic values and beliefs.

definition of the situation (5) An interpretation of social reality that lends meaning and order to social interaction.

demographic transition (11) A model describing stages of change from high to low birth and death rates.

demography (10) The study of human populations.

dependency ratio (10) The number of people younger and older than working age divided by the number of working age, usually assumed to be ages 15 to 64.

dependent variable (2) The behavior or phenomenon influenced or caused by the **independent variable**.

deviant subculture (3) A group whose norms run counter to those of the larger society.

differential association (3) Sutherland's theory that deviant behavior is learned by associating with others who engage in such behavior, often in a small, intimate group.

diffuseness (5) An open-ended pattern of social relations involving several kinds of interaction. Compare **specificity**.

division of labor (6) The assignment of different functions or tasks to different parts or positions of an organization.

dual labor market (9) The theory that the labor market is not a single opportunity structure but is divided into two or more segments that are only weakly connected.

dyad (4) Two interacting persons.

ego (4) According to Freud, the part of the self that has rational self-preservation as its goal. Compare **id** and **superego**.

elite (9) People at the top of the social hierarchy.

ethnic group (8) A grouping whose members share a common language, religion, or culture.

ethnocentrism (3) The feeling that one's own culture or group is superior.

ethnomethodology (5) A sociological approach that emphasizes the methods or practical understandings people use in the course of action and interaction.

experimental variable (2) The particular factor that is being studied in an experiment.

expressive (5) An action chosen because it is personally satisfying rather than directed toward a definite goal. Compare **instrumental**.

expressive symbol (3) A symbol that connotes an idea or feeling, as the word ''home'' connotes comfort and security.

familistic (1) A society in which the family is the main type of social group.

fecundity (10) The biological maximum number of births possible.

fertility (10) The rate at which reproduction occurs in a population.

field experiment (2) An experiment that is conducted in a ''natural'' social situation.

folkways (3) Norms that can be broken without serious consequence.

formal organization (6) A system of consciously coordinated activities established for a specific purpose.

formal structure (6) An officially approved pattern of rules, goals, powers, and procedures.

functional theory of inequality (9) The theory that

high rewards are necessary to get the ablest people to perform the society's most important tasks.

Gemeinschaft (5) A community based on shared tradition and a sense of kinship.

gender (7) Characteristics of males and females that are social and psychological in origin. Compare **sex**.

gender identity (7) A person's socially assigned label and self-definition as male or female.

gender roles (7) Socially defined rights and responsibilities assigned to males and females.

general fertility rate (10) The number of births per 1,000 women aged 15–44 in a given year.

generalized other (4) The perspective of organized group life as it enters into the moral awareness of the individual.

Gesellschaft (5) A society based mainly on purposive organizations (e.g., corporations) and on contract rather than kinship.

guinea pig effect (2) Behavior influenced by the knowledge of being observed.

hierarchy of authority (6) A chain of command in which some individuals and groups can give orders to others.

horizontal mobility (9) A change, usually in occupation, that does not involve a major vertical movement in social rank.

hypothesis (2) A generalization that can be tested.

the "I" and the "me" (4) According to Mead, the "I" is the more active part of the self, and the "me" is the more conventional or socially controlled part.

id (4) According to Freud, the part of the self that attempts to gratify basic urges or instincts. Compare **ego** and **superego**.

identity (4) A person's self-concept built up over a lifetime.

impersonality (6) Application of universalistic rather than particularistic standards.

independent variable (2) The causative factor or source of change influencing the **dependent variable**.

infant mortality rate (10) The number of infants who die in their first year, per 1,000 live births.

informal structure (6) Patterned interactions of persons and groups within an organization. Compare **formal structure**.

instinct (4) A complex behavior pattern for which a species is biologically programmed.

institution (5) An established way of organizing social life; a pattern that is valued by a group, community, or society.

institutionalization (5) The process by which a way of organizing social life becomes valued and established.

instrumental (5) A rational action or choice directed toward efficiently seeking a definite goal. Compare **expressive**.

intentional community (5) A voluntary association of people who live according to a specific plan of organization and code of conduct.

intergenerational mobility (9) A change in the social position of offspring compared with their parents.

interpersonal relation (1) The social connection between two or more people.

labeling theory (4) The theory that being socially defined as "deviant" is crucial to the formation of deviant identities.

labor force (7) All of the people in a society who are working or looking for work.

life course (7) The sequence of events and stages that occur during the lifetime of individuals.

line (6) Organizational officials responsible for getting the main job done, as distinguished from auxiliary staff officials. Compare **staff**.

looking-glass self (4) The way we imagine other people see us and our actions, and the way we think they judge that picture.

marginal (4) A person who is part of two cultures but is not completely socialized by either.

maternal mortality rate (10) The number of maternal deaths in childbirth per 100,000 live births.

micro-order (5) The pattern of interpersonal contacts in small-scale situations.

minority (8) A racial or ethnic group that is at a

disadvantage relative to the rest of the population.

mores (3) The norms considered most important in a culture.

net reproduction rate (NRR) (10) The number of female children born per woman in a cohort of women passing through the childbearing period.

norm (3) A specific guide to conduct.

oligarchy (6) According to Michels, management by a few leaders who tend to perpetuate their control over the organization.

participant observation (2) Observation in which the observer is a part of the social situation being studied.

participatory socialization (4) A pattern of child-rearing that tries to involve the child in his or her own socialization.

particularistic (5) A decision based on personal ties and obligations rather than general principles. Compare **universalistic**.

pattern variable (5) A set of contrasting terms that refer to ways of relating to oneself and to others.

perceived role (5) The individual's own conception of what his or her role demands.

performed role (5) Actual role behavior.

plural society (8) A society composed of different peoples who do not combine into a single community.

population (2) The whole group being studied.

population pyramid (10) A graph that shows a population's age and sex composition in a given year.

prescribed role (5) The ideal role, that is, what the group expects of a husband, worker, friend, etc.

primary group (5) A setting in which intimate, person-centered interaction takes place.

primary relation (5) A relation characterized by response to the whole person, in-depth communication, and personal satisfaction.

proletariat (9) According to Marx, under capitalism the working class, including agricultural laborers, that possess only their labor power. Compare **bourgeoisie**.

purposive sample (2) See **theoretical sample**.

race (8) A population whose members share inherited traits, such as skin color.

random sample (2) A sample chosen so that all individuals in the population being studied have an equal chance of being included.

rational-legal authority (6) Bureaucratic authority based on rules and clearly defined procedures and jurisdiction.

reference group (9) A group of people with whom one compares oneself, for example, when placing oneself in the class system.

referential symbol (3) A symbol that denotes a specific idea or thing.

repressive socialization (4) A pattern of childrearing that stresses obedience.

resocialization (4) Giving up one way of life for another that is different from and incompatible with it.

rite of passage (7) A ceremony marking the transition from one social status to another.

role (5) The behavior pattern that is associated with a given status.

role gain (7) The taking on of a new role upon entering a new phase of the life course.

role loss (7) The loss of an old role upon concluding a phase of the life course.

role set (5) All of the roles generated by a given status.

role strain (5) The tension produced when a particular role calls for conflicting behavior.

salient (master) status (5) A status that tends to fix a person's social identity.

sample (2) A group of subjects specially selected for the purposes of a study.

secondary relation (5) A relation in which people respond in relatively controlled ways to particular aspects of other persons; a nonprimary relation.

segmental participation (6) Participation that involves only a part of a person's life or personality.

self (4) A person's unique and lasting identity.

sex (7) The biological and physical characteristics of males and females. Compare **gender**.

sex ratio (SR) (10) The number of males per 100 females in a population.

significant other (4) The person with whom an individual's most important interactions occur, and from whom a child gains his or her initial conception of self.

social category (1) A set of individuals who have similar characteristics but who are not a social group; also known as a *statistical aggregate.*

social mobility (9) Significant change in social position, life chances, or life-styles.

social order (1) A society characterized by lasting and distinctive patterns of social organization.

social organization (3) A pattern of individual or group relations, for example, the division of labor or the system of social stratification.

social stratum (9) Individuals or families located at about the same level on a given dimension of social rank, such as power, prestige, or income.

socialization (4) The process by which individuals become part of a culture and gain a self.

societal (1) Whatever relates to or is affected by the general structure of a society.

sociogram (5) A diagram of a group showing members' choices of friends, leaders, etc.

specificity (5) A sharply defined pattern with clear limits, such as a legal contract. Compare **diffuseness.**

staff (6) Officials and other employees of an organization whose roles are mainly advisory or otherwise auxiliary to the main task. Compare **line.**

status (5) A position within a social system.

status group (9) According to Weber, a cohesive grouping that shares a common life-style and values.

stereotype (8) An oversimplified and often prejudiced belief about members of a group.

stigma (4) An act or trait that is perceived as highly negative and therefore sets the stigmatized person apart from ordinary people.

structural mobility (9) Change in social rank caused by industrial or technological change. Compare **circulation mobility.**

subculture (3) A cultural pattern that is distinctive in important ways but has much in common with the dominant culture.

superego (4) According to Freud, the part of the self that internalizes social norms. Compare **ego** and **id.**

symbol (3) Anything that stands for or represents something else.

symbolic interactionism (1) A perspective that emphasizes process rather than structure, and finds the core of social reality in the way persons interpret cues they receive from each other and from the social situation.

theoretical (purposive) sample (2) A sample of subjects selected for study because they have some special characteristic, knowledge, or experience.

total institution (4) An organization that almost completely controls the lives of its members or inmates.

traditional authority (6) Authority based on custom and accepted practice.

type Z (6) Organization in which workers actively participate and involve themselves in decision-making.

underclass (9) The lowest social stratum, consisting of people who are usually unemployed and otherwise out of the mainstream of social and economic life.

universe (2) The entire population from which a sample is drawn.

universalistic (5) A rule applied equally to all. Compare **particularistic.**

variable (2) A factor or characteristic under study (e.g., age, income, absenteeism) which varies over time or from one individual or situation to another.

vertical mobility (9) An upward or downward change in the rank of an individual or group.

voluntary association (6) An association formed by people who join together to pursue mutual interests.

white-collar crimes (3) Crimes committed in the course of their occupations by people of relatively high social status.

zero population growth (ZPG) (11) A stationary population with birthrates and death rates in balance.

References

Alba, Richard D., and Gwen Moore
1982 "Ethnicity in the American Elite." *American Sociological Review*, 47 (June):373–383.

Alves, Wayne, and Peter Rossi
1978 "Who should get what?: fairness judgments of distribution of earnings." *American Journal of Sociology* 84:541–564.

Andrews, Alice
1978 "Spatial patterns of higher education in the Soviet Union." *Soviet Geography* 19(September):443–457.

Angell, Robert Cooley
1936/1965 *The Family Encounters the Depression*. Gloucester, Mass.: P. Smith.

Argyris, Chris
1957 *Personality and Organization*. New York: Harper & Row.

Ariès, Philippe
1960/1962 *Centuries of Childhood*. New York: Knopf.

Ausubel, David P., and Pearl Ausubel
1963 "Ego development among segregated Negro children." Pp. 109–141 in A. Harry Passow (ed.), *Education in Depressed Areas*. New York: Columbia University Press.

Bakke, E. Wight
1935/1940 *The Unemployed Worker*. New York: Dutton.

Balswick, Jack O., and Charles W. Peek
1971 "The inexpressive male: a tragedy of American society." *The Family Coordination* (October):363–368.

Baltzell, E. Digby
1958 *Philadelphia Gentlemen: The Making of a National Upper Class*. New York: Free Press.
1966 *The Protestant Establishment: Aristocracy and Caste in America*. New York: Random House (Vintage Books).

1976 "The Protestant establishment revisited." *American Scholar* (Autumn):499–518.

Bane, Mary Jo
1976 *Here to Stay: American Families in the Twentieth Century*. New York: Basic Books.

Banfield, Edward C.
1958 *The Moral Basis of a Backward Society*. New York: Free Press.

Barnes, J. A.
1972 *Social Networks*. Reading, Mass.: Addison-Wesley.

Baron, James and William Bielby
1980 "Bringing the firms back in: stratification, segmentation, and the organization of work." *American Sociological Review* 45:736–766.

Barrett, Carol J.
1977 "Women in widowhood." *Signs* 2(Summer):856–868.

Bean, Frank D., Allan G. King, and Jeffrey S. Passel
1983 "The number of illegal migrants of Mexican origin in the United States." *Demography* 20(February):99–109.

Becker, Howard S.
1963 *Outsiders: Studies in the Sociology of Deviance*. New York: Free Press.

Bell, Carolyn Shaw
1976 "Working wives and family income." Pp. 239–262 in Jane Roberts Chapman (ed.), *Economic Independence for Women*. Sage Yearbooks in Women's Policy Studies, Volume 1. Beverly Hills: Sage Publications.

Bendix, Reinhard, and Seymour Martin Lipset (eds.)
1966 *Class, Status, and Power*. Second edition. New York: Free Press.

Benet, Mary Kathleen
1972 *The Secretarial Ghetto*. New York: McGraw-Hill.

Bennis, Warren G.
1968 "Beyond bureaucracy." Pp. 53–

76 in Warren G. Bennis and Philip E. Slater, *The Temporary Society*. New York: Harper & Row.
1970 "Warren Bennis, a conversation." *Psychology Today* 3(February):48–54, 68–71.

Berger, Bennett
1971 *Looking for America*. Englewood Cliffs, N.J.: Prentice-Hall.

Berger, Bennett, Bruce Hackett, and Mervyn Millar
1972 "Child rearing practices of the communal family." Pp. 271–300 in Hans Peter Dreitzel (ed.), *Recent Sociology, No. 4*. New York: Macmillan.

Berger, Peter L.
1963 *Invitation to Sociology, A Humanistic Perspective*. New York: Doubleday.

Berle, A. A., and G. C. Means
1933 *The Modern Corporation and Private Property*. New York: Macmillan.

Bernstein, B.
1958 "Some sociological determinants of perception." *British Journal of Sociology* 9(June):159–174.

Blau, Peter M., and Otis Dudley Duncan
1967 *The American Occupational Structure*. New York: Wiley.

Blau, Zena Smith
1956 "Changes in status and age identification." *American Sociological Review* 21(April):198–203.

Blauner, Robert
1964 *Alienation and Freedom: The Factory Worker and His Industry*. Chicago: University of Chicago Press.

Blumer, Herbert
1969 *Symbolic Interactionism: Perspective and Method*. Englewood Cliffs, N.J.: Prentice-Hall.

Bogue, Donald J.
1967 "The end of the population explosion." *Public Interest* 7(Spring):11–20.

Bongaarts, John
1975 "Why high birth rates are so low." *Population and Development Review* 1(December):289–296.

Booth, Charles
1889–1902/1970 *Labour and Life of the People of London*. New York: AMS Press.

Bordua, David J.
1961 "Delinquent subcultures: sociological interpretations of gang delinquency." *Annals of the American Academy of Social and Political Science* 338(November):119–136.

Bottomore, T. B., and Maximilien Rubel (eds.)
1956 *Karl Marx: Selected Writings in Sociology and Social Philosophy*. New York: McGraw-Hill.

Briggs, Asa
1968 "Robert Owen." *Encyclopedia of the Social Sciences* 11:351–352.

Bronfenbrenner, Urie
1958 "Socialization and social class through time and space." Pp. 400–425 in E. E. Maccoby, J. M. Newcomb, and E. L. Hartley (eds.), *Readings in Social Psychology*. New York: Holt, Rinehart and Winston.

Broom, Leonard, and Robert G. Cushing
1977 "A modest test of an immodest theory: the functional theory of stratification." *American Sociological Review* 42(February):157–169.

Broom, Leonard, and Norval D. Glenn
1967 *Transformation of the Negro American*. New York: Harper & Row.

Broom, Leonard, and F. L. Jones
1969 "Father-to-son mobility: Australia in comparative perspective." *American Journal of Sociology* 74(January): 333–342.

Broom, Leonard, Cora A. Martin, and Betty Maynard
1971 "Status profiles of racial and ethnic populations." *Social Science Quarterly* 52 (September): 379–388.

Broom, Leonard, and Betty J. Maynard
1969 "Prestige and socioeconomic ranking of occupations." *Social Science Quarterly* 50(September):369–373.

Broom, Leonard, and Philip Selznick
1963 *Sociology: A Text with Adapted Readings*. Third edition. New York: Harper & Row.

Broverman, Inge et al.
1972 "Sex role stereotypes: a current appraisal." *Journal of Social Issues* 28(2):59–78.

Bugental, J. F. T., and S. L. Zelen
1950 "Investigations into the self concept." *Journal of Personality* 18:483–498.

Burghes, Louie
1979 "The old order." Chap. 1 in Frank Field (ed.), *The Wealth Report*. London: Routledge and Kegan Paul.

Burnight, Robert G., and Parker G. Marden
1967 "Social correlates of weight in an aging population." *Milbank Memorial Fund Quarterly* 45:75–92.

Campbell, Angus, Philip E. Converse, and Willard L. Rodgers
1976 *The Quality of American Life: Perceptions, Evaluations, and Satisfactions*. New York: Russell Sage.

Canada Year Book.
See Statistics Canada.

Canadian Royal Commission on Bilingualism and Biculturalism
1967–1970 Volumes 1–5. Final Report.
1969 Volume 3A. The Work World: Part 1, Socioeconomic Status; Part 2, The Federal Administration. Volume 3B. The Work World: Part 3, The Private Sector; Part 4, Conclusions. Ottawa: Queen's Printer for Canada.

Canadian Royal Commission on the Status of Women
1970 *Report of the Royal Commission on the Status of Women in Canada*. Ottawa: Information Canada.

Caplow, Theodore
1980 "Middletown fifty years after." *Contemporary Sociology* 9(January):46–50.

Caplow, Theodore, and Howard M. Bahr
1979 "Half a century of change in adolescent attitudes: Replication of a Middletown survey by the Lynds." *Public Opinion Quarterly* 43(Spring):1–17.

Caplow, Theodore, Howard M. Bahr, Bruce A. Chadwick, Reuben Hill, and Margaret Holmes Willlamson
1982 *Middletown Families: Fifty Years of Change and Continuity*. Minneapolis: University of Minnesota Press.

Carr-Saunders, A. M.
1936 *World Population*. Oxford: Clarendon.

Cather, Willa
1926 *My Antonia*. Boston: Houghton Mifflin.

Centers, Richard
1949 *The Psychology of Social Classes*. Princeton, N.J.: Princeton University Press.

Chalmers, James A., and Michael J. Greenwood
1980 "The economics of the rural to urban migration turnaround." *Social Science Quarterly* 61(December):524–544.

Chen, Muhua
1979 "Birth planning in China." *Family Planning Perspectives* 11 (November/December): 348–354.

Cherlin, Andrew
1982 "Middletown III: The story continues." *Contemporary Sociology* 11(November):617–619.

Cicourel, Aaron V.
1968 *The Social Organization of Juvenile Justice*. New York: Wiley.

Clark, Kenneth B., and Mamie P. Clark
1947 "Racial identification and preference in Negro children." Pp. 169–178 in Theodore M. Newcomb, Euguene L. Hartley, and Guy E. Swanson (eds.), *Readings in Social Psychology*. New York: Holt, Rinehart and Winston.

Cohen, Albert K.
1955 *Delinquent Boys*. New York: Free Press.

Colclough, Glenna, and Patrick M. Horan
1983 "The status attainment paradigm: an application of a Kuhnian perspective." *The Sociological Quarterly* 24(Winter):25–42.

Coleman, James S. et al.
1974 *Youth: Transition to Adulthood.* Report of the Panel on Youth of the President's Science Advisory Committee. Chicago: University of Chicago Press.

Coles, Robert
1967 *Children of Crisis.* Boston: Little, Brown.

Connor, Walter D.
1972 *Deviance in Soviet Society: Crime, Delinquency, and Alcoholism.* New York: Columbia University Press.
1979 *Socialism, Politics and Equality: Hierarchy and Change in Eastern Europe and the USSR.* New York: Columbia University Press.

Cooley, Charles Horton
1902/1964 *Human Nature and the Social Order.* New York: Schocken Books.
1909 *Social Organization.* New York: Scribner.

Cooper, A. A.
1842 "A speech before the House of Commons, UK, June 7, 1842." Reprinted in *Speeches of the Earl of Shaftsbury, K. R.* London: Chapman and Hall, 1968:31–58. Quoted in Skolnick, 1973:348.

Coser, Lewis A.
1976 "Sociological theory from the Chicago dominance to 1965." *Annual Review of Sociology:*145–159.

Cox, Kevin R.
1976 "American geography: social science emergent." *Social Science Quarterly* 57(June):182–207.

CPR (Current Population Reports) Citation given parenthetically in text.

Cripps, Thomas R.
1967 "The death of Rastus: Negroes in American films since 1945." *Phylon* 28(Fall):267–275.

Curtin, Philip D.
1969 *The Atlantic Slave Trade: A Census.* Madison: University of Wisconsin Press.

Dahrendorf, Ralf
1959 *Class and Class Conflict in Industrial Society.* Stanford, CA: Stanford University Press.

Dalton, Melville
1959 *Men Who Manage.* New York: Wiley.

Davenport, T. R. H.
1977 *South Africa: A Modern History.* London: Macmillan.

Davies, A. F.
1967 *Images of Class: An Australian Study.* Sydney: Sydney University Press.

Davis, David Brion
1966 *The Problem of Slavery in Western Culture.* Ithaca, N.Y.: Cornell University Press.

Davis, Kingsley
1940 "Extreme social isolation of a child." *American Journal of Sociology* 45(January):554–565.
1947 "A final note on a case of extreme isolation." *American Journal of Sociology* 52(March):432–437.

Davis, Kingsley, and Wilbert E. Moore
1945 "Some principles of stratification." *American Sociological Review* 10(April):242–249.

DellaPergola, Sergio
1980 "Patterns of American Jewish fertility." *Demography* 17(August):261–273.

Demeny, Paul
1979 "On the end of the population explosion." *Population and Development Review* 5(March):141–162.

Dennis, Wayne
1968 "Creative productivity between the ages of 20 and 80 years." Pp. 106–114 in Neugarten, 1968.

Denzin, Norman K.
1970 "The work of little children." *New Society* (July):13–15.

DHEW
See U.S. Department of Health, Education, and Welfare.

DHHS
See U.S. Department of Health and Human Services.

Domhoff, G. William
1967 *Who Rules America?* Englewood Cliffs, N.J.: Prentice-Hall.

Dorn, Harold F.
1950 "Pitfalls in population forecasts and projections." *Journal of the American Statistical Association* 45(September):311–334.

Douglass, Frederick

1960 *Narrative of the Life of Frederick Douglass, An American Slave.* Edited by Benjamin Quarles. Cambridge: Harvard University Press (Belknap Press).

Doyle, Bertram Wilbur
1937 *The Etiquette of Race Relations in the South.* Chicago: University of Chicago Press.

Dreitzel, Hans Peter (ed.)
1970 *Recent Sociology No. 2: Patterns of Communicative Behavior.* London: Macmillan. See articles on ethnomethodology.

Dunn, Marvin
1980 "Miami riots." TV interview on The MacNeil/Lehrer Report, May 19. New York: Educational Broadcating Corporation.

Durkheim, Emile
1895/1938 *The Rules of the Sociological Method.* New York: Free Press.
1897/1951 *Le Suicide.* English translation by George Simpson. New York: Free Press.
1912/1947 *The Elementary Forms of the Religious Life.* New York: Free Press.

Edwards, Meredith
1981 Financial Arrangements Within Families. Canberra, Australia: National Women's Advisory Council.

Efron, David
1941 *Gesture and Environment.* New York: Kings Crown Press.

Ehrlich, Paul R., Anne H. Ehrlich, and John P. Holdren
1977 *Ecoscience: Population, Resources, Environment.* San Francisco, Freeman.

Epstein, Cynthia Fuchs
1970 "Encountering the male establishment: sex-status limits on women's careers in the professions." *American Journal of Sociology* 75(May):965–982.

Erikson, Robert, John H. Goldthorpe, and Lucienne Portocarero
1979 "Intergenerational class mobility in three Western European societies." *British Journal of Sociology* 30(December):415–551.
1982 "Social fluidity in industrial nations." *British Journal of Sociology* 33(March):1–34.

Fahy Committee (President's Committee on Equality of Treatment and Opportunity in the Armed Forces)
1950 *Freedom to Serve! Equality of Treatment and Opportunity in the Armed Forces*. Washington, D.C.

Fairfield, Richard
1972 *Communes, U.S.A.* Baltimore: Penguin

Feshbach, Murray
1978 "Population and manpower trends in the U.S.R.R." Pp. 81–92 in *The U.S.R.R. and the Sources of Soviet Policy*. Occasional Paper No. 34. Washington, D.C.: Kennan Institute for Advanced Russian Studies.

Feuer, Lewis S. (ed.)
1959 *Marx and Engels: Basic Writings on Politics and Philosophy*. Garden City, N.Y.: Doubleday.

Foner, Anne
1979 "Ascribed and achieved bases of stratification." *Annual Review of Sociology* 5:219–242.

Foner, Laura, and Eugene D. Genovese (eds.)
1969 *Slavery in the New World: A Reader in Comparative History*. Englewood Cliffs, N.J.: Prentice-Hall.

Foner, Philip S.
1950–1955 *The Life and Writings of Frederick Douglass*. Four volumes. New York: International.

Frankland, Mark
1979 "Will Russia's Muslims join march of Islam?" *London Observer* (April 1).

Frenkel-Brunswick, Else
1968 "Adjustments and reorientations in the course of the life span." Pp. 77–84 in Neugarten, 1968.

Freud, Sigmund
1923 *The Ego and the Id*. New York: Norton.

Furnivall, J. S.
1948 *Colonial Policy and Practice*. London: Cambridge University Press.

Galbraith, John Kenneth
1967 *The New Industrial State*. Boston: Houghton Mifflin.

Gallup Organization, Inc.
1981 *Americans Volunteer: 1981*. Conducted for Independent Sector. Princeton, N.J.

Garbin, Albeno P., and Frederick L. Bates
1961 "Occupational prestige: an empirical study of its correlates." *Social Forces* 40:131–136.

Garfinkel, Harold
1967 *Studies in Ethnomethodology*. Englewood Cliffs, N.J.: Prentice-Hall.

Garraty, John A.
1971 *The American Nation: A History of the United States to 1877*. Second edition. New York: Harper & Row and American Heritage.

Genovese, Eugene D.
1972 *Roll, Jordan, Roll: The World the Slaves Made*. New York: Random House.

Gerth, H. H., and C. Wright Mills (eds.)
1946 *From Max Weber: Essays in Sociology*. New York: Oxford University Press.

Gillis, John R.
1974 *Youth and History*. New York: Academic Press.

Ginzberg, Eli, Ethel L. Ginsburg, and Dorothy L. Lynn.
1943 *The Unemployed*. New York: Harper & Row

Glenn, Norval D.
1963 "Some changes in the relative status of American nonwhites, 1940–1960." *Phylon* 24(Summer).
1977 *Cohort Analysis*. Beverly Hills: Sage Publications.

Glick, Paul C.
1977 "Updating the life cycle of the family." *Journal of Marriage and the Family* 39(February)5–13.

Goff, Regina Mary.
1949 *Problems and Emotional Difficulties of Negro Children*. New York: Columbia University Press.

Goffman, Erving
1955/1967 "On face-work: an analysis of ritual elements in social interaction." *Psychiatry: Journal for the Study of Interpersonal Processes* 18(August):213–231. Also as pp. 5–45 in Goffman, 1967.
1956/1967 "The nature of deference and demeanor." *American Anthropologist* 58 (June): 473–502.

Also as pp. 47–95 in Goffman, 1967.
1959 *The Presentation of Self in Everyday Life*. Garden City, N.Y.: Doubleday (Anchor Books).
1963a *Behavior in Public Places*. New York: Free Press.
1963b *Stigma: Notes on the Management of Spoiled Identity*. Englewood Cliffs, N.J.: Prentice-Hall.
1967 *Interaction Ritual: Essays on Face-to-Face Behavior*. New York: Doubleday (Anchor Books).
1971 *Relations in Public: Microstudies of the Public Order*. New York: Harper Colophon Books.

Goldenweiser, Alexander.
1937 *Anthropology*. New York: Appleton.

Goldman, Nathan
1963 *The Differential Selection of Juvenile Offenders for Court Appearance*. New York: National Council on Crime and Delinquency.

Goldthorpe, John, and Keith Hope
1972 "Occupational grading and occupational prestige." Pp. 19–79 in Keith Hope (ed.), *The Analysis of Social Mobility: Methods and Approaches*. Oxford: Clarendon Press.

Golovensky, D. I.
1952 "The marginal man concept, an analysis and critique." *Social Forces* 30:333–339.

Goode, William J.
1960 "A theory of role strain." *American Sociological Review* 25(August):483–496.
1967 "The protection of the inept." *American Sociological Review* 32(February):5–19.

Goodsell, Charles T.
1983 *The Case for Bureaucracy*. Chatham, N.J.: Chatham House Publishers.

Gordon, Chad
1968 "Self conceptions: configurations of content." Chapter 11 in Chad Gordon and Kenneth J. Gergen (eds.), *The Self in Social Interaction*. Volume 1. New York: Wiley.

Gouldner, Alvin W.
1954 *Patterns of Industrial Bureaucracy*. New York: Free Press.

Griffiths, Martha W.
1976 "Can we still afford occupational segregation?" *Signs* 1(Spring):7–14.

Hall, Edward T.
1959 *The Silent Language*. Garden City, N.Y.: Doubleday.
1966 *Hidden Dimension*. Garden City, N.Y.: Doubleday.

Hall, G. Stanley
1904 *Adolescence*. New York: D. Appleton & Co.

Harbison, Frederick, and C. A. Myers
1959 *Management in the Industrial World*. New York: McGraw-Hill.

Harrison, B.
1977 "Education and underemployment in the urban ghetto." Pp. 252–263 in D. M. Gordon (ed.), *Problems in Political Economy*. Lexington, Mass.: Heath.

Hayflick, Leonard
1980 "The cell biology of human aging." *Scientific American* 242(January):58–65.

Heer, David M.
1979 "What is the annual net flow of undocumented Mexican immigrants to the United States?" *Demography* 16(August):417–423.

Henripin, Jacques, and Jacques Légaré
1971 "Recent trends in Canadian fertility." *Canadian Review of Sociology and Anthropology* 8(May):106–118.

Hewlett, Sylvia Ann
1981–1982 "Coping with illegal immigration." *Foreign Affairs* 60(Winter):358–378.

Hickson, D. J.
1966 "A convergence in organizational theory." *Administrative Science Quarterly* 11(September):224–237.

Hirschman, Albert O.
1970 *Exit, Voice, and Loyalty*. Cambridge: Harvard University Press.

Historical Statistics of the United States. *See* U.S. Bureau of the Census.

Hodge, Robert W., Paul M. Siegel, and Peter H. Rossi
1964 "Occupational prestige in the United States, 1925–1963."

American Journal of Sociology 70(November)286–302.

Hodge, Robert W., Donald J. Treiman, and Peter H. Rossi
1966 "A comparative study of occupational prestige." Pp. 309–321 in Bendix and Lipset, 1966.

Hollander, Paul
1973 *Soviet and American Society: A Comparison*. New York: Oxford University Press.

Holt, John
1974 *Escape from Childhood*. New York: Dutton.

Horner, Matina S.
1968 "Sex differences in achievement motivation and performance in competitive and non-competitive situations." Unpublished Ph.D. dissertation, University of Michigan.

Hraba, Joseph
1972 "The Doll Technique: A Measure of Racial Ethnocentrism?" *Social Forces* 50(June):522–527.

Hraba, Joseph, and Geoffrey Grant
1970 "Black is Beautiful: A Reexamination of Racial Preference and Identification." *Journal of Personality and Social Psychology* 16(November):398–402.

Hughes, Everett C.
1943 *French Canada in Transition*. Chicago: University of Chicago Press.

Hyman, Herbert, and Charles R. Wright
1971 "Trends in voluntary association memberships of American adults: replication based on secondary analysis of national sample surveys." *American Sociological Review* 36(April):191–206.

ILO (International Labour Organisation)
1977 *Yearbook of Labour Statistics*.

Ise, John
1940 *Sod and Stubble: The Story of a Kansas Homestead*. New York: Wilson-Erickson.

Jackman, Mary R.
1979 "The subjective meaning of social class identification in the United States." *The Public Opinion Quarterly* 43, No. 4(Winter):443–462.

Jaffe, Frederick S., and Deborah Oakley
1978 "Observations on birth planning in China, 1977." *Family Planning Perspectives* 10(March/April):101–108.

James, William
1891 *The Principles of Psychology*. Volume I. New York: Holt, Rinehart and Winston.

Johnson, Charles S.
1943 *Patterns of Negro Segregation*. Third edition. New York: Harper & Row.

Jones, Elise F., and Charles F. Westoff
1979 "The end of 'Catholic' fertility." *Demography* 16(May):209–217.

Kagan, Jerome
1973 "Do the first two years matter?" *Saturday Review of Education* 1(April):41–43.

Kanter, Rosabeth Moss
1968 "Commitment and social organization: a study of commitment mechanisms in utopian communities." *American Sociological Review* 33(August):499–517.
1977 *Men and Women of the Corporation*. New York: Basic Books.

Kasarda, John D.
1980 "The implications of contemporary distribution trends for national urban policy." *Social Science Quarterly* 61(December):373–400.

Keely, Charles B.
1977 "Counting the uncountable: estimates of undocumented aliens in the United States." *Population and Development Review* 3(December):473–481.

Keely, Charles B., and Ellen Percy Kraly
1974 "Immigration composition and population policy." *Science* 184(August 16):587–593.
1978 "Recent net alien immigration to the United States: its impact on population growth and native fertility." *Demography* 15(August):267–283.

Kennan, George F.
1971 "Hazardous courses in Southern Africa." *Foreign Affairs* 49(January):218–236.

Kennan Institute for Advanced Russian Studies
1978 "The U.S.S.R. and the sources of Soviet policy." Occasional paper No. 34. Washington, D.C.

Kerner Report
See National Advisory Commission on Civil Disorders.

Kett, Joseph F.
1973 "Adolescence and youth in nineteenth century America." Pp. 94–110 in Theodore K. Rabb and Robert I. Rotberg (eds.), The Family in History. New York: Harper & Row.

Kirk, Dudley
1971 "A new demographic transition?" Pp. 123–147 in National Academy of Sciences, Rapid Population Growth: Consequences and Policy Implications. Baltimore: Johns Hopkins Press.

Kluckhohn, Clyde
1962a Culture and Behavior. New York: Free Press.
1962b "Universal categories of culture." Pp. 304–320 in Sol Tax (ed.), Anthropology Today: Selections. Chicago: University of Chicago Press.

Koch, Fred C.
1977 The Volga Germans in Russia and the Americas. University Park: The Pennsylvania State University Press.

Kohn, Melvin L.
1977 Class and Conformity. Second edition. Chicago: University of Chicago Press.

Kohn, Melvin L., and Carmi Schooler
1982 "Job conditions and personality: a longitudinal assessment of their reciprocal effects." American Journal of Sociology 87(6):1257–1286.

Korner, Anneliese F.
1974 "The effect of the infant's state of arousal, sex, and ontogenetic stage on the caregiver." Pp. 105–122 in Michael Lewis and Leonard A. Rosenblum (eds.), The Effect of the Infant on its Caregiver. New York: Wiley.

Kroeber, A. L., and Clyde Kluckhohn
1963 Culture: A Critical Review of Concepts and Definitions. New York: Random House (Vintage Books).

Kuper, Leo, and M. G. Smith (eds.)
1969 Pluralism in Africa. Berkeley and Los Angeles: University of California Press.

Landman, Lynn C.
1977 "Birth control in India: the carrot and the rod." Family Planning Perspectives 9(May/June): 101–110.

LaPiere, Richard T.
1934 "Attitudes versus actions." Social Forces 13(December):230–237.

Laslett, Peter
1971/1973 "Age at menarche in Europe since the eighteenth century." Journal of Interdisciplinary History 2(Autumn) (special number of "The Family in History"). Also as pp. 28–47 in Theodore K. Rabb and Robert I. Rotberg (eds.), The Family in History. New York: Harper & Row (Torchbooks).

Latane, Bibb, and John M. Darley
1968 "Group inhibition of bystander intervention in emergencies." Journal of Personality and Social Psychology 10(November):215–221.

Laws, Judith Long
1976 "Work aspirations of women: false leads and new starts." Signs 1(Spring):33–49.

Leach, E. R. (ed.)
1960 Aspects of Caste in South India, Ceylon and North West Pakistan. New York: Cambridge University Press.

Lemert, Edwin M.
1967 Human Deviance, Social Problems, and Social Control. Englewood Cliffs, N.J.: Prentice-Hall.

Lever, Henry
1978 South African Society. Johannesburg: Jonathan Ball.

Lewis, Oscar
1951 Life in a Mexican Village: Tepoztlán Restudied. Urbana, IL: University of Illinois Press.

Lifton, Robert Jay
1968 "Protean man." Partisan Review 35:13–27.

Likert, Rensis
1961 New Patterns of Management. New York: McGraw-Hill.

Lind, Andrew W.
1938 An Island Community. Chicago: University of Chicago Press.

Linton, Ralph
1933 The Tanala: A Hill Tribe of Madagascar. Anthropological Series Volume XXII. Chicago: Field Museum of Natural History.
1936 The Study of Man. New York: Appleton.

Lipset, S. M., M. A. Trow, and J. S. Coleman
1956 Union Democracy: The Internal Politics of the International Typographical Union. New York: Free Press.

Lipset, S. M., and Hans L. Zetterberg
1959 "Social mobility in industrial societies." Pp. 11–75 in Lipset and Bendix.

Little, Roger W.
1964 "Buddy relations and combat performance." Pp. 195–223 in Morris Janowitz (ed.), The New Military. New York: Russell Sage.

Long, Larry H.
1970 "Fertility patterns among religious groups in Canada." Demography 7(May):135–149.

Long, Larry H., and Diane DeAre
1982 "Repopulating the countryside: a 1980 census trend." Science 217(September 17):1111–1116.
1983 "The Slowing of Urbanization in the United States." Scientific American 249 (July):33–41.

Long, Larry H., and Kristin A. Hansen
1979 "Reasons for interstate migration." Current Population Reports. P-23. No. 81

Lopreato, Joseph
1967 Peasants No More. New York: Chandler/Harper & Row.

Lopreato, Joseph, and Lionel S. Lewis
1963 "An analysis of variables in the functional theory of stratification." The Sociological Quarterly 4(Autumn):301–310.

Lord, George F., III, and William W. Falk
1982 "Hidden income and segmentation: structural determinants of

fringe benefits." *Social Science Quarterly* 63, No. 2(June):208–224.

Lydall, Harold
1968 *The Structure of Earnings*. London: Oxford University Press.

Lynd, Robert S.
1939 *Knowledge for What?* Princeton: Princeton University Press.

Lynd, Robert S., and Helen Merrell Lynd
1929 *Middletown*. New York: Harcourt Brace Jovanovich.
1937 *Middletown in Transition: A Study in Cultural Conflicts*. New York: Harcourt Brace Jovanovich.

Macaulay, Stewart
1963 "Non-contractual relations in business." *American Sociological Review* 28(February):55–67.

McClelland, David C.
1961 *The Achieving Society*. New York: Van Nostrand Reinhold.

McClendon, McKee J.
1976 "The occupational status attainment process of males and females." *American Sociological Review* 41(February):52–64.

Maccoby, Eleanor Emmons, and Carol Nagy Jacklin
1974 *The Psychology of Sex Differences*. Stanford, CA.: Stanford University Press.

McGregor, Douglas M.
1960 *The Human Side of Enterprise*. New York: McGraw-Hill.

Malabre, Alfred L., Jr.
1980 "Underground economy grows and grows." *The Wall Street Journal* (October 20):1.

Marquard, Leo
1969 *The Peoples and Policies of South Africa*. Fourth edition. New York: Oxford University Press.

Marshall, T. H.
1950/1964 *Class, Citizenship, and Social Development*. Garden City, N.Y.: Doubleday.

Maslow, Abraham, H.
1965 "Criteria for judging needs to be instinctoid." Pp. 33–48 in Marshall R. Jones (ed.), *Human Motivation: A Symposium*. Lincoln, University of Nebraska Press.

Matthews, Mervyn
1978 *Privilege in the Soviet Union*. London: Allen & Unwin.

Mead, George H.
1934 *Mind, Self, and Society*. Chicago: University of Chicago Press.

Meier, August, Elliott Rudwick, and Francis L. Broderick
1971 *Black Protest Thought in the Twentieth Century*. Second edition. Indianapolis: Bobbs-Merrill.

Merton, Robert K.
1948/1968 "The self-fulfilling prophecy." Pp. 475–490 in Merton, 1968.
1968 *Social Theory and Social Structure*. New York: Free Press.

Meyer, Herbert E.
1978 "The coming Soviet ethnic crisis." *Fortune* (August 14):156–166.

Meyer, Marshall
1979 "Debureaucratization?" *Social Science Quarterly* 60(June):25–34.

Miller, Walter B.
1958 "Lower-class culture as a generating milieu of gang delinquency." *Journal of Social Issues* 14(July):5–14.

Millett, Kate et al.
1973 *The Prostitution Papers*. New York: Avon Books.

Mills, C. Wright
1956 *The Power Elite*. New York: Oxford University Press.
1959 *The Sociological Imagination*. New York: Oxford University Press.

Moorehead, Alan
1966 *The Fatal Impact*. New York: Harper & Row.

Moreno, J. L.
1934/1953 *Who Shall Survive?* Beacon, N.Y.: Beacon House

Morris, Richard T., and Raymond J. Murphy
1959 "The situs dimension in occupational structure." *American Sociological Review* 24(April):231–239.

Mortimer, Jeylan P., and Roberta G. Simmons
1978 "Adult socializaton." *Annual Review of Sociology* 4:421–454.

Moskos, Charles C., Jr.
1966 "Racial integration in the armed forces." *American Journal of Sociology* 72(September):132–148.
1970 *The American Enlisted Man*. New York: Russell Sage.

Mukerji, C.
1978 "Bullshitting: road lore among hitchhikers." *Social Problems* 25, No. 3:241–252.

Muramatsu, Minoru
1971 "Japan." *Country Profiles*. New York: Population Council.

Murdock, George Peter
1934 *Our Primitive Contemporaries*. New York: Macmillan.
1945 "The common denominator of cultures." Pp. 123–142 in Ralph Linton (ed.). *The Science of Man in the World Crisis*. New York: Columbia University Press.

Murphy, Cullen
1983 "Watching the Russians." *Atlantic Monthly* 251(February):33–52.

Myles, John F.
1978 "Institutionalization and sick role identification among the elderly." *American Sociological Review* 43(August):508–521.

Myrdal, Gunnar, with the assistance of Richard Sterner and Arnold Rose
1944 *An American Dilemma*. New York: Harper & Row.

Nadelson, Carol, and Malkah T. Notman
1972 "The woman physician." *Journal of Medical Education* 47(3):176–183.

National Advisory Commission on Civil Disorders
1968 *Kerner Report*. New York: Bantam Books.

Norbeck, Edward
1953 "Age-grading in Japan." *American Anthropologist* 55:373–384.

Norland (Yam), Joseph
1974 "Population composition: age and sex." Pp. 31–39 in Leroy O. Stone and Andrew J. Siggner (eds.), *The Population of Canada*. Ottawa: Statistics Canada.

Nortman, Dorothy L.
1978 "India's new birth rate target." *Population and Development Review* 4(June):277–312.

O'Hare, William P.
1983 "Wealth and Economic Status." *Focus* 11 (June):3–5.

Oakley, Ann
1974a *Woman's Work: The Housewife, Past and Present*. New York: Random House (Vintage Books).
1974b *The Sociology of Housework*. London: Martin Robertson.

Orleans, Leo A.
1972 *Every Fifth Child: The Population of China*. London: Eyre Methuen.

Ouchi, William G.
1981 *Theory Z: How American Business Can Meet the Japanese Challenge*. New York: Addison Wesley.

Park, Robert E.
1937 "Introduction." Pp. xi–xxiv in Doyle.

Parsons, Talcott
1951 *The Social System*. New York: Free Press.

Parsons, Talcott, and Edward A. Shils (eds.)
1951 *Toward a General Theory of Action*. Cambridge: Harvard University Press.

Passin, Herbert
1955 "Untouchability in the Far East." *Monumenta Nipponica* 11(October):27–47.

Pauli, Hertha
1962 *Her Name Was Sojourner Truth*. New York: Avon Books.

Pearl, Robert B., and Matilda Frankel
1982 "Composition of the Personal Wealth of American Households at the Start of the Eighties." Presented at the American Statistical Association Annual Meeting, August.

Pfeiffer, John E.
1978 *The Emergence of Man*. Third edition. New York: Harper & Row.

Pfohl, Stephen J.
1977 "The 'discovery' of child abuse." *Social Problems* 24 (February):310–313.

Piliavin, Irving, and Scott Briar
1964 "Police encounters with juveniles." *American Journal of Sociology* 70(September):206–214.

Pilling, Doria, and Mia Pringle
1978 *Controversial Issues in Child Development*. New York: Schocken Books.

Piore, M.
1977 "The dual labor market: theory and implications." Pp. 93–97 in D. M. Gordon (ed.), *Problems in Political Economy*. Lexington, Mass.:Heath.

Polsky, Ned
1967/1969 *Hustlers, Beats, and Others*. Garden City, N.Y.: Doubleday (Anchor Books).

Pöntinen, Seppo, Matti Alestalo, and Hannu Uusitalo
1983 *The Finnish Mobility Survey 1980: Data and First Results*. Helsinki: Suomen Gallup Oy Report no. 9.

Porter, James
1974 "Race, socialization, and mobility in educational and early occupational attainment." *American Sociological Review* 39 (June):303–316.

Porter, John
1968 *The Vertical Mosaic*. Toronto: University of Toronto Press.

Pratt, Henry J.
1976 *The Gray Lobby*. Chicago: University of Chicago Press.

Presthus, Robert
1962 *The Organizational Society*. New York: Knopf.

Price, John
1966 "A history of the outcaste: untouchability in Japan." Pp. 6–30 in George De Vos and Hiroshi Wagatsuma (eds.), *Japan's Invisible Race*. Berkeley and Los Angeles: University of California Press.

Rainwater, Lee
1974 *What Money Buys: Inequality and the Social Meanings of Income*. New York: Basic Books.

Redfield, Robert
1941 *The Folk Culture of Yucatan*. Chicago: University of Chicago Press.

Redl, Fritz, and David Wineman
1951 *Children Who Hate: The Disorganization and Breakdown of Behavioral Controls*. New York: Free Press.

Riesman, David, in collaboration with Reuel Denney and Nathan Glazer
1950 *The Lonely Crowd*. New Haven: Yale University Press.

Riley, Matilda White, and Anne Foner
1968 *Aging and Society*. Volume 1: An Inventory of Research Findings. New York: Russell Sage.

Rioux, Marcel
1971 *Quebec in Question*. Translated by James Boake. Toronto: James Lewis & Samuel. First published in French in 1969.

Rivers, W. H. R.
1922 *Essays on the Depopulation of Melanesia*. Cambridge, England: Cambridge University Press.

Robinson, John P., Philip E. Converse, and Alexander Szalai
1972 "Everyday life in twelve countries." Pp. 113–114 in Alexander Szalai (ed.), *The Use of Time*. The Hague: Mouton.

Roethlisberger, F. J., and W. J. Dickson
1939 *Management and the Worker*, Cambridge: Harvard University Press.

Rosen, Bernard C., and R. D'Andrade
1959 "The psychosocial origins of achievement motivation." *Sociometry* 22(September):185–217.

Rosenfeld, Jeffrey P.
1979 *The Legacy of Aging: Inheritance and Disinheritance in Social Perspective*. Norwood, N.J.: Ablex Publishing.

Rosenfeld, Rachel A.
1978 "Women's intergenerational occupational mobility." *American Sociological Review* 43(February):36–46.

Rossi, Alice
1964/1967 "Equality between the sexes: an immodest proposal." Pp. 98–143 in Robert Jay Lifton (ed.), *The Woman in America*. Boston: Beacon Press.
1971 "Women in science: why so few?" Pp. 110–121 in C. F. Epstein and W. J. Goode (eds.), *The*

Other Half. Englewood Cliffs, N.J.: Prentice-Hall.

Royce, C. C.
1887 *The Cherokee Nation of Indians, Fifth Annual Report.* Bureau of American Ethnology. Washington, D.C.: GPO.

Rushing, William A.
1980 "Organizational size, rules and surveillance." Pp. 396–405 in Joseph A. Litterer (ed.), *Organizations.* New York: Wiley.

Rutter, Michael
1972 *Material Deprivation Reassessed.* Harmondsworth: Penguin.

Ryder, Norman B.
1973 "Recent trends and group differences in fertility." Pp. 57–68 in Westoff et al., 1973.

Ryder, Norman B., and Charles F. Westoff
1971 *Reproduction in the United States, 1965.* Princeton, N.J.: Princeton University Press.

Sapir, Edward
1924 "Culture, genuine and spurious." *American Journal of Sociology* 29(January):401–429.
1929/1958 "The status of linguistics as a science." Pp. 160–165 in David G. Mandelbaum (ed.), *Selected Writings of Edward Sapir.* Berkeley and Los Angeles: University of California Press.
1934 "Symbolism." *Encyclopedia of the Social Sciences* 14:492–495.

Sassower, Doris
1972 "Women in the professions." Pp. 350–358 in Eleanor Holmes Norton (ed.), *Women's Role in Contemporary Society.* New York: Avon Books.

Schlesinger, Arthur.
1933 *The Rise of the City.* New York: Macmillan.

Schlozman, Kay Lehman, and Sidney Verba
1978 "The new unemployment: does it hurt?" *Public Policy* 26(Summer):333–358.

Schnier, Miriam (ed.)
1972 *Feminism: The Essential Historical Writings.* New York: Random House.

Schutz, Alfred
1962 *Collected Papers, I: The Problem of Social Reality.* The Hague: Martinus Nijhoff.

Schwartz, Richard D., and Jerome Skolnick
1962 "Two studies of legal stigma." *Social Problems* 10(Fall):133–142.

Seiden, Anne M.
1976 "Overview: research on the psychology of women." *American Journal of Psychiatry* 133(October):1111–1123.

Selznick, Philip
1957 *Leadership in Administration.* New York: Harper & Row.
1969 *Law, Society, and Industrial Justice.* New York: Russell Sage.

Seneker, Harold, with Jonathan Greenberg and John Dorfman
1982 "The Forbes four hundred." *Forbes,* September 13:100–186.

Sewell, William H., and Robert M. Hauser
1975 *Education, Occupation and Earnings: Achievement in the Early Career.* New York: Academic Press.

Shariff, Zahid
1979 "The persistence of bureaucracy." *Social Science Quarterly* 60(June):3–19.

Sharp, Harry, and Leo F. Schnore
1971 "Public response to the 1970 census: a Wisconsin survey." *Demography* 8(August):297–305.

Shils, Edward A.
1950 "Primary groups in the American army." Pp. 16–39 in Robert K. Merton and Paul F. Lazarsfeld (eds.), *Continuities in Social Research.* New York: Free Press.

Shils, Edward A., and Morris Janowitz
1948 "Cohesion and disintegration in the Wehrmacht in World War II." *Public Opinion Quarterly* 12(Summer):280–315.

Shodara, Hide
1962 "Honorific expressions of personal attitudes in spoken Japanese." *Center for Japanese Studies, Occasional Papers, No. 2.* Ann Arbor, Mich.: University of Michigan Press.

Sills, David L.

1968 "Voluntary associations: sociological aspects." Pp. 362–379 in *International Encyclopedia of the Social Sciences.* Volume 16.

Silverberg, James (ed.)
1968 "Social mobility in the caste system of India." *Comparative Studies in Society and History.* Supplement III.

Silverstein, Barry, and Ronald Krate
1975 *Children of the Dark Ghetto.* New York: Praeger.

Singelmann, Joachim
1978 *From Agriculture to Services: The Transformation of Industrial Employment.* Beverly Hills: Sage.

Skolnick, Arlene
1973 *The Intimate Environment: Exploring Marriage and the Family.* Boston: Little, Brown.
1978 *The Intimate Environment.* Second edition. Boston: Little, Brown.

Smith, David H.
1975 "Voluntary action and voluntary groups." Pp. 247–270, *Annual Review of Sociology, 1975.* Palo Alto, Calif.:Annual Reviews, Inc.

Smith, James D.
1982 "Hearing on the distribution of income and wealth." Testimony before the Joint Economic Committee, February 10.

Smith, M. G.
1960 "Social and cultural pluralism." *Annals of the New York Academy of Sciences* 83(January 20):763–777.

Smith-Rosenberg, Carroll
1978 "Sex as symbol in Victorian purity." *American Journal of Sociology* 84(Supplement):212–247.

Smuts, Robert W.
1959 *Women and Work in America.* New York: Columbia University Press.

Sowell, Thomas (ed.), with the assistance of Lynn D. Collins
1978 *Essays and Data on American Ethnic Groups.* The Urban Institute.

Spence, Janet T., Robert Helmreich, and Joy Stapp
1975 "Ratings of self and peers on sex-role attributes and their relation to self-esteem and conceptions of masculinity and femininity." *Journal of Personality and Social Psychology* 32(1)29–39.

Spitz, Rene A.
1945 and 1947/1964 "Hospitalism." Pp. 399–425 in Rose L. Coser (ed.), *The Family: Its Structure and Functions*. New York: St. Martin's Press.

Srinivas, M. N.
1962 *Caste in Modern India, and Other Essays*. Bombay: Asia Publishing House.
1966 *Social Change in Modern India*. Berkeley and Los Angeles: University of California Press.

Statistics Canada
1979 *Canada Year Book, 1978–79*. Ottawa: Statistics Canada.

Steinem, Gloria
1973 "Women and money." *Ms. Magazine* (June):37ff.

Stevenson, H. N. C.
1967 "Caste (Indian)." *Encylopaedia Britannica* 5:24–33.

Stinchcombe, Arthur L.
1963 "Some empirical consequences of the Davis-Moore theory of stratification." *American Sociological Review* 28(October):805–808.

Stone, Lawrence
1977 *The Family, Sex and Marriage in England 1500–1800*. New York: Harper & Row.

Stonequist, E. V.
1937 *The Marginal Man*. New York: Scribner.

Stouffer, Samuel A., Arthur A. Lumsdaine, Marion Harper Lumsdaine, Robin M. Williams, Jr., M. Brewster Smith, Irving L. Janis, Shirley A. Star, and Leonard S. Cottrell, Jr.
1949 *The American Soldier, Combat and Its Aftermath*. Volume 2. Princeton: Princeton University Press.

Strauss, Murray A.
1962 "Deferred gratification, social class, and the achievement syndrome." *American Sociological Review* 27(June):326–335.

Summers, Gene F., Richard L. Hough, John T. Scott, and Clinton L. Folse
1969 *Before Industrialization: A Social System Base Study of a Rural Area*. Urbana, IL.: Illinois Agricultural Experiment Station, Bulletin 736.

Sumner, William Graham

1906/1960 *Folkways*. New York: New American Library.

Sutherland, Edwin H., and Donald R. Cressey
1978 *Criminology*. Tenth edition. Philadelphia: Lippincott.

Svalastoga, Kaare
1957 "An empirical analysis of intrasociety mobility determinants." *Working Paper No. 9*, submitted to the Fourth Working Conference on Social Stratification and Mobility, International Sociological Association (December).
1959 *Prestige, Class, and Mobility*. Copenhagen: Gyldendal.

Tannenbaum, Frank
1947/1963 *Slave and Citizen: The Negro in the Americas*. New York: Random House.

Tanner, J. M.
1971 "Development of boys and girls aged twelve to sixteen." Pp. 1–24 in Jerome Kagan and Robert Coles (eds.), *Twelve to Sixteen: Early Adolescence*. New York: Norton.

Teitelbaum, Michael S.
1975 "Population theory and the LDCs." *Science* 188(May 2):420–425.

Terry, Robert M.
1967 "The screening of juvenile offenders." *Journal of Criminal Law, Criminology, and Police Science* 58:173–181.

Thibaut, John W., and Harold H. Kelley
1959 *The Social Psychology of Groups*. New York: Wiley.

Thomas, W. I., and Dorothy S. Thomas
1928 *The Child in America*. New York: Knopf.

Thompson, Edgar T.
1958 "The plantation as a race-making situation." Pp. 506–507 in Leonard Broom and Philip Selznick, *Sociology: A Text with Adapted Reading*. Second edition. New York: Harper & Row.

Townsend, Peter
1957/1963 *The Family Life of Old People:* An Inquiry in East London. Harmondsworth, England: Penguin

Treiman, Donald J.
1977 *Occupational Prestige in Comparative Perspective*. New York: Academic Press.

Treiman, Donald J., and Kermit Terrell
1975 "Sex and the process of status attainment: a comparison of working men and women." *American Sociological Review* 40(April):174–200.

Tucker, Nicholas
1977 *What Is a Child?* London: Fontana Open Books.

Tumin, Melvin M.
1953 "Some principles of stratification: a critical analysis." *American Sociological Review* 18(August):387–393.

U.N. (United Nations)
1979 *Demographic Yearbook*.
1983 *Monthly Bulletin of Statistics*.

U.S. Bureau of the Census
1971 *The Two-Child Family and Population Growth: An International View*. Washington, D.C.: GPO.
1975 *Historical Statistics of the U.S.: Colonial Times to 1970*. Bicentennial edition. Washington, D.C.: GPO.
1976 *Statistical Abstract of the United States*. 97th edition. Washington, D.C.: GPO.
1978 *World Population: 1977*. Recent Demographic Estimates for the Countries and Regions of the World. Washington, D.C.: GPO.
1980 *A Statistical Portrait of Women in the United States: 1978*. Washington, D.C.: GPO.
1981 *Statistical Abstract of the United States*. 102d edition. Washington, D.C.: GPO.
1982 *Statistical Abstract of the United States, 1982–83*. 103d edition. Washington, D.C.: GPO.

U.S. Bureau of Labor Statistics
1980 *Employment and Earnings*. Volume 27(April, May, June).
1982 *Employment and Earnings*. Volume 29 (September, November).

U.S. Commission on Civil Rights
1978 *Social Indicators of Equality for*

Minorities and Women. Washington, D.C.: GPO.

U.S. HEW (Department of Health, Education and Welfare)
1975 *Monthly Vital Statistics Report. Annual Summary, 1974: Births, Deaths, Marriages, and Divorces.* Volume 23(May).
1977 Publication (PHS) No. 78-1650. Series 11, No. 165 (November).

U.S. Department of Health and Human Services
1980 *Monthly Vital Statistics Report.* PHS 80-1120. Volume 29, No. 1(April).

U.S. NCHS (National Center for Health Statistics)
1977 *Vital and Health Statistics.* Series 11, No. 165(November).

U.S. Public Health Service
1978 *Facts of Life and Death.* PHS 79-1222.

U.S. Senate Committee on Labor and Public Welfare
1973 *Work in America: Report of a Special Task Force to the Secretary of Health, Education, and Welfare.* Washington, D.C.: GPO.

Uphoff, Norman
1977 "Hope not income is what matters." *Development Forum* 5(January–February):4–5.

van den Berghe, Pierre L.
1966 "Racial segregation in South Africa: degrees and kinds." *Cahiers d'Etudes Africaines* 6(3):408–418.

Vanek, Joann
1974 "Time spent in housework." *Scientific American* 23(November):116–120.

van Gennep, Arnold
1908/1960 *The Rites of Passage.* Translated by M. B. Vizedom and G. L. Caffee. London: Routledge & Kegan Paul.

Verba, Sidney, and Norman H. Nie
1972 *Participation in America.* New York: Harper & Row.

Waldron, Ingrid
1976 "Why do women live longer than men?" *Social Science and Medicine* 10(July/August):349–362.

Wallis, W. Allen, and Harry V. Roberts
1956 *Statistics: A New Approach.* New York: Free Press.

Warner, W. Lloyd
1959 *The Living and the Dead.* New Haven: Yale University Press.

Warner, W. L., and J. O. Low
1947 *The Social System of the Modern Factory.* New Haven: Yale University Press.

Warner, W. L., and P. S. Lunt
1941 *The Social Life of a Modern Community.* New Haven: Yale University Press.
1942 *The Status System of a Modern Community.* New Haven: Yale University Press.

Warner, W. L., and Leo Srole
1945 *The Social Systems of American Ethnic Groups.* New Haven: Yale University Press.

Wax, Murray L.
1971 *Indian Americans: Unity and Diversity.* Englewood Cliffs, N.J.: Prentice-Hall.

Webb, Eugene J., Donald T. Campbell, Richard D. Schwartz, and Lee Sechrest
1966 *Unobtrusive Measures.* Chicago: Rand McNally.

Webber, Everett
1959 *Escape to Utopia.* New York: Hastings House.

Weitzman, Lenore J.
1978 "Contracts for intimate relationships." *Alternative Lifestyles* 1(August):303–378.

Weitzman, Lenore J., Deborah Eifler, Elizabeth Hokada, and Catherine Ross
1972 "Sex-role socialization in picture books for pre-school children." *American Journal of Sociology* 77(May):1125–1150.

Wesolowski, Wlodzimierz, and Kazimierz Slomczynski
1968 "Social stratification in Polish cities." Pp. 175–211 in J. A. Jackson (ed.), *Social Stratification.* Cambridge, England: Cambridge University Press.

Westoff, Charles F.
1978 "Marriage and fertility in the developed countries." *Scientific American* 239(December):35–41.

Westoff, Charles, et al.
1973 *Toward the End of Growth: Population in America.* Englewood Cliffs, N.J.: Prentice Hall.

Westoff, Charles F., and Elise F. Jones
1977a "Contraception and sterilization in the United States, 1965–1975." *Family Planning Perspectives* 9(July/August):153–157.
1977b "The secularization of U.S. Catholic birth control practices." *Family Planning Perspectives* 9(September/October):203–207.

Westhoff, Charles F., and N. B. Ryder
1977 *The Contraceptive Revolution.* Princeton: Princeton University Press.

Whorf, Benjamin Lee
1940/1956 *Language, Thought, and Reality.* New York: Wiley.

Whyte, William F.
1961 *Men at Work.* Homewood, Ill: Dorsey.

Whyte, William H., Jr.
1956 *The Organization Man.* New York: Simon & Schuster.

Williams, Gregory
1979 "The changing U.S. labor force and occupational differentiation by sex." *Demography* 16(February):73–87.

Williams, Maurice J.
1977 "Development cooperation." *OECD Review* (November).

Williams, Raymond
1960 *Culture and Society, 1780–1950.* Garden City, N.Y.: Doubleday.

Wittmer, Joe
1971 "The Plight of the Old Order Amish." *Current Anthropology* 12(February):106–107.

Woodward, C. Vann
1966 *The Strange Career of Jim Crow.* Second revised edition. New York: Oxford University Press. A Galaxy Book.

Wrong, Dennis
1961 "The oversocialized conception of man in modern sociology." *American Sociological Review* 26(April):183–193.

Zablocki, Benjamin David
1971 *The Joyful Community.* Baltimore: Penguin Books.

Credits

Name Index

Subject Index

The Book Manufacture

Essentials of Sociology, Third edition was typeset at Autographics, Inc., Monterey Park, California. Printing and binding was at Kingsport Press, Kingsport, Tennessee. Cover design was by Quarto, Inc., Morton Grove, Illinois. Internal design was by Mead Design, San Diego, California. The typeface is Times Roman with Helvetica display.